MEN OF AIR

By the same author

Bomber Boys

MEN OF AIR

Doomed Youth of
Bomber Command, 1944

KEVIN WILSON

Weidenfeld & Nicolson
LONDON

First published in Great Britain in 2007
by Weidenfeld & Nicolson

1 3 5 7 9 10 8 6 4 2

A CIP catalogue record for this book
is available from the British Library.

ISBN 978 0 297 85321 3

Typeset by Input Data Services Ltd, Frome

Printed and bound in Great Britain at
Mackays of Chatham plc, Chatham, Kent

Weidenfeld & Nicolson

The Orion Publishing Group Ltd
Orion House
5 Upper Saint Martin's Lane
London, WC2H 9EA
An Hachette Livre UK company

The Orion publishing group's policy is to use papers that
are natural, renewable and recyclable products and made
from wood grown in sustainable forests. The logging and
manufacturing processes are expected to conform to the
environmental regulations of the country of origin.

www.orionbooks.co.uk

To Declan, Julia, Nicholas and Martin

Contents

List of Illustrations

SECTION ONE

1. The crew of P/O Jim Catlin, who brought their Lancaster into a crash landing at Manston after it had been shot up by a night fighter on the Leipzig raid in February (*Private collection*)
2. The happy crew of F/Sgt Bill Yates outside their spartan Nissen hut at East Kirkby. (*Private collection*)
3. LACW Dorothy Mason, the teleprinter operator at RAF Bardney. (*Private collection*)
4. Sgt Kenneth Dobbs volunteered for the Nuremberg raid and was shot down, being pulled from the wreckage of his Halifax. (*Private collection*)
5. F/Sgt Don Gray, whose aircraft exploded on the Nuremberg operation. (*Private collection*)
6. W/O Lawrence Woolliscroft, whose Lancaster was also lost on the raid. (*Private collection*)
7. The international crew of F/O Jim Lord mark the end of their tour at North Killingholme. (*Private collection*)
8. Releasing the tension: the crew of 83 Sqn skipper P/O Alan Edgar fool around outside their billet. (*Private collection*)
9. Navigator F/O Jim Wright, who nearly lost an arm from frostbite, pictured with crew members and ground staff at East Kirkby in the spring of 1944. (*Private collection*)
10. Evader F/O Bob Farnbank with a French Resistance woman, and three USAAF flyers, outside the Normandy farmhouse. (*Private collection*)
11. Evader Harry Fisher. (*Private collection*)
12. S/Ldr Gordon Carter and his skipper S/Ldr Julian Sale, who were shot down in February. (*Private collection*)
13. Great Escaper S/Ldr Jimmy James as a POW. (*Private collection*)
14. S/Ldr Steve Cockbain poses for the press the day after bringing home his damaged Lancaster from the Wesseling raid in June after ordering four of his crew to bale out. Inset is one of them, W/O Albert Bracegirdle, whose picture was taken by the Luftwaffe. (*Private collection*)
15. The Fillingham crew celebrate the end of a tour on 101 Sqn. (*Private collection*)
16. WAAF driver Marian Smith, pictured with a friend at Kirmington. (*Private collection*)
17. Flight engineer Ron Brown. (*Private collection*)
18. W/O Harry Ball, wearing the Caterpillar Club emblem beneath his signaller's brevet for a successful bale-out. (*Private collection*).

19. W/O Roy Ollerhead. (*Private collection*)
20. Canadian F/O Don Cheney with the crew of 617 Sqn's 'Dark Victor'. (*Private collection*)
21. F/O Rhys Thomas lines up with his crew and ground crew in front of their Lancaster at North Killingholme, the day after finishing their tour in September. (*Private collection*)
22. The 9 Sqn crew of Australian S/Ldr James Hancock at RAF Bardney. (*Private collection*)

SECTION TWO

23. A Dornier Do217 about to take off to engage British bombers. The Do217 was one of the first German night fighters to be equipped with the deadly *Schräge Musik* upward-firing cannon. (*SV-Bilderdienst*)
24. The result of tracerless *Schräge Musik*: a bomber explodes. This official picture was printed in the *Daily Express*, in April 1944, with the claim it was a German 'Scarecrow' shell, which the RAF told aircrew were fired to simulate doomed aircraft. In fact there were no 'Scarecrow' shells, only exploding bombers. (*Private collection*)
25. The dawn of 31 January 1944 in a typical Berlin street hours after approximately 2,000 tons of bombs had fallen on the Reich capital in less than fifteen minutes. (*Bildarchiv Preussischer Kulturbesitz*)
26. A bomb aimer crouches over his sight in the nose of a Lancaster, his head surrounded by the glow of a burning German city as he prepares to release his load. (*Private collection*)
27. The devastation in the centre of Munich after the highly accurate raid of 24 April. (*SV-Bilderdienst*)
28. Bombs from higher-flying Lancasters have hit this Halifax over a V-weapon site in France in July 1944, removing part of its tailplane. (*AKG Images*)
29. There were dangers even without meeting the enemy for Bomber Command airmen, ten percent of whom died in training. This Lancaster of 35 Sqn crashed on take-off at Graveley in July. It was the favoured aircraft of F/Lt Harold Hoover, who returned from leave to find his much-loved C-Charlie wrecked. (*Private collection*)
30. A Doodlebug arrives near Drury Lane in mid-July. (*Topfoto*)
31. and 32. The raid on the Panzer training base at Mailly-le-Camp cost forty-two Lancasters, 11.6 per cent of the force which set out, but the camp was wrecked. *Above*: the repair sheds and billets of the 21st Panzer Group before the attack; and *below*, afterwards. (*Imperial War Museum*)
33. The Nazi hierarchy forced inmates of local concentration camps to dispose of unexploded bombs after bombing attacks. Here such prisoners are seen digging in the rubble after the heavy raid on Bremen in August 1944. (*Bildarchiv Preussischer Kulturbesitz*)
34. Stuttgart was devastated in three heavy raids in July, particularly the night of 25/26, in which the centre of the old city southwest of the main station, as shown here, was virtually destroyed. (*National Archives*)
35. The three raids also left their mark on the RAF. Pictured is the Halifax of F/Lt Jim Weaver of 102 Sqn shot up by a nightfighter on the way back from the first operation of 24/25 July. The aircraft is leaning to port because of a bullet-ridden tyre, which caused it to groundloop on landing. (*Private collection*)

List of Maps

'When we first arrived on 101 Sqn the intelligence officer told us: "You're now on an operational squadron, your expectation of life is six weeks. Go back to your huts and make out your wills." It was simply accepted that two out of three of us would be killed.'

Sgt Dennis Goodliffe, a 19-year-old flight engineer, who completed a thirty-three-operation tour in sixteen weeks in the spring and summer of 1944.

Prelude

~~~~~~~~

As always for those who waited in the night across the flat fields of bomber country, the first faint droning they now heard in the southern sky was both welcome and worrying. First came relief at hearing the young heroes of the night return from raiding Germany, then the nagging question of how many there would be. In this particular, frosty dawn such anguish was acute. For this was the end of the first raid in 1944 in the Battle of Berlin, a campaign that was draining the lifeblood from Bomber Command.

As the Lancasters descended in the darkness, lurching up England's eastern edge, pilots and bomb aimers peered fretfully into the gloom for the first uncertain glimmer of navigation beacons. Airframes creaked, whistled and whispered, advertising fresh flak holes from the target all crews feared. Engineers tapped fuel gauges and anxiously eyed oil temperatures as the ragged armada thundered on, swinging ever deeper into the blackness. And slowly, as altimeters wound back, the sense of unspoken unity that had kept this loose gaggle of airmen linked across miles of sky was lost. Now each individually coded contributor to the cacophony sought its own airfield. It was then that the reverberation of their passing rattled slates in sleepy villages as the Lancasters began the closing letdown to base, debriefing and fuggy billet.

On the airfields WAAF drivers waited by their trucks to pick up crews from dispersal, intelligence officers sharpened pencils and wits to pick from weary airmen the latest clues to Luftwaffe tactics, and beaming chaplains stood poised in ops rooms by tea urn and rum jar to dispense warmth and comfort for tension-stretched nerves. Crews not flying that night stirred beneath rough blankets at the sound of bombers touching, then gratefully holding, the glistening concrete of the stretching runway. First elements of the force of 421 bombers that had struggled into the overcast at midnight, turned off the flarepath and trundled, power plants popping, into the open arms of dispersal bays and shut down. Hot engines cooled and ticked clock-like in contraction from the efforts of the night, as crews climbed down stiffly into the silence, then stood awkwardly, almost shyly, anticipating the crew truck driven by their welcoming WAAF.

In the chill of ops rooms, station commanders and other earthbound souls gathered anxiously to count the tally as the airmen trudged in, heavy-legged in their flying gear, and flopped into stiff-backed chairs ranged in rows before smart intelligence staff. The officers waited, bright-eyed and with pencils poised, as they faced the weary warriors, ready to interpret the halting accounts of the night. In fact, it was the same old story of attrition for insufficient return.

The ops boards would show a final toll of twenty-eight Lancasters missing, a percentage loss of 6.7 – the latest appalling statistic in an eroding campaign that seemed without hope of remission. The gloom of 1/2 January in this fifth year of war had seen Bomber Command raid the Reich capital for the ninth time since the Battle of Berlin had opened the previous November, and for the second time in four nights. Before the campaign began the Command's C-in-C, Sir Arthur Harris, had promised Churchill it would cost Germany the war and Britain 'between 400 and 500 aircraft'. It was not ending the war for Germany, but so far it had cost Bomber Command 211 aircraft and the crews in them.

The latest raid had been mounted despite little hope of Pathfinders being able to visually mark the target. The reality had been a reliance on uncertain skymarkers, which drifted above nine-tenths cloud and caused a scattering of bombs among the thickets of the Grünewald south-west of Berlin. Only one industrial building had been destroyed. In fact, it had been another encouraging night for the Luftwaffe. The operational plan had called for route markers, to keep the bomber force on track. The Luftwaffe's seasoned *Nachtjäger* had then been able to orbit and swoop between these flares, which signalled the bomber stream's progress to the target as clearly as a glaring window in the blackout. A total of 168 airmen who had climbed into the darkness nine hours before were now dead and thirty-four were prisoners. In Berlin itself only seventy-nine people had died.

Unknown to the aircrew, who now bottled up their terror and instead spilled out tales of frustration, the Battle of Berlin still had three months to run. The toll among the bomber boys on these raids and those on other German cities in the period would be greater even than in the nineteen weeks of the Battle of the Ruhr in 1943. It would be the apogee of Luftwaffe success, demonstrated by the losses in the final operation of the Battle of Berlin, by Leipzig in February and by Nuremberg at the end of March. In February, 1,529 aircrew would fail to return; in March – which would see the highest loss by Bomber Command on any single raid by far – 1,880. But it was the month that had just begun which would prove the cruellest in that bleak winter. In thirty-one days a total of 2,256 aircrew were lost, only 464 of whom were later found to be prisoners of war. January 1944 was the worst period of the war to be an airman in heavy bombers.

It wasn't just the likelihood of death but the method of dying that kept young aircrew awake in their billets. The choices were stark. If they didn't perish from searing flak or fighter bullet, they might fall without parachutes from suddenly disintegrating aircraft, drown in the cold waters of the North Sea, or for a few, slowly suffocate from lack of oxygen. This was the year when the aircrew strength of Bomber Command reached its zenith and the time when a broader scythe than ever swished through its ranks. The cream of Britain and young bloods of the Commonwealth died in this period – well-educated youngsters with a desire to experience the adventure of flight who had stepped forward, then been subjected to rigorous physical and mental tests before being passed for aircrew training. The comparison with subalterns of the First World War who suffered an equal attrition has been made before and is worth repeating. The elite of the Second World War generation had volunteered to fly and, in the attrition of 1944, found the likelihood of survival in the bomber war so slim they were no more substantial than men of air, ghosts already, waiting to vanish this night or the next.

A grateful nation was well aware, hearing on the fireside radio just how many aircraft were missing after each raid, what sacrifices these young men were making. Girls were often anxious to be seen in the company of a winged airman. But to the young aircrew themselves it was an unglamorous, pitiless war, in which they pitched themselves against barrages of flak and other young, enemy flyers in the dark and freezing cold, as searching eyes grew heavy-lidded and limbs ached for rest. Death often came suddenly out of the darkness. Most of the men who lived to tell their tales in this book only did so because they vacated their aircraft within seconds of it being set ablaze, sometimes with parachutes only partly attached. Those who hesitated, even for a fraction, were lost.

For the airmen involved in this battle against the Luftwaffe there was usually little cheer to be found on the ground. Just a few squadrons were based on pre-war airfields where brick-built billets and ablution blocks could provide some of the comforts of home. Only one unit of aircrew, those of 617 Sqn, were based in a requisitioned luxury hotel. The rest made do with draughty Nissen huts and the insanitary conditions of hastily constructed wartime airfields. It was the sergeants' and officers' messes and the village pub where they could find some solace and where many of their memories of the intoxication and impetuosity of youth are placed. They lived as if there was no tomorrow, because for many there wasn't.

This is the heart of this book, the personal experiences of the airmen who fought the titanic battle of the RAF and Commonwealth bomber offensive through the winter, spring and summer of 1944. Much of it was a deadly, demoralising period to be an airman and some of it was the most intense of the war, as the bombing campaign progressed from the Battle of Berlin and other targets deep in Germany to the pre-D-Day containment of the enemy by attacks on transportation targets, through the invasion itself, to the demands of being asked to fight four campaigns at once. It was in this period as the Command raided communication targets, was called on to defeat the new menace of the flying bomb, to support army operations and also begin an onslaught on the enemy's oil supply, that many aircrew found themselves in the new, unfamiliar role of evader, on the run in Occupied Europe, anxiously existing from day to day in the hope Allied troops would gain ground to find them before the Germans did. They would experience the same, lonely anxiety as their comrades from earlier raids, who weeks before had tunnelled through the Silesian sand of Sagan in what became known as the Great Escape.

But it was also at this time that the efficiency of Bomber Command would improve dramatically; several targets would be attacked in one night and the groups themselves would start the process of operating as separate entities, led by 5 Group and the resurgent 617 Sqn, who under W/Cdr Leonard Cheshire would develop their technique of low-level target marking.

The bomber boys' experiences of ops were recorded within hours in the debriefings that formed the basis of their squadron operational record books, now part of the National Archives. But the ORBs only give the bare bones of the deadly, nightly game with the Luftwaffe. Sixty years later in 115 private interviews spanning three continents I have been privileged to learn the true nature of what each of those traumatic tussles meant in personal terms, what the bomber war meant for the WAAFs who waited for the airmen to return, what it meant for the Luftwaffe pilots who opposed the bombers and what it meant for those on the ground in Germany and Occupied Europe beneath the bombs.

Many of the airmen's accounts begin in January 1944, the month of greatest bloodshed for Bomber Command. That attrition lay ahead as the crews who had been to Berlin on the night of New Year's Day told their tales of facing flak and fighter as they went through Berlin's three rings of defences and out again. The intelligence officers had heard it all before. Some, more usually female, were sympathetic as they probed for more relevant details of target indicators seen, size of fires on the ground and new concentrations of anti-aircraft fire both en route and homeward. Others were impatient for information. When no more could be gleaned chairs were scraped back and the exhausted airmen, with one last glance at the names of the missing on the ops board, stumbled away to shed their heavy gear in the crew room, to bolt down the post-op bacon and eggs in the mess, then to gratefully sink on their beds in billets. For most sleep swiftly followed, but for some – on the edge of breakdown – it wouldn't come. Within a few short hours in this bleak midwinter most of them would be called again for another raid.

Let's join them then as the young men of Britain and its Commonwealth crowd noisily into briefing rooms in the alphabet of airfields sprawled along eastern England from Binbrook to Warboys, to hear what their brief futures hold on this bitter evening of 2 January 1944 ...

WINTER

I

An Op Too Many

It was not a good night to die. Earlier in the day it had been snowing and the tired crews, whose memories of the Berlin defences had haunted their dreams, were sure as they stumbled into briefing rooms that commanders would come to their senses and call the operation off. There were fewer of them this time, 383 crews instead of the 421 dispatched the previous evening. More than 200 airmen who had sat on these same seats 24 hours earlier were now missing and only thirty of them were in the hands of the Germans. There was more than the usual nervousness as crews waited in each long room for the screens to be drawn from the map covering much of the end wall. The target it revealed would, after all, decide how many of them lived or died. There had been no easy targets since the Battle of Berlin began, even a diversion from the campaign to Frankfurt less than two weeks before claiming forty-one aircraft. But they could always hope against the odds for a mining operation or an op to a German city less of a haul than distant Berlin.

The airmen sat together in crews, seeking comfort in familiarity. They were identical in blue battledress, but that was as far as similarity served. Ranged before that mysterious end wall were a diverse range of characters from disparate classes, backgrounds and even nations. More than two-thirds of aircrew on any RAF Bomber Command squadron were from the British Isles, including a significant number from neutral Eire. The rest were from Canada, Australia and New Zealand and a few from South Africa, the West Indies and even farther parts of the Commonwealth such as India and Ceylon. A sprinkling were Americans, entrants to the

RCAF before Pearl Harbor, and now serving out their tours before the US Army Air Force claimed them. They sat there, close in their own thoughts – the callow and the cultured; the novice and the knowledgeable; the profound and the profane; all waiting for their immediate futures to be revealed. Cigarettes were passed round and the chatter rose. Occasionally there would be a burst of nervous laughter as a crewman recalled a raucous incident at the pub, a bumpy landing or a lucky escape on ops the night before.

There was often a theatricality about airmen's lives in Bomber Command as step by step they prepared for their night's performance over an arena of bright destruction, and no aspect was more histrionic than the lifting of the curtain to reveal the target. Eyes restlessly roamed the walls as tense pilots and fraught gunners waited for the drama to begin. Most of them were crowded into the cold of corrugated-roofed Nissen huts. The lucky few serving in pre-war stations spread out along their benches between the permanence of brick partitions in purpose-built operations blocks. But the view and the atmosphere were much the same. The uniform drab green paint on the walls, the identical Air Ministry posters urging stream concentration as in 'Don't be proud, stay with the crowd'; or in the likely event of bale out, 'Remember tell them nothing but your name, rank and number'; the ubiquitous Station Standing Orders. It had a depressing familiarity. And all the time as the smoke swirled and the gossip flew back and forth, eyes kept flicking nervously to that curtained end wall.

P/O Dick Starkey, a 20-year-old pilot on 106 Sqn in the winter of 1944, recalls the atmosphere at hastily constructed Metheringham: 'In the briefing room there was a table for each captain with his name on and during the Battle of Berlin if you got there early you could see as the other lads came in they only had eyes for the map at the end of the Nissen hut.' And when the target was known, he remembers, 'You could hear them saying, "Oh, no, not the Big City again."'[1]

It was with relief, therefore, that the airmen who had waited so impatiently at briefing rooms throughout bomber country were called to attention as their COs strode in. The waiting was over; for the final time talismans were nervously twiddled as the senior officer mounted the dais. Then, so slowly it seemed, he was handed his billiard-cue pointer and the target was illuminated. It was Berlin again. And this time there was more than the usual involuntary gasp of indrawn breath as the target was revealed. Now there was open disbelief on many squadrons.

To add to the shock, Bomber Command headquarters at High Wycombe seemed to have abandoned any attempt to fool the Reich's awesome defences and opted for a straight route all the way beyond Bremen, cutting north-west past Hamburg, then dog-legging through the target and south of Hanover before joining up with almost the same route out as in. The beginning and end of the track over the Zuider Zee, a favourite point for *Nachtjäger* to catch the unwary or plain weary, had been used seven times already. Eyes stayed riveted on the skein of crimson ribbon outlining the route as COs handed over to the section leaders for times on target, bomb loads, wireless frequencies and airfield marshalling procedure. Outside lowly aircraftsmen were sweeping snow from the runways.

Now the automatic preparation for the night's perils began. The thoughtful crews assembled their own personal ephemera for what lay ahead, navigators shuffled charts, bomb aimers collected target maps, flight engineers packed fuel logs, wireless operators filed code flimsies. Then they filed out to their messes for the operational meal, which always included a fresh egg – a luxury virtually unknown to civilians, who were by now well used to cooking their ration from powdered form. Cynical servicemen referred to it as the propaganda meal, claiming it was provided so that they would be able to tell any Nazis they met after bale-out how well fed the RAF were.

What followed for the airmen as plates were picked clean was acknowledged as the most anxious time. There was a stirring, bustling energy about Bomber Command stations – each home to approximately 2,500 men and women and therefore the size of a township – as the fine detail of mounting an operation against the Reich capital entered its final stages. The fuel bowsers topped up the last of the 2,143 gallons each Lancaster would need for the return trip to Berlin; armourers checked bomb racks and the bombers' eight individual machine guns; WAAFs prepared flying rations of coffee, sandwiches, boiled sweets and chocolate; chest-type chute packs were piled ready for collection in the high-roofed parachute store; escape kits with sturdy, silk maps for the correct area crews would be flying over, and perhaps coming down in, were stacked in locker rooms.

But the crews themselves had little else to do from pre-op meal to take-off except think. Some ambled off to the mess ante-room to try to read, or play table tennis or bar billiards. Others went back to their billets to quiet their nerves and still their imaginations. Dick Starkey remembers:

> I did nine Berlin trips and after we'd been briefed we often got a couple of hours rest in our Nissen huts. We'd lie on our beds and not a word would be spoken. Instead we would all have our thoughts. When the time came to go up to the flights we were like men going to the gallows. In the locker room there might be a hundred of us putting on our kit and it was as quiet as anything. That winter was the lowest point for Bomber Command.[2]

F/Sgt Cliff Hill, a veteran rear gunner on 35 Sqn at Graveley who took part in the Battle of Berlin, recalled:

> We went to the locker room about an hour before take-off, calling at the parachute section on the way. For me there was the lengthy process of getting into my flying clothing – silk and woollen underwear, shirt, heavy white roll-neck sweater, battledress uniform, electrical suit, white woollen knee socks, then the Irvin flying suit made of fleece-lined leather. Finally there were the fleece-lined, brown suede flying boots and a scarf – often different WAAFs' scarves worn as a favour, so they could say this scarf has been over Berlin. The last act was to hang my lucky charm, a miniature pair of Dutch shoes given to me by my mother, from my B/D jacket.[3]

There followed the train of crew buses and utility trucks out to the frozen dispersals where the Lancasters – snow now swept from their wings – sat heavily on their huge, smooth tyres, brooding almost in silent anticipation, waiting for the first stab of a gloved finger on starboard inner engine starter button to begin the mechanical chain that would see each crew taking approximately 5 tons of high explosives and incendiaries to the Reich capital. For the airmen themselves, layered and lumbering in their bulky clothing, there was an opportunity for a final cigarette and a nervous pee against the tail wheel for luck, before they climbed aboard, some for the last time. F/O Dennis Thorman, a bomb aimer on 77 Sqn, later recorded how difficult that could be. 'Our flying clothing, with all the parachutes and everything else that we carried, was a terrific weight, which meant that we struggled up the steps of the aircraft, then inside to our various positions,' he wrote. 'I was in the nose where I laid flat on my stomach most of the time ... I had a marvellous view, but it could be a bit terrifying.'[4]

The tension of preparation was now released in a burst of sound, which rolled and echoed across the wide expanse of an airfield as engines were started at dispersal after dispersal in orchestrated succession and the snaking lines of Lancasters began their ungainly procession down narrow perimeter paths, barking and rumbling, each following the white tail light of the one in front. At runway thresholds the WAAFs and ground-staff officers were gathering to wave the boys off.

Dorothy Mason was a 20-year-old WAAF teleprinter operator at RAF Bardney, near Lincoln, and remembers the scene. Her boyfriend, Sgt Cliff Williams, was a flight engineer on 9 Sqn at the base and their courtship continued throughout the Battle of Berlin. 'Working in the teleprinter office I used to get the instructions through that operations were on, giving the code for the German city Bomber Command would be going to: Berlin, for instance, was Whitebait. Security was such that I couldn't tell my boyfriend where he was going that night even though I knew. It was very difficult,' she remembers.[5]

The first of the processing Lancasters turned, tyres squealing, onto the active runway and waited, propellers whirling furiously in a yellow-tipped arc against the banks of cleared snow, as the pilot held the aircraft against the brakes. Inside the cold, dark, dripping and shaking fuselage, booming and echoing with the beating of four Merlin engines at full bore, the skipper sat, taut and captive in his seat harness, eyes locked in the direction of the Watch Office mid-way and to the right of the flarepath. It seemed a lot longer than 48 hours ago that new sooty footprints were added to the ante-room ceiling on New Year's Eve, as pint after foaming pint was served through the mess serving hatch to slake throats dried by endless choruses of the popular air force ditty named 'Bloody Hell'. It had been adapted to suit isolated, grim bomber stations throughout the country and ran: 'This bloody town's a bloody cuss, no bloody trains and no bloody bus and nobody cares for bloody us, bloody [East Moor, East Kirkby or wherever].' It seemed almost like another age and many a poised pilot considered at this moment that nobody did in fact care for the airmen now locked in a battle of attrition with the Luftwaffe, in which more and more was being asked each night without it ever seeming enough.

There it was! A glaring green light flicked on, then as quickly disappeared. Now it could begin. Heart in mouth, the skipper snatched off the brakes and the first of the night's bombers bounded away down the flarepath into uncertain fate. This was the most dangerous part of all until enemy territory was reached. A swing off the centre line, a missed beat from one of the four engines and the laden Lancaster would plough into the frozen mud, the undercarriage quickly collapsing and the resulting red flash and rolling boom from its thin-cased 4000-lb Cookie exploding, signalling the end of another crew.

The flight engineer called out the gathering velocity from the air speed indicator as the tail came up, his splayed out, gloved left hand holding in the vibrating throttle levers while the skipper now grasped both sides of the wide U-shaped control column, correcting each miniscule variation to port or starboard as the aircraft so rapidly approached the dark unknown at the end of the grey concrete. Reluctantly it seemed the wheels unstuck and as the aircraft lifted away the rear gunner waved rude signals to the waiting WAAFs. Dorothy Mason says: 'I only went to wave Cliff's crew off on an operation once. I saw them having a last cigarette before they got in their big, ugly heavy aircraft, then it roared off down the runway. I found it too sad to go again. They were all scared I know.'[6]

MIDNIGHT ticked away 2 January to 3 January as the bombers climbed over their airfields into the gloom and set course for Cromer and the North Sea. The Lancasters of 1 Group took longer to orbit base. Its squadrons were carrying an average of 330 lbs more bombs than those of other comparable Lancaster squadrons because of a policy of its commander, Air Vice Marshal Edward Rice, to load his bombers to a point just short of where the undercarriage oleo legs started to buckle. One aircraft of the group, from 460 Sqn, failed to climb and crashed six minutes later near Binbrook village, killing all its Australian crew.

As the rest of the stream headed out to sea the imperfections of aircraft that had returned from a gruelling operation only 24 hours before began to show up. The crews also found themselves in ten-tenths cloud and now low morale among those who had felt it an op too many competed with the press-on spirit so encouraged by group commanders. Not surprisingly sixty crews turned back, the highest rate of early returns in the whole of the Battle of Berlin. A quarter of those early returns were blamed on a signals error giving a diversionary landing site for 1 Group's Wellingtons out sowing mines. Fifteen 1 Group Lancaster crews later reported they thought it was a general recall and came home. There had already been telltale splashes of bombs being jettisoned over the water from 1 Group Lancasters in a bid to gain extra height.

The depleted stream of brave airmen going on to Berlin now began to string out as pilots battled with ice building up on airframes in the freezing conditions and static lightning flashing on windscreens. The weather had closed many Luftwaffe airfields but more than 150 fighters did manage to take off. Oberst Hajo Herrmann, who had formed the Luftwaffe's Wilde Sau squadrons of single-engined night fighters the previous summer, had been given strict orders from the head of the Luftwaffe himself, Hermann Goering, not to fly operationally. But he felt he needed to show an example to his younger pilots in such poor visibility. He was airborne in his FW190 at 0130,* breaking out of the overcast at 22,000 feet and heading for Berlin where flak crews were firing flares above the clouds to guide the Wilde Sau.

Only ten minutes later P/O Thomas Spink of 432 Sqn was attacked by a Focke Wulf not far from Bremen, where several fighters had been held to orbit beacon Marie. 'The enemy aircraft opened fire from ahead slightly to starboard and 300 yards above,' he later reported. 'I immediately made a diving turn to port and the attack was broken off.'[7] As his damaged Lancaster climbed out of the corkscrew and resumed course the enemy aircraft came into the attack once more. Spink dived into cloud and stayed there for the next fifteen minutes. He then called on his crew to check the aircraft for damage and found it had been considerable. The navigator reported that his oxygen had been cut off and the Gee† set was wrecked, the bomb aimer had found the electrical bomb release was now unserviceable, and the rear gunner and mid-upper gunner reported several holes through the rear of the fuselage and tailplane. Far worse, the engineer reported a bullet through the instrument panel that had put a hole in the oxygen regulator, causing a leak. The engineer estimated the oxygen would run out in three-quarters of an hour. The crew would need to keep on oxygen until they had bombed at the required height of 20,000 feet or suffer anoxia, where a condition

---

* Luftwaffe times were one hour ahead of RAF clocks.
† Gee was a radio receiver by which a navigator was able to plot his exact course on a grid.

akin to drunkenness would be rapidly followed by unconsciousness, then probably death. Berlin, however, was an hour away. 'Having arranged with my wireless operator to release our 4,000-lb bomb manually over the target and to collect all the oxygen bottles and bring them to the navigator I decided to carry on and hope our oxygen supply would last until reaching Berlin,' Spink reported.

Aboard another Lancaster in the stream was a navigator who knew all about the dangers of lack of oxygen. F/O Jim Wright, a navigator with 630 Sqn, had reported at the East Kirkby base only two weeks before from the RAF hospital at Ely, where he had lain for five weeks recovering from frostbite and anoxia. The frostbite had occurred because he lost consciousness when pieces of cannon shell stitched across his navigation desk during an attack by three fighters over Kassel at 20,000 feet, clipping his oxygen tube away. After evading the enemy aircraft the crew had dumped him by the main spar, presuming he was dead. Wright remembers:

> I eventually came to when the skipper, Ken Ames, lost height over the North Sea. I think they thought I was a ghost when I finally appeared as the aircraft went below 10,000 feet. My left arm was useless because it had become frostbitten lying against the cold floor of the aircraft. We had lost a lot of fuel and the crew didn't know where they were and whether they should ditch. I managed to get the Gee box working and there was enough fuel left to get us into Coltishall, a fighter station at that time. We got down at the second attempt and ran out of fuel at the end of the runway. The aircraft looked awful, there were holes all over it.[8]

F/O Wright, his frostbitten arm a distinctive blue, was put to bed at Ely with an oxygen cylinder alongside, while doctors debated whether to amputate the limb. He managed to persuade them not to and when he was released rejoined his crew at East Kirkby, from where he was now flying his third Berlin trip in five days. Within an hour he would face a new ordeal from the *Nachtjäger*.

Over Berlin itself the Luftwaffe had now gathered, racing there after most of its fighters had failed to penetrate the stream near Bremen. The first of the Pathfinders were by then banking over the last turning point to the north-west, the Müritsee, which showed up well on radar sets, and starting their fast run-in to Berlin, chased by an 80 mph tail wind, but early returns had cut their number from fifty to forty-two and the Wilde Sau fell on them, further reducing their number. As a result the marking was scattered and Main Force arrived to find no concentrations to guide it. Most of the bombs began to go down in open country.

The oxygen supply for P/O Spink and his crew ran out five minutes before they reached Berlin. He went on to bomb at 20,000 feet, risking anoxia. 'We completed our detail except for dropping our incendiaries which would have had to be dropped individually,' he later reported. 'Immediately after leaving the target I descended to 8,000 feet at which height I managed to stay until reaching the enemy coast although each member of the crew was affected by lack of oxygen.'[9]

More than 150 *Nachtjäger* were now over Berlin as the bombers searched for target indicators to aim at. The flak had been ordered to fire no higher than 21,000 feet to give the Wilde Sau their chance and searchlights were sweeping the underside of the cloud base to silhouette the bombers flying above. Flares from Luftwaffe illuminator units were lighting the path of the bomber stream. Hajo Herrmann later wrote:

I saw our first illuminating flare ... the second the third ... and more. Splendid! In we go! I could see a 'heavy' approaching from the south. I swept in astern of it, throttled back, dived and fired into its wings and cockpit, a burst of several seconds. My aim was good. I pulled up over him and a large object flew past my aircraft. 0257 hours: I reported a probable kill. I turned into the bright, colour-filled arena. Just below me and between 500 and 1,000 metres away I saw another bomber silhouetted against the 'shroud'. For a few seconds our flares dazzled me, then I opened up. The bomber caught fire. I gave a further burst. The bomber was blazing furiously; it was 0305 hours and I reported one bomber destroyed.

However, immediately afterwards the hunter became the hunted as Herrmann was caught by a Mosquito night fighter. He related later:

There was a loud banging, crashing noise all around me. I felt something hit my leg. There was a sudden loss of pressure in the cabin. Shooting past me and ahead and fading I saw the tracer of an enemy night fighter. I had become a victim of my own shroud; the blazing bomber had made it even brighter. I lost all the feeling in my right leg. I looked down cautiously. It was there.[10]

Herrmann could not make contact with his ground station because his R/T was dead, so decided to fly west where he had been told the weather was better. He followed guidance flares, fired for the night fighters, to head towards Dortmund in a blizzard.

P/O James McIntosh of 432 Sqn, who had watched tussles with fighters on the Berlin raid of the night before, arrived later than planned over the Reich capital. His rear turret had developed a fault just before take-off and he had had to wait more than half an hour to get it working again, then after cutting corners to catch up with the stream his air speed indicator had packed up twenty minutes before the target.

McIntosh later reported:

I continued climbing and bombed from at least 23,000 feet. I had just turned for home and had gone about two minutes when the rear gunner [Sgt Andrew De Dauw] yelled: 'Fighter.' I was already weaving but really got going. Just as he gave the warning I felt the cannon shells hitting the kite like a sledgehammer and saw other tracers hitting the wings and passing by the cockpit. The first few shells did most of the damage. The control column jumped forward when a shell hit the elevator putting the aircraft into a vertical dive. All this happened within five seconds as the gunners had replied to the fighter and shot him down before he could finish us off.

We were going straight down and by getting both feet on the instrument panel and one arm around the control column and the other hand on the elevator trim I managed by giving it everything I had to force the aircraft out of its dive at 10,000 feet. I was heading in what I figured was the right direction, so I began calling up the crew to see if they were OK. When the kite first went into its dive it threw the crew about badly as well as scattering their equipment from one end of the kite to the other. The bomb aimer [Sgt Robert Elvin] answered OK, the flight engineer [Sgt Walter King] was beside me with his chute on and mine in his hand. I'd given the order to prepare to abandon when my controls were knocked out of my hands. The navigator [P/O Alexander Small] replied 'OK' as did the wireless operator [W/O Clyde Schell]. The rear gunner replied 'OK', but there was no response from the mid-upper gunner

[Sgt Leo Bandle], so I detailed the w/op to go back and see if he was all right. When he got plugged in he reported the mid-upper was OK, but he had become entangled in shot-away wires and a foot had stuck in the flare chute. He also reported the fuselage was full of holes and the floor covered with oil.

Having found the crew were all OK I detailed them to ascertain damage. The rear gunner reported cannon holes in his turret and the turret u/s, the mid-upper reported his turret u/s – his hydraulics shot away, and many large holes in his part of the fuselage. The w/op reported his wireless set still OK, but most of his equipment lost. The navigator's equipment was scattered all over the floor, but he managed to approximate a course for me to fly. The flight engineer reported the instruments to the starboard outer engine as u/s except the tachometer which showed OK, so I left the engine going. The bomb aimer reported the bomb doors hanging open, so I detailed the flight engineer to try pumping them up. This failed so we knew the hydraulics had gone. The flight engineer and bomb aimer then tried reaching the bomb doors from the bomb aimer's compartment, but they were unable to pull them up.

My compasses were u/s, the rudder controls had jammed and I could get very little response from the elevators. It necessitated both arms around the control column to hold my height. The P4 compass finally settled down well and I was able to steer an approximate course. The navigator was unable to fix his position so attempted astro navigation, despite the aircraft being unstable. His fix put him fairly well on track but with a very low ground speed, so I figured there must be more than the bomb doors dragging although there was nothing I could do except keep flying as best I could. We were now far behind the rest of the bombers and our only chance was to stay in the cloud tops despite the severe icing which was encountered. There were fighters' flares dropping around us and the flak positions en route were bursting their stuff at our height, but because of the cloud cover the fighters were unable to pick us up.[11]

THE Luftwaffe harried the Lancasters past Hanover and along their route back to Holland, picking them off as the bombers bucked and plunged in the blizzard. The 630 Sqn Lancaster of navigator Jim Wright, who had suffered such an ordeal from frostbite, was attacked three times, by an Me109, a Ju88 and an Me110, each time the gunners hitting back as the aircraft went into corkscrew after corkscrew.

The then F/O Wright remembers:

When you're a navigator strapped into your desk with a night-flying curtain around you, you are cocooned, shielded from the outside. I heard the corkscrew call then just held tight and hoped for the best. I was trying to keep an eye on the instruments as the aircraft went sideways, downwards then upwards. I think it was worse for a navigator in many ways because you just had to trust in everybody else. There was absolutely nothing you could do except hope and pray that all the other guys were doing their job. The one thing to try to hang on to was where you were on the Mercator's chart with the ground plot and air plot on it. Every six minutes we had to have something down there, whether estimated position, actual, forecast or whatever, with its associated air plot and the difference between the two is your estimated wind, speed and direction you hope.[12]

In his own Lancaster P/O Spink was able to reduce height further for his crew, who were sick for lack of oxygen over the target, as the battered and strung-out stream reached the Dutch coast. 'But due to the condition of the weather and strain caused by flying without oxygen I found it necessary to land at an airfield before reaching our own base,' he related in his combat report.

Oberst Herrmann hadn't got home. Without radio and still gradually descending towards Dortmund he hoped to pick up the welcoming searchlights of an airfield, but at 600 feet as the snowflakes whirled past his windscreen he realised it was hopeless, so pulled up into the stars shining above the clouds, jettisoned the canopy and shoved the nose down. Herrmann wrote:

I was free. I pulled the ripcord quickly. My motion and the force of gravity took control of me. My head went forward, the parachute harness cut into me, and I was swinging from one horizon to another. Below me I heard the scream of an engine, then a dull thud when the aircraft impacted. Weak and half-conscious I fell into the clouds. It was cold and damp. Soon wet snow was falling before my eyes. All around me it was as quiet as the grave . . . a thump and a pain, I had landed.[13]

Herrmann had come down near Hagen and he crawled to an isolated house from where he was taken to hospital. While there he had a telephone call saying the Führer sent personal congratulations on his escape and would be decorating him on his recovery. A later message from Goering asked him in harsh terms to explain why he had disobeyed orders.

Jim Wright's Lancaster came over the windmill at Old Bolingbroke and landed at East Kirkby as dawn was creeping across the sky at 0754. Within minutes his pilot, F/O Ken Ames, was sitting at a table in the debriefing room and reporting: 'Target conditions ten-tenths cloud. Reflected explosions of 4,000-lb bombs seen. Fighters were active and three enemy aircraft claimed as damaged, an Me109, a Ju88 and an Me 110.'[14]

At Bardney Dorothy Mason was relieved to find all of 9 Sqn's aircraft had returned safely. She remembers:

We worked three shifts in the teleprinter room and on nights I would listen for the sound of the Lancasters returning after an operation. Sometimes I would have to go over to debriefing with a teleprinter message for an intelligence officer and I would see the aircrew coming in. A friend of mine on the telephone exchange would tell me what crews were back and who wasn't. I didn't get to know a lot of crews, several would go missing on their first three or four operations and we put it down to inexperience, but you would get to know a few who went on for quite a number of ops and it was very sad when those didn't return.[15]

At East Moor P/O McIntosh was sitting down in the debriefing Nissen hut relating his own adventures, and his fellow 432 Sqn skipper, P/O Spink, had already been accounted for, but missing from the ops board was another squadron mate, the married F/Lt John Allen, who had been making his third Berlin raid in three weeks at the start of his second tour. His was one of the twenty-seven bombers shot down that night. The previous night one of 630 Sqn's pilots, 20-year-old Londoner F/Sgt John Homewood, who had seen two bombers shot down, had reported at debriefing: 'The route was too familiar to enemy fighters.'[16] That route had proved so again and Berlin would claim Homewood himself before the month was out. The loss rate for 2 January had been 7 per cent compared to 6.7 on New Year's Day. There was little to show for it. The bombing had been more scattered than the night before and the damage was disappointing. The Command was being drained away on what for some seemed a tide of despair.

BUT if the despondency in Bomber Command was increasing so too was the depression in Berlin. The last two raids had not achieved anything like the success that the planners at High Wycombe had hoped for. However, the Reich capital, the third largest city in the world at that time, was so vast that any bombs – concentrated or not – created changes in the landscape, and raids particularly in November had drastically altered the face of central Berlin.

On 3 January Marie Vassiltchikov, a Russian-born aristocrat who worked in the German Foreign Ministry's Information Department, found herself looking at the fresh damage to her home city. She had left Berlin for Leipzig on 28 November after bomb damage to her home in the Lutzowstrasse in the heavy raid of 22 November, but had received an order to return to her job. On the night of 1 January her train had been held up outside Berlin for four and a half hours because of the latest raid. Dawn was approaching before she got to her home district. 'Two mines fell on either side of the Lutzowstrasse and a third at the entrance to our little square and all the villas around ours are gone,' she wrote in her diary. 'I went through the house with old Martha, the cook. It is a dreary sight, the windows are gaping holes, the rain comes in onto the piano.' Then at 2 a.m. the sirens had sounded again as Bomber Command made its second visit within 24 hours. 'My nerves are not improving and I was jolly frightened when some bombs came whizzing down in our vicinity,' she wrote. 'Also having to sit up every night, sometimes for hours, is becoming exhausting.'

The next day she was at her office, reporting that nerves were so strained two secretaries had got into a fist fight. She wrote:

> Work is pretty much at a standstill, with everyone leaving at 4 p.m. to be home by nightfall before the raids start. Some people travel several hours to get into town. One secretary takes seven hours to make the return trip, so she spends only about an hour at work. I find the harassed faces of the people more depressing even than the desolate aspect of the town. It must be this constant insomnia that never gives one time to recuperate, be it only a little.[17]

The Battle of Berlin had many weeks to run. For both airmen and those beneath the bombs there would be further ordeals to face and for the bomber boys the defences of Berlin in bitter January would leave a cruel scar no less obvious than the gaps evident in Berlin's skyline.

2

The Cauldron

It was with some trepidation that surviving skippers checked into their flight offices in the early afternoon of 3 January. There was a genuine fear that they might be going to Berlin again. But the bad weather and the need to restore losses brought the more encouraging news of a stand-down. In fact, they and the other demoralised young men who made up their crews were rested for a full 48 hours, before many of them were called for another long-distance haul, to Stettin.

Leafing through the papers as a new week began, aircrew could take satisfaction in reports of what the last three out of five nights had meant to Berlin, though the more experienced were aware the information from the Air Ministry's press department bent more towards maintaining morale than accuracy. 'Fires started by the RAF in Berlin on Sunday morning were still burning early today when our bombers made another heavy attack on the German capital,' the *Yorkshire Evening Press* reported under a headline of 'RAF Strikes Again While Berlin Burns'. 'An Air Ministry communiqué says a pilot reconnoitring the city after the raid reported two large concentrations of fires.' But for those who could read between the lines there was a note of caution further down, stating, 'The last three RAF raids on Berlin were all made under exceptionally unfavourable weather conditions with visibility on the ground nil, says the German Overseas News Agency.'[1]

There were the usual ads for married officers looking for accommodation for their wives near RAF stations – though it was not encouraged by most squadron commanders. Sometimes there was a reminder that not everybody in the RAF died as a direct result of Luftwaffe action. The *Yorkshire Evening Press* reported on 3 January that Marie Hemingway, a 20-year-old WAAF, had fallen down the steps of the Railway Institute, in York, and died of a fractured skull. She had been leaving a dance, and had lost her footing in the blackout. In 5 Group's area south of Lincoln the local paper carried a picture of a belly-landed Lancaster on its front page with the somewhat over-optimistic caption: 'Ready for another trip ... Lancasters damaged in the hammering of Berlin are reconditioned and made airworthy again in a few hours.'[2] Aircrew turned the pages, flicking over the ads exhorting savings schemes – not much point for those with a short future – and pausing perhaps over the one for teenage troubles such as acne. Then they and looked up what was on at the cinema as they planned nights out.

Ranks of blue uniforms crowded the streets of York, Lincoln, Boston, Cambridge, Doncaster and the other towns and cities of bomber country in the two-night stand-down. The Fred Astaire film *The Sky's the Limit*, at the Odeon, proved a popular choice for the 4 and 6 Group squadrons stationed around York, and 5 Group crews flocked into Lincoln for a few restorative pints and to see Ann Mathew and Betty Johnson strut the stage of the Theatre Royal in the pantomime *Robinson Crusoe*.[3] Squadrons based further south in Lincolnshire looked forward to a 'Super Special Dance' being advertised for the Assembly Rooms, Boston mid-month. The band of Frank Dey, 'acknowledged as the best ever for dancing', was promised, guaranteed to set toes tapping and skirts whirling from foxtrot to jitterbug.[4]

As the early weeks of January drizzled by the memory of what a cauldron Berlin had been lessened, though raids on Stettin and particularly on Brunswick on the 14th, made their own savage impact. In fact bomber aircrew would not be asked to return to the Reich capital again until the 20th. Their respite was not due to a sudden kindness of their commanders but to the moon period, a period four days before the full moon and four days after it began to wane, when it was considered at this stage of the war too dangerous to operate on a target such as Berlin. As operational airmen lolled in sergeants' and officers' messes restoring frayed nerves with warm beer, wads and banter, they could almost work out their future over the next few months of their tour. In early January several local newspapers had printed for the benefit of farmers the moon periods for the year. The current one would run until the 18th, the next would be from 1 to 13 February; the third from early March to the 17th and the fourth would begin on 30 March.[5] Aircrew could correctly forecast they would be over Berlin again at the end of the month, the middle of February and towards the end of March. It was certain the cycle of the moon would mean no ops on 30 March. They were wrong; in fact, that night would be Bomber Command's apocalypse.

THE moon period also gave Harris and his planners at Bomber Command an opportunity to reflect on what the cost had been so far in the Battle of Berlin and to review strategy in the technical war with the Luftwaffe. The retrospection was made more bitter by remembrance of how encouragingly the campaign had begun. On only the second raid of the series, that of 22 November, bombs had tumbled through cloud onto the German Ministry of Justice, the Foreign Office, the Propaganda Ministry, the Treasury, the Ministry of Transport, the Gestapo head-quarters, even the official residence of Himmler – and all for a loss rate of only 3.4 per cent. The Germans had made much of the fact that several embassies, including the British, had been hit, giving a huge clue to the fact the bombs had fallen around the administrative area of the Wilhelmstrasse. But it was not until 20 December that reconnaissance pictures were available to the RAF's Photographic Interpretation Unit at Medmenham, near Aylesbury, as Mosquitos crossed the city in clear skies. There had been four more raids since then and there would be five more before the weather was kind enough for reconnaissance again.

Harris was now truly operating in the dark, to less effect and at mounting cost. Not only was the constant overcast preventing recon-naissance flights, that other source of possible intelligence, bomb-run photoflash pictures – as their bomb load impacted, all crews had to hold steady in the flak to record where their tonnage had hit – were showing nothing but cloud. It was impossible to tell what was being destroyed apart from Bomber Command itself. The Air Ministry had to rely for much of its information on British journalists based in Sweden – who got most of their news from Swedish businessmen travelling by train through Germany – or from broadcasts from Reich radio stations. For instance, readers learned from the newspapers of 3 January that 'Trav-ellers from Berlin confirmed that the Reich Chancellery was hit in Sunday night's raid and three parts destroyed. The Leipzigstrasse in central Berlin was also hit.'[6]

The lack of intelligence was frustrating for a commander for whom

Berlin had always been the major prize. After the cataclysmic Battle of Hamburg the previous July, in which a firestorm had largely taken the city out of the economic equation and Hitler's Armaments Minister, Albert Speer, had warned that six more city raids of such magnitude would probably bring the Reich's total armament production to a halt, it was natural to turn to Berlin in the hope of administering the Hamburg treatment. Not only was it the administrative heart where the Reich's leaders schemed and dreamed, it was also home to about 10 per cent of Germany's industrial workers, had a rail centre in which twelve main lines converged and was Europe's focal point for air transport. From north to south and east to west Greater Berlin housed factories, scientific and army institutions, machine plants and railway workshops.

The construction of Berlin, however, was not that of Hamburg. Where in Hamburg there were narrow old streets in which tongues of flame could leap and greedily seek out and devour the nooks and crannies of ancient timbers, Berlin was made of solid apartment blocks on wide thoroughfares where the twinkling flames of 4-lb incendiary bombs had little chance of linking into a howling firestorm sweeping all before it. The Pathfinder Force, too, was not up to the task at that stage, the long haul across fighter-infested skies in foul weather – usually carrying gremlin-ridden H2S airborne radar of inadequate precision – inevitably leading to scattered marking. The weather on most nights was so poor PFF had to drop a mixture of ground markers and skymarkers, which would evolve into a standard practice known as the Berlin Method.

There had now been ten raids in the campaign. Many more would be needed if Harris was to make good his somewhat rash promise by letter to Churchill the previous November that it would cost Germany the war. That promise had carried the condition 'if the USA will come in on it', thereby increasing the force available to at least half of the 4,000 bombers Harris had originally wanted for his bomber offensive.[7] So far there had been little sign of the USAAF coming in on it, by night or by day. The Americans were not trained for night bombing and were still regrouping after the 20 per cent losses of the Schweinfurt raid of October, which proved the necessity of a long-range day fighter. A brave attempt had been made by briefing groups on 23 November, just after the opening of the Berlin campaign, but the mission had been scrubbed before take-off.[8] The Merlin-engined Mustang, the P-51B, which would transform the capabilities of the USAAF, would not arrive in adequate numbers until the end of January and the Americans would not bomb Berlin until March.[9]

It was becoming clear Bomber Command was in this costliest of campaigns alone. The battle had already undergone many changes and would see many more, not least in the types of heavy bombers employed. Harris had had to withdraw his Stirling squadrons within less than a week of opening his campaign because their maximum ceiling of 14,000 feet made them easy meat for fighters. Before the end of February the older marks of Halifax, the under-powered Mk IIs and Vs, would also disappear from Bomber Command's front line because they had become prime fighter bait in turn. These two reductions cost Harris about one-third of his total nightly strength of approximately 750 heavy bombers. It was fortunate the steady increase in Lancaster production and that of the excellent Halifax Mk III was able to counter the loss of the less useful older aircraft. But these reductions and the constant attrition meant Harris was constantly having to play catch-up in his campaign at a time when Bomber Command was building up to its peak of trained aircrew available for operations and efficient aircraft available to do the job.

He was also now conducting a campaign against a Luftwaffe at the zenith of achievement. There had been many improvements in Germany's air defence since the Battle of Hamburg. That battle had seen the advent of Window, foil strips dropped in their thousands by the bombers, which effectively blinded the Würzburg radar sets controlling both the night-fighter interceptions and radar-laid flak guns. The strips had also swamped with false echoes the airborne Lichtenstein radar sets, which the night fighters used in the final stages of intercepting a bomber. It was a triumph for the RAF and a disaster for the Luftwaffe, as their defensive Himmelbett system of interceptions in controlled sky 'boxes' became permanently useless overnight. New systems had to be developed and it was these novel techniques that were now cutting a swathe through the ranks of Bomber Command.

First Hajo Herrmann had been allowed to fully form his Wilde Sau of single-engined fighters to engage the bombers over target cities, then the tactic of Zahme Sau (Tame Boar) was developed for the twin-engined fighters whose previously controlled interceptions Window had rendered obsolete. These Me110s, Ju88s and Do217s usually orbited beacons along the likely routes of the bombers, then were fed into the stream. Window, which had once proved such a protection to individual bombers, now often signalled the presence of the stream by its very direction, fluttering across the sky in a formless glittering ballet.

A *Luftreportage* running commentary by the German controller of the likely target of the bomber force gave every Luftwaffe *Nachtjäger* crew a good chance of making an interception, not just the aces who had been favoured by the Himmelbett system. As the target neared, Ju88s would drop flares above and ahead of the stream for the bombers to fly through, lighting the way like a pre-war boulevard. If the *Nachtjäger* didn't intercept before the target, there was another opportunity to do so as the Tommies flew home. The night fighters would be guided to the heart of the stream by the obscene multi-coloured splash of bombers exploding then burning on the ground.

Those pyres were there because of another Luftwaffe development, perhaps the most important of all in raising the attrition rate among the Men of Air and lowering their morale even further as they waited their turn for the chop, as they termed it. Its use was unsuspected by the Air Ministry for the first three months of the Battle of Berlin, and never fully fathomed, and it would not be officially revealed until the war was over to the bomber crews who saw its deadly effect.

It was called 'Schräge Musik', a brilliantly simple development in aerial gunnery consisting of two machine guns, or more usually cannons, installed in the roof of a twin-engined German night fighter at an angle of 70 to 80 degrees. Schräge Musik took much of the danger out of an aerial engagement for a Luftwaffe crew, allowing them to creep slowly into the blind spot below the RAF machine instead of tackling it from astern in full view of the rear gunner. Once the *Nachtjäger* pilot had confirmed his angled sight was positioned between the two engines on either wing of the bomber, he fired a quick burst of tracerless ammunition, which almost inevitably set fire to a petrol tank. The *Nachtjäger* then dived away as the bomber plunged in the opposite direction and usually exploded within a minute or two. Hardly any Luftwaffe crews reported return fire. As the debriefing reports of more and more Bomber Command airmen featured stories of aircraft exploding without apparent cause the Air Ministry told base intelligence officers to explain them away as 'scarecrow' shells, fired by the Germans to lower aircrew morale by making them think they were seeing an exploding bomber.

But by no means all the recent developments in aerial warfare were on the side of the Luftwaffe. The Allies, too, had introduced many changes in the deadly nocturnal game of cat and mouse played above Germany, not least with the formation of the bomber support unit, 100

Group, in December. It was now controlling Beaufighter and Mosquito squadrons to fly Ranger patrols over the German night-fighter bases, to shoot down the *Nachtjäger* at their most vulnerable time of take-off or landing. It also dispatched Mosquito units equipped with the Serrate homing device to lock on to *Nachtjäger* radar transmissions by which the RAF aimed to make hunters the hunted.

Spoof raids were routine by January 1944. They could be mounted by a force of minelaying aircraft regularly dropping Window en masse as they flew out over the North Sea to give the appearance of many bombers and confuse the German controllers into thinking they were the night's major raiders, or by large numbers of training aircraft droning towards the enemy coast then turning back before it was reached. Mandrel screens of airborne and ground-based radar jammers were set up to blank out the course of the real bombers. Mosquitos dropped Window and Cookies on German cities away from the main bomber stream to make the *Nachtjäger* fly there. And occasionally, to keep the enemy guessing, two major forces on the Luftwaffe radar screens would in fact be huge forces of bombers carrying out separate raids on German targets at the same time to split the defences. But as January advanced, and the Germans also had time to reflect in the moon period, it was obvious that any raid in force was more than likely to be on Berlin.

ON the night of the 20th the waiting was over for the men of Bomber Command and the sirens wailed again over the Reich capital. For the crews of thirty-five of the 769 aircraft that set out it was a one-way trip. The operation broke new ground for the Luftwaffe. More than 400 of the twin-engined long-range Me110s and Ju88s, which had been blinded in their search for encroaching bombers by the introduction of Window, had by now been equipped with a new radar set, SN-2, which could not be jammed by the metallised strips. Allied to the ground-based Korfu and aircraft-fitted Naxos radar, which locked onto the ground-tracking H2S radar emissions of bombers, it released the Zahme Sau fighters to patrol Germany for the bomber stream, then once located pick up individual aircraft for rapid dispatch by Schräge Musik cannon.

The operation also marked the return to the Battle of Berlin for the first time since 29 December of the less efficient Halifaxes. Their inability to climb out of trouble and the new radar aids of the Luftwaffe would have a lethal effect on some Halifax squadrons, 102 for instance losing five of the sixteen Halifaxes it dispatched on the raid and two more crashing in England. From Croft, 434 (RCAF) Sqn would lose four of its Halifax Vs and three of 76 Sqn's would not return to Holme-on-Spalding Moor; 77 Sqn at nearby Elvington would lose another two Halifaxes.

F/O Dennis Thorman, the bomb aimer on 77 Sqn who found clambering aboard a bomber so difficult in heavy flying clothing, was on his seventh operation that night. He had arrived at Elvington in a period almost as bleak for its weather as its losses. 'As officers we lived in what was supposed to be the best accommodation, long lanes of hutments each with a coke stove,' he remembered. 'It always seemed to be raining or snowing in Yorkshire.'[10] In the dismal late afternoon of 20 January F/O Thorman found himself smoking a last cigarette outside his Halifax at dispersal as it was prepared to join the 263 other Halifaxes bound for Berlin. He reflected on the chances of collision, with so many bombing within the space of fifteen minutes.

Sgt Alan Dearden, a 21-year-old flight engineer, was on the ill-fated 102 Sqn at Pocklington and remembers:

We had been on 102 about seven or eight weeks, after crewing up at HCU at Riccall, when we were called for the maximum effort on Berlin. We were as green as grass, but didn't know it. The aircraft we were given was O-Orange, which had been left parked by the bomb dump for a couple of weeks and was rumoured to be u/s. Because the operation was a maximum effort the aircraft was resurrected as a bit of an afterthought and given to the spare crew, our crew, to go to the Big City. My strongest impression at the time was that with full fuel tanks plus an overload tank Berlin was obviously a long way to go. It was pretty outrageous that a new crew was asked to go to Berlin as their first trip, but we were full of enthusiasm as we rolled down the runway in the late afternoon and climbed out over Flamborough Head. It was a question of getting everybody airborne who could fly and you always think it will happen to the other fellow. We thought we were invincible.[11]

A pilot in another 4 Group squadron was also making his first operational flight. F/Sgt Joe Hitchman had arrived at 158 Sqn's base at Lissett shortly before the squadron's Halifaxes were changed for the much improved Mk III. Hitchman, whose entire crew would be commissioned and decorated by the end of his tour, remembers:

We arrived at Lissett as a crew on 10 December right in the middle of the Battle of Berlin. We knew it was going to be a little bit difficult as we finished our training. My navigator went on a trip with another crew to Berlin and was shot down so I then had to do a few cross-countries with another navigator before we operated otherwise I would have done a few more of the Berlin raids. I did my first raid as a second dickey on the Berlin raid of 20 January in a Halifax Mk III.

When I saw Berlin on the board at briefing I wasn't surprised, I expected it. I was flying with our flight commander, S/Ldr S. D. Jones. Going into the target through the three rings of defences I just hoped for the best. Sometimes when there was a box-type barrage of flak in front of you at your height it was daunting, but you just had to fly through it. I thought the Mk III was wonderful, better than the Lancaster in my opinion. It could fly up to 26,000 feet without a bomb load.[12]

The Mk III Halifax was indeed a remarkable aircraft, but the reputation of the Mk IIs and Vs would be confirmed as death traps on the night of 20 January. Their inability to climb to the height of the Lancasters in the stream cost their crews dearly as the Zahme Sau were launched, with interceptions taking place at intervals along the bombers' track from south of Kiel to the target. The straight route, which had proved so daunting to crews on the two Berlin raids at the beginning of the month, had been abandoned and spoof raids had been launched against Kiel and Hanover. But as the Mosquitos tasked with these raids did not carry H2S, the German controllers were not fooled. In fact, the British radio listening service identified that 'freelance fighters' were airborne forty minutes before the first of the bombers reached the north German coast. They also discovered the new Luftwaffe tactics being demonstrated with chilling effect, though bad weather again meant less than 100 Zahme Sau aircraft were out hunting.

The later analysis of Bomber Command's Operational Research Section noted:

The controller directed the main effort into getting fighters into the bomber stream rather than identifying the main objective. In the target area conditions were particularly favourable to night fighters since a layer of cloud at 12,000 feet illuminated from below by searchlights provided a background against which aircraft could be silhouetted.

About 100 twin-engined fighters were sighted over Berlin (including 46 Ju88s), but only 10 of these attacked our aircraft; similarly only one of the 70 single-engined fighters observed in this area opened fire. The position of the bomber stream was plotted by the commentator until they had passed Magdeburg and fighters pursued our aircraft at least as far as Bitterfeld. Six aircraft were lost to fighters on the way out distributed evenly over the route; at least six over Berlin; and four more on the first leg of the homeward journey. One PFF Lancaster shot down an Me110 over the target.[13]

The 77 Sqn Halifax II of F/O Thorman came under attack four times, the first by an Me110. F/O Thorman held on as his aircraft corkscrewed clear with only superficial damage, but saw 'an aircraft about 100 metres from us shot down in flames. I could see it all going on with aircrew struggling to get out of the aircraft,' he related. The second and third attacks were over Berlin itself, where twin-engined Zahme Sau were evident. 'We suffered from determined attacks by Ju88s. It seemed to me there were quite a lot of aircraft being shot down and I could see a number of aircrew in parachutes. Both our rear and mid-upper gunners were firing at the Ju88s and we were corkscrewing to get out of their way. It was getting quite hair-raising. I could see through the cloud all the various fires on the ground.'[14] After leaving the target they were attacked once more by a Ju88, which slightly damaged the Halifax again before disappearing into the night. The fires F/O Thorman saw were not what Harris had hoped for. The bombs were falling in an 8-mile spread along the eastern side of the city, hitting railways, industrial premises and a power station, but many of them were also falling in open country.

Alan Dearden remembers what it was like that night over Berlin as a young airman.

There weren't a great many searchlights over the target as the raid was very scattered and the visibility was atrocious, but I could hear the occasional crump of heavy flak nearby and see bits of light appearing in the Perspex on the starboard side as pieces of flak came through. It wasn't very alarming because everybody was busy and it was all pretty hard work. Coming back we got off track and flew over Hanover. We got a bit of a buffeting from the flak, but we got out as quick as we could and we weren't damaged. As we approached the North Sea I could see we were pretty short of fuel as we had had to increase the power to give us the performance with that aircraft.

Of the 102 Sqn Halifaxes lost four were claimed by night fighters in the Berlin area, a fifth by flak over the target and two more crashlanding in Britain. One of those was Sgt Dearden's.

I told our pilot, Sgt Richard Proctor, we seemed to be running on fresh air as we crossed the sea. We tried to land at the emergency airfield at Woodbridge, but we were refused and advised to try elsewhere. We got rejected at various other stations and I suggested we bale out, but eventually we got accepted for Hethel, a USAAF base, near Norwich. I was trying to keep the engines going by transferring fuel and even tried to get the last drops out of the overload tank, but the starboard outer packed up for lack of petrol as we were coming over Norwich. We must have crossed it at zero feet. We were on final approach and I was in the rest area juggling the tanks when we struck slightly rising ground.

There was an almighty crash. As the undercarriage was down it absorbed the initial impact, but the aircraft then disintegrated. Suddenly from all the noise in the world there was an eerie silence. I had been thrown backwards and was tangled up in the ammunition racks at the side of the mid-upper turret. It was pandemonium. The skipper got hold of the front of my Mae West and dragged me out.

The bomb aimer, F/O Jock Turnbull, had been killed. I think he was coming out of the front of the aircraft to get in the second dickey's seat when we hit the ground. After the aircraft stopped he went on through the windscreen. I found him lying about 15 yards ahead of the aircraft up in the hedge at the edge of the field. He was bleeding badly from the skull and I covered him with a parachute. He was later reported as having died in the outpatients department of Norwich Hospital, but I think he had already gone when I found him.

As there was no fuel left there was no smell of petrol and no fire, but after we got out we could see a chap coming across the field smoking and we all bellowed out at the same time, 'Put that cigarette out.' The local ARP section came out to the crash and later the Americans from Hethel. I was put in the back of an ARP ambulance. My right elbow was broken, I had had a bash on the head and my knee and ankle were badly bruised. I also had tiny bits of the shattered aircraft in my forehead. The wireless operator was also injured, his leg had been broken in two places. I remember going over a ford and a train went by at a level crossing. It must have been the midnight service from Norwich and I remember the sudden glow of the firebox being stoked up, which showed up a line of saplings. The crew was split up after the crash. I spent six months in hospital.[15]

The attrition had been heavy among the squadrons equipped with the low-ceiling Halifax. A total of twenty-two Halifaxes had not returned to base, almost twice the number of Lancasters lost. Sgt Montague Clarke, another 102 Sqn flight engineer, remembers the mind-numbing misery of serving in a flak-and-fighter-bait Halifax squadron in the Battle of Berlin.

That winter of 1943/4 aircrew were going down with flu and they were ordering maximum efforts, so to make up crews they used to take people from other crews. I flew two operations myself as a replacement. Our 19-year-old rear gunner, Sgt Hugh Addison, was killed on one raid operating with a different crew and then the next night the mid-upper gunner, F/Sgt Kermit Peterson, was killed after being called on for another crew. It was a blow to us all. I had joined the crew in August at a heavy conversion unit at Rufforth and we had gone out drinking together many times.

In January 1944 102 Sqn entered its worst period. I went to Berlin on the 20th and it was obviously a very bad raid for us. Several times I saw tracer in the sky, then fire as an aircraft was hit and started to go down. I knew losses were going to be particularly savage.[16]

IT WAS with relief, therefore, that the Halifax squadrons found themselves left off the battle order for the next Berlin raid a week later. Instead Harris sent out 515 Lancasters with fifteen Mosquitos and, having learned from the experience of the 20th that small H2S-bereft spoof raids didn't fool the Luftwaffe controllers, mounted two large diversions. A mine-laying force of eighty Stirlings and Wellingtons was sent out to the north of the route where it crossed the Dutch coast and another force of H2S-equipped aircraft laid mines even further north around Heligoland.

There were further intelligent tactics in planning the Main Force route itself. Instead of flying directly to Berlin, it headed south-east towards Leipzig then abruptly banked north-east towards the Reich capital, while Mosquitos droned on, dropping Window and dummy fighter flares. Another wrinkle was the introduction of extra Pathfinder 'Supporter' aircraft from 1 Group, equipped solely with high explosive bombs so as not to start fires, and accompanying the 8 Group Pathfinders, who were locating the aiming point and spreading a Window screen. On the previous two Berlin raids the Pathfinders – who stood out alone on radar, which made them prime targets for predicted flak – had suffered grievously. From Warboys 156 Sqn had lost five crews on the 2 January raid – with another five missing less than two weeks later on Brunswick, including the squadron commander – and the Wyton-based 83 Sqn lost three on 20 January.

This time there were fewer early returns – thirty-eight, just over 7 per cent of those dispatched – but the pressure of constant long-distance raiding of difficult targets in January was still showing up deficiencies caused by quick turnarounds in battle-bruised aircraft. In one of those aircraft, from 166 Sqn, was flight engineer Sgt Barry Wright, who would win the Conspicuous Gallantry Medal in February. He was coming towards the end of a tour that had included six Berlin raids so far and would require two more. He remembers:

We had been briefed for Berlin on the 27th but our Lancaster, Q-Queenie, was unserviceable and we had to take another, J-Jig. It had a lot of equipment we didn't know about and a long way into the trip the batteries flattened and we lost all the electrics, including H2S. We had to jettison our bombs and put into Manston after being airborne for seven hours and fifty-five minutes, so we were a long way on. The same day they sent an aircraft down to Manston. We were back on ops the same night.[17]

After all the planning and tactical innovations there had been a whiff of victory in the air as aircrew were briefed for the operation of 27 January, pointing to a devastating raid of the like of 22 November. Instead, the weather drew a shroud over High Wycombe's hopes, with Berlin screened by ten-tenths cloud once more. As the Pathfinders' skymarker target indicators tumbled from bomb bays just before 2030 and blossomed over the stratus, a fierce tail wind blew them across the metropolis. More than fifteen communities in Berlin itself reported damage, but more frustratingly so did sixty-odd in the countryside outside the city.

Lali Horstmann, the wife of a German aristocrat, whose ancestral home was at Kerzendorf, 15 miles from the centre of the capital, later described what it was like to live in a rural community as the capital underwent its siege that winter. Her home was one of those destroyed by stray bombs. Earlier she had been enjoying a relaxing dinner and had just gone into the garden with her pet dachshund when she looked up. 'What I saw made me catch my breath,' she later wrote. 'In the stillness of the night gigantic globes of light were raining down from the sky, coloured like precious rubies or emeralds, more beautiful than anything I could have imagined. I stood transfixed not understanding the meaning of the magic fireworks when suddenly there was a terrible crash.' The process had begun whereby Lali Horstmann became one of the bombed-out.[18]

W/O Bruce Sutherland, a Canadian navigator, was on his first operation over Germany, in a 622 Sqn, operationally tired Lancaster skippered by Scotsman, F/Sgt Hugh Craig. He remembers:

The aircraft was not able to climb to operational height and we fell far behind of the stream, unable to reach and bomb the target We had turned for home over Germany when we were suddenly hit hard by a fighter. The pilot was trying to evade with a corkscrew manoeuvre and as he went into the dive I found myself suspended from the ceiling. By the time I got back on the floor the fighter had gone and I heard the skipper telling us to put our chutes on.

I had clipped mine on when we were hit again and the front turret was blown off. The aircraft was spinning and the only way I could move was to crawl along the floor. I was heading towards the escape hatch when I think the aircraft exploded as shells hit the bomb bay I assume. At this point I passed out. I came to swinging backwards and forwards beneath my opened parachute. I managed to stabilise the swinging, then I tried to put my gloves on because I felt cold and wet. The next thing I remember I was in a wood on the ground.

I got rid of my chute, checked my escape kit and started walking generally westward. I walked all that night and throughout the next day. The following evening I came across a group of large buildings. I was pretty tired and I stepped inside one. I found myself at the head of a large corridor with many doors. The rooms appeared to be the female living quarters of some sort of industrial complex. Someone got hold of me and took me to the factory canteen, but I was unable to communicate with anyone. Eventually a Nazi Party official came along and identified me as shot-down aircrew and took me into custody and I was taken under guard to Dulag Luft at Frankfurt.[19]*

F/O James Hancock was an Australian skipper with 9 Sqn, halfway through his tour, and a veteran of raiding Berlin. Over the capital his Lancaster was hit by flak yet again, now becoming as much a routine as the inevitable fighter attacks over the target. Hancock remembers:

We did nine Berlin raids in all and had fighter attacks on each raid, but over the target they were only sharp firefights, not sustained attacks. We probably would average one sustained fighter attack on the way to the target, then two or more sharp exchanges over the target and two or so sustained attacks on the way home.

On one Berlin raid we were attacked by two Me109 fighters in combination. One stood just out of range of the rear gunner and flashed his navigation lights, thus obviously signalling a second fighter. The mid-upper gunner then focused to the starboard beam and saw the second fighter come in. It appeared in his sights as a non-deflection shot and it caught fire from his bullets. The rear gunner also hit the other fighter, which had then attacked at the same time, and it left, streaming smoke from its engine. We suffered considerable damage, but claimed one Me109 shot down and another hit.

On the way home, now that the enemy knew where we were and where we were going, they would be in the air waiting as we approached the French coast and we would get one or two sustained attacks. The reason we survived the sustained fighter attacks was due to the rigorous carrying out of the defensive corkscrew manoeuvre.[20]

Oberleutnant Wilhelm Johnen shot down four of the bombers lost in the raid of 27 January. He had reached the bombers' route in with difficulty, seeing his new CO crash before his eyes as he took off in severe icing conditions from Parchim. Over Wismar the SN-2 radar antennae recently installed in the nose of his Me110 had found the first of his targets and he saw it spin through the clouds at 2036.

* W/O Sutherland later discovered only he and his bomb aimer had survived the explosion.

Twenty minutes later a second crashed just outside the capital.

'The British drew a square above the clouds with their parachute flares,' he later recorded. 'Thousands of flak bursts confirmed our arrival over the target. Wave after wave of bombers flew across the square of light and dropped their loads within.' Johnen spotted two Lancasters directly above the city.

> After a short attack the first bomber exploded and fell in burning debris through the clouds. The second banked steeply to starboard, trying to escape. The Tommies fired at me with all their guns, framing my aircraft with gleaming tracers. I pressed home the attack; the tail unit grew ever larger in my sights. Now was the time to shoot. The fire power of my guns was terrific. My armour-piercing shells riddled the well-protected wing tanks and the pilot's armoured cockpit; the tracers set fire to the petrol and the HE shells tore great holes in the wings. Despite the valiant efforts of the crew the aircraft plunged to the ground in flames.[21]

The powerful tail wind, which had so helped the Germans by scattering the skymarkers, now helped them again as the bomber stream turned into it to fly home, slowing the heavy bombers down. The Luftwaffe was able to continue pecking away at the stream as it headed south-west to clear the Ruhr and the raid cost a total of thirty-seven Lancasters, an insupportable 6.4 per cent. The scythe had swung particularly heavily among the Canadian squadrons of 6 Group operating radial-engined Lancaster IIs. The pre-war station of Linton-on-Ouse, near York, lost no fewer than seven aircraft divided between 408 and 426 Squadrons in which all but seven of fifty crewmen died. The bar of Linton's aircrew pub, the Alice Hawthorn in idyllic Nun Monkton, where a BBC programme had been made in November for beaming to Canada, was becoming a lonely and draughty place as bitter January ground deeper.

FRUSTRATED by the loss for little gain of the night before, Harris sent his force back to Berlin the next night and this time the Halifax squadrons, which had suffered so much previously, were called upon again. A huge force of 432 Lancasters and 241 Halifaxes took off around midnight and flew an unusual route, north-east over the North Sea then across Denmark and south-east over the Baltic, returning the same way. But as with the double blow of 1 and 2 January there was the inevitable result of calling on aircraft that had taken the long haul only the night before and nearly 10 per cent made early returns.

Earlier in the evening Mosquitos had carried out their own nuisance raid on Berlin in a bid to convince the Germans the capital was not scheduled for a heavy raid that night and now sixty-three Stirlings went out mine-laying off Kiel aided by Pathfinder Halifaxes to further puzzle the Luftwaffe about where a major blow might fall. Mosquitos also bombed night-fighter bases in Holland to make the German controller think any bombers out that night would pass through there.

Serrate patrols by Mosquito night fighters were also sent out hunting for individual *Nachtjäger* radar transmissions. From 141 Sqn F/O A. R. Hurley found a back blip on his airborne interception radar at 12,000 feet as the bomber stream approached Berlin from the Baltic and asked his pilot, F/O N. Munro, to turn hard to get behind the contact. 'The aircraft was travelling northwards straight and level and was recognised as an Me110,' Munro reported back at West Raynham later. 'After a two-second burst of 20 mm cannon it was seen to burst into flames and break up, one of its wings going past our aircraft which was hit by flying debris.'[22]

The contact was a sign the German controller had not been fooled by Bomber Command's planning and had ordered the *Nachtjäger* to head straight for Berlin itself. The resultant gathering brought an attrition rate worse than ever, forty-six aircraft being shot down. The percentage loss chart was inexorably rising and now it hit 6.8. On the positive side the damage was considerable, particularly in the centre where the public buildings hit included the new Chancellery, but again there was a scattering of bombs outside the city on a large scale.

F/O Jim Wright, the 630 Sqn navigator whose Lancaster had been attacked three times in the Berlin raid of 2 January, was over Berlin that night and found himself under fighter fire again. He remembers:

We were attacked by a Ju88, but not damaged. We had experience by that time. We were used to being shot at, used to being hit by flak and used to being coned. By that particular time we had been to Berlin four or five times. Of course I was worried to death being shot at, but there was nothing I could do as a navigator. My main task was to make sure my pilot had the next heading.[23]

F/O Wright's squadron, which had been formed at East Kirkby only weeks before, suffered a particular blow that night. Its new CO, W/Cdr

John Rollinson, had taken over from the American S/Ldr Malcolm Crocker, who had originally led the squadron, but was shot down and killed on his fifty-third operational sortie. Another 630 Sqn crew was also lost, no one surviving from a total of fourteen airmen.

As always the squadrons equipped with the older marks of Halifaxes had suffered most of all. The Canadian 434 Sqn lost five, 10 Sqn lost four, 466 Sqn had three missing, 77 Sqn another three and 102 Sqn, which was being battered out of existence, another two. One of those, captained by F/Sgt Dai Pugh, came down in the North Sea after flak had holed its fuel tanks over Berlin. The whole crew were able to take to the dinghy, but three were later lost as it capsized in the freezing, tumultuous waves. Pugh, the navigator, the wireless operator and the rear gunner were finally rescued by an Air Sea Rescue launch from Montrose after three days and two nights of being pitched around in the thin craft. The navigator died in the launch before it reached base and the remaining three crew suffered so badly with exposure and frostbite they never flew operationally again and were eventually invalided out of the RAF.[24]

Generally, the morale of Bomber Command was drooping by the day. Each time crews were called to the briefing room they saw the tape stretched across Europe to the Reich capital and each morning there were fewer at the mess tables to share the post-op bacon and egg. It was with sinking hearts, therefore, that aircrew were called to test the defences of Berlin again after only one night off. To add to the risks the lunar period was beginning and the bombers would fly out under a half moon. For those who still survived on the squadrons equipped with the old Mk II and Mk V Halifaxes respite had come at last and they were left off the battle order. It meant Harris was able to send only eighty-two Halifaxes to join the 440 Lancasters on the raid. It is some testimony to how much improved the Mk III Halifax was over its forebears that only one was lost on the operation, alongside thirty-two Lancasters.

The planned northern route was to follow virtually the same track to the target as the one of the 28th, then come back out over Holland, with a spoof raid by Mosquitos on Brunswick. The gremlins soon began to appear and forty-three skippers turned back, 8 per cent of those dispatched. However, the routing did fool the controller and it was not until the stream was nearing Berlin, by then under thick cloud, that any fighters were able to gather. As the TIs bloomed, signalling another concentration of bombs on the city centre, the *Nachtjäger* swooped and the sky flared with the flash and crash of cannon. Again many subsequent bombs went down in open country and the Zahme Sau and Wilde Sau followed the bombers through the target and most of the way to the Dutch coast, burning aircraft turning the clouds red at cruelly regular intervals.

P/O Starkey of 106 Sqn was over Berlin for the third time in four nights. He remembers:

A Berlin raid had to be seen to be believed. The Pathfinders used to drop flares two minutes before the raid was to begin. Everywhere in the sky there seemed to be these sparklers of flares. Then there were hundreds of searchlights and the red flashes of the 88 mm guns. On the bomb run trying to fly straight and level the bursting of the flak would knock the aircraft over 90 degrees, but the wing would come back by itself. You were going up and down all the time and there were combats taking place around you. It was like being in an arena. Inside were all the pyrotechnics with the glow of the fires below on the wings and bellies of the bombers, coloured target indicators going down, searchlights coming across, the tracer of combats. It was no wonder bombing started falling short. Then you had to hold it steady for up to two minutes after your bombs went to take the photograph. Immediately afterwards you put on full power to get out of that arena and, of course, often you'd be followed into the darkness. There would be 600 miles to go before you got home. The German defences were fantastic.[25]

As January closed Sgt Alan Morgan, a flight engineer in a 49 Sqn Lancaster from Fiskerton, was on the sixth of seven raids he would make on Berlin in a unit where the aircrew he knew were getting fewer and fewer. 'The mid-upper gunner scared off any fighters we saw and we took evasive action, corkscrewing into cloud, then popping out again,' he remembers. 'At the time of my tour fighters only tended to attack if you were on your own. If you could see aircraft ahead and behind you you were pretty safe.'[26] Sgt Morgan's tour would end abruptly on his 21st birthday the following month.

John Hennessey, a married flight engineer on the same squadron, kept a diary during his own tour. After the Berlin raid of 30 January he wrote:

Too much moonlight for the Big City and too many fighter flares to make one feel happy!! We watched seven people going down in flames as we went in to bomb and I also noticed a parachute opening and it was drifting towards the flames!! Stan Weedon's [the mid-upper gunner] turret was u/s and so he could not have fired his guns had we been attacked. We arrived home twenty minutes early and that was how I spent my wedding anniversary!![27]

Many of the aircraft Hennessey saw falling in flames were victims of Schräge Musik. Sgt Roy Child was an 18-year-old in a 7 Sqn PFF Lancaster, which narrowly escaped in a Schräge Musik attack that night.

I was the mid-upper gunner on the night we were hit. I and the other gunner Al Grange often used to change positions even though I might be down for tail gunner. When they checked on the base the next day they could see it was cannon shells that had hit the mainplane. It was a massive hole in the wing, about 6 feet wide. I don't know how the plane didn't blow up. A couple of wingless wonders came out to look at it and were muttering away to themselves. I think they knew what it was. It was obviously shells which had hit us. They took photographs of it.

The German fighters used to fly underneath, fire one burst then go on to the next plane hoping the one they fired at was going down. In our case they just made a great big hole in the wing then went on to some other aircraft. We used to talk on the squadron at that time about planes coming underneath us and that they were equipped with a sort of H aerial. We didn't know about this upward-firing cannon, just that fighters came from underneath. Looking down sometimes you could see them with the aerial. Some of the targets we went to were like going down a street with fighter flares each side. The fighters used to wait at the target for us, but there were also fighters en route and coming out who were underneath. We didn't believe in this story of 'scarecrow' rockets when we saw a plane blow up.[28]

The combat report filed within days by the skipper, S/Ldr Ken Davis, detailed:

Outbound at 19,700 feet Lancaster U was fired on and hit by an unidentified aircraft, not using tracer, from beneath. Five minutes previously the wireless operator [F/O Ken Marriott] had reported a 'blimp' on the Fishpond and warned the gunners. Just before the attack the mid-upper gunner observed an unidentified aircraft 1,500 feet below passing from the starboard beam to port beam. The Lancaster was weaving. The next indication of the enemy aircraft was an explosion in the starboard wing. At the time it was thought that the aircraft had been hit by flak. The Lancaster jettisoned its bombs and returned to base. It has since been established that the damage was due to cannon fire. No rounds fired.

S/Ldr Davis would be dead less than three weeks later.[29]

HARRIS'S squadrons had two weeks to rest and replenish in the moon period covering the first two weeks of February, but the agony was by no means over for the shattered aircrew or for those beneath the bombs.

By the end of January Harris had lost 384 aircraft in the Battle of Berlin and as February opened he was under considerable pressure from the Chief of the Air Staff to show dramatic results or turn aside to other targets, preferably linked to the coming invasion. The mounting blood list from the Berlin campaign was proving a cost too high. There had been talk amid the backbiting at the Air Ministry of sacking Harris, Sydney Bufton, Director of Bomber Operations, being asked by Sir Charles Portal in January whether he thought a change of leader might be a good idea.[30]

There were now only a few weeks left for Butch Harris to stubbornly prove the point he had made in a letter to Portal in December that Bomber Command's Lancasters could produce in Germany by 1 April 'a state of devastation in which surrender is inevitable'. He was convinced in the rightness of his cause to continue and was encouraged to do so by two factors. Increased output from the aircraft factories and the operational training units was showing how rapidly Bomber Command could recover in replacing lost crews and aircraft after the devastating raids of January and there were indications from General Carl Spaatz of the USAAF that he was at last ready to join him in raiding the Reich capital with the Eighth Air Force's daylight bombing groups of B-17s and B-24s. The Americans' first daylight raid on Big B, as they called it, would follow on 6 March.

As new crews reported to their squadrons in the first weeks of February and replacement Lancasters joined the flight lines, Harris prepared for a colossal new blow against Berlin, in which he would send his largest number of aircraft so far. A force of 891, composed of 314 Halifaxes and sixteen Mosquitos as well as Lancasters, was being prepared – the biggest bomber fleet to leave Britain's shores since the 826 sent to Dortmund the previous May, capable of dropping a record total of 2,642 tons of bombs, more than those in the firestorm raid on Hamburg. Surely nothing could prevent so many aircraft delivering a catastrophic blow.

As before it was the weather that dashed Harris's hopes. With the closing of the moon period in the second week of February came heavy snow, which had erks and aircrew alike sweeping runways, and it was not until 13 February that ops were ordered. The weather intervened once more and the operation was postponed to the next day, then cancelled again. Finally it was laid on for 15 February. Reading their names on a battle order and going through the turmoil of preparing for deadly danger to then see an op scrubbed at the last moment did little for the nerves of aircrew, two-week rest or not.

It was with the anxiety born of experience that the old sweats listened to the details of the plan for 15 February. Their fresh-faced colleagues, who had replaced those 'gone for a Burton' in January, had little idea of what lay ahead. The route in would now avoid the coastal flak belt of Holland and northern Germany by crossing over Denmark into the Baltic, then turning east of Rostock and heading down to Berlin, making one small dog-leg after leaving the target and coming out over the Zuider Zee. And this time, as well as the night-fighter attacks on German airfields and mine-laying diversion by a large force – in the Kiel area – a double bluff would be employed to fool the German controller. Mosquitos would precede the Main Force to Berlin, dropping target indicators and bombs that it was hoped the Luftwaffe would see as a decoy. Then just before the real raid opened on Berlin, twenty-four H2S-equipped Pathfinder Lancasters would simulate the opening of a major attack on Frankfurt-on-Oder 50 miles further east, which it was thought the Germans would think was the actual target. On the way home the returning bombers would split into two elements, flying 40 miles apart to confuse the fighters.[31]

The plan had two flaws. If Zahme Sau pilots picked up the stream early they would follow them all the way to the actual target, and on the return lack of ability by the average navigator would lead to a melding of the two elements resulting in a broad gaggle of bombers, giving controlled Zahme Sau the advantage again.

In fact, the bomber force was detected not long after crossing the English coast and the night-fighter crews in Holland and Belgium were alerted to fly north, leaving those in Germany to conserve their fuel. As the bombers set out across the North Sea the usual gremlins of faulty turrets, low engine oil pressure and failure of oxygen supply set in and seventy-five bombers turned back early from the raid, many of them the Halifax IIs and Vs of 4 Group. Sgt Frank Jones was in one of the Halifax IIs. The 20-year-old flight engineer was just beginning his tour, with 10 Sqn. He says:

It was a bad time to start operations. While we were on our way we developed trouble with the constant speed unit on one engine and had a bit of trouble with the oil pressure. Probably if we had had a bit more experience we would have continued, but being a sprog crew we decided to turn back at the Danish coast. It was rather upsetting to have to turn back, but the loss rate, of course, was extremely high. The skipper got a bit of a rollocking for coming back.[32]

The crew were wise not to proceed further with a faulty machine. The German fighter controller's running commentary to the Zahme Sau quickly began and they started to shoot down bombers into the Baltic as the stream crossed the east coast of Denmark. Attempts by special radio operators in the Lancasters of 101 Sqn to jam the running commentary of the German controller were unsuccessful and night fighters followed the latter half of the stream all the way to Berlin, blasting bomber after bomber.

F/Sgt Jim Davies, a 21-year-old Welshman, was one of the 101 Sqn special radio operators on the raid, doing his bit to try to stop the *Nachtjäger* gathering by jamming Luftwaffe radio wavelengths. He recalls:

It was one of the heaviest raids on Berlin and I found it very alarming. Positioned where I was in the body of the aircraft between the wireless operator and mid-upper gunner and tuning in to the German night-fighter broadcasts I had little idea of what was happening until we got to the target. Then I walked forward to the front of the aircraft and saw the biggest pyrotechnic display in Europe. It was utterly fantastic. There were planes being shot down, the red bursts of flak, yellow tracer and white searchlights all over the place. It was quite terrifying. Below the city was burning. I watched fascinated for minutes and it was a great feeling when we turned onto a homeward course and I was very relieved when we got back to Ludford Magna.[33]

The teenaged Pathfinder air gunner Sgt Roy Child, whose aircraft had been so badly shot up by Schräge Musik on the Berlin raid of 30 January, was back aboard the newly repaired U-Uncle going to Berlin. He found himself under attack once more – outbound, over the city, and on the way home. Back at 7 Sqn's base of Oakington the crew filed a combat report on the routine Form 439. The cold, crisp words of the RAF file do little justice to the crew's night of terror. It reads:

Outbound at 2100 a Ju88 was sighted at 500 yards on the starboard quarter. The e/a made two attacks and the rear gunner [F/Sgt Grange] and mid-upper [Sgt Child] opened fire each time. The e/a was seen to fall in flames and is claimed as destroyed. Seven minutes later U sighted an Me109F carrying no lights, on the starboard quarter above. The mid-upper gunner immediately opened fire with two bursts and strikes were observed on the enemy aircraft which broke away and was not seen again. The enemy aircraft is claimed as damaged.

At 2139 over the Berlin area homeward bound the mid-upper gunner and rear gunner opened fire on an unidentified e/a which immediately broke away and was lost to view. No claim is made. At 2316 hours U sighted an e/a following astern. The rear gunner ordered to corkscrew port and the e/a was then identified as a Ju88 at 600 yards range. Both gunners opened fire, one machine gun failed to work due to freezing up, U then dived to starboard and e/a for a short time was lost to view, but four minutes later re-appeared on the starboard quarter. The rear gunner gave orders to corkscrew starboard and the e/a was lost again. The e/a once more attacked from the port beam. U made an orbit to port and the e/a was again lost to view. The e/a made a final appearance on the starboard beam. U did an orbit to starboard losing height rapidly into cloud where visual contact was lost and the e/a was not seen again. No contact was made. Rounds fired: Rear gunner 700, mid-upper 800.[34]

Roy Child remembers: 'We had about six attacks that night. When we were coming back the crew were punch-drunk from it all. I went on the intercom and said: "I'm going to live until the year 2000," and not one of them answered me.'[35]

The 77 Sqn bomb aimer F/O Dennis Thorman was in one of the Halifax IIs on the raid now suffering so much from the *Nachtjäger* because of the plane's inability to climb out of trouble. He recorded later:

> On the way into Berlin we were attacked twice, fortunately with only superficial damage. But going over Berlin the flak was fairly intense, much heavier than we had experienced on any previous raid. There seemed to be lots of fires in the city with aircraft going down around us and we were being thrown around all over the place with the flak explosions.[36]

The diversionary raid on Frankfurt-on-Oder had been completely ignored by the night fighters.

A young journalist, Ursula von Kardorff, was among those who heard and felt the shock waves of the high explosive released from the bomb bays of the aircraft of F/Sgt Davies, F/O Thorman, Sgt Child and their countless comrades. She had a flat in the Pariser Platz, off the Unter den Linden, very close to the Adlon Hotel, whose cellars had been deepened and turned into two-tier air raid shelters – the lower one for VIPs and diplomats.

As the bombs fell just after 9 p.m. on 15 February she occupied herself by writing in her diary, surrounded by others packed tight on the hard benches provided courtesy of the Adlon management.

> How lucky I am to be living next door to this shelter, which is supposed to be the safest in Berlin. I had some difficulty making way through the crowded passages ... Every now and then the lights go out. Perhaps a bomb has fallen nearby? Would it be better to be stifled here if panic broke out, or to be roasted to death as they were in the shelters of Hamburg? There has just been the most frightful rush of wind and everything is rocking ... 'they' are bound to come back tomorrow.[37]

Tomorrow looked a dim prospect to the men of the RAF as they turned homeward from Berlin. The night fighters fell on the stream again, flaming wreckage marking the bombers' path all the way to the Dutch coast. F/O Thorman wrote:

We dropped our bombs and were attacked again by a Ju88 shortly after we left the target area and then had our final attack just before we reached Kiel, this time by an Me109. Actually damage to our aircraft was quite slight. We thought that we were very lucky to get away with it so far, but we knew that undoubtedly our time was going to come.[38]

Ursula von Kardorff emerged from the shelter underneath the Adlon Hotel at 11.30 p.m. to find that it and her home next door had in fact escaped the bombs despite fires all around, but another famous Berlin hotel, the Bristol, just across the Unter den Linden's junction with the Wilhelmstrasse had not been so fortunate. 'I stood for a moment or two in front of the Hotel Bristol which has just been rebuilt. A mine dropped on it,' she wrote. 'They say that people are buried in the shelter ... the whole of the Unter den Linden is bathed in a strange, pale greenish light, interspersed with the red of fires.'[39]

A total of forty-three aircraft had been lost over enemy territory in the raid and another five either crashed or were abandoned over Britain. The target had been covered by cloud yet again, preventing a hammer blow. However, those who had bombed accurately had caused considerable damage, some in the centre, but particularly in the western and southern parts most frequently hit. Among the blasted war industries were those at the large Siemensstadt complex. Only 320 people had been killed, a reflection of the mass evacuation from the capital as the Battle of Berlin intensified. It is significant that eighty of the dead were foreign workers, who were unable to leave.

The next day Fräulein von Kardorff was back at the Adlon for a surreal dinner given by the Nazi Secretary of State, Herr Steengracht, as the German Salvage Corps started to clear the rubble of the Bristol, where so many civilians were missing. 'It is said that tapping can still be heard from the shelter, but that it is growing feebler,' she recorded in her diary. 'If I had known that only a few houses away people were slowly suffocating to death, I would have choked over the food at the dinner party ... but we went on eating and drinking and making polite conversation.[40]

The Battle of Berlin, which had burst on the centre of the capital so dramatically in November, had created a feverish, siege-like atmosphere among its citizens as they struggled to cope three months later with the constant uncertainty and nights without sleep. The normal farewell of

'*Auf wiedersehen*' as workers left their desks and work benches for the prospect of another fitful night underground was now more often replaced by '*Wach auf, morgen*' ('Wake up, tomorrow'). The sleeplessness and the infections that spread in the fetid conditions of shelter living were also having an effect on production. A report from Stockholm during the Battle of Berlin claimed: 'Absenteeism in war industries is said to have risen from 10 per cent to between 30 and 40 per cent as the raids affect the health of the people.'

For the better-off in Berlin society the prospect of imminent death created an instability that was reflected in abandon, the like of which surpassed that of the nihilistic Weimar Republic following the First World War. Ingeborg Wells, a young actress at the city's UFA film studios during the Battle of Berlin, wrote three years later: 'What orgies took place during those months! I don't suppose there has ever been such unabashed drinking and debauching in Berlin as during that period. It was not surprising really, considering that one was always in a state of nervous tension, that rumours were flying and that no one really knew whether he would live to see another day.'[41]

Harris still clung to the hope of producing in Berlin the Hamburg-like blow that had eluded him and follow-up mass raids to the capital were ordered over the next three days, each time being cancelled because of predicted poor weather over the target. Finally on 19 February, in response to yet another testy signal from the Air Ministry two days before asking why he wasn't attacking aircraft factories, Harris turned to Leipzig, a centre of Messerschmitt and Junkers production. What the Zahme Sau did to his force on that operation meant there would be no hope of fighting the Battle of Berlin to a conclusion. There would be one more Berlin raid, but not for more than five weeks and that, too, would be a disaster for Bomber Command. Some historians see the raid of 15 February as the true end to the Battle of Berlin and the raid of 24 March as the last tragic footnote, which seemed almost an afterthought to all but Harris. However, the Berlin raid in the third week of March was the most important of all because of what it did to Harris's men. Morale in his command would plummet to its lowest of the war and before the week was out plunge even further because of another disastrous operation.

But all that lay ahead. By the end of January a total of 1,792 RAF and Commonwealth bomber airmen who had celebrated the beginning of 1944 and hoped at least to see the spring were dead. Another 464 were prisoners. These were the worst month's personnel loss statistics in the whole course of the bomber boys' war. Two weeks later another 273 were dead and a further sixty-five prisoners of war. To the young men of Bomber Command suffering in the terrible months of January and February it seemed nothing could possibly get any worse and it wasn't just the defence of Berlin that was killing them in great numbers. Other raids had been mounted in the period to confound and confuse the enemy. One of them alone in January had cost fifty-nine aircraft, almost all of them falling to a German night-fighter force now at its zenith. The name of the target was Magdeburg. The legend of the Luftwaffe's efficient and deadly defence of that city would echo through the corridors of Bomber Command from billet to admin block for weeks to come.

3

The Cost of Courage

It came as a welcome relief to many crews, eyes riveted on the wall map in briefing rooms, to discover the red tape that stretched between Hamburg and Hanover on a familiar route to Berlin stopped short at a town they had seldom heard of. Magdeburg, lying along the Elbe, south-west of the Reich capital and with a population of 320,000, had in fact never been attacked in strength, though it had been subjected to two nuisance raids by Mosquitos in January. Now it had two attractions to make it the night's target for Bomber Command.

Its heavy engineering and tank and aero-engine factories established it as a centre of industry prime for an obliterating attack by a mighty force of aircraft, and it was sufficiently close to Berlin for the High Wycombe planners to hope the Luftwaffe would be fooled into gathering over the capital instead of the actual target. Harris's command, which had lost thirty-five aircraft on a Berlin raid only the night before in a month of increasing attrition, required a respite in losses while keeping the pressure on. Squadrons equipped with the older marks of Halifax, the Mk IIs and Mk Vs, particularly needed to see a reduction in the chop rate after the mauling they had had in the Battle of Berlin. No crews were more apprehensive than those on 102 Sqn. They cycled to briefing at Pocklington that day past the empty dispersals of seven aircraft lost the night before on a raid to the Reich capital. But there was to be no reprieve and for many of the young airmen now dismounting outside the operations hut it was the last briefing they would attend.

Flight engineer Sgt Montague Clarke, who would be shot down less than a month later, remembers the atmosphere on the Yorkshire base after 102 had lost so many men from the Berlin raid of 20 January. He says:

> Four new crews arrived on the squadron next morning and that night they were put on the operation to Magdeburg. Again I saw a lot of aircraft going down. We lost four aircraft that night and three of them were those of the new crews. Nobody had had a chance to talk to them. In two nights the squadron had been nearly wiped out. It was a very depressing time. You didn't know who you might still see in the mess the next day. There was a very gloomy atmosphere. People just stopped talking. We went from having a real old laugh in the mess to people just sitting around, looking despondent. It was obvious nobody was going to get through a tour. Nobody talked about it, but everybody was low.
>
> Morale was so bad that at briefing one night the medical officer came in with some kind of concoction to boost our spirits and we all had to take a drink before we went out to the aircraft. We were flying the Halifax Mk II 1A with Merlin engines, which didn't have the height and speed of other aircraft, and after the night we were shot down I believe they changed the squadron to the much better Halifax Mk IIIs. The 1A was fizzled out for operations.[1]

The crews now listening at briefing to the plan being outlined of how they would hit Magdeburg were told they were part of a force of 648 aircraft. A total of 421 Lancasters, 224 Halifaxes and three Mosquitos, would head north-east in four waves towards the island of Sylt then turn south-east to make landfall into Germany between Hamburg and Hanover, heading as if for Leipzig, then Berlin, but turning 90 degrees in the area of Stendal for the final run in to Magdeburg. A small force of twenty-two Lancasters from 5 Group plus twelve PFF Mosquitos would fly on to Berlin, Windowing furiously, to make the Germans think the Reich capital was the target once more. Each of the heavies in the main Magdeburg force would dispense Window at one bundle per minute from the moment they entered enemy airspace, then increase it to two bundles within 40 miles of the target.[2]

The weather promised to be fair with variable patches of thin cloud and the wind, expected to be at a slight angle to the force on the latter part of the route, was not likely to be excessive. As plans went it had a major flaw. The outward route was similar to that of the night before when the German controller had been able to feed his Zahme Sau aircraft into the stream early, only low cloud over the Luftwaffe airfields preventing a worse casualty rate. The winds tonight would also prove to be stronger than forecast, putting many navigators off track. Following the attrition of the past few weeks new crews were now making up a major part of Bomber Command, even among the Pathfinders. Lacking experience they would be easily led astray by decoy markers laid by the Luftwaffe as they headed for Magdeburg.

German radar picked up the bomber fleet crossing the North Sea. As it made its turn off the coast of Schleswig-Holstein the first Luftwaffe fighters were vectored into position and two bombers were shot down into the water. The force had still more than an hour to run before making landfall and listening stations in Britain heard that the German controller had already ordered Zahme Sau to assemble at a beacon between Hamburg and Cuxhaven, almost on the very track of the bombers. He later ordered them to Hamburg itself and then to Leipzig just south of Magdeburg, but by this time the SN-2 radar of the Me110s and Ju88s had found the stream and between Cuxhaven and Lüneburg south of Hamburg another eleven attacks were made, resulting in four more losses. The night fighters then stayed with the bombers all the way to the target. Bomber Command's Operational Record Section later recorded: 'The fighters' route to Leipzig lay within 20 miles of the route markers which they must have passed just as they were being dropped.'[3]

The feint to Berlin was largely ignored, though at least one bomber found itself off track heading for the capital because of confusion over the forecast winds. The 9 Sqn Lancaster of wireless operator Sgt Gordon Penfold was operating with a replacement navigator after the previous one had been killed over Stettin less than two weeks before. Penfold remembered:

We were on the bomb run over Stettin and I could feel the aircraft being rocked by the flak and it was jumping with the explosions. The navigator, Sgt Freddie Forshew, who was right next to me in the aircraft called out: 'I've been hit.' I saw him slump forward and he was bleeding badly. Apparently a stray piece of flak had come in by his desk. On the Magdeburg operation the squadron had been given the wrong wind at briefing, so we found we had a tail wind. We found

54

ourselves over Berlin and were getting shot at. I could feel the flak buffeting the aircraft. We dived out of it and the navigator had to work out a course back to Magdeburg.[4]

Losses along the final part of the route as most of the bombers approached Magdeburg might have been even worse if the forecast winds being used had not proved faulty, thinning out the now obvious stream as navigators tried to gauge what the actual wind on the route was. Several of Main Force now carried H2S and the strong winds brought some of these over the target before the Pathfinders. Pursued by an alerted enemy they were anxious to unload and they opened the attack before PFF arrived. Main Force were supposed to bomb red target indicators and later greens, but when the first two primary blind markers attacked – one load of flares being plotted 2½ miles south of the aiming point – they found red and green TIs 'apparently lit by the enemy' already burning, and some Pathfinders unable to identify the aiming point held onto their reds. The result was confusion for assembling Main Force crews. 'There is no doubt the enemy made extensive use of decoy red and green TIs,' the ORS later reported.[5]

The bombing was now going astray east and south of the target as blazing aircraft plunged from the sky while the *Nachtjäger* swooped and soared over the arena of bursting TIs and exploding flak. Ten attacks were reported over Magdeburg itself by returning crews who confirmed seeing six bombers go down over the target. Alert gunners in the bomber force shot down an Me110 and a Ju88. One of the Junkers fell to the guns of the Lancaster skippered by Australian F/O James Hancock in which Gordon Penfold was the wireless operator. Hancock remembers:

When the raid started we were still thirty minutes away. By the time we arrived over Magdeburg the fires were very bright and lit the aircraft up like daylight. We were alone over the target and were attacked by a Ju88 with all the aces in firepower, eight machine guns and four cannon all mounted on the wings and set to concentrate at a point about 200 metres in front. It was advisable not to be in that position when he opened fire.

In fact, he made three attacks in all and damaged us in the first attack. After each attack as the fighter broke away I followed him around for as long as I could, giving the mid-upper gunner and the bomb aimer – now in the front turret – longer to attack, until he did a loop and roll over the top (known as an Immelman turn). On the second attack our gunners set fire to his port engine. He made another attack and our gunners then hit his starboard engine. Then after this attack as we were now right behind him the bomb aimer and mid-upper gunner poured a continuous fire into the Ju88 and it exploded. When not on ops we practised the corkscrew manoeuvre endlessly with a Hurricane fighter – both of us using camera guns – which no doubt saved our lives.[6]

The diabolical lightning of combats in the night sky had indeed not all been one way and paradoxically the *Nachtjäger* would lose two of its aces this night. Sharp-eyed and well-practised gunners in the mould of F/O Hancock's may well have accounted for Hauptmann Manfred Meurer, of I/NJG1. Meurer, in fourth place on the *Nachtjäger*'s table of aces with sixty-two kills, took off from Venlo and disappeared. But it was a Mosquito night fighter, part of a growing force now ranging the skies of Germany since the formation of 100 Group, that shot down the ace leading the *Nachtjäger* list, Major Heinrich Prince zu Sayn-Wittgenstein.

Wittgenstein had been promoted to command NJG2 at Deelen from 1 January and was rapidly increasing his score. Defending Berlin on 20 January he shot down three Lancasters, but the final one collided with his Ju88 and he had to make a wheels-up landing. Now, as the bomber fleet headed towards Magdeburg the next night, Wittgenstein was within five places of overtaking Major Helmut Lent, who had seventy-eight victories. Wittgenstein shot down four bombers at regular intervals as the bombers approached Magdeburg, positioning himself in the blind spot underneath them, then letting fly with his Schräge Musik cannon.

His radar operator Friedrich Ostheimer quickly found on his SN-2 screen a fifth victim, which followed the others earthwards, but immediately afterwards there was a banging and crashing in the aircraft, the port wing caught fire and Wittgenstein called '*Raus!*' for the crew to bale out. Ostheimer found himself flung from the aircraft and came down in a copse, eventually finding habitation where he later admitted calling out '*Deutscher Flieger – nicht schiessen!*' in case a German farmer might mistake him for RAF and open fire with a shotgun or beat him up. Two days later Wittgenstein's body was found in the wreckage of his Ju88.[7]

Meanwhile, the tail wind that had brought many of Main Force over Magdeburg before the Pathfinders now brought reverse problems as they turned for home pursued by the night fighters, who would leave a trail of plunging, burning bombers all the way to the coast and even over the North Sea. Sgt Harry Ball was on his second operation as a wireless operator on 158 Sqn at Lissett, near the east coast resort of Bridlington. His skipper, Canadian P/O Allan Van Slyke, had had to turn back from the op the previous night to Berlin because of engine faults.

Sgt Ball remembers:

> Coming back from Magdeburg we were flying into a severe head wind and got very low on fuel. The pilot gave the order to prepare to ditch, but the bomb aimer who was lying flat in the nose of the aircraft said he could see waves breaking as if on a shore. The pilot immediately changed the order to 'Bale out'. I was busy on the wireless set sending out SOSs. When I got the order I went immediately to the rear to go out. The rear gunner, Sgt Lewis Collingwood, and our navigator that night – a replacement for ours, who was sick with jaundice – were sitting on the edge of the escape hatch. I threw myself straight out between them and immediately pulled the ripcord.
>
> Within seconds I was in a ploughed field, having landed between the inner and outer perimeter lights of our home base. I must have gone out at around a thousand feet. The gunner and the nav, Sgt Cyril Evans, came straight after me and their chutes didn't open. I had a guardian angel looking after me that night. The pilot went on to make a straight-in, wheels-down landing on the airfield. The ground mechanics said they found only about a pint of fuel in the tanks afterwards.[8]

In fact, four bombers had gone down in the sea as they ran out of fuel. Apart from the inaccurately forecast winds crews were also unimpressed by the routing, so similar to that of the night before when only poor weather over the night-fighter bases had saved Bomber Command from a worse loss, and they were particularly angry at having to fly back over exactly the same few miles of German coastline south of Hamburg that they had crossed on the way in. One experienced pilot on 158 Sqn blurted out at debriefing: 'The routing took aircraft over the most heavily defended coastal area ever encountered. The flak along 40 miles of coast was heavy and accurate and searchlight activity great. A better way out should have been possible.'[9]

The final tally showed a total of fifty-nine bombers missing, a chop rate of more than 9 per cent. It was Bomber Command's heaviest loss in the war so far. In addition, fifty-eight other aircraft that had struggled home were showing damage by flak or fighter and several would never fly again. Cruellest of all was that the attrition had been heaviest among those very squadrons that most needed a reprieve, the ones equipped with the old Halifax IIs and Vs. Their loss rate amounted to an eviscerating 15.6 per cent. From Holme-on-Spalding-Moor 76 Sqn had lost five of its Halifaxes, 77 Sqn at Elvington had four missing, the Leeming-based 427 Sqn another four and the much-mangled 102 Sqn was now displaying a further four empty dispersals as testimony to the fact that its crews were paying the price of having to fly in aircraft that couldn't reach the height of the main stream of Lancasters.

For many of the young crews of Bomber Command – who had suffered a loss rate of 7.6 per cent on another non-Berlin target, Brunswick, only a week before – Magdeburg tore away any last shred of hope at a time when morale was plummeting and causing serious concern. The disastrous operation had been a classic for the Luftwaffe. Its night-fighter force, now fully restored and more skilful than ever, was defeating the RAF's incursions into its territory on a rising tide of efficiency. The irony was that the triumph of Magdeburg had also cost the *Nachtjäger* two of its aces, Meurer and Wittgenstein.

AS Bomber Command's squadrons replaced their losses with raw new aircrew, over the next 48 hours Marie Vassiltchikov was going through her own trauma. The diarist, who had known Wittgenstein well, was casually told of his death at a Berlin dinner party. She noted:

> I froze. Only a few days ago, in Berlin, Heinrich had rung me up at the office. He had just been to Hitler's HQ to receive from the hands of 'the Almighty' the Oak Leaves to his Knight's Cross. He said on the phone, 'I have been to see our darling' and added that to his surprise his handgun had not been removed before he entered the 'Presence' (as is customary nowadays) so it might have been possible to 'bump him off'.

Marie Vassiltchikov, worried that their conversation might be overheard, stopped him short, but met Wittgenstein a little later when he speculated about blowing himself up with Hitler the next time they met.

> Poor boy. Little did he suspect that he had only a few more days to live. And yet he seemed so fragile that I always worried about him ... He had become Germany's most successful night fighter, was constantly in action and was clearly worn out. He often spoke of the agony he felt about having to kill people and how, whenever possible, he tried to hit the enemy plane in such a way that the crew could bale out.[10]

Mercy notwithstanding Wittgenstein and the other *Nachtjäger Experten* had already accounted for hundreds of British and Commonwealth aircrew in the winter of 1943/4. Magdeburg and the other targets of that bitter January were demanding a price among the young airmen of Bomber Command that they could only meet for so long before the debt of despair was called in. Most convinced themselves – as they watched bombers bloom into dripping blobs of orange fire in the blackness or vanish in an instant of oily smoke – that it could never happen to them. But the evidence of a growing army of strangers in the mess gave the lie to that faith and in the quiet of the night many an airman lay awake in his billet counting the odds on future life as others snored around him. Even those hardy souls who still clung to an irrational belief in their own immortality would eventually find that creed demolished by the evidence of empty beds in their spartan Nissen huts as fellow crews failed to return.

Conversely, some found themselves caught by the adrenalin rush of war. Sgt Alan Morgan, the 49 Sqn flight engineer, says: 'I was never upset by operating. I was trained for it and it was exciting. We had a good skipper who we knew would always bring us back.' However, he admits: 'I was only at Fiskerton for three months and in that time I saw three crews go missing from my Nissen hut. These were your pals, you cooked food on the stove together, you wrote letters together. Losing crews you were billeted with was more upsetting than the actual raids.'[11]

For most it was a struggle to call on their reserves of courage each time they found themselves on the battle order. Sgt Dick Raymond, a 19-year-old flight engineer on 83 Sqn at Wyton, who would eventually be shot down, was fully aware in hospital in January how tenuous his grip on life was after reporting for the Berlin raid of 26 November. He recalls:

> We had been dropped off at the aircraft OL-K as per normal before the operation and I had been in and done my checks leaving the navigator and the wireless operator still in the aircraft with an armourer working on the photoflash. The usual procedure was to have a cup of tea with the ground staff in their Nissen hut 100 yards away. I was sitting in the hut when there was a sensation as if somebody had hit me in the left ear and I found I was lying under a piece of corrugated iron and the aircraft had disappeared with its full bomb load. It seems the armourer had done something to the photoflash. Nothing was found of the navigator and wireless operator, they are remembered on the Runnymede Memorial to the missing.
>
> I only had minor injuries, with bits of rubbish in my head and a leg. But the station sick quarters was inundated with the injured and with the dead, which included a WAAF MT driver. I finished up in the RAF General Hospital in Ely because my leg turned septic. I next flew again operationally on 15 February with a new crew on another Berlin raid. This word trauma didn't exist in 1944 and I came back to the squadron from Ely without any survivor's leave. I sat in the mess until a pilot, F/Sgt Ken Lane, came up to me and said, 'You're flying with me.'
>
> To be honest, after what had happened with the explosion the smell of an aircraft nearly made me vomit. It was shocking to re-enter a Lancaster. The survival rate in those days was so low you felt you were almost under a death sentence. Once you saw your name on the battle order and went to briefing and saw the target and had time to think, that was the worst time. When you were on your way it was better. So many aircraft were being hit and blowing up or crashing on the ground the last thing I thought was that I would be a prisoner of war.[12]

Sgt John Harrison, who joined 106 Sqn at Metheringham as an 18-year-old rear gunner as the Battle of Berlin raged, found himself under attack three times on his first Berlin trip, which also happened to be his first operational flight. The final attack was by two Ju88s one and a half hours into the return journey.

One came in straight away from the rear and I opened fire and it sheered off. But another came in from the side. The whole thing lasted about twenty-fve minutes, the pilot was corkscrewing and we kept thinking we had evaded them. Why they didn't come in and finish us off I don't know. It's possible they were trying to avoid being silhouetted. We weren't damaged at all, even though they had kept pecking away at us. After we got back to Metheringham I thought, 'What am I doing here, on ops?'[13]

On his next trip to Berlin a rocket exploding near by took the head off the flight engineer.*

F/Sgt Bill Isaacs also found the air force didn't always play by the rules it had instituted as its young airmen struggled to complete the recognised tour of thirty operations. He was serving at East Kirkby as a flight engineer on 630 Sqn in the winter of 1944. The squadron had been formed in a rush in December from B Flight of 57 Sqn, which originally had the station to itself. F/Sgt Isaacs says:

We had a very long tour before we were finally shot down. We were in 57 Sqn's B Flight and were senior crew with fifteen or sixteen ops in when 630 Sqn was formed. Because it meant we had changed squadrons we were told we were starting our tour again from scratch. It was simply assumed we would do it. We just accepted it, we were in the air force and that's what happened.

I had done about forty-two ops when I was shot down, including fourteen Berlin raids in all. This was a particularly bad time for Bomber Command and we had had our share of incidents. We had to land at an American base one time after being hit by flak, which damaged the flaps and hydraulics and set an engine on fire we had had to feather. We were frequently attacked by night fighters and Bill Yates our pilot was awarded the DFC for successfully evading an attack one night over Hanover. We were coned by searchlights about four times.[14]

In the aftermath of Magdeburg, particularly, there were other worries for aircrew to add to those of being ejected without a parachute, being burned to death in a blazing fuselage or watching life darkly seeping

* Sgt Alexander Braid, aged 26, a married man who had remustered from ground duties.

away from a flak wound. P/O Dick Starkey, the pilot on 106 Sqn who remembers the tension at misty Metheringham that winter of the Battle of Berlin, says: 'After Magdeburg there were lots of rumours on the squadron that several airmen had been killed by civilians. I don't know how they knew, but it was a talking point.'[15] Douglas Hudson, a navigator on 100 Sqn at Waltham, near Grimsby, in January 1944, also recalls: 'Because Berlin covered such a large mass it was obvious that if you had to bale out you were likely to come down in a built-up area rather than the countryside. We were warned on the squadron that if we had to give ourselves up to make sure it was to someone in uniform, because the women would tear us apart.'[16]

Harris was fully aware of the pressures his offensive imposed on the bomber boys he somewhat ironically referred to as his 'old lags'. Because of it he was content to turn a blind eye to practically all the transgressions of his crews so long as they continued to take war to the enemy. Saluting was not expected on operational bomber stations and when airmen weren't on ops or on standby they could leave the base for nights out on a whim. Should an operational airman survive he could expect seven days' leave every six weeks, considered essential for morale by the few married men – who were strongly discouraged from moving their wives to a town near their base.

Female companionship, even of an innocent nature, was a welcome diversion for most airmen with the prospect of only a few weeks to live. Dick Starkey recalls:

We were very friendly with the local Land Army girls. There were about twenty of them at a hostel in Martin village nearby. A Canadian pilot and I wanted some female company one Sunday so rang up the hostel. The first thing they wanted to know was 'Are you good-looking airmen?' We told them, 'Not bad,' and met them outside the Martin village church that evening and went to the service with them. Two of the girls in the hostel were sisters. Their father had a public house near Leeds and I was very friendly with them.

That friendship went on until we were shot down. The female friendship was very welcome to us in that terrible period. They were so familiar with us I remember the Land Girls asking us what the next target was – not that we knew. When I came home on leave there was always eggs and other food from them for me to take with me. The girls I was friendly with knew where our dispersal was and if we arrived back at 7 or 8 a.m. they would have made their way to greet us and were waiting for us on the other side of the fence.[17]

But if Harris was happy for his airmen's short life to be a merry one, his superiors at the Air Ministry were not. They fought a different war, far removed from bloody fuselages and the operational strain evidenced by twitching faces in the mess, and on 6 January Harris was summoned to a meeting in Whitehall to discuss morale and discipline in the RAF. A special committee had been formed the previous December to see how it could be improved. One of the matters worrying the Whitehall warriors was the lax attitude towards other ranks by aircrew hastily promoted to officer status, as the Battle of Berlin cut a swathe through squadrons. The committee's recommendations to the January meeting were that 'All newly commissioned aircrew should be given officer training' and 'training in their responsibilities as NCOs to be given to all aircrew'.[18]

The Air Ministry had awarded qualified aircrew the minimum rank of sergeant since May 1940. Most aircrew NCOs and junior officers carried their rank extremely lightly and considered others should do the same, particularly if those others were non-operational types. A memorandum to the Air Ministry of the previous August, which had helped to push the Chief of the Air Staff, Sir Charles Portal, into setting up the committee, had read: 'At one Personnel Despatch Centre over a long period no less than 90 per cent of aircrew were guilty of insubordination or failure in some form to comply with orders, many of them appeared on marching out parades, often held at night, drunk and even incapable of standing.'[19]

Harris and Portal respected each other, but the Bomber Command chief did not see eye to eye with many of his Air Ministry colleagues, complaining in his post-war memoirs of 'the multiplicity of directives embodying one change of plan after another', often so cautiously worded 'that the authors were in effect guarded against any and every outcome of the orders issued'.[20] He, alone of the air rank officers heading their own RAF commands, had resisted sending his newly commissioned men for training, pointing out it would mean breaking up crews between the beginning of OTU courses and the completion of an operational tour. Harris, who had lost sixteen of his rank-ignoring, devil-may-care crews on Stettin the night before, reacted at the 6 January meeting with predictable bluntness to the complaints of those who made war on paper. The only problem with the morale of his men he suggested was in watching 'the mounting wages of civilian war workers some of whom in the aircraft industry were reported to be getting £25 a week'. Junior RAF officers now felt they were the 'paupers of the community', he said. In fact, pilot officers on flying duties were being paid just over £5 weekly.[21]

The C-in-C of Coastal Command, Air Marshal Sir John Slessor, suggested P/O Prune could do with a smartening-up and was perhaps now doing more harm than good. This clueless, much-loved character, who appeared in the RAF periodical *Tee Emm* magazine – invariably wearing patched uniform and battered cap – had spawned an award for the silliest aircrew errors of the month. February's would be to a pilot who flew through telephone wires because he said, 'he was avoiding strong winds at higher altitudes'.

The committee would rumble and grumble on, meeting on average every two months throughout 1944. In May, not long after forty-two Lancasters had been lost hitting a Panzer base at Mailly-le-Camp and as Bomber Command continued targeting transportation links in the run-up to D-Day, the committee was worrying about all-ranks dances. It ruled they should only be in addition to separate dances for officers or NCOs, not instead of.

In August, as Bomber Command carried out heavy attacks in the Normandy battle area supporting the coming break-out and even raided in strength a German port city within 70 miles of the Russian Front, Harris received a directive that the Air Council wanted to see an 'improvement in the general appearance and bearing of officers, airmen and airwomen, especially when they are in London'. What the Air Council was complaining about was 'walking in a slovenly manner with hands in pockets' and other crimes such as caps worn at an angle, long, untidy hair, and the wearing of irregular emblems, including the Caterpillar Club badge for a successful bale-out.[22] Harris's crews tended to get on with fighting the war and let Whitehall worry about discipline.

But for those who did seriously upset their commanding officers there was the somewhat euphemistically titled Aircrew Refresher School at RAF Norton in Sheffield. The unit had been temporarily closed down in May 1943 and its personnel absorbed by another disciplinary unit at Brighton. However, as Bomber Command expanded, it was reopened in July 1943 and became the main unit for processing aircrew the RAF considered weren't making a full contribution to the war effort.[23] These included the harshly treated Lack of Moral Fibre cases, airmen who often had carried out operation after operation and then finally found their well of courage had run dry and refused to fly any more. Almost invariably for NCOs a quick interview with their squadron commander was followed by a stripping of their rank and flying brevet and a posting to a demeaning job in an unpleasant part of the country. For hostilities-only officers the process would begin of having them cashiered and drafted into the army as privates. Those with permanent commissions, more difficult to take away, would be 'invited' to resign. In many cases the process would involve a disciplinary course at RAF Norton. And in all circumstances, whether officer or NCO, their files were marked with a large red W for 'Waverer'.

Aircrew, by contrast, usually had a sympathy for those who had cracked under the strain. Rear gunner W/O Cliff Hill, who had already completed one tour in 1943 and finished a second ending in the late summer of 1944, winning the DFM, said:

> I only met one chap who went LMF. He had done a tour and been posted to 35 Sqn for a second. He was married with a child and he did two or three ops, then he told me he wasn't doing any more. He said, 'They can have my stripes, I can't risk my life any more because of my wife and family.' I must say I respected his decision, he had after all done a tour. He was posted LMF and I suppose lost his rank. We never showed fear to each other. After the war we told one another how frightened we had been.[24]

There was little understanding to be found on the parade ground at Norton. On 3 January 1944 the unit recorded seventy-nine aircrew as beginning a disciplinary course, of whom twenty were officers. By April, following raids of ever-increasing losses in February and March, it had risen to twenty-nine officers and sixty NCOs. After the D-Day support operations in June thirty-two officers and sixty-two NCOs would be pounding the parade ground.[25] The harsh 'syllabus' of the three-week course was concentrated on the barrack square. Approximately one-third of it was made up of forty-two hours of drill, twelve hours of morning and evening runs and six hours of parades. Then there was thirty hours of airmanship, law, discipline and administration, fifteen hours of physical training and unarmed combat, nine hours of organised games, six hours of musketry and use of personal defence weapons, and three hours of hygiene and sanitation. Many airmen found it too much to bear and went over the wall. A total of twenty-two aircrew were court-martialled at Norton up to the middle of May 1944 for being absent without leave.[26] What was surprising – considering what a dreadful, strange war Bomber Command aircrew fought, in which the stomach-churning tension of seeing fellow-airmen's lives snuffed out with the ease of nipping a spluttering candle was replaced the next night by a merry time round the pub piano – was how few tours were ended by a refusal to fly any more.

A 1945 survey by an officer of the Air Ministry Personnel Department showed that 746 officers and 3,313 airmen had their files submitted for classification as LMF in the course of the war. A number of these included airmen who had not specifically refused to fly, but had 'lost the confidence of their commanding officers' because of failures to carry out operations through early returns or – in the view of the CO – displaying other evidence of a desire to avoid danger. Out of the 4,059 cases submitted, only 2,726 were actually branded as LMF. It was NCOs proportionately who were more likely to carry the slur than officers, 2,726 being so classified, compared to 389 of commissioned rank.[27] There was a greater chance that someone would notice signs of operational strain in officers before it was too late. RAF doctors shared a mess with aircrew officers. If they saw someone displaying increased excitability, even truculence, or conversely unusual quietness and then depression, they could quickly act on it by recommending a period of leave.

F/Lt Bob Brackenridge, a newly qualified doctor at 27, was the medical officer at the heavy bomber station RAF Lissett throughout most of the Battle of Berlin. He remembers:

> Aircrew tended to suffer from very little, but there was always the minor thing that was enough to put them off flying such as upper respiratory infections which could affect the ears. They would be grounded temporarily. Now and again, of course, there were the psychiatric troubles – not surprisingly. It wasn't very great, funnily enough, but sometimes their troubles were disguised as other things. The headaches they complained of, for instance, would in fact be stress. You could treat them symptomatically for headaches or insomnia and put them off flying for a week to see what would happen. But if there was no improvement we had to get rid of them to psychiatric specialists.
>
> I know the term LMF, but I don't think we used it. I think the usual plan was that if treatment wasn't helpful they had to get to the bottom

of it and treat them and ground them. I never saw one returned to the squadron. They were outside my orbit after they left. Some weren't treated kindly by the service. I remember one aircrew chap not complaining of anything which should have put him off flying, but maintaining he couldn't fly. He was treated rather roughly. There was no specific medical reason why he couldn't fly, but obviously underneath there was.

And yet I remember an officer at this time, who I knew rather well, Andy Holmes from Northern Ireland, a very good pilot, who was in the thick of it in the Battle of Berlin and we could see he was suffering from stress. I suggested he went off for a bit, but he refused. He wanted to carry on and the poor chap was shot down eventually. In the mess I could see aircrew officers who were suffering severe stress and could suggest they came to see me. At the height of the Battle of Berlin the percentage of casualties was really terrible. I could see people getting twitchy, but very often they would joke about it and laugh it off. It was awfully sad. I was amazed at the way they went out night after night.

I remember one tail gunner who went on leave towards the end of his tour and came back to find he had been put down to fly as a replacement gunner that night with a very new crew. He was so mad – stamping up and down the control tower. He said, 'Why don't you shoot me now and save the petrol?' But he went and I'm glad to say he came back.[28]

Going to war surrounded by strangers undoubtedly added to the burden of uncertainty Bomber Command airmen suffered. A few found their crews suddenly broken up and from then on being fed into the war machine haphazardly. Sgt Kenneth Dobbs, a wireless operator on 78 Sqn, was one it happened to after an operation in the Battle of Berlin that winter he was lucky to survive. He recalls:

The Berlin op was a horrific experience, we were picked up by a single searchlight at the start of the bomb run and then witnessed every searchlight panning across the sky towards us. Consequently the whole of the Berlin anti-aircraft defences were targeting us. We could hear the explosions of the flak bursting all around. I left my wireless operator's position while we were over the target and stood up in the second pilot's position to see what was going on and I could see the flashes of the flak around the aircraft. The Halifax suffered a real pounding. The bursting of anti-aircraft shells could be clearly heard through our flying helmets and above the engine noise. It was a question of nose down to pick up air speed and violent evasive action. I don't know how we got through. On return to Breighton we found forty-seven large holes in the aircraft. The Canadian rear gunner, who was slow of movement and speech, so we called him Flash, had come back from Berlin sitting in a turret which was held up by one strut. All four of his guns had been clipped off by flak, but he had no idea he was virtually sitting on nothing.

Following this op the pilot did not fly again, for what reason I don't know and I have never queried it. It resulted in the crew being disbanded and me being dispatched to 158 Sqn at Lissett. I hoped to get crewed up there because a crew is a crew, you live and eat together, but I was just a spare bod at Lissett. I was called in as a spare wireless operator to fly with the squadron commander twice.[29]

It was while flying as a spare crew member, asked to volunteer at the eleventh hour, that Sgt Dobbs was shot down within weeks.

What position a man held in a crew could throw up its peculiarities of stress. Pilots suffered because they realised that on their actions depended the lives of six others. Bomb aimers, heads exposed inside the bubble of thin Perspex as the flak roared over the pulsating target, could well see how the next burst might be specifically meant for them. Many navigators refused to leave the curtained-off cocoon of their compartment from take-off to touchdown, thus able to convince themselves the maps and mathematics were part of a classroom exercise. But it was the tail gunners who probably suffered the most. With their backs to the rest of the crew and a long way from the comfort of their presence they sat in their cramped turrets for hour after hour, their imaginations running wild as they waited for death to wink in the darkness. Married men, particularly, went through agonies for the wives and children they might soon be leaving behind for ever.

Practically no airmen, whether officers or NCOs, were made to face a court martial for actions that might be considered to show a 'lack of moral fibre'. They were 'got away from the station at the earliest possible moment', COs being aware that a court martial would require individuals to remain in the unit for a considerable time, thus affecting the morale of others.[30] However, on 44 Sqn at Dunholme Lodge, near Lincoln, a married air gunner faced such a court martial in the spring of 1944. He had pleaded not guilty to 'imperilling the success of part of His Majesty's forces' by damaging an oil feed pipe to his turret after taking off for a raid on Frankfurt on 18 March.[31]

The 23-year-old sergeant and his crew had been posted to Dunholme Lodge at the height of the Battle of Berlin, arriving on the last day of 1943 as the effects of two crews missing from the raid on the Reich capital the night before were being sorted. It was a period when approximately eighty-five NCO aircrew and twenty of their officers were being posted into the station each month to fill gaps. The story of the man's rapid disintegration under the strain of ops is revealed in the court record.

The sergeant told the court martial he was often able to leave the base to spend nights at home in the industrial city he came from – an unsettling quick change from combat, which was the very reason Harris did not want wives near bases to take the airman's mind off his job. The NCO flew on three ops with his crew, to Schweinfurt, Augsburg and Stuttgart, once seeing his Lancaster nearly collide with another, and all the time he was worrying about his wife, shortly to give birth. 'I couldn't sleep at nights and I couldn't eat my food properly and I began to get jittery,' he told the court martial. He said he reported to the station medical officer with 'ear trouble and pains in the chest'. On the morning of 18 March after returning to base from a night at home with his wife he asked for an interview with his CO 'with regards to being taken off aircrew'. The slip went in the CO's in-tray and within a short time the gunner found ops were listed and he and his crew were already on the battle order. The sergeant said he was so 'nervous and jumpy' even his crew commented on it. He hoped his fear would pass after take-off. 'But I was in that turret all by myself, back away from the rest of the crew,' he said. 'I tried to steady myself but could not manage it.' The air gunner said he got up, grabbed the fire axe from its position above the Elsan toilet and struck one blow to the oil feed pipe to his turret. He then reported the turret u/s and the pilot, who had not yet reached the North Sea, turned back.

In mitigation the court was told the gunner had volunteered for aircrew the previous February, but had already been in the RAF for three years and had been knocked unconscious and buried when his airfield gun post had been attacked by a marauding German aircraft. 'You may think it was a very bad thing he was able to get home so often and his mind was disturbed by these visits,' the defence said in summing up. The members of the court were not in a mood for pity in this fifth year of the war and the sergeant was reduced to the ranks and sentenced to three years' penal servitude, later commuted to two without hard labour. Almost inevitably in this period his crew, now with a replacement rear gunner, were all killed on another operation shortly after the incident with the oil pipe.

IT WAS the lucky ones showing signs of operational strain who escaped being graded LMF. F/Lt Brackenridge, the Lissett station medical officer, remembers:

> I knew convalescent, psychiatric homes existed for aircrew, but I didn't know where. It was usually an executive matter to send aircrew to one of these centres. The recommendation often came to me and I would tell the flight commander and the business was taken from there right up to squadron commander and very often the matter didn't come through me at all. The squadron commander, the flight commanders and the various section leaders had very good experience of the people underneath them. They could sift the wheat from the chaff. They knew very well those who would probably benefit and would return to flying duties, so would be referred to the centre, whereas on the other hand, they also knew very well those who were swinging the lead and were unlikely to return to full flying duties.[32]

In fact, there were several such centres dotted around the country, including a section of the RAF Hospital at Rauceby, Lincolnshire and at Wharncliffe Hospital, Sheffield. The RCAF had one all to itself at Hackwood Park, Basingstoke. But the most frequently used was the Rockside RAF Hospital at Matlock, Derbyshire. The hospital was busy throughout the war, though it was as the RAF geared up for the bomber offensive that its need became apparent and by 1943 it was treating more than 850 patients a year. Many of them arrived showing obvious signs of stress such as facial twitches and sedation figured largely in the first few days, but a third recovered sufficiently to eventually return to ops in an attempt to complete their tours.

There is no doubt it took courage of the kind it's difficult to comprehend today to fly into the apparently unbroken wall of bursting flak that was Berlin or the Ruhr, then – having survived by an apparent miracle – do it again the next night or the one after that. Occasionally a new pilot or other crew member found it a challenge too difficult to overcome, such as the recorded incident of a bomber skipper who set out on an op but found it impossible to keep to the navigator's course, wallowing to port and starboard, and eventually turning back. When he did it again on the next op he was rapidly packed off the station.

But mistakes could be made. F/Lt Brackenridge remembers:

A pilot took off along with the others one night and when he had reached about 14,000 feet his head began to swim and the moon began dancing in front of him like a football, so he turned back. Any plane that turned back without completing its mission was a serious business and called for investigation. When his symptoms were described to me it was obvious it was oxygen lack and the engineers found a fault in the oxygen supply, so he was let off the hook. He was a good pilot. There was no question about him coming back unnecessarily.[33]

On another station, however, and with a less efficient or sympathetic medical officer, the pilot may well have found himself up before the CO accused of LMF and a second early return, perhaps because of a mechanical fault over which he had no control, could have found him on his way to RAF Norton.

The US Eighth Air Force, which would suffer its own terrible attrition in 1944 as round-the-clock bombing became the norm, took a more enlightened view. Combat airmen who showed signs of battle fatigue were sent to rest homes, usually in requisitioned country houses. Extensive sport and amusement facilities were available as was the best of food, two eggs for breakfast being the routine. Airmen who showed little sign of recovery were normally sent home without shame.

Despite the constant battle to hold down their fear aircrew, whether RAF or USAAF, were generally keen to complete their tours or die in the attempt. F/Lt Brackenridge says:

I remember one navigator reporting to me off leave with bowel looseness. I think the crew had three operations to complete their tour. I told him he couldn't fly and would prescribe a chalk and opium mixture to seal him up and he would be OK in a couple of days. But he refused this and said: 'I want to fly, I don't want the rest of the crew to take off without me,' so I relented and he took the chalk and opium with him. He came up to me at a squadron reunion recently and said in good humour, 'Doc, you were responsible for me being taken prisoner.'

That night his aircraft had been shot up and he and his crew spent a couple of years in Stalag Luft III.[34]

The airman had been joined in prison camp by several airmen who knew the coastline pubs and the country lanes around Lissett as well as he did as the winter of 1944 turned even more cruel and January blustered into February. One deep-penetration operation in February saw a shocking tally of bombers shot down, establishing a fresh record for the war. Leipzig would become the new name of dread, not least on 158 Sqn itself, which lost three crews.

4

The Lesson of Leipzig

It would perhaps have been little comfort for Butch Harris's boys, who predicted a short future for themselves after the savage reductions in their ranks caused by Magdeburg and Berlin in January and February, to know that the prospects of their commander-in-chief were also taking a downward turn. Harris's boss, Sir Charles Portal, had at first been supportive as Harris struggled to succeed in the Battle of Berlin. The bomber offensive was after all being carried out on Portal's direct orders. But there was growing alarm at the Air Ministry that the tail was now wagging the dog, which Harris's considerable enemies were quick to take advantage of. The Air Ministry was exasperated with what was now being seen as Harris's insubordination in failing to obey the Pointblank Directive issued to both him and the head of the Eighth Air Force in June 1943 to make first priority 'the attack on German fighter forces and the industry upon which they depend' so that the Eighth Air Force particularly could play its part in the bomber offensive without annihilation. There was now further urgency, as D-Day approached, that the Luftwaffe fighter force be reduced, so that it could not wreak havoc through ranks of shivering khaki.

Harris had interpreted his part of the plan as hitting the cities that contained the aircraft factories, since his crews could not carry out precision attacks in darkness. But those cities were mainly in eastern and southern Germany, too far away to attack in the short summer nights. Then came the Battle of Berlin, which Harris was convinced was a war winner. It was now becoming clear to all but Harris and Churchill – and even the Prime Minister would soon begin to question – that though the damage had been impressive the cost was too high and there would be no whirlwind of destruction as with Hamburg.

Harris received three Air Ministry directives from mid-January to mid-February urging him to concentrate on the aircraft industry. The first, from the Deputy Chief of the Air Staff Air Marshal Sir Norman Bottomley on 14 January read:

> The closest co-ordination is essential to the successful prosecution of the Combined Bomber Offensive and without it, the reduction of the German fighter strength which is a prerequisite to the launching of Overlord as well as to the effective conduct of Pointblank may not be achieved in the time available. I am accordingly to request that you adhere to the spirit of the directive forwarded in the Air Ministry letter dated 10 June, 1943, and that you attack, as far as practicable, those industrial centres associated with the German fighter air-frame and ball-bearing industry.[1]

The raid on Magdeburg, which contained plants supporting the German aircraft industry, came six days later, then Harris went straight back to hitting Berlin again. Even after the loss of forty-three aircraft on the night of 15 February the C-in-C refused to accept that the Reich capital was too tough a nut to crack and only the poor weather prevented him sending his force back to Berlin on succeeding nights. It is some indication of the pressure he was now under that finally, in response to yet another testy signal from the Air Ministry two days before, Harris turned to Leipzig, a centre of Messerschmitt and Junkers aircraft production. It was intended to be a double-strike with the Americans, which would so effectively deal with Leipzig, and then Harris would be able to return to trying to produce a cataclysm in Berlin. In fact, the losses of Leipzig would effectively sound the death knell for that campaign.

THE USAAF, having recovered from crippling losses on the Schweinfurt mission against Germany's ball-bearing industry the previous October, was now joined in a round-the-clock campaign with Bomber Command. The haphazard weather conditions of January had kept many groups grounded at their East Anglian bases, but on 11 January a 650-aircraft mission had been launched on centres of aircraft production in the Brunswick area – Bomber Command had carried out its part three nights later at some cost – and the Americans had then followed up with short-range raids against V1 sites now springing up in the Pas-de-Calais area.

In February leaders of the Eighth Air Force were itching to hit the aircraft production factories of Leipzig. Harris's command got there the night before they did. His first serious attack on Leipzig, one of the more distant on the British target list, had been the previous October by 358 Lancasters, of which surprisingly only sixteen were lost in 'appalling' weather conditions of snow, hail and electrical storms. The resultant scattered bombing necessitated a return on 3 December by more than 500 aircraft, which caused considerable damage, particularly to Junkers factories in the old World Fair exhibition site, but twenty-four bombers had been lost.

On Saturday, 19 February Mosquito weather reconnaissance reported an extensive high pressure area moving south-east across central Germany bringing the prospect of clear skies. Harris ordered a maximum effort to take out Leipzig. Skippers reporting at flight offices were quietly told: 'You're on tonight,' and the machine of administration was set in motion, as crews of more than 560 Lancasters and 255 Halifaxes began the round of paperwork, equipment checks and briefings that would end with the yawning uncertainty of a flarepath and a green light from flying control.

F/Sgt Jim Davies, whose first operation had been the Berlin raid of four days before, was still settling in at Ludford Magna where he had joined 101 Sqn as a special radio operator at the end of January. 'Ludford itself was pretty grim, being known as Mudford, but I got one opportunity to get off the camp in those days after Berlin and had a night out in Louth,' F/Sgt Davies remembers. 'I never really got to know the crew well before we were briefed for Leipzig and shot down.'[2]

At Pocklington in 4 Group's area near York 102 Sqn flight engineer Sgt Montague Clarke, who had found morale worsening as losses mounted in the Battle of Berlin, was looking forward to starting ten days' leave after the operation that night. He normally flew in W-Willie, but on 19 February his crew were allocated B-Boomerang – which belonged to an Australian crew on leave – because it, unlike his usual plane, was equipped with H2S.

At Fiskerton the crew of flight engineer Sgt Alan Morgan were meant to go on leave that very day and were surprised to find themselves on the battle order for Leipzig. They were recovering from celebrating two 21st birthdays following the 15 February Berlin raid – Sgt Morgan's and that of the bomb aimer, Sgt Victor Mackew. Morgan remembers:

I got drunk in the Saracen's Head in Lincoln. I didn't like the taste of beer. I just used to have a lemonade or a shandy, but that night the rest of the crew got me really drunk on cherry brandy. I liked it because it was sweet. We celebrated the bomb aimer's 21st birthday shortly before in the sergeants' mess. His parents had sent him £100 – a lot of money. Our skipper had to tell him to calm down because he was getting all 49 Sqn drunk. He told him to save his money, but he just wanted to get rid of it. He bought a motorbike because I had one. He just spent money like mad.*3

Within 48 hours Sgt Morgan would begin a long ordeal in hospital. At Kirmington 166 Sqn flight engineer Sgt Barry Wright went out to check on Q-Queenie, the Lancaster his crew had flown since the autumn. By the following morning he would have won the Conspicuous Gallantry Medal. At Elvington F/O Thorman woke up to a bitterly cold day, watching the snow fall, and hoped ops didn't mean Berlin again.

Sgt John Harrison, the 18-year-old 106 Sqn rear gunner, was actually pleased when he saw at the Metheringham briefing the target was Leipzig. 'We had found we were going to Berlin every trip,' he says. 'At briefing when the cloth was pulled back and you saw the little red line going to Berlin you thought, "Oh my God, not again." Every night it seemed to be Berlin, Berlin, Berlin. When we saw Leipzig as the target we thought, "Oh, marvellous, not Berlin."'4 In fact, it would be Leipzig, not Berlin, which would claim Sgt Harrison and his crew.

At Graveley 35 Pathfinder Sqn's navigation leader, now working out the final details of the route before take-off, would also not be returning from Leipzig. In the case of S/Ldr Gordon Carter, who had just been awarded a bar to his DFC, it would be his third bale-out. He had been shot down over Brittany in 1943 and evaded capture, then forced to bale out from a burning Halifax over Graveley in December 1943 when hung-up TIs exploded as the aircraft came below their barometric fuse altitude of 1,500 feet.

The route S/Ldr Carter and the rest of the Pathfinders took ahead of

* Sgt Mackew was perhaps right to spend his money in a hurry. He was killed by a piece of flak over Brunswick on 22 April and his dead body was brought back by his crew.

Main Force to Leipzig went towards Denmark then down to Zwolle in Holland – where it became familiar to both Allied and German airmen, it being the direct approach to Berlin – across Holland and between Hamburg and the Ruhr. It was hoped a small force of Mosquitos carrying on due east to Berlin as Main Force turned sharply south to Leipzig at Brandenburg would fool the Germans that yet another Berlin raid was in progress. The Mosquitos failed in this because the Luftwaffe detectors picked up the whole force over the North Sea and then Zahme Sau followed the bombers all the way to the target.

In fact, the congested bomber stream ran into trouble in the freezing night air even before reaching the enemy coast. S/Ldr Johnny Miller, a flight commander on 49 Sqn, had to take the risk of turning back against the stream when well over the sea after both engine generators of his Lancaster failed. He wasn't the only pilot to find the extreme weather conditions and heavy workload for Bomber Command causing problems with his aircraft, necessitating an early return. He reported back at Fiskerton three hours after take-off: 'The North Sea was filled with aircraft flying in every direction, some wiser ones with navigation lights on, most without. Three aircraft were seen to explode in the air, probably due to collision.'[5]

The weather now showed it was on the German side rather than the Allied. The bomber crews had been told to expect a steady head wind, but in fact there was a tail wind in excess of 100 mph. The stream rapidly lost its cohesion as navigators tried to balance the forecast wind against what their instruments were showing them.

It was the last flight for gunner Roy Child. He remembers:

Once we got over the sea we discovered George the automatic pilot wasn't working. Instead of being sensible and turning back we carried on. Because the winds were bad that night the skipper Ken Davis decided to zig-zag across the bomber stream, so that we wouldn't get to the target area too early. We were nearly hit by another Lanc. I could have touched it it was so close as it went over the top of us. I said, 'We've got to stop doing this, Ken, or we are going to get knocked out of the sky.' He said, 'We've got to get to the target,' but I told him it was going to get us killed.[6]

Once the stream crossed the enemy coast it turned into a night of unparalled victory for the German night-fighter arm in which the twin-engined Zahme Sau left a trail of shattered, burning British-made wreckage pointing the way as clear beacons to their as yet unblooded comrades. Eventually flare-dropping Ju88s and Dorniers attracted by the pinpoints created their own illuminated roadway across the sky.

The 101 Sqn aircraft of special radio operator Jim Davies was one of the early aircraft to be shot down. He recalls:

We were flying over Holland on our way into Germany when we were attacked by a night fighter. I was tuned in to the German broadcasts and didn't hear a thing. It was just a bit of luck that I saw a red warning light go on at my desk, switched on the intercom and heard the pilot telling everybody to bale out. Apparently he had said it three times and I only caught the last one. The fuel tanks in both wings were on fire. The whole of the front was an inferno. I picked up my parachute, put it on and headed for the rear door. It was already open and the mid-upper gunner, Sgt William Bolt, was hesitating in the doorway. I just hoped he would jump, then as he went out I went straight after him, head first.* I was the last of the crew to get out OK. The wireless operator, Sgt Cassian Waight, who was from British Honduras, died in the flames I believe. He always refused to wear his parachute harness in the aircraft because he found it so uncomfortable.

As I tumbled through the cold air I counted very hurriedly to ten and pulled the ripcord. It opened with a jerk and I came down in the middle of a field near the village of Tolbert in the area of Groningen. I buried my chute and started back towards the coast.

F/Sgt Davies was taking the first steps on a journey that would end in his betrayal almost six months later.[7]

The Pathfinders had crossed Holland and were heading into Germany when the 35 Sqn aircraft of navigator S/Ldr Carter was lost.

It was clear to us after we crossed the sea that the Germans knew where we were going because they had stacked up night fighters all along the route and they lit up the cloud below with searchlights, setting us off against the glare. We knew from the start we were going to be in bad trouble and Leipzig was such a long way into Germany.

* The body of Sgt Bolt was later found with his chute unopened.

We were hit by a Ju88 armed with Schräge Musik. We didn't know about the upward-firing cannon at the time. I discovered it after the war, but I assumed that was what got us because there was no warning. I know it was a Ju88 because at a Luftwaffe airfield I was detained at temporarily as I went through the interrogation system a German officer came up to me and said he was the 88 pilot who shot us down.

We didn't see a thing, just the port inner catching fire. He had fired up into the aircraft and had an easy job of it because the exhaust flames from the four engines were 3 or 4 feet long and anyone in his right mind can aim between four exhausts. The pilot called: 'Bale out, bale out, bale out!' and I immediately went into the abandon routine. You had to get it dead right or everybody was cooked. I lifted my desk up to make room and turned the handle of the hatch, hoping it wasn't frozen in by people wrongfully lubricating it, then removed the hatch and threw it into the nose of the aircraft. If you didn't do that it could get jammed in the entrance. I turned round so that I was facing to the rear, called: 'Navigator baling out,' and, because I had been through it twice before, removed my helmet. A lot of chaps were hanged by their intercom leads going out. I had one hand on the edge of the hatch and went out and pulled the ripcord straight away. We were at about 23,000 feet, very high for a fully loaded Halifax, and I descended through the entire slipstream of the better part of 800 aircraft. I remember seeing vague aircraft shapes, any one of which could have hit me or collapsed the chute. It was about minus 50° Centigrade and I had no oxygen, so there must have been a period of blackout, but I came to early enough to realise I was falling through a stream of bombers.

I remembered I had a revolver on me and decided I had better get rid of it. I had bought it in Huntingdon in case I ever fell into a city because I reckoned civilians would mob me. It was to take my own life with. We were told that in Hamburg aircrew were killed on the ground, particularly because of the firestorm raid, and Hitler had threatened to have killed every airman who fell on German soil. We even carried Sten guns for a while until someone realised it was preposterous.

I went through the cloud cover and saw a wood, but managed to slip the chute so that I landed in a lane in the forest. I was bang in central Germany near Celle. I had on my back, under my parachute harness, a pack of escape items such as wire cutters and some civilian clothes bought in France during my evasion a year earlier, so I went into the forest and put the clothes on.[8]

S/Ldr Carter's ordeal would continue for the next 48 hours.

The wrongly forecast winds meant that many Main Force navigators were now giving their pilots dog-legs to fly as they crossed Germany between Hamburg and the Ruhr, to avoid arriving over the target before the Pathfinders. Those course changes were being made as the *Nachtjäger Geschwader*, airborne from their airfields in Germany, were being swilled into the stream, giving them more time to find victims. An earlier force sent to intercept fifty-four mine-laying aircraft in Kiel Bay soon joined in. The later inquest by Bomber Command's Operational Research Section concluded: 'They assembled at a position from which they were easily directed into the outgoing stream. The necessity for bombers to lose time, due to forecast wind errors, in this fighter-infested area aggravated this main cause of loss.'[9]

Sgt Child was shot down about 80 miles further along the route than S/Ldr Carter in the area of Wittenberg, north of Magdeburg. He remembers:

The first indication we had of a fighter was when it hit us from underneath in the middle of the plane. The wireless operator, Ken Marriott, was killed in the first attack. The pilot ordered us to bale out. I was the mid-upper that night and Al Grange was in the tail. I went out through the rear door and the others except the pilot and Ken Marriott went out of the front. The engineer we had that night was a replacement, making his first trip, because our own engineer was ill. He was already standing on the escape hatch. It wasn't until I had baled out and was going down that I realised the pilot couldn't get out of the plane because George wasn't working. Al Grange, the gunner, I believe was killed by the Germans. A Luftwaffe chap told me he was in hospital when we demanded to see him, but his body has never been found.*[10]

As Sgt Child came down he could see the fighter that had got his aircraft, still buzzing around. After the war he wrote:

I landed in deep snow and was not able to bury my chute. I started walking to the north and at about 3 a.m. I saw lights which looked like

* F/Sgt Al Grange, DFM, is remembered on the Runnymede Memorial to the missing.

a small village, ahead I could see a church which I thought might be a good place to hide ... alas two German soldiers were waiting for me with the words, 'For you the war is over.' I was taken to a large house and during the next half hour the village turned out to look at me. They all wore the Nazi badge and were very hostile.

Later a Wehrmacht officer arrived with a man in civilian clothes and the villagers were sent away. Sgt Child was screamed at by the officer and was surprised to find the official with him spoke perfect English. The air gunner remembers: 'I said, "I want Luftwaffe officers to take me prisoner." For that I was placed in the corner of the room looking at a picture of Hitler.' Later Luftwaffe officers arrived and Sgt Child began the journey that would eventually end in a prisoner-of-war camp at Fallingbostel.[11]

Rear gunner Sgt John Harrison was one of those shot down in the final stages of the route. He remembers:

We had had to dog-leg to avoid reaching the target too early. We were at about 21,000 feet approaching the last turning point when we were hit from underneath. Our pilot, Dickie Leggett, always weaved to give us a chance to look underneath and as we tipped towards the port side I saw this damned reddish tracer coming at me. It was an Me210, obviously fitted with what we didn't know at the time were upward-firing cannon. I shouted to 'Dive, port', but the bomb aimer thought afterwards we dived starboard. We were hit in the port wing fuel tank and as the German pilot fired he must have drifted from the front to back because the back door was riddled and twisted. The pilot said, 'This is it lads, we've got to go.' The bomb aimer pulled the hatch and was out straight away followed by the navigator and wireless operator. I and the mid-upper gunner Stan Payne were supposed to go out through the rear door, but Payne told the pilot on the intercom we couldn't get it open, so the pilot said: 'Come to the forward hatch, I'll hold her as long as I can.'

We went forward and by that time everyone else but Dickie had gone. I looked across to him and he put his thumb up. That was the last I saw of him as I leaped out at about 10,000 feet. I heard the burning aircraft go over me and I could hear it descending in a half-circle ending in a burst of flame, then I hit a frozen lake near a forest on the edge of Neubrandenburg. I found out after the war that the aircraft had gone into the lake and the German report said the pilot's feet were trapped beneath the pedals.

I got my parachute off and pushed it into some bushes. There was an airfield near by and I saw a tram track, so I walked across it and into some woods to take stock. As dawn broke I saw two or three German soldiers coming my way, so it was obvious they knew where I was. I was taken to the Luftwaffe base. There is no doubt Dickie Leggett gave his life to save ours and I and a couple more of the crew wrote to the Air Ministry after the war in the hope of him getting a posthumous medal, but we heard nothing of it. If any man deserved an award he did.[12]

Sgt Montague Clarke's aircraft was also shot down as it approached the final turning point. He says:

We were a fairly experienced crew because we had done nine operations so we were briefed to drop a marker flare over the Stendal–Brandenburg area at 2.30 a.m. to signal the last turning point to Leipzig. We were told there would be head winds, but crossing the North Sea the wireless operator picked up a message from Bomber Command saying the head winds were now tail winds of up to 150 mph. The route was towards Denmark, then southerly towards Zwolle in Holland. We found we were seven minutes early at Denmark, so had to reduce speed. We lost about four minutes by the time we reached Zwolle. At Zwolle we turned due east to make the Germans think we were going to Berlin. At Stendal where we were supposed to release the flare and turn south for Leipzig we were still two minutes early. It gave a night fighter time to track us. It came up from underneath. We didn't know about Schräge Musik at the time, but that's what got us. There were several loud explosions as he set the port inner engine on fire and he had also hit the bomb bay.

It was so cold that night the rear gunner's breach blocks had iced up, so he couldn't open fire, but Bill Stenning, the mid-upper gunner, had swung his turret to face forward and saw the night fighter appear on our starboard side, climbing, and Bill gave it a good burst. I was in the astrodome and saw the port engine of the night fighter burst into flames and it went over on its back and down.

I shut off the main fuel supply then looked through the inspection panels to the bomb bay and saw that it was on fire. That night we were carrying several canisters of the type of incendiary bomb that exploded two minutes after igniting on the ground and when I told the Canadian pilot, Bill Dean, the bomb bay was on fire he immediately said, 'Right, bale out.' I went to get the pilot's parachute, which was stored with mine just behind my position, and clipped it on for him, then went back for mine, but I couldn't find it. I didn't panic and found it had got buried under bundles of Window. By the time I found it and clipped it on I discovered the pilot's seat was empty, so I was the last.

I dropped my legs through the forward escape hatch and leaned forward. I pulled the ripcord straight away as I went out and there was a terrific tug and the parachute hit me under the chin, cutting me. When I looked up the chute was fully open. I had seen the burning aircraft pass over me and within a matter of seconds there was a loud explosion. I looked down to what I thought was low cloud, but it was ground mist. I landed and when I got up immediately fell over. I was on a frozen lake. The whole country was covered by about 6 inches of snow. The shoreline was only a few yards away, fortunately. I got into some bracken and covered myself with the parachute.

Sgt Clarke would begin evading the next day.[13]

P/O Dick Starkey, whose previous trip to Leipzig in October had been a battle against icing conditions with cumulus clouds up to 20,000 feet, remembers the starkly lit route to the target on 19 February.

I saw a lot of fighter flares going down from high-flying Dorniers. The flares were put down all the way from before the turning point south, to Leipzig itself, about 80 miles. We were flying a corridor of flares and, of course, the fighters were waiting on the outside and just coming in and bumping off the bombers. I could see the combats taking place and aircraft being shot down. It was like daylight. The gunners were calling in that they could see aircraft being knocked down. When we got towards Leipzig we were about five minutes early because the winds weren't as forecast, so I veered off course a bit to lose time. Then I saw the flares going down and went in and bombed.[14]

In one of those aircraft shot up on the turning point to head south to Leipzig was flight engineer Sgt Barry Wright. The crew were on the alert for enemy fighters after seeing so many combats and had already reported fifteen. Wright remembers:

Two fighters moved in and one attacked from close range. The bomber was raked along the whole length of the fuselage, wounding four of us. The mid-upper gunner was most severely wounded. He was hit in his left lung, which collapsed. A lot of Perspex was gone from his turret and the crew couldn't get him out. I had been hit in the back by a piece of cannon shell, which came upwards towards my stomach and stopped just under my skin. The ailerons and rudder had been damaged so the pilot, Jim Catlin, couldn't take evasive action. He was battling all the time to keep the aircraft straight and level. We were shot up so badly that the main electrical panel on the right side of the cockpit had been blown right out and had landed at the back of the navigator. The RAF roundel on the starboard side had just gone we were told later. I was told I lost consciousness three times and when I came round I fiddled with the engines to keep us going.[15]

In fact, the first fighter's attack had also wounded the navigator and left a piece of shrapnel in the arm of the wireless operator, Sgt Tom Hall. A shell had also gone through the main electrical panel and suddenly all the aircraft lights came on. The second Me110 then turned in to attack the fully lit-up aircraft, but the rear gunner Sgt Bill Birch shot him down although the hydraulic controls to his turret were no longer working.

Tom Hall remembers:

We had to jettison the bombs short of the target. I had served as a radio mechanic and this gave me sufficient knowledge to remove the correct fuses and put the lights out and bring the intercom back. I went to attend to the mid-upper gunner, not realising I was walking over gaps in the floor where I could easily have lost a leg.[16]

Barry Wright recalls:

The pilot told us to prepare to bale out, so the bomb aimer jettisoned the front hatch and what with that and the hole in the side where the roundel had been the slipstream was going right through the aircraft. When it was realised we couldn't get the mid-upper gunner out, the pilot told us to hang on as he seemed to have some control.[17]

P/O Catlin's struggle to reach home was just beginning as his flight engineer, whose wounds meant he was unable to stand unaided, tried to keep the engines going despite fainting. The bomb doors were open because the hydraulic controls had been shot away and as the trim controls were locked for a full bomb load the aircraft could only be prevented from climbing by forcing the control column forward. Rudder damage meant it could only be flown in a general westward direction by pushing one rudder pedal fully down. As soon as P/O Catlin reduced the pressure the aircraft flew in a circle.

IT WAS now chaos over the target with some bombers that had not made dog-legs unloading before the Pathfinders, others orbiting to wait then colliding with incoming aircraft, but most holding on for the Pathfinders then charging in to catch the target indicators, causing other collisions. Bursting flak in the crowded sky is thought to have shot down twenty bombers and the Wilde Sau single-engined fighters had also now arrived.

The 630 Sqn bomber of engineer F/Sgt Bill Isaacs was one of those shot down over the target by a fighter. He recalls:

We arrived over Leipzig five to seven minutes too early for the Pathfinders and had to orbit with a lot of other bombers. We were like a hundred moths around a light bulb and that's how they got our aircraft. The first indication we had of the fighter attack was flares going down to starboard, then the rear gunner shouted, 'Dive port,' but as he did so the mid-upper gunner called, 'Dive, starboard,' as he had seen a second fighter coming in and that one was definitely attacking. We went to starboard into a corkscrew and I could see the tracer going over the top of the canopy. We came up to the top of the corkscrew and thought we had got rid of him and opened the bomb doors. We had already gone into the emergency drill, so I handed parachutes to the navigator Alan Spence and Reg Findlow our Canadian bomb aimer and put my own on. Then the second fighter attacked across us and the aircraft exploded. I didn't have any sensation of it happening, I just felt myself out in the cold air. I think the chute was blown open. I landed in a snowdrift to the north side of Leipzig. I had a broken shoulder and a broken ankle and couldn't move. Don Scott, our wireless operator, had landed near by and pulled me out of the snow and we saw another parachute come down. We didn't know at the time but it was Reg Findlow, the only other survivor. Don, who was unwounded, stayed with me until it was light when a German soldier found us.[18]

F/O Thorman's Halifax from Elvington had been attacked three times on the way to the target, but managed to evade the fighters, then over Leipzig itself two Ju88s severely damaged the aircraft. He wrote later:

> They caused a fire in the starboard inner and a glycol leak from the starboard outer. The flare in the flare chute exploded causing more fires inside the aircraft. We dived over the target area from 20,000 feet to 10,000 feet which put out the fires, then lined up and dropped the bombs. By now we were on three engines, but the starboard outer was causing trouble, so we were quickly reduced to two.
>
> We were then attacked by another Ju88 which further damaged the aircraft extensively. Both gunners were hit and there was a fair amount of chaos. Then we were hit in the nose where I was and I got bits of shrapnel in my arms and legs and small bits all over my face. My parachute and another had gone out of the nose with all the navigational equipment. Fortunately we did not fall out of the aircraft. It was bitterly cold and one of the port engines was now giving trouble.[19]

Flight engineer Sgt Frank Jones, whose 10 Sqn tour had begun only four days before, was in another Halifax struggling to make it home in the conditions.

> The winds were all to cock. Most of the bombers finished up over the Ruhr in moonlight on the way back including us. The Germans really slaughtered us. We were picked up by searchlights over the Ruhr and coned. It was a really hot place. The skipper corkscrewed, dived and climbed, he did everything in the book to escape, but it just went on. The flak was coming up. We were coned for twenty minutes in all and were just giving up hope of ever getting out of the beams when the lights slipped away. Whether we got out or they just got fed up I don't know, but it seemed like a lifetime. It was terrifying, particularly with being new. Fortunately we escaped without any serious flak damage.[20]

BY NOW more than seventy bombers had been lost and the crews of several shot-up aircraft were still desperately trying to make it to the sea and safety. F/O Thorman's shattered Halifax flew towards Hanover where the pings of flak were heard hitting the fuselage and hydraulic pressure was found to be ebbing away. 'It was decided that the crew should start to abandon the aircraft,' he wrote later. 'Unfortunately two of the parachutes had gone out of the aircraft in all the pandemonium.' Three of the remaining four chutes were given to the wireless operator and the two gunners, who had all been injured. The three officers left in the aircraft had no navigation equipment, but assumed they were near Cologne, then Liège, as the aircraft gradually lost height. F/O Thorman wrote:

> We decided when we were somewhere near Cambrai that Derek Measures, the navigator, should jump out with the one remaining parachute. By this time we were in a blinding snowstorm at 1,500 feet and heading we hoped for the French coast. Unfortunately it got worse and worse until eventually the aircraft fell out of the sky and we hit a hillside covered in thick snow which broke our fall and the aircraft more or less disintegrated.[21]

F/O Thorman and F/O Thomas scrambled out and tried to destroy the secret H2S equipment with an aircraft flare, not very successfully, then headed in opposite directions. F/O Thorman was soon caught by Waffen SS and taken to the Gestapo jail in Lille where he slept on the floor of a bitterly cold cell. He was interrogated but not physically harmed. Two weeks later he and F/O Thomas were in Stalag Luft III, now a hive of illicit industry in anticipation of the mass escape that would come towards the end of March.

As F/O Thorman's Halifax crashed, the shot-up Q-Queenie of 166 Sqn was not far away, heading for the emergency airfield of Manston. When the Kent coast was crossed and Sgt Wright and the bomb aimer had got the wheels down with the emergency air bottle, P/O Catlin realised both tyres had been burst and ordered his crew to crash stations. The battered and broken Lancaster careered down the runway in a shower of sparks and as it pulled off onto the grass another unannounced aircraft landed.

Sgt Wright says:

> All I remember was crawling down the fuselage to get out of the door, then lying on my back on the grass looking at the wreck of poor old Q-Queenie. The aircraft was so badly damaged that the salvage crew had to break it up where it lay. We four who were wounded were in Margate hospital for a week, then they sent us on to the RAF hospital

at Halton. We had done twenty-five trips and the pilot had done twenty-seven. He had ten Berlin trips in and we had nine so the air force decided we had done enough.'[22]

Apart from being screened from operations Sgt Wright learned the whole crew had been decorated. He had won the Conspicuous Gallantry Medal, the officers in the crew the DFC and Sgt Hall and the two gunners the DFM. Sgt Hall also read in a national newspaper, under the headline 'Lancaster Was All Lit-Up', an accolade to his enterprise in finding and removing the correct fuses to plunge the aircraft back into the safe anonymity of darkness.

As aircrew were debriefed in the cold dawn at airfields that now displayed empty dispersals like missing pieces of a jigsaw it was being realised that something had gone terribly wrong, which couldn't be easily explained away. Alan Morgan remembers: 'I saw three bombers explode. The nav logged them and at interrogation afterwards the intelligence officer said they were scarecrow shells, but I knew damn well they were bombers. There's no mistaking that vivid big red flash and the plane going down.'[23] It was in fact tracerless Schräge Musik that had accounted for many of the seventy-eight bombers lost that night and Bomber Command was at last beginning to wake up to the fact that the new tactics now being employed by the Luftwaffe included a mysterious method of attack from below at an acute angle.

AS airmen in 3 Group at East Anglia were being debriefed there was the hum and splutter of other, American-made, engines being run up at airfields near by, as US airmen manned their Flying Fortresses and Liberators to strike their own blow at Leipzig. The bombers rose like angry gnats in the dawn, orbiting their fields in a pulsating roar and then joining with other groups, to finally form a 90-mile long phalanx of aircraft droning across the North Sea. More than 1,000 heavy bombers were aloft, heading for aircraft plants at Leipzig, Oschersleben, Halberstadt, Tutow and Rostock.

After the massive reaction by the Luftwaffe the night before many fighters were dispersed across Germany and the American bombers were virtually unopposed, creating great destruction at their assigned targets, not least those at Leipzig where damage was such that it was impossible to separate what the RAF had achieved the night before from what the USAAF now caused. It was the most successful operation by the Eighth

Air Force yet. The true meaning of round-the-clock bombing, in which the German people and their defence resources would have no rest, was now being assessed at Reichsmarschall Goering's headquarters in Berlin. Other missions combined with RAF attacks on Stuttgart and Augsburg would follow within days in what became known as Big Week to the USAAF. German fighter production plunged in March as a result. And the Eighth Air Force, with operational heavy bombardment groups, would soon exceed RAF Bomber Command, which had borne the flame for so long, in terms of aircraft and crews available.

A later USAAF report on the mission, sifted and regurgitated by the Air Ministry, read: 'An outstanding feature of the operation is the small loss – 21 bombers and four fighters ... it is apparent that the German Air Force was surprised and overwhelmed by the large force and its employment, particularly following the large-scale RAF attack on Leipzig the previous night.'[24]

The RAF Photographic Interpretation Unit at Medmenham produced its own document on the Leipzig double-strike following reconnaissance flights. 'The recent raids on Leipzig have damaged some of the city's most important industries and out of the ten works listed as being of the very highest priority, five have suffered severely,' it revealed. On the west side of the city there was a heavy concentration of damage mainly from fire in a closely packed industrial area, east of Plagwitz station, most likely to have been caused by the RAF alone. 'Between 20 and 30 firms have suffered. The most important of these is the largest wool spinning and dye works in Europe, over three-quarters of which was destroyed by fire. Business and residential damage was very slight compared to industrial.'[25]

Ilse McKee, a young nursing student who had been studying in Westphalia, returned to her former home in Leipzig not long after the raid to pick up some belongings. After the war she described the acres of RAF destruction that met her eyes as her train drew into Plagwitz station. 'I was shocked at what I saw,' she wrote. 'The gigantic hall was just a mass of tumbled-down girders, grotesquely bent metal structures and splintered glass. In order to get out of the station I had to climb over several great mounds of rubble.' As she ceased clambering she was stunned by the wilderness of what had been a thriving city centre.

> I looked around and I could see nothing but ruins. The big square in front of the station, which was usually so busy, was almost deserted.

There were hardly any trams or buses running ... I went across the Bahnhofsplatz up to the Bruhl and turned to the left towards Augustplatz. I stopped and looked around, searching for the spire of the Thomaskirche which should have been quite near, but I couldn't find it ... not a building was left intact ... everything was still.[26]

She finally arrived at her former lodgings to discover it was just a heap of bricks.

The scale of damage in Leipzig had indeed been considerable and there were those among the population, worked into a frenzy by press and radio descriptions of *'Terrorfliegers'* and *'Luftgangsters'*, who wreaked their revenge. In the days following the double-strike captured aircrew saw evidence of that rage. F/Sgt Bill Isaacs, who had lain with broken bones in a snowdrift north of the city, remembers:

A horse and cart was brought to take me to hospital in Leipzig. As we entered the city I saw six airmen strung up from lamp-posts. We didn't know whether they were RAF or American. The Gestapo were at the hospital and slapped us around a few times. Fortunately when I went into the actual ward at the Leipzig hospital I was treated pretty well, by a Polish doctor. There were about twenty other airmen in there, some with burns.[27]

F/Sgt Isaacs was in hospital until May, then transferred to prison camp at Heydekrug in Lithuania where he finally met up again with the other two members of his crew who had successfully baled out.

Sgt John Harrison, who came down near a Luftwaffe airfield at Neubrandenburg, also found evidence of how vengeful the German public now were as the heavy raiding period that accompanied the Battle of Berlin drew to a close. He recalls:

From the Luftwaffe base four or five of us shot-down airmen were taken by truck to Berlin to be taken by train to Dulag Luft. Before we got on the truck the *Oberfeldwebel* accompanying us said, 'Now look, Berlin is in a terrible state, just act like a prisoner who is completely fed up and don't show any interest because if the people attack you, there is no way I can stop them.'

We hung our heads very low as we went out of the train into the station. Berlin was in fact in a terrible mess, great swirls of streets which were just rubble. You had a tiny sense of guilt when you thought, 'My God, I helped to do this,' but then you thought about Coventry and Plymouth and the other bombed British cities and that the Germans had started it all. The Germans had, of course, developed the V-weapons at that time and if we hadn't finished the war in time they would have come up with something bigger, perhaps the atom bomb.

At Dulag Luft it was the usual treatment with first the heat turned up very high, then down low, but when I was first taken across for interrogation I couldn't help but crack out laughing when the officer actually used the words we used to joke about at home and said, 'For you the war is over.' He wasn't very happy.[28]

Like F/Sgt Isaacs, Sgt Harrison finished up in Heydekrug.

They were joined by Montague Clarke, the last man out of 102 Sqn's doomed B-Boomerang, who came down on the frozen lake near Stendal and had then been on the run. He remembers:

The next morning after baling out I cut the parachute up and wrapped various panels round my arms and legs to camouflage myself against the snow. I got out my escape compass and started heading for Lübeck. At briefing the night before we had been told that if we were shot down to go for Lübeck as there would be a Swedish vessel in the harbour for four days and we could identify it by a clothes line at the stern of the ship with washing all hung upside down. I started walking in that direction by night, hiding up in a forest by day, but after five or six days of this I got frostbite in my toes and decided I had to give myself up.

I went up to a farm and knocked on the door. The farmer's wife opened it and screamed because I was all blood down the front from where the parachute had hit me. Two farmers came running out and I held my arms up and said: *'Englander Flieger,'* but the next thing I was being knocked about quite a bit and they were shouting. It never entered my head that they might kill me. They bundled me in a cart and took me to what I think was the kitchen of the burgomaster's house in a place called Perlberg. He ranted and raved at me in German, then went out and came back with a girl aged about 14 or 15 who could speak English. She asked me questions, but I would only answer with name, rank and number. It was very warm and eventually I fell asleep.

The next thing I felt a stinging cut across the face and when I looked up there was a Luftwaffe officer with two guards. He told me to stand up and salute a German officer. He asked me what had happened to my escape kit, which contained German marks and French francs of course. I told him I had thrown it away and I think the idea of him losing that money upset him more. He put me in the back of a car with the two guards and we drove to Berlin.

As we entered Berlin I saw the body of an airman hanging from a lamp-post. They took me to an aerodrome and placed me in a cellar. A little while later a young Luftwaffe officer came in and tried to question me but I wouldn't answer anything. He got one of the guards to bring me a can of soup and just before he left he tapped his left arm and said it was wooden. He said he had lost his arm bombing York.[29]

Gordon Carter, the 35 Sqn navigation leader, was free for 48 hours after landing in a forest near Celle. All the crew had got out except the captain, S/Ldr Julian Sale – a legend in Bomber Command – and the rear gunner, 19-year-old F/Sgt Kenneth Knight. S/Ldr Sale had crash-landed the Halifax because the gunner had not answered the call to abandon and was very badly injured as a result. The gunner was found dead. S/Ldr Carter, an Englishman who had volunteered for the RCAF in 1941 while studying in the United States, recalls:

I walked, mainly by night, about 100 km westward. It was minus 20° Centigrade and there was deep snow on the ground. The streams and rivers in that part of Germany flow from south to north and were mostly frozen over. The first indication I had of a river was the cracking of ice beneath me, so I had to decide to turn left or right to find a crossing. I hit a real river, the Weser, and knew the only way was to find a bridge.

I had encountered several Germans along the way and had even walked right through a hydro-electric plant, but I was in civilian clothes and wasn't stopped. It was a Sunday so there were not too many people around. Finally I came across a bunch of schoolchildren. One said something to me in German and I answered briefly in French, saying I was a French labourer. The child disappeared and the next thing I knew I was facing a sailor in uniform holding a gun he had been using for shooting crows.

He escorted me to a house where a lady and her two daughters offered me a glass of Schnapps and told me to come back and see them after the war. I was on the outskirts of Nienburg-am-Weser. I was taken into the town hall by the local police and rather rough-handled. I was put in a cell, still wearing my French civilian clothes, of course. I was taken to various places over the next few weeks and at one point, when I was in the cells of a Panzer battalion barracks I realised that in my escape kit, which I still had, was a photograph taken for escape document purposes, which showed me in the civilian suit I was still wearing. Sooner or later an interrogation officer was bound to ask the question, 'What was he doing in that suit in England?', so I chewed and swallowed the photograph piece by piece. Eventually I was inter-rogated at Dulag Luft in Frankfurt and practically the first words of the *Hauptmann* who questioned me were, 'Were you trying to do what Julian Sale, your skipper, succeeded in doing last year?'

He told me they had read about it in the Toronto ski club magazine. He said: 'You must prove to me you are who you say you are,' so I opened my shirt and showed him my RCAF dog tags. He said, 'Most interesting,' and opened his shirt up and showed me the same Canadian dog tags. But he knew who I was anyway. It was incredible what they knew. He showed me a scrapbook on 35 Sqn.

My pilot also had a set of clothes with him he had bought in France during his own evasion. After Sale crashlanded the aircraft he was taken to a Luftwaffe hospital near Frankfurt and died there, nobody is sure in what circumstances.[30]

Within a short time S/Ldr Carter was sent to Stalag Luft III at Sagan, where he was asked to play his part in assisting the coming break-out.

F/Sgt Jim Davies, the 101 Sqn novice, was in the hands of the Dutch resistance when S/Ldr Carter was being interrogated at Dulag Luft and would remain so for months. He had walked from the Groningen area of Holland, hiding up in barns during the day. He remembers:

By the time three days had passed I had become very cold and knew I needed help, so I approached a farm, knocked on the door and said 'RAF', but the farmer, who had young children and an old lady in the house, was very scared. He didn't want to help, so I gave the old lady my silk flying gloves and the farmer 100 guilders from my escape kit. He then gave me a bicycle and told me to follow him to another farm about 3 km away.

From there I was put in touch with the Resistance and passed down through an escape line for about five months. Eventually I was taken to a safe house in Antwerp where I had to wait for a Resistance leader known as The Captain, but unknown to me he was working for the Germans. He took me out to a car where I was told I would begin a journey that would eventually take me to the south of France. But in fact it took me straight to a Gestapo jail. I was in civilian clothes with two sets of false papers and the Gestapo threatened to shoot me. This was now August, however, and the war was entering its closing stages so I didn't believe them. The Gestapo began to see people like me as bargaining chips with the Allies and eventually I was transferred to Dulag Luft and sent to a prisoner-of-war camp, Stalag Luft VII at Bankau in Silesia.[31]

IT was clear within those four days of February as the RAF and Commonwealth losses from Leipzig and Berlin were assessed that Bomber Command could not continue without a change of tactics. The USAAF's Big Week arrived in the nick of time. Harris was able to switch his night bombers away from northern and central Germany to southern targets associated with the aircraft industry, such as Augsburg and Stuttgart, to complement daytime raids by the Eighth Air Force.

The routes to these targets lay mainly through France, away from the busy chain of northern night-fighter bases, and it reduced the average loss per operation for the month considerably. The chop rate of the Leipzig raid, approaching 10 per cent, had been absorbed into a mean average of 5.1 per cent by the end of February. On the debit side the removal from the battle order for Germany of Halifax Mk IIs and Vs after Leipzig had reduced Harris's strength considerably. He lost eight squadrons at a stroke until they could be re-equipped with the much better Halifax III.

There was a further important change following the debacle of crews arriving too early over Leipzig because of the wrongly forecast winds. From then on there was a switchable zero hour, so that the time on target could be altered by transmission of a code with the wind broadcasts to aircraft.

But a solution would never be found to the most serious lossmaker of all – Schräge Musik, the upward-firing cannon, which came unannounced out of the darkness and proved deadly in combination with the hunting *Nachtjäger*'s SN-2 radar, unaffected by Window. Bomber

Command's monthly review of losses and interceptions for February noted that: 'A number of surprise attacks in which the attacking fighter was not seen at any stage – 16 in all – points to fairly frequent use of some tactic by which the attack is delivered from steeply below.' It went on: 'Very few cases are reported, however, in which the enemy aircraft is actually seen attacking from such a position ... so it is not possible to discover from the combat reports the method by which such attacks are made i.e. whether by a special manoeuvre or by use of a free gun.'[32]

Significantly there was no mention in the report of 'scarecrow' rockets, though debriefing officers – undoubtedly under instruction from senior officers – continued to tell crews until the war's end that this was what they were seeing, rather than exploding aircraft hit by tracerless cannon from Schräge Musik. The Air Ministry even put out a press statement a few weeks later insisting under headlines such as 'The "Scarecrow" Flare Is A German Bluff' that crews had nothing to worry about. One pilot was quoted underneath a picture of a vivid air explosion: 'When these scarecrows burst there is a sheet of orange flame for about half a minute, followed by oily black smoke. A shower of coloured fragments shoots outwards and drops slowly. The whole show lasts for about three quarters of a minute.'[33] What better description of an exploding bomber?

So the raids continued in February, though Schräge Musik proved not such a threat in southern Germany at that time. The prospects of finishing a tour temporarily improved: for instance, the loss rate on the Stuttgart operation the day after Leipzig was only 1.5 per cent, or nine aircraft out of nearly 600 dispatched. But for the unlucky the pitiless penalties of air warfare were still waiting.

For young 5 Group flight engineer Alan Morgan that day would shape the rest of his life. He remembers:

We took off for Leipzig at 2359 and came back at 0705 on my 21st birthday. Then we took off for Stuttgart at five minutes to midnight, so I was on two raids on my birthday. This was a period of intensive bombing. You often at that time did an op, were debriefed, got two or three hours sleep, then checked your aircraft and got briefed for another op that night. Some went three nights running, but eventually group stopped that because of fatigue. We were losing aircraft that way. Even on the Leipzig raid when I saw the planes exploding in the sky I didn't think it would happen to me.

We met heavy flak over the target on the Stuttgart raid and we had just dropped our bombs when the mid-upper gunner said the rear door had blown open. The skipper sent the wireless operator with a portable oxygen bottle to check, then after a while the skipper said to me, 'Go and see what's happening, there's no communication with him.' I grabbed an oxygen bottle and went to him. I could see he was groggy so I took my leather gloves off to help him. I normally wore silk under-gloves, but that night I just had the leather. I took him back to his position and plugged him into the main oxygen supply and he recovered. I then went back to the door and managed to close it, but then my own oxygen bottle packed up and I slumped to the floor. My bare hands were touching the cold airframe at the bottom of the door and it was minus 45° Centigrade.

I found out from Air Ministry later that the portable oxygen bottles we were using were only half full. The ground crew would test them and all the testing half-emptied them. The skipper had decided to dive down from 22,000 feet to 10,000 feet and at that height I began to recover. At that point my hands were blistering up and the bomb aimer came and helped me to the rest bed. The pilot decided to land at RAF Ford to get help for me. A blood wagon came out to the Lanc and took me straight to Chichester hospital. There I got the wrong treatment. They put me in a warm room with warm, saline gloves and it made my hands worse. In ten days gangrene had set in. The plastic surgeon Dr Archibald McIndoe from East Grinstead had heard of me and had me taken to his hospital. My hands were put in ice buckets over my bed, but it was too late, the fingers went black and within two months they amputated them.*[34]

For LACW Dorothy Mason, too, that intensive winter period of operations and the Stuttgart raid in particular would be painful. The young teleprinter operator, who had been at RAF Bardney from the beginning of 1943, had joined the WAAFs after her neighbours' house had been bombed, killing the whole family. She remembers:

I met a young air gunner, Freddie Coote, one night at Bardney who I used to dance with in my home town of Nuneaton before I joined up.

---

* Plastic surgery over many months gave Sgt Morgan the ability to grip and in the final few months of the war he returned to flying.

I was walking up one side of the road on the camp and he was on the other. He said, 'What the heck are you doing here?' It was lovely to meet someone from home. He told me he had just arrived at Bardney and we talked a lot, but I never saw him again. He went missing only a few nights later.[35]

Sgt Coote, rear gunner to P/O Patrick Nice, was killed with his entire 9 Sqn crew on the same Stuttgart raid in which Alan Morgan suffered his injuries. The crew had arrived at Bardney only fourteen days before. It was their first operation. They thus became one of the thousands of crews to be killed in the first five operations of a tour, the most likely time for a crew to be shot down.

THE freezing weather of February was followed by an almost equally cold March and Harris could find little warmth to comfort him in what lay ahead. Berlin had proved too hard a task and the Luftwaffe had shown in devastating fashion what it could achieve when Bomber Command launched raids on distant targets in northern and central Germany. He had been forced to turn aside and there were other factors now militating against him. The target cities selected in the last two weeks of February included the ball-bearing centre of Schweinfurt. It was attacked against Harris's wishes on the direct orders of the Air Ministry. The C-in-C's continued leadership of Bomber Command was under threat from Whitehall. And it seemed that even Churchill, until now Harris's greatest advocate for the bomber offensive, was beginning to lose faith as Hitler forced Goering to show that his Luftwaffe could still act offensively as well as defending the Reich.

5

Revenge and Recrimination

The bloom of doom casting shadows through the ranks of young aircrew spread in a new direction in the bitter period before hopeful spring among civilians in Britain. Hitler, stung by the smouldering piles of debris choking productive life out of his own cities, ordered revenge attacks on England and air raids returned to London after a long period of relative nocturnal calm. There was one in late January and a total of five in February. The third of these, on 19 February started a fire in the roof of Westminster Hall as Bomber Command was taking a beating over Leipzig.[1] The following night two bombs on Horse Guards Parade blew out all the windows in 10 Downing Street and another in the same stick shattered nearly all those in the War Office.[2]

Churchill was at Chequers, so did not suffer, but he was back in London for the subsequent February raid and five March attacks. He went back to his old habits of the 1940–41 Blitz, donning his tin hat and climbing to the roof of his residence to watch the fireworks. He also liked to visit his daughter Mary, a junior officer at a Hyde Park mixed Royal Artillery/ATS anti-aircraft battery, to hear her command the guns to fire during a raid.[3] He was pictured with her in the *Daily Express* the day after the second February raid, he in RAF uniform, she in khaki, watching firemen fight to save a blazing building. The *Express* claimed nine bombers had been brought down, partly by AA rocket guns 'which fire flaming red balls which shower in the sky'. And in a reference to the Clark Gable/Vivien Leigh American Civil War epic now enjoying a revival in the West End, the newspaper said: 'They are 20-minute raiders – gone with the wind.'[4]

The short, sharp raids, which became known as the 'Little Blitz', caused little damage, apart from the final two, in February, in which the bombers dived to as low as 2,000 feet to release their bombs in central London, but in total 279 people were killed in a campaign that used bombs as heavy as 2,500 kg. It was not a sufficient balance for the Luftwaffe's Fliegerkorps IX, which had been tasked with bringing a scale of retribution on Britain to cause the War Cabinet to rethink its bombing policy. Its leader Generalmajor Dietrich Peltz, who had himself bombed London in the real Blitz of 1940–41, never managed to put up more than 170 aircraft at one time and could only report to Berlin diminishing returns for an average loss of 10 per cent.[5]

By April the raids died away, the *Daily Express* reporting in late March that even the Berlin newspapers now relegated news of bombing London to an inside page. They also denied the German claim that the Bank of England had been destroyed.[6] The Luftwaffe high command were now incapable of pursuing an offensive war. Thanks to Bomber Command, their energies were devoted to the defence of the Reich. Gone were the days of conquest in 1940 when 26 per cent of German military aircraft production was devoted to bombers. Now it was 11 per cent, and 78 per cent of the planes rolling off the production lines were fighters.[7]

However, the fact that the Luftwaffe could return at all to London's night skies, in a period when Harris had pledged Bomber Command would finish Hitler, irritated Churchill, not at his best following a near-fatal bout of pneumonia in Tunis in December. He was now impatient for Harris to show signs of making good on his somewhat rash personal promise of the previous November that his concentrated winter campaign against the Reich capital would cost Germany the war.[8]

Persistent cloud cover over Berlin had allowed practically no reconnaisance photographs of the Reich capital since the previous year for Harris's staff to paste in his famous Blue Book, and so impress important visitors that Bomber Command was turning Nazi ambitions to dust. Churchill, in a sign of his growing irritation, demonstrated his infuriating habit of sticking his finger into every aspect of the war by asking if some new method could be employed to assess damage, if cloud was preventing visual evidence. In a bizarre memo a member of the PM's staff wrote to Harris on 14 March asking if 'deductions could be made by reading the local (Berlin) newspapers ... in particular that the number of theatres and cinemas open to the public is reduced might provide a useful guide as to the extent and locality of damage'.[9] The Air Ministry itself, anxious to halt this deviant trend of intelligence gathering at No. 10, rapidly dispatched a reply pointing out that 'during the past year ... German press censorship has been considerably tightened and little now appears that is of value save notices concerning alterations of tram or bus routes'.[10] Churchill's method of damage analysis by theatre reduction quietly disappeared.

There was by now considerable destruction across vast areas of Berlin, particularly in the west and south-west as well as the centre, extending to 2,180 acres, or more than 4 square miles, and this did not include damage in the outlying suburbs. Reports were prepared by Swiss intelligence and diplomatic sources during the whole of the Battle of Berlin to evaluate how the war was going and decide whether Germany would ever be in a position to settle its considerable debts. In January and February the Swiss officials had been able to add the names of Daimler-Benz, AEG, Lorenz, BMW, Dornier and Heinkel to the list of aeronautical, chemical, locomotive, electrical and precision-engineering firms destroyed or severely damaged in the campaign, which had even by mid-December's calculation left a shortfall of unfinished armament orders valued at nearly 300 million Reichsmarks.[11]

By early March the US Eight Air Force also had made its important psychological contribution to the Battle of Berlin, 702 Flying Fortresses and Liberators penetrating enemy airspace on the 6th with an escort of 644 fighters. The force had encountered the same problems as its nocturnal RAF colleagues had throughout the campaign, first pervasive cloud, which led to scattered bombing of Berlin, and secondly, fierce flak and fighter defence in great depth. It cost the Americans sixty-nine bombers and eleven fighters, the highest numerical – though not percentage – loss on any single USAAF mission over Europe in the Second World War.[12]

Goebbels had had a seven-minute film made for neutral countries, *Bombers Over Berlin*, intended to demonstrate that Berliners could take it, as had Londoners in 1940 and 1941. Copies were shown in ten Stockholm cinemas that winter.[13] There was rare truth in Goebbels propaganda. Despite its stark ruins Berlin was still functioning. There was no sign of an approaching collapse as Harris had promised and as newspaper headline after headline trumpeted of growing bomb tonnages on each successive raid, some in Britain began to question the morality of what they saw, somewhat simplistically and erroneously, as a war against women and children. Richard Stokes, Labour MP for Ipswich and a fierce critic of area bombing, had reacted as early as December to the publicity blitz accompanying the tumbling incendiaries and careening blockbusters in the Battle of Berlin, by asking in the House of Commons 'whether the policy of limiting the objectives of Bomber Command to targets of military importance has, or has not been changed to the bombing of towns and wide areas in which military targets are situated?' The answer from Air Minister Sir Archibald Sinclair was, 'There has been no change of policy.'[14]

It was a typical government fudge. There certainly hadn't been a change of policy from the Casablanca Directive of February 1943, which had ordered the C-in-Cs of RAF Bomber Command and that of the US Eighth Air Force to 'undermine the morale of the German people to a point where their capacity for armed resistance is fatally weakened' and that Berlin 'should be attacked when conditions are suitable for the attainment of specially valuable results'. But Sir Archibald had refused to answer on security grounds Richard Stokes's question 'Within what area in square miles was it estimated that the 350 blockbusters recently dropped on Berlin fell?', thus being forced to admit area bombing as a matter of record.[15] The man in the street may not have known it, but even the lowliest clerk in the corridors of Whitehall was aware that Bomber Command's raids were area attacks for the simple reason that specific targets could not be hit at night.

It was a pragmatic policy few could disagree with as Britain struggled to survive and hoped for victory, but as the Battle of Berlin raged throughout January and showed no end in February, the fiercest critic of area attacks dropped his own bombshell. George Bell, the Bishop of Chichester – which like much of Sussex had seen German bombers aplenty heading for London in the early war years – had been a consistent opponent of the RAF bombing doctrine, even voicing his disquiet during the closing stages of Britain's own 1940–41 Blitz and the subsequent retaliation, making a speech the night after an RAF raid on the centre and shipyards of Hamburg in May 1941. In it he described the 'night-bombing of non-combatants as a degradation of the spirit for all who take part in it'. He called for negotiations to take place between Churchill and Hitler to bring an end to the policy of bombing civilian areas and in July 1943 Bell attempted to persuade the Archbishop of Canterbury, William Temple, to oppose area bombing. Temple, no doubt briefed about how impossible it was to be accurate at night, refused.

By 9 February 1944 Bell had had enough. He stood up in the House of Lords and asked the government to make a statement as to its policy of bombing enemy towns 'with special reference to the effect of such bombing on civilian as well as objects of non-military and non-industrial significance'.[16] He was careful to point out that 'no criticism was intended of the pilots, the gunners and the aircrews who in circumstances of tremendous danger, with supreme courage, carried out the simple duty of obeying their superior's orders', but instanced how in Berlin half the city was said to be destroyed and 74,000 (sic) killed. Area by area was carefully plotted out until, to use the language of the chief of Bomber Command, 'the heart of Germany ceases to beat'. 'How could there be discrimination?' he asked.[17]

The government had no one more senior in the Lords that day than Viscount Cranborne, the Secretary of State for Dominion Affairs, to make its case and he somewhat weakly replied: 'The RAF has never indulged in purely terror raids.' He dealt with Bishop Bell's concerns about destruction of non-military targets – in other words fine and ancient architecture – by saying it was not the government's intention to drop bombs within the Vatican or Rome itself.*[18]

Bishop Bell was an important though minority voice as a spokesman for the nation's conscience, and both national and regional newspapers were not slow to seek the opinions of others in the Church of England. The *Daily Mail* sent a reporter to the Sussex county town of Lewes, which he described as a local 'stronghold of the church'. 'Lewes is in revolt against the opinion of Dr Bell that the RAF's area bombing of Germany should stop,' he reported. 'Following a day of debate in the diocese the Rural Dean of Lewes, Canon E. Griffiths (whose son was a Bomber Command squadron leader with a DFC), said, "I am convinced that the great majority of people are opposed to the bishop's anti-bombing view."'[19]

On the same day the big cannons of the *Church Times* reacted to Bishop Bell's statement in an editorial. 'The bishop, supported by Archbishop Lord Lang, pointed out with conspicuous ability and moderation that the (bombing) policy had received a large extension. Originally the targets were military installations, ports, communications and individual factories of outstanding size and importance. Now they are entire towns.'

---

* This was so. However, the ancient abbey of Monte Cassino, which the Germans had turned into a fortress barring the Allies' path to Rome, was destroyed by tactical bombing on 16 February.

Crucially, the *Church Times* then came down firmly on the side of the government and showed a knowledge of Bomber Command's problems of target-finding, by continuing:

> We do not suggest the extension lacks reason or justification, though Lord Cranborne's reply struck us as halting and in part irrelevant.
>
> We do maintain, however, that the public should be told clearly what is going on. Merely to bomb big factories is not enough to put German production out of action. Garages and small works on every street are engaged in war work. To destroy them the whole area must be destroyed ... without houses it is impossible to maintain workers ... horrors are inseparable from war.[20]

Harris, certainly, had no doubt about what area bombing meant. He knew what his orders were and even before the fudging of the issue to Richard Stokes in December 1943, had written to the Air Council demanding a more honest approach. Harris complained that 'the aims of Bomber Command are presented as the destruction of "specific factory premises" rather than "the destruction of German cities, the killing of German workers and the disruption of civilized community life throughout Germany"'.[21]

On 15 December two weeks after Stokes's questions in the House, Sir Arthur Street, the Permanent Under-Secretary of State for Air whose bomber-pilot son was in Stalag Luft III, had replied, reminding Harris that the requirements of the Casablanca and Pointblank directives still stood, requiring the undermining of German morale. To achieve this he continued: 'The Council recognize, of course, that night attacks directed against the German war economy involve the virtual destruction of those German cities which are essential to the enemy's war effort and that such destruction entails heavy casualties to the civil population.'[22] No attempt had been made, it was said, to conceal from the public the immense devastation that was being brought to German industrial cities. 'Everyone knows that in attacking the sources of Germany's war potential, Bomber Command is bound to destroy large areas of German cities.' But the under-secretary continued that it was desirable

> to present the bomber offensive in such a light as to provoke the minimum of public controversy and so far as possible to avoid conflict with religious and humanitarian opinion. Any public protest, whether

reasonable or unreasonable, against the bomber offensive could not but hamper the Government in the execution of their policy and might affect the morale of the aircrews themselves.[23]

If Harris didn't know before, he certainly knew at that point that he was expected to wage a successful campaign whatever the problems and criticisms and any reproof would be falling his way – not on Whitehall. However, he still had the *public* backing of Churchill whatever quibbles about Berlin damage the Prime Minister had raised earlier. In a speech in the House twelve days after Dr Bell's protest Churchill had promised that not only would there be no let-up in the Allied bomber offensive against the Reich, but, in fact, it would increase. 'The whole of this air offensive constitutes the foundation upon which our plans for overseas invasion stand,' the Prime Minister said. 'The scale of the attacks will reach far beyond the dimensions of anything which has yet been employed or, indeed, imagined.'[24]

AS debate ebbed and flowed about the success and morality of the Battle of Berlin the Joint Intelligence Committee reporting to the War Cabinet had been preparing its own analysis of how effective the bombing campaign was proving, culled from German newspapers, reports of neutral embassies and its own agents' stories. The file was sent to Harris by Air Marshal Sir Douglas Evill, Vice Chief of the Air Staff, on 29 March.

Like many intelligence summaries spurred by a specific premise the report slanted towards what Churchill and the Cabinet might wish to hear rather than absolute accuracy, and in its litany of Berlin gloom it revealed that a conference of Japanese service attachés in Germany had concluded as the year turned that morale in areas under the bombs 'was deteriorating and that this downward progress could only be checked by the employment of drastic repressive measures'. It also pointed out that a Swedish military attaché had reported that the Berlin raids at the end of January had depressed morale to a new low level. Anti-Nazi sentiment, it was indicated, was considerably stronger than before. Subversive slogans appeared overnight on hoardings and curses were directed against the party and its leaders. In the words of one source there was 'a marked tendency not to give a damn about what the Führer had said', to avoid work where possible or at least to work at minimum efficiency. Tellingly, however, it concluded:

The factor of concentration in time which made so significant a contribution to the success of the Hamburg attacks, has been absent in
the Berlin raids which were spread over a number of months, and
while therefore the sequence of attacks has had a great and progressive
effect, it has not caused the break in morale which the German authorities themselves seem to have feared might result from attacks on the
capital.[25]

It was clear by now that the bombing of Berlin, with its wide boulevards
rather than narrow streets, would not produce the kind of cataclysm
achieved in Germany's second-largest city the previous summer. Yet it
was with just such hopes that the Battle of Berlin had begun. The
sentiment of the British public, however, was still strongly for hitting
Germany as hard and as often as possible to prepare the path for D-Day
and make it a road to ruin for the Nazis. The bomber boys, taking that
war to Germany on a nightly basis, were greater heroes now not less.
And as the dreadful losses in aircraft were announced in BBC news
broadcasts to anxious men and women gathered round the family radio,
who among them could *not* empathise with the anguish of young aircrew
making such a sacrifice for the nation? The ranks of winged airmen,
many of them in Commonwealth uniform, were guaranteed a sympathetic glance from the girls they passed in London's streets, and
newspapers telling of Bomber Command's impact on Germany were
avidly read. Terence Rattigan's play *Flare Path*, featuring wives waiting
in a Lincolnshire hotel for their husbands to return from a bombing
operation, had just closed in the West End in February, after a run of no
less than eighteen months.

Advertisements of the time, often among the keenest tests of a nation's
mood, portrayed aircrew as supremely glamorous figures, one promoting
Odol toothpaste showing a delighted-looking RAF officer with a pretty
girl and urging: 'Cheer up and smile – keep smiling even if you're
running risks.'[26] A joke in *Blighty*, a sought-after magazine in RAF
messes because of its drawings of pretty girls, carried a cartoon showing
a cinema usherette asking a woman with a pilot on her arm, 'I haven't
two together, would the lady care for a seat next to another airman in
the cinema?'[27] So popular in fact were aircrew, particularly those from
the Dominions, proving with some girls in the easy here-today-gone-
tomorrow morals of wartime that it was creating a minor crisis among
the brasshats at the Air Ministry. Statistics showed some girls had been

grateful with too many aircrew and venereal disease was appearing with monotonous regularity in Bomber Command sickness returns.

Tit-Bits, another magazine popular with airmen and delivered free to camps and air bases by its publishers, carried an article on 25 February headed 'The Truth About Britain's Good-Time Girls'. It complained that: 'Many mothers find it impossible to control their 16-year-old daughters who stay out till all hours of the night and will brook no interference with their liberty.' It continued: 'The Bishop of Chelmsford has said the home life's very foundation is crumbling before our eyes.'[28] The following month the magazine carried a prominent advertisement reading: 'VD – Do you know the facts?'[29]

As from January 1944 the Air Ministry had asked for separate VD figures for aircrew and ground crew of Bomber Command to be tendered on a monthly basis after a survey late the previous year showed Bomber Command had the highest incidence in all the air commands with an average of 43.9 cases per 1,000 aircrew, compared to an average of 11.2 per 1,000 ground personnel. As a comparison Coastal Command's figures were 24.1 and 7.6. A report in 1943 had wondered 'whether this was connected with the stress and strain of the increased intensity of bomber operation'. The figures and the report were put before the March 1944 meeting of the Air Ministry's Morale and Discipline Committee, apparently to stem the expected increase in venereal disease infection to the bomber boys in the approaching light, warm evenings from May to September. The committee continued with its policy decided in December of declining to issue free condoms to RAF personnel to prevent disease.[30]

Harris considered VD was the least danger the young aircrew he referred to as his 'old lags' had to face. He was planning another assault on Berlin, with the inevitable heavy losses it would entail. The non-moon period would run from 17 to 30 March and Harris, desperate to see a telling blow against the Reich capital before his command was drawn away to the needs of pre-invasion targeting, and fighting increasing pressure from the Air Ministry to end the Berlin blood-letting, prepared a last gamble with the Luftwaffe. His airmen would run the greatest risks again, but hopefully losses would be less than in February.

In fact, the operation would be a disaster, because as on the Leipzig raid the winds forecast by Met officers for navigators to make their calculations were wildly inaccurate as to strength. That error would spread and weaken the bomber stream to make individual aircraft easy prey for Schräge Musik night fighters. It would begin a week that was the nadir of despair for Bomber Command.

6

Berlin or Bust

The operation that brought the Battle of Berlin shuddering to a close in such a bloody fashion for Bomber Command lacked nothing in ambition and effort. Harris was able to call on more not fewer aircraft and crews in March as the nation's factories and the Commonwealth Air Training Plan not only replaced those hundreds of airmen and scores of aircraft lost over the previous month, but also considerably exceeded them. The reduced need for the services of the bomber boys in the moon period during the first two weeks in March had also allowed crews to ease their jagged nerves as they wondered at the innocence of ebullient replacements repopulating vacant billets and echoing messes after the decimation of Berlin and Leipzig. The Command now had more than 800 Lancasters and efficient Mk III Halifaxes as the squealing and grinding of trucks depositing the fresh faces at guardrooms was added to by the roar of landing bombers restoring strength to the flight line.

In the meantime the losses of the Berlin raids and other targets in northern Germany in the first six weeks of the year had caused Harris to switch his aim to the southern cities of the Reich, defended by fewer and less experienced night-fighter *Gruppen*. It was a sign of Bomber Command's rapidly recovered strength that he had been able to commit 617 Lancasters and 230 Mk III Halifaxes to an attack on Stuttgart under a waning moon on the night of 15/16 March at the same time as 140 of the older Halifaxes and Stirlings were bombing railway yards at Amiens and twenty-two Lancasters of 5 Group were flying out to bomb an aero-engine factory near Metz.

It was disappointing, therefore, that although the defences in southern

Germany were thought to fall short of those in the north, they could prove savage enough to cause losses rivalling those of a Berlin raid. On that March night the German controller guessed the target correctly in sufficient time for him to rally his forces just before Stuttgart was reached, and thirty-seven bombers were shot down. To those replacement crews who had listened to the old sweats in the mess telling them how treacherous the Big City was it must have seemed that nothing could be worse than Stuttgart.

Flight engineer Sgt Dennis Goodliffe was one of those beginning a tour at that time, on 101 Sqn. He reported at Ludford Magna as it was still recovering from the Berlin raids and his first operation was the Stuttgart raid, which claimed a 101 Sqn aircraft. 'When we had first arrived on 101 Sqn,' he remembered, 'the intelligence officer told us: "You're now on an operational squadron, your expectation of life is six weeks. Go back to your huts and make out your wills." It was simply accepted that two out of three of us would be killed.'[1]

As before, the losses from the Stuttgart operation were rapidly replaced and as March headed into the blackness of the moonless period the experts at High Wycombe worked on their meticulous plans to answer Harris's gnawing need for a telling strike against Berlin before the lighter nights took long-distance targets off the list. It was with some trepidation that the approximately 1,100-mile route to Berlin was being charted once more. There was little choice in deciding which way to fly in to or out of Berlin, it was either north-east across the North Sea to Scandinavia and then down, coming out the same way or across northern Germany and the Low Countries; or more or less directly in across Holland and back out slightly to the south-east or north, crossing Denmark or even Sweden. The possibilities were well known to the Luftwaffe high command and night-fighter groups were positioned accordingly. It was strange, therefore, that a route in should be chosen similar to that used on the night of 28 January when losses had been among the highest of the Berlin raids at forty-six aircraft (6.8 per cent). However, on that night the bombers had returned by virtually the same route as they took in, all the while pursued by fighters.

On this occasion, although the route in would cross Denmark as before – at a point too far north for most of the night-fighter bases – the return route would be south-west of Berlin, turning almost due west near Magdeburg, north-west below Hanover, making a sharp turn north-westerly to clear the deadly Ruhr defences and finally out over the Zuider

Zee. It had been noted that on the Berlin raid of 20 January most of the fighters had departed near Hanover.

There was also another facet that night that, it was hoped, would draw off the Luftwaffe. A huge sweep would be mounted over France west of Paris by 146 aircraft from training units in the hope it would fool the German controller into thinking Bomber Command's target for the night was another raid on southern Germany. A total of forty-two bomber Mosquitos from 8 Group would also be out, twenty-seven of them striking at night-fighter fields to further dissuade interference and the rest causing confusion with raids on Duisburg, Kiel and Münster. Ten Mosquitos of 100 Group would mount Serrate patrols in the hope of turning the hunters into the hunted.[2]

There was a popular song at the time, 'Berlin or Bust', and Harris was determined this last gamble with the Luftwaffe for Berlin before pre-invasion needs intervened would succeed as no other. One of his trump cards was to reintroduce the concept of a master bomber, not seen since the Berlin raid of 23 August the previous year. The Canadian W/Cdr R. J. Lane of 405 Sqn was briefed for the task with the radio call sign of Redskin and was told that just in case he was shot down there would be a deputy in a Mosquito, W/Cdr E. W. Anderson, an experienced Pathfinder navigator. A total of 112 Pathfinder Lancasters would be over Berlin, in the hope of starting fires their colleagues in Main Force could not fail to turn into massive conflagrations. The Pathfinders were also told that for the first time in the Battle of Berlin they would be expected to identify their aiming point visually, not by H2S. Only one factor still needed to be considered – the weather.

After so many disappointing results caused by bombing through cloud that winter Harris had been prepared to wait for clear conditions to hit Berlin accurately. On 21 March the weather report was favourable in the morning and the teleprinters chattered at the bomber fields for a maximum effort to the Big City, but it was scrubbed at 6 p.m. because a later report forecast cloud over the capital. It was three days before conditions improved and the plan was resurrected. However, frontal cloud was moving east. It might not clear Berlin in time, so a scheme to raid Brunswick as an alternative was prepared. Finally two Mosquitos of the Meteorological Flight attached to 8 Group brought back a report of encouraging conditions along the outward route and Berlin was selected. There were still doubts, however. The pre-raid weather report read: 'Berlin – good chance of clear skies, but the possibility of ten-tenths thick strato-cumulus. Better prospects at Brunswick.'[3] Harris, however, was determined to hit Berlin no matter what.

A 20 mph wind was expected, blowing almost at right angles to the first part of the route over the North Sea, then increasing to 44 mph as the planned course turned more acutely east nearer the Danish coast.[4] Navigators would have to calculate on their hand-held Dalton computers a compass heading considerably further to the north than their actual route to stay on track, the pencil line drawn on their maps. They would be assisted in ensuring that all navigators were making the same calculations and thus keeping the stream compact, by the 'found-wind system' in which selected navigators had the wind strength and direction they discovered en route broadcast to their group headquarters every thirty minutes. The mean was taken of all these calculations then rebroadcast to the bombers, so that all navigators used the same wind statistics, thus keeping the bomber force concentrated. The found-wind system had been used the last time Bomber Command had ventured into northern Germany, the ill-fated Leipzig raid of more than a month before, when groups had broadcast to the bombers en route that the forecast head wind had become a fierce tail wind.

What no one knew as preparations were made to raid the Reich capital on 24 March was that the wind that night would develop a strength never before encountered in that part of the world at the bombers' normal altitude of 20,000–22,000 feet, a phenomenon now known as the jet stream. It would be so dramatically different from that forecast that some of the selected navigators would reduce the figures before sending them back to their group as they seemed so unbelievable. Then when the groups sent the statistics on to Bomber Command headquarters navigation experts there would also not believe the figures they were getting from the bombers and would scale back the supposed-found strength of the wind before rebroadcasting a wind back to the groups for retransmission to the bombers for all navigators to use. It meant more experienced navigators stayed with the figures they had found themselves while the novices obeyed orders. The cohesion of the stream was thereby lost and the first ingredients were added to a recipe for disaster as many bombers were blown a long way off track to the south, thundering into flak and fighter territory alone.

As 24 March dawned, however, there was every hope of a successful raid after all the planning. On that day aircrew had been able to see in the *Daily Express* as they went for breakfast a five-column picture across the front page headed 'Skeleton City: Berlin, as seen this month by the RAF'. There was a key alongside the image of roofless buildings on shattered streets, numbering wrecked structures from the Reichstag to the Berlin Post Office and Sorting Office.[5]

Some airmen had already seen the fuel bowsers trundling out to dispersals and soon they would hear from ground crew that tanks were being topped up to the maximum. It meant another long trip, deep into southern Germany, or even worse a return to Berlin. For forty-two aircrew of 78 Sqn taking breakfast at Breighton, near Selby, that day it would be their last in freedom and for twenty-eight of them their final breakfast of all. The squadron, which had converted from Halifax IIs only weeks before, would lose six of the new Mk IIIs, more than 200 of which would be going to Berlin from various 4 Group units.

At Kelstern, in 1 Group's area north of Lincoln, three crews of 625 Sqn, which had seen several new faces since Leipzig and Berlin, would also be taking off on their last flight. Mid-upper gunner Sgt Russell Margerison was one of the novices newly drafted into the squadron. He had begun his tour with two trips to Frankfurt in the past six days and on the first of them realised how little he and his comrades knew as a crew. He remembers:

In the turret I was supposed to be facing backwards, but as it was my first target I briefly rotated my turret to the front to see what was happening. I couldn't believe what I was looking at. I thought nobody could fly through it and get away with it, but we didn't get a touch. Over the target itself the wireless operator, who was in the astrodome, saw a night fighter flying below us and asked we gunners if we had spotted it. Quite frankly we hadn't, we were looking above and all round the place at that stage. When I looked down it was so close I could see the turquoise-blue lighting in his cockpit. Both myself and the rear gunner trained our guns on him. We then had a silly debate whether to open fire. We realised our job was to get there and back and not get tangled up with night fighters where we wouldn't have had a cat in hell's chance. We were total novices. I was looking straight down on him and could see him reflected on the fires below. He either didn't see us or had upward-firing cannon – which we were totally unaware of – as while we were having the debate he slid underneath us and we didn't see him again.[6]

Sgt Margerison would be going to Berlin with an American pilot, 1st Lt Max Dowden, USAAF, one of three ex-RCAF American pilots at Kelstern who had volunteered for combat before the USA came into the war and were now serving their tours in American uniform on considerably higher American pay before the USAAF planned to call on their services at the end of their thirty trips.

At East Kirkby, in 5 Group south of Lincoln, 57 Sqn flight engineer Sgt Ken Hulton was another newcomer, but he and his crew were learning fast. Only six days before, on his second operation, an incendiary bomb from an aircraft above had come through the port wing between the outer and inner engines as they made their bomb run on Frankfurt. Also at East Kirkby was Tony Leyva, a 21-year-old navigator on 630 Sqn. F/Sgt Leyva was in the crew of 22-year-old Yorkshireman P/O Clifford Allen and would be flying on his sixth operation in just under a month. It would be Leyva's last, his crew would be among five from the base failing to return.

Among the Pathfinders of 8 Group, leading the attack, was the crew of F/O Harold Hoover, a Canadian with a DFC who had just started his second tour on 35 Sqn at Graveley. He had brought many of his first-tour crew members with him from a heavy conversion unit, including his rear gunner, F/Sgt Cliff Hill, and the wireless operator, F/O Jack Mossop, who held the DFC and DFM. Two nights earlier the crew had made the first trip of their second tour to Frankfurt. F/Sgt Hill was still coming to terms with how many trips he now had ahead of him.

> After a nine-month rest the pilot said he was going back on ops. We knew it was only a matter of time before we were recalled, so we thought it was a case of 'Better the devil you know' and agreed to go back with him. Then he said, 'There's only one snag, I want to get back to Canada so I'm going on Pathfinders.' We didn't know much about PFF then apart from what happened over targets, so we agreed. When we arrived at 35 Sqn we got a surprise because we thought we would only have to do twenty ops, which was the requirement for a Main Force second tour, but then we were told it would be forty-five as we were Pathfinders.[7]

F/O HOOVER'S crew joined the throng of bicycles converging on the Graveley operations block in the late afternoon and shuffled along the hard benches in the briefing room as the murmur of quizzical chatter rose and the nervous puffing of a hundred cigarettes left a blue haze in the air. Eyes stayed riveted on the curtained end wall where the target waited to be revealed. The crews rose to their feet as the door opened and the CO, W/Cdr Pat Daniels, strode down the aisle between them and swiftly drew back the curtain. It confirmed the suspicions of many, including F/Sgt Hill. 'Berlin it was. The usual buzz of excitement increased, loud talk mingled with expletives and a measure of apprehension could always be felt when it was the Big City,' F/Sgt Hill wrote shortly after the war. 'The atmosphere was electric. Jack the wireless operator was smiling broadly. Turning to me he said, "Chop night tonight, Clifford, we'll be able to get a drink in comfort in the mess tomorrow."'[8]

W/Cdr Daniels outlined the route on the map with a billiard cue, emphasising it was vital to keep north of the island of Sylt off the Danish coast on the way in thus avoiding the German defences in Schleswig-Holstein, and gradually trailed the cue to the final turning for the target over the large lake known as the Tollense See at Neubrandenburg, which would show up well on H2S screens. In fact, that last 180 degrees heading into Berlin with the jet stream immediately behind would give the bombers a ground speed of 360 mph, removing the last possibility of an accurate attack as the Lancasters and Halifaxes rocketed over the target while the Pathfinders desperately tried to pinpoint the aiming point at the east end of the Tiergarten through thick scattered cloud. 'The other section leaders followed in quick succession – Signals, Engineering, Gunnery and finally the Met Officer, who was always greeted with a loud cheer,' F/Sgt Hill wrote. 'He outlined the weather. It was expected to be relatively clear over the target with average winds en route and clear at base for our return.'[9]

That night there was another departure from the usual in the run-up to an operation. Harris was so keen to see this last maximum effort in the Battle of Berlin succeed he had sent a message to the crews to be read out at briefing. It acknowledged how the weather had dashed so many hopes in the campaign so far. He said:

Although successful blind bombing attacks on Berlin have destroyed large areas of it, there is a substantial section of this vital city more or less intact. To write this off it is of great importance that tonight's attack should be closely concentrated on the Aiming Point. You must not think that the size of Berlin makes accurate bombing unimportant.

There is no point in dropping bombs on the devastated areas in the west and south west. Weather over the target should be good. Go in and do the job.[10]

F/Sgt Hill remembered the reaction among his fellow, battle-experienced airmen: 'Cryptic to the point of bluntness, no good luck remarks at all. It annoyed some of us.'

The thoughtful crews filed out to their messes for the fresh-egg operational meal followed by the edgy atmosphere of the ante-room – quick bursts of conversation, sudden silences, raucous laughter at jokes that in normal times would not have been funny at all and desultory games of bar billiards as others wrote letters to parents, wives and girlfriends. Many heartfelt final letters that aircrew wrote in the hope they would never be posted would be found in their lockers the next day and mailed to newly grieving relatives.

'This was the worst part, waiting to get off,' F/Sgt Hill recorded. 'At last it was time to go. We drew our purse and Pandora – the purse containing approximately £30 in Dutch, French, or Belgian money according to where you were flying over – the Pandora the escape kit in which was a silk map, Horlicks tablets, chocolate and a compass.'[11] There followed the long, silent process of donning flight clothing in the crew locker room, then another brief period of nerve-racking inactivity. Finally it was broken throughout bomber country as WAAF drivers arrived outside crew rooms and the doors of their trucks and buses slammed shut as the bomber boys, valiantly affecting jauntiness, were taken out to dispersals where their Lancasters and Halifaxes waited, laden with atmosphere in the fading light.

Out at the flight line there were further delays as the latest weather reports were sifted to judge that conditions would be right for a gigantic, successful strike against the Big City. Wisps of fog hung over several airfields in 5 Group and as the minutes ticked by many thought the operation would be scrubbed. At East Kirkby Sgt Ken Hulton waited in his Lancaster for the start-engines signal. It was a long time coming. He remembers:

Take-off was delayed for two hours. They had fired a red Verey cartridge signifying it was scrubbed, but we had been told to stay in our aircraft. It had been my 21st birthday on 9 March and we hadn't had a chance to celebrate.

Behind the fence to our dispersal was the local pub, the Red Lion, and there was a hole in the fence, so we decided we would go and have an odd jar because we were sure it was going to be scrubbed. We all went into the pub except the navigator, who stayed in the aircraft. We had just had one drink when one of the ground crew came in and said: 'Come on, it's on again.' I'd had a whisky I think and was quite happy.[12]

The Red Lion was also the favoured pub of navigator Tony Leyva and his crew.

We got all the information we needed from there about where we were going in Germany. I suppose the chaps who put on the petrol and bomb load had a pretty good idea. If you popped into the Red Lion for a drink before lunch the barmaids would tell you you were off to Berlin or wherever because the ground staff had told them their guess. The pub didn't always get it right, but nine times out of ten they did. It was rather a joke.[13]

At Kirmington, in 1 Group's area, flight engineer Sgt Roy Keen climbed aboard a brand-new Lancaster of 166 Sqn, I-Item. The operation would be the crew's eighth, so instead of having to make do with the Lancasters of airmen on leave they had been given their own aircraft. 'Before we took off, I'll never forget that the wireless operator [22-year-old Sgt Frank Fountaine] said: "We're going to get the chop tonight." The skipper immediately pounced on him, but of course he was dead right.'[14] Sgt Fountaine's Lancaster was one of four that 166 Sqn would lose on the raid.

THE last of the bomber boys tasked with this final blow against Berlin scrambled aboard and the heavy machines began to trundle onto the perimeter track and follow each other nose to tail, engines popping and snarling, down to runway thresholds. There they turned, at airfield after airfield from Durham to Huntingdonshire, seemingly one long queue down the whole of eastern England, bursting to launch themselves into the night. In 8 Group, at the geographic tail of that assembly of might but in the vanguard of the operation, the first of the Pathfinders opened up just after 6.30 p.m. and went bounding down the concrete, its navigation lights flashing past the waiting crowd of WAAFs who waved good luck at departure point, then lifting into the gloom. At Fiskerton 49 Sqn

he crew of P/O Jim Catlin, who brought their Lancaster into a crash landing at Manston
er it had been shot up by a night fighter on the Leipzig raid in February. The whole crew
s decorated. From left: wireless operator Sgt Tom Hall; rear gunner Sgt Bill Birch;
nadian bomb aimer Fred Sim; Catlin; flight engineer Sgt Barry Wright; mid-upper
nner Sgt Tom Powers; navigator P/O Tony Pragnell. The aircraft was so badly damaged
was broken up where it lay.

he happy crew of F/Sgt Bill Yates outside their spartan Nissen hut at East Kirkby. They are
m left: flight engineer Sgt Bill Isaacs; Canadian bomb aimer F/Sgt Reg Findlow; Yates;
reless operator Sgt Don Scott; navigator Sgt Alan Spence; and Australian rear gunner Sgt
ocky' Roche. Findlow and Isaacs were the only survivors when their aircraft was shot down
a night fighter on the Leipzig operation.

LACW Dorothy Mason, the teleprinter operator at RAF Bardney. Tight security meant she couldn't tell her flight engineer boyfriend she knew he would be flying to Berlin.

Sgt Kenneth Dobbs volunteered for the Nuremberg raid and was shot down, being pulled from the wreckage of his Halifax.

F/Sgt Don Gray, whose aircraft exploded on the Nuremberg operation. His black eyes were caused by the pressure of his terrifying parachute descent, upside down, with the open harness loosely tangled round his boots.

W/O Lawrence Woolliscroft, whose Lancaster was also lost on the raid. Fearful of being killed by German civilians, he knelt down and prayed after coming to earth in a German forest.

The international crew of F/O Jim Lord mark the end of their tour at North Killingholme. From left: flight engineer Sgt Ken Down; F/O Lord; bomb aimer Sgt Gus Vass (RCAF); wireless operator P/O Jock Elliott; mid-upper gunner Sgt Pat Scully; navigator F/Sgt Bob Lubaski (RCAF); rear gunner Sgt Jack Schomberg (RAAF).

Releasing the tension: the crew of 83 Sqn skipper P/O Alan Edgar (front) fool around outside their billet. On one operation wireless operator Sgt Alf Ridpath, far left, had counted from the astrodome fourteen British bombers going down within minutes.

Navigator F/O Jim Wright, who nearly lost an arm from frostbite, is pictured (third from left bottom row) with crew members and ground staff at East Kirkby in the spring of 1944. The Australian wireless operator P/O Harvey Glasby, who was bitterly disappointed at miss ing operations on D-Day, is top left, next to the skipper Ken Ames.

Evader F/O Bob Farnbank (top left) with a French Resistance woman, and three USAAF flyers, outside the Normandy farmhouse where they hid in August, anx- iously awaiting the Allies' advance.

Evader Harry Fisher. He was captured by th Germans in the Pyrenees and was released l the Maquis in Toulouse after the invasion of the south of France.

...dr Gordon Carter and his skipper S/Ldr Julian
...e, who were shot down in February. It was
...rter's third bale-out. Picture copyright Gordon
...rter.

...ght) Great Escaper S/Ldr Jimmy James as a
...OW. He was the thirty-ninth out of the Sagan
...nel and was recaptured within days. Fifty of
...companions were shot, but James was sent to
...chsenhausen concentration camp, from where
...escaped again.

...Ldr Steve Cockbain, second from left, poses for the press at Dunholme Lodge, the day
...er bringing home his damaged Lancaster from the Wesseling raid in June after ordering
...r of his crew to bale out. Inset is one of them, W/O Albert Bracegirdle, whose picture
...s taken by the Luftwaffe.

The Fillingham crew celebrate the end of a tour on 101 Sqn. Clockwise from left, back, Sgt Dennis Goodliffe (flight engineer); P/O Ken Fillingham (pilot); Sgt Jimmy Law (rear gunner); Sgt Jack Soulsby (mid-upper gunner); P/O Ken Connel, RCAF, (bomb aimer); Sgt Phil Medway (wireless operator); F/O Stan Licquorish, RCAF (navigator and car owner) ABC operator P/O Adrian Marks (RAAF).

WAAF driver Marian Smith, pictured right with a friend at Kirmington. An aircraft exploding on the runway brought the ceiling down on her in her cottage near the airfield.

Flight engineer Ron Brown. He had been to marry on D-Day, but instead found himself in a Stirling in the pre-dawn over Normandy towing a glider.

O Harry Ball, wearing the Caterpillar
b emblem beneath his signaller's
vet for a successful bale-out. He did it
ce, the second time over Berlin.

W/O Roy Ollerhead told intelligence officers
that his Lancaster crew had bravely taken on
the formidable firepower of a flak ship on
D-Day, but his skipper was ticked off for it.

adian F/O Don Cheney (centre, bottom) with the crew of 617 Sqn's 'Dark Victor'.
e wireless operator Reg Pool (top left); rear gunner Noel Wait (top, third from left) and
igator Robert Welch (bottom, left) were all found dead in the Channel after the aircraft
shot down bombing Brest.

F/O Rhys Thomas lines up with his crew and ground crew in front of their Lancaster at North Killingholme, the day after finishing their tour in September. The navigator, F/Sgt Vic Farmer, is fourth from the left, and the Australian bomb aimer, F/Sgt Harry Stack, is front.

The 9 Sqn crew of Australian S/Ldr James Hancock, far left, at RAF Bardney. The wireless operator Sgt Gordon Penfold, who saw the mortal wounding of their first navigator, is between the pilot, far left, and the replacement navigator. The flight engineer, Sgt Cliff Williams, boyfriend of LACW Mason, is bottom right.

flight engineer John Hennessey, who had seen seven Lancasters shot down over Berlin on the raid of 30 January, would record in his diary the next day: 'There was mist hanging over the 'drome when we took off to visit the "Big City" once more. As we rolled down the runway I could see we were not getting as much power as we could, but skip [F/Lt Don Bacon] just managed to pull her off in time.'[15]

The initial aircraft of what would eventually be an aerial armada 5 miles wide and 70 miles long headed out towards the last British landfall of Cromer. As the Pathfinder navigators began to take readings from their Gee sets halfway over the North Sea the tragic error in weather forecasting quickly became evident. The grid system of signals from England gave good pinpoints, but German jamming rapidly decreased Gee's efficiency the further east a bomber flew. As Windfinder navigators sent back their readings to their groups of wind speeds approaching 120 knots their results caused astonishment among the navigation experts appointed to assess them. The mean – and very much reduced – statistics those experts then rebroadcast arrived in the last hour before the Danish coastline could be checked with H2S screens and as Gee deteriorated to the point of uselessness under German jamming. Many navigators now plotted their aircraft way off track to the south and the stream began to lose its vital solidarity.

F/Sgt Hill in F/O Hoover's Q-Queenie near the head of the stream realised the plan was unravelling as the aircraft passed Sylt off the Danish coast and the bomb aimer, who could see it, began arguing with the navigator, who could not, as to which side of the aircraft the island was on. The wireless operator then chipped in with the news that he had received a new wind strength from base of 80 knots. F/Sgt Hill recalled:

The navigator disagreed, saying, 'That's not what I'm getting, I calculate more like 110 to 120 knots.' Hoov answered, 'Bloody impossible.' The H2S operator replied, 'We must have drifted well off track, navigator could well be right on the wind velocity.' Then the navigator said, 'Of course I'm bloody well right, group are way out, they are not here.' I spoke: 'We're passing something, somebody is getting hell knocked out of them over to starboard.' A plane was held in searchlights and was taking a hell of a battering, then it glowed red and began to fall. 'It's in the drink,' someone said.[16]

F/Sgt Leyva, not far back in the stream in his 630 Sqn Lancaster, found the same problems.

By golly it was a strong wind. Across the North Sea we lost Gee and I was never very good at astro-navigation, although it was never very certain anyway from a moving platform. Of course there was no way we could get a fix as the H2S showed nothing over the sea. By the time I got my first fix on the Danish coast I discovered we were a hell of a long way further south than we should have been. We had blundered over Sylt, which had an awful lot of ack-ack. I ignored the rebroadcast winds we were getting and used my own found winds. We went on and did a few semi-circles and dog-legs and went down south past Stettin to Berlin.[17]

The usual mechanical malfunctions on over-stretched aircraft from faulty turrets to overheating engines had by this time evidenced themselves as they did on any operation. One skipper, P/O Howard Farmiloe from 61 Sqn, suffered an engine failure over the North Sea, but decided to press on to Berlin. Before the night was through he would be in line for the DSO, one of very few awarded to RAF junior officers in the war. A total of fifty-three crews had already turned back, however. Australian P/O Keith Simpson radioed his 158 Sqn aircraft was returning with serious engine trouble then ditched less than an hour later off Winterton-on-Sea, Norfolk. The Halifax exploded in a coastal minefield.

There were now 755 bombers thundering across the Baltic at surprising ground speeds in a scattered widening stream, making landfall east of Rostock. The force of 146 training aircraft mounting a sweep east of Paris had already turned for home and their blips on German radar screens had been recognised as a spoof. The German controller became certain Berlin was the target as the force bypassed Stettin and briefed his night fighters by running commentary. Among the Zahme Sau flying that night was the ace Hauptmann Paul Zorner, aloft in his Me110 from St Trond in Belgium. It had been the usual confused picture since the Luftwaffe had been alerted to a major raid pending earlier in the day by the radio tests of bombers being prepared for the night's operation. He recalls:

We had quite an early warning from the *Nachtjäger* command of a raid, but for a long time it was uncertain what we could expect. There were intrusions reported in the direction of southern Denmark and others in northern France. Bit by bit it was decided that the enemy aircraft in northern France were just a red herring and the mass of bombers was in the north. We got the 'go' shortly before 2030 and took off five minutes later heading north-east. After about an hour there was a report from the *Luftreportage* that the bombers were pretty scattered, but had now changed direction to the south-east. At that time I was north of the Ruhr at 6,000 metres, so decided to head east. The visibility was perfect in a cloudless sky, but there was nothing in sight. After about another thirty minutes flying east I saw searchlights, flak and soon burning aircraft crashing. I then saw the bombing and fires beginning and realised it must be Berlin. I doubted that I could get there in time.[18]

Hptmn Zorner would claim his thirty-seventh victim before the night was through.

THE full force of the jet stream, at this time almost directly behind them, had been felt as those bombers still on track turned over the clearly outlined lake at Neubrandenburg in clear weather and headed for Berlin. Some aircraft began to be picked up by Zahme Sau night fighters at this point. One of the *Nachtjäger* was that of the ace Major Helmut Lent, *Kommodore* of NJG3 and a Protestant pastor's son. He shot down two four-engined bombers in the Berlin area aided by his *funker* (radar operator) Oberfeldwebel Walter Kubisch. They had the unit's official war correspondent on board, Leutnant Werner Kark, and his report, high on propaganda, later appeared in the *Oberdonau Zeitung* newspaper.

Kark, who would later be killed with Lent, described how the first victory came as the flak fire intensified over Berlin, which lay ahead of them. Suddenly there was a whip-like crack along the fuselage, which meant they had run into the slipstream of an enemy bomber.

'I've got him – I can see him,' comes from the front seat. Slowly we creep up on the enemy. The *Kommodore* opens fire. Dull thuds vibrate through the fighter's fuselage. There are dazzling flashes in the cockpit. All our guns are sending a long burst into the heavy four-engined bomber aircraft ahead of us. 'He's burning,' says Lent, 'he's really burning!' It comes from his mouth as casually as if he were sitting at his office desk. At the same time we catch sight of the burning enemy. Its wide wings are swathed in flame. In a steep dive it races towards the earth like a torch. Searchlights pick it up and follow it down over the silent landscape until it hits the ground. A blazing pyre, black smoke, then fiery embers. The first kill this memorable night and certainly a Pathfinder.*[19]

THE power of the jet stream meant that many aircraft overshot the target. F/O Harold Hoover's Q-Queenie of 35 Sqn, scheduled as a supporter for the more experienced twenty-five Pathfinder blind markers asked to mark the Tiergarten aiming point visually, was one of them. The captain decided to fly a half-circuit to bring his Lancaster back into the main stream of early Pathfinders.

Among those blind markers, S/Ldr Keith Cresswell, a veteran flight commander on 35 Sqn, had arrived over Berlin at 2227 to find nine-tenths cloud at about 8–10,000 feet, but good horizontal visibility. He could see two skymarkers going down on arrival, but had to identify the aiming point on H2S and dropped only his Cookie and selected markers. He later reported back at Graveley: 'The attack was very scattered at first, improving in the later stages with a better concentration of skymarkers. The attack seemed to be a terrific overshoot. A large bunch of reds and greens were seen about ten miles south-west of the target on the way out. The remainder of my load was brought back as conditions did not permit visual marking.'[20] The intelligence officer conducting the debriefing, who had heard countless tales of daring before, failed to record that S/Ldr Cresswell had had a tussle with an FW190, his mid-upper gunner Sgt Randolph Rhodes shooting it down.

P/O Dick Starkey of 106 Sqn, who remembers the doomed atmosphere among aircrew at Metheringham that winter and was now making his ninth Berlin trip, also arrived early in the target area after telling his navigator to plot on the winds he had found himself because it was obvious the rebroadcast winds from their group were wrong. He says:

I did a circuit on the eastern side of Berlin to wait for PFF. By the time we came back round the markers were going down. The activity over the target was awesome as it was on all Berlin raids. The fighters no longer waited on the outside, they flew amongst the anti-aircraft

* This was probably the Lancaster of New Zealander F/O John Mee DFC, of the Pathfinder 7 Sqn, the only aircraft known to have been shot down as it approached Berlin from the north-east.

fire. On the bombing run with two other Lancasters a fighter flew past our nose firing at one of the bombers. There were tracers all over the sky as the gunners from my aircraft and the third Lancaster joined in with the gunners of the one targeted, but the Lancaster the fighter was going for turned over and went down in flames.[21]

F/Sgt Leyva's Lancaster was over the target at the same time. He remembers:

They had advanced the time on target by five minutes because of the strong wind. Our particular role was as backers-up to the Pathfinders arriving a minute before Main Force to put bombs down as far forward as we could on PFF's circle of fire on the principle there was always creepback later as people dropped their bombs as soon as possible and pushed off. We bombed virtually on the front row of the Pathfinders' flares, turned right and proceeded back. I never looked out at a target. On our first raid on Augsburg it frightened me so much I never looked again and stayed in my compartment working out the next course.[22]

F/O Hoover's Lancaster with F/Sgt Hill in the rear turret completed its orbit and came into the attack as green and red target indicators started to fall. 'Odd gaps could be seen, but little of the ground, which appeared hazy, glowing red with flashes from scattered exploding bombs,' F/Sgt Hill wrote. 'From the rear turret it looked as if it had the makings of a shambles. The bomb aimer could not find a concentration of target indicators that appeared accurate enough to release our bombs on. "We'll go round again," Hoov said.'[23]

The attack was indeed deteriorating into a shambles. It had been intended that a co-ordinated stream of five waves would release 2,493 tons on Berlin from the Tiergarten to the largely undamaged north and east of the centre in a twenty-minute cataclysm of sound and fire to knock out the air raid defences. Instead aircraft were arriving haphazardly from the west, north and north-east, well off track because of the strong wind and then overshooting cloud-covered Berlin and turning back to bomb. The extensive cloud cover with occasional gaps meant some Pathfinders dropped their red and green target indicators visually, but most had to resort to Wanganui skymarking with parachute-held TIs, which were quickly blown across the target in the jet stream.

It was not the night to reinstitute the role of master bomber, often known as master of ceremonies. Neither W/Cdr Lane nor his deputy W/Cdr Anderson had any chance of being able to stop the chaos. The Bomber Command intelligence narrative into the raid the next day stated: 'The Master of Ceremonies was heard in spite of jamming and was generally more helpful in giving encouragement than in directing the bombing.'[24]

Flight engineer Sgt Frank Jones was over Berlin in a low-ceiling Mk II Halifax, officially barred from German targets, but put up by 10 Sqn, who were still re-equipping, because of the maximum effort order. He remembers:

The rumour on the squadron at that time was that the Germans were using captured British and American bombers to drop flares to illuminate the bomber stream from the right altitude. Sure enough, as we approached the run-in to bomb, an avenue of fighter flares dropped from above, making it like brilliant daylight. Those flares lasted for quite a long time and they stretched right into the target. You could only see the flash of the explosion as bombers were hit. The gunners were watching all the time for night fighters coming in and I stood in the astrodome to keep a watch, but we escaped without an individual attack.[25]

P/O Farmiloe arrived over Berlin in H-Hellzapoppin and began his bomb run on three engines amid bursting flak. At 18,500 feet the second of his starboard engines failed, but Farmiloe was able to bomb the target before turning for home, trailing fire from the newly damaged engine. The 22-year-old pilot was unable to put out the blaze and expecting to be pounced on by a night fighter at every mile he flew westward like a beacon. He eventually made it to the North Sea, all the while with his bomb aimer, Sgt Ken Vowe, clasping the starboard rudder pedal in an arm lock to stop the descending aircraft flying in circles.[26]

The 166 Sqn Lancaster of F/Sgt Roy Keen reached the target twenty minutes early because of the fierce tailwind. He later recalled:

We couldn't find anything to bomb the first time, so we went round again – we assume it was a fighter that actually took us out from underneath, but nobody saw it, none of the gunners reported anything. There's a step from the flight engineer's position down to the bomb aimer's compartment – I was sitting on that step looking out of the window and we had this horrible crash, a funny kind of sound, very loud, and I looked around and my panel had disappeared. There was a fire between me and the bomb aimer. We immediately got the order to bale out, which we decided to do. The trouble was it was so quick and violent that there was nothing anyone could do – we were just straight down, screaming down. It was very hard to move with the G-forces.

F/Sgt Keen took his gloves off to put his chute on, then tried to bale out head first through the narrow front escape hatch, but as must have happened to many others who didn't live to tell the story he got stuck. He came to falling through the night sky, feeling very sick with the risers to his chute pressing against his head.

I felt like going back to sleep – I must have passed out again and eventually woke up with my arms round a tree trunk wondering what the hell had happened! When I landed, the fur collar of my suit was all burnt, so there must have been fire getting through the hatch.

In fact the aircraft had exploded, only the pilot and the flight engineer, who had been wounded in the leg and posterior, surviving.

I was trying to decide what to do when I heard a whistle, which I thought odd at that time of night as it was pitch black and freezing cold, but it was my skipper! His face was covered in blood, but he said, 'How, are you?' and I said, 'I'm all right apart from I can't walk! I can hop along.'

The two wounded men 'agreed it wasn't a time to be heroic' and eventually knocked at a forester's house. 'The chap came out in a bit of a temper, calling us *Schwein*, *Terrorfliegers* and goodness knows what! The lady eventually took us in and bathed my skipper's face ... then they phoned the army. I was taken to hospital.'[27]

Flight engineer Ken Hulton, from 57 Sqn, who had been so sure the op would be scrubbed, was in the closing waves of the attack.

Everybody wanted to do a Berlin raid, but people had told us it was a daunting target. We had been warned of the searchlights and heavy flak and they came up to expectations. There was heavy and light flak inside the defences and fighters outside. We thought the actual markers were dummies, so we bombed small fires which turned out to be an oil dump. There were so many searchlights it was just like a dartboard and first a master searchlight locked on us then the others converged. We were coned, so we went over and dived, then pulled out. Everybody put their parachutes on and I could see the navigator's maps and pencils floating in the air. Being coned put everything else out of your mind. You didn't know what was happening elsewhere, just what was happening to your own aircraft. After we finally escaped the searchlights it took both me and the pilot pulling back on the controls to get out of the dive. The skipper was rather short and we had to put our feet on the instrument panel to manage it. We then had to go through the outer defences to go home.[28]

From 49 Sqn P/O Frank Clark also bombed in the closing stages of the attack on the centre of red TIs and flew away to collide with another Lancaster over Osnabrück just over an hour later, ripping off his tail wheel and giving his rear gunner a nasty shock. Yorkshireman Clark made it back to Fiskerton but was killed a month later.[29]

THERE was a refinement being used by the defences that night, apart from the usual three rings of searchlights and flak guns enclosing the city like a fortress. Hajo Herrmann, who had formulated the Wilde Sau system of night fighting the previous year, had taken over command of the 1st Fighter Division, containing all the fighter units in central Germany, only 48 hours before. Its headquarters were in Berlin. For some time he had wanted to employ a technique of igniting thousands of phosphorus flares at the same time as searchlights were used to light the underside of a cloud layer, giving the single-engined Wilde Sau a vision of scores of targets below as they hunted. That night the conditions over Berlin turned out to be near perfect.

It was feared that gaps in the cloud of the size that had allowed the searchlights to catch Sgt Hulton's aircraft might dazzle the fighter crews above, but as Herrmann stood on the roof of his headquarters and the first wave of Pathfinders flew away from the city, the decision to ignite the flares and shine battalions of searchlights onto the cloud base was taken. Herrmann later wrote:

Suddenly it was as bright as day on the ground. Blackout orders had become irrelevant. The light not only penetrated into the stratus, but was bounced back to the ground and then up again. The amount of electricity that was used in the ensuing half-hour and the number of tons of phosphorus that were burned were incalculable. The scene was intoxicating.

The Me109s and FW190s of the Wilde Sau now began to wreak havoc among the bombers. Meanwhile, the twin-engined Zahme Sau waited outside the defences to catch them as the stream flew homewards. Herrmann continued:

Fighters were brought in from everywhere. The battle was on: blow after blow ... with the extra thrust [of the tailwind] those who had not dropped their bombs early or to one side were able to overfly the danger zone, the 'shroud', very quickly. Had it been different, the fighters would have been able to make more attacks.[30]

Major Lent was guided by his radar operator onto another bomber over Berlin and opened fire on its massive bulk above him. The newspaperman Kark wrote:

A broad sheet of flame from the centre of the fuselage tells us that he is badly hit. Behind him he is trailing thick banners of smoke. Once, twice, three times a small shadow sweeps past the tail unit of the bomber. The British are baling out! But the pilot must still be at the controls. The bomber is still capable of flying, and he is trying to escape. A second attack! Our cannon and machine guns hammer out again. It is the *coup de grâce*. The bomber loses height more and more swiftly, descending towards the wide countryside in a steep dive. Like a shadow, careful and alert in case despite everything the enemy still recovers, we follow him until finally, some distance from us, a huge ball of fire on the ground marks his end.[31]

Halifax wireless operator Sgt Harry Ball, who had baled out near his home airfield of Lissett coming back from Magdeburg, was in one of those bombers shot down in the immediate Berlin defence zone. He recalls:

We had just reached the target area when I heard a thud, thud, thud of cannon shells striking the aircraft from underneath where we had no protection. The skipper shouted, 'For Christ's sake, get out of this aircraft.' I felt a lurch and the kite went into a dive and started spinning. I went to bale out through the front hatch and the Canadian bomb aimer [F/Sgt J. McDonagh] was kicking it, trying to get it open. Apparently he had pieces of metal in him from the cannon shells. He was lying down in the nose when the fighter shells came up and copped the lot. I remember one of his flying boots was cut to ribbons and he was wounded all down his right side. The hatch opened and I could see a massive bed of red flames below – we were right over the target. We were still spinning and I thought I had no chance, but I threw myself straight through and gradually I drifted away from the flames and everything went black. My guardian angel must have been looking after me again. I landed in a dyke and was pulled along like a motor boat for a while, before I managed to collapse the chute. I was really soaked. I buried my chute and started walking until I found a farm where I could get into the loft.[32]

He was captured the next day.

Among the last to bomb Berlin that night was the intrepid young F/O Hoover of 35 Sqn, one of the first to arrive over the target and now turning to make his second run over the Berlin defences. His rear gunner, F/Sgt Hill, remembered:

As we made a wide circuit heavy flak was coming up, but it didn't seem as thick or concentrated as on other occasions – just a few black puffs; and then I realised why, the guns went silent and the searchlights were directed at the cloud base, lighting it up and silhouetting the incoming bombers. I saw two night fighters flying in the opposite direction. They were FW190s and the speed of them amazed me.

F/O Hoover started his bombing run, the bomb aimer releasing on fires illuminating the cloud base at 1102. It was seventeen minutes after the attack had been intended to cease and there were no other aircraft coming in behind.

Before the navigator could give a course for home the mid-upper gunner opened fire and shouted, 'Corkscrew starboard. Go!' Hoov took evasive action immediately turning into the attack, I couldn't see it back in the tail. In unison Hoov and I both shouted, 'Where is he?'

The mid-upper replied: 'It's an FW190 on the beam – he's cleared off now.' 'Where for Christ's sake?' I asked. I covered the port side. Fighters had a habit of hunting in pairs over the target or anywhere, one for distraction and the other making an attack. Eventually I could see nothing behind or below. We all breathed a sigh of relief.

'The most deadly part of the night was now beginning as the bombers, scattered across the sky by the jet stream and the defences, turned westward skirting Magdeburg and heading towards home. The Zahme Sau twin-engined night fighters were waiting and so was the flak over the Ruhr that many would find themselves blundering over in the fierce wind, blowing them ever further south off track.

Hauptmann Paul Zorner had been heading north-east in his Me110 when he saw the bombs beginning to fall over Berlin. He remembers:

I doubted that I could get there in time, but then saw some more aircraft shot down closer to me so realised I was in the direction of the bombers leaving and decided to fly 'barrier', but we had already been in the air two hours and the petrol would not last long. My *Funker* [radar operator], Heinz Wilke, reported: 'Captain, I have a target from right to left, Marie* 4,000, a lot higher.' I flew straight north and started to climb. 'Target still a bit right, Marie 3,000, little bit higher … Target in front of us, Marie 2,000, on the same height … three times Lisa, Marie 1,500, yet another three times Lisa, Marie 1,000 … once Lisa, Marie 700 in front of us.'

Now I saw the bomber a bit higher in front of us at 6,700 metres. There were no clouds below and it was therefore ideal for an attack with Schräge Musik. It was 2252. I flew under the bomber's right wing and opened fire. Nothing happened to the bomber, but high above me I saw the explosions of the shots. I pulled the trigger for the second time with the same result and again, still nothing. God damn it the calibration of the Schräge Musik was absolutely wrong, therefore I had to attack from the back.

I stayed behind a moment, pulled my Me up in a gentle ascent and let the left wing of the bomber wander through the sight. A short burst of fire and one more and the wing began to burn. It took just one

* Marie was R/T code for 'distance', Lisa for 'turn 10 degrees port'.

minute and there was no defence. The result came suddenly. The bomber started to go down vertically and crashed at 2257.* I asked Wilke where we were and he said he could see the Xantippe beacon, north of Magdeburg, in front of us. 'Good, we have gas left for a maximum of thirty minutes,' I said. 'I will fly zick-zack in a westerly direction. Maybe we will find something.' We found nothing and realised later we had searched too far to the north. After another fifteen minutes we landed at Wesendorf at 2335, exactly three hours after leaving St Trond.[34]

The flak, always so formidable over Berlin, was no less a danger on the homeward route. It caused particular problems for F/Sgt Bernard Downs, making his fifth journey to the Reich capital. After the first trip in November the 20-year-old had been surprised to find photographers waiting for a youthful-looking pilot at dispersal, he and his crew being pictured in the *Daily Telegraph*.[35] By the end of March he was one of 78 Sqn's most experienced skippers and had been detailed to take an artillery expert on this particular Berlin raid. He remembers:

We had no particular problem going out to Berlin and there was some cloud cover, which was good, because the searchlights couldn't get through. I had a hang-up with a 2,000-lb bomb, which I didn't want to waste. It was far too dangerous for us to go round again for fear of hitting one of our own aircraft, so I asked the navigator for another place to drop it on the way back. We found Magdeburg by H2S and dropped it there, just off our route, and got picked up by some very unpleasant predicted flak. The army major ack-ack expert was quite cross because I was taking evasive action and he wanted to see what this predicted flak was all about. I wasn't prepared to do it.

We picked up this jet stream that was coming at us and suddenly I saw searchlights ahead which I recognised as Cologne by the pattern of the lights. We were 60 or 70 miles south of track. I berated Bill Hendry, my unfortunate navigator, but it wasn't his fault at all. He was

---

* This was one of the four 12 Sqn aircraft lost that night. PH-L was flown by F/O Galtan de Marigny, of St Pierre, Ile Maurice, Amirante Islands, in the Indian Ocean, who was on his eighth operation. Three members of his crew survived.

working on winds sent to us from our group. Rather than try to pick up track I thought the best way was to head south of Cologne. We headed from there to the nearest point of the coast and didn't have any further problems, but I saw some poor sods who took the direct route right across between Cologne and the Ruhr valley and they did get hell. I can't see how many survived it. There was fierce flak coming up.[36]

Sgt Russell Margerison, the 625 Sqn mid-upper gunner, whose tour had begun less than a week before, had reached Berlin without incident, then found his aircraft battling to stay on track as it headed for home. He recalls:

There were plenty of other people bombing when we were over the target, but on the return journey we were blown all over the sky. We knew we were out of the bomber stream because there was no slip-stream buffeting. A lot of poor devils found themselves blown over the defences of the Ruhr valley. We were fortunately to the north of it and we could see these lads getting pasted. As we flew on into Belgium we were caught in the beam of a blue master searchlight. I immediately called, 'Corkscrew port,' but the pilot was already on his way down and we were out of it. I could see the searchlight swinging around though and it settled on a bomber above and to starboard. The Germans sent up just one shell and the aircraft exploded, then the sky was black again.[37]

As F/O Hoover finally left Berlin his navigator also found it a struggle to stay on track. His rear gunner F/Sgt Hill remembered:

As we wheeled out of the target area we went like a bat out of hell. The winds were terrible. Hoov attempted to catch up with the main stream of home-going aircraft. Combats were taking place miles away. We saw some poor chaps coned in searchlights way over to port, then the inevitable tiny glow of flame increasing until as a burning ball of fire the aircraft went down ... the route home was a journey lasting a lifetime.[38]

THE intended bomber stream had now become a gaggle spread across 50 miles of sky and stretching back for another 150 miles. Most of the bombers were well south of track and many wandered over the Ruhr defences where the flak gunners were plentiful and deadly efficient, but most aircraft were brought down by *Nachtjäger*. The entire northern strength of the German night-fighter arm was aloft and conditions were ideal for tracking blips on the radar screen.

One of those blips struggling to stay clear of the Ruhr was A4-K of 115 Sqn. In the next few minutes the Lancaster's rear gunner, Sgt Nick Alkemade, was about to escape death in a manner that was among the most amazing of Bomber Command's remarkable war. The wireless operator, Sgt Geoffrey Burwell, told the story of that night to his local newspaper. 'After bombing Berlin successfully we were coming out of the city when we were attacked from behind by a Ju88 night fighter. It came in right underneath us and absolutely rocketed us with cannon shells and we went on fire like an incendiary bomb from top to bottom,' Sgt Burwell said.

Sgt Alkemade, who had set one engine of the Ju88 ablaze with his return fire, felt the heat of the raging inferno down the fuselage against his turret doors and as there was no communication with the rest of the crew rotated his turret to reach for his parachute on its stowage shelf just inside. He saw it burning brightly and realised it was now useless. He then felt his rubber oxygen mask beginning to melt against his face and, preferring to die from hitting the ground rather than being burned alive, flipped out backwards through the open turret doors into the cold night air at 18,000 feet. He had time to wonder how long it would be before his body slammed into the earth bringing merciful release, before he lost consciousness.

At that point Sgt Burwell and the aircraft's navigator, Sgt Joe Cleary, who would also escape, were still in the aircraft. Sgt Burwell said:

> All inside communication in the bomber was lost. The bomber then exploded and I was blown out. I blacked out and when I came to, realised I was falling free. I thought my parachute had gone, but then found the pack was trailing behind me. I pulled the ripcord and the parachute opened, checking my fall, and almost immediately I landed in the top of a huge pine tree with a terrific jolt.[39]

Sgt Cleary was also blown out in the explosion. He described to his family later finding himself 'ejected in an instant from searing heat to intense cold as he plunged through the night air beneath an impressive canopy of glittering stars'. His chute pack had been damaged in the explosion and without him pulling the ripcord the chute spilled out and snapped open, one flying boot falling away into the blackness. Sgt Cleary hit a pine tree in the Arnsbergerwald near Schmallenberg, on the edge of the Ruhr and quickly lost consciousness, hanging in his harness from the tree. Villagers found him in the morning suffering from severe frostbite of the leg and took him to a small hospital run by nuns, who managed to save his limb.*[40]

Sgt Alkemade's swift journey to earth had ended in the same forest. Unconscious he also had plummeted into the top of a tall pine tree, then broken one supple branch after another as he plunged through it, each one slowing his descent from terminal velocity until the last one tipped him into a small snowdrift against the tree trunk. It was only a few feet deep yet had been enough to save his life. The next day the Gestapo would not believe he had landed without a parachute until he pointed out that the rivets which held his harness snap hooks flat to the chest, and would break once the ripcord was pulled, were still intact.

THE Lancaster of F/Sgt Tony Leyva was shot down north of Osnabrück and very close to the Dutch border. The navigator had found that, unlike on the outward route, now that he knew what the winds were and could get fixes with H2S, being over land, the strong wind wasn't so much of a problem. He remembers:

> We came back pretty well on track and were quite high, about 27,000 feet. Our pilot always flew as high as he could as a general principle, though it was very unofficial. We were almost on the border with Holland over Lingen when a night fighter armed with Schräge Musik came underneath us. Nobody saw him. The first I knew was a bang, the pilot shouted: 'Jump, jump,' and I think he was probably hit because he fell over the control column. I got my chute and clipped it on and we immediately started going down vertically on full power. I fell and slid down the aircraft over the

---

* Sgt Cleary's wife Betty heard her missing husband was safe as a prisoner of war via an acquaintance who heard it from Lord Haw Haw on Hamburg Radio. Sgt Cleary was finally repatriated, arriving in Liverpool on the *Arundel Castle* on 6 February 1945.

steps to the bomb aimer's compartment and as the escape hatch was open I fell straight out. Either someone had managed to open it or just by luck it was damaged in the attack.

I felt almost outside myself as if I was looking at myself. Once I got into the slipstream I pulled the ripcord and it didn't work, it came away in my hand. I was a bit anxious to put it mildly and I started tearing the pack apart and it opened. I discovered then I had only connected it to my harness by one hook. The previous day I had taken my parachute to be repacked. This one was a replacement one from the WAAF parachute packer, who cracked the usual joke of, 'If it doesn't work come back and tell us.' As it was a spare parachute it was probably over-packed. I wasn't the least worried after it opened even though I was only attached on one hook. It was a very gentle descent and I fell into a ploughed field. I didn't see it coming up and as I wasn't tensed up therefore I didn't hurt myself.

I lay on the ground for a moment and thought, 'Well thank God, here I am,' then rolled up the parachute and stuffed it in a hedge, following the bale-out rules. I found I only had one shoe on, which didn't help much, but I knew I was in that little bit of Germany which bulges into Holland and started walking along a road. I ran into some farm workers who must have heard the aircraft hit the ground. They got hold of me and took me to the farm where there were two or three German soldiers looking after French prisoners of war working there. I was well treated. I managed to give my escape kit to one of the French prisoners of war and as I had on me some false German ration cards which we had carried on the previous trip to drop over Germany I gave them to the farmer's wife. The rate she put them in her apron pocket they must have looked rather good.[41]

He would be shown his wrecked aircraft, deep in a marsh, the next day. F/Sgt Leyva was the sole survivor.

IN all fifty-six aircraft were shot down on that 370-mile return route to the Dutch coast, most by Schräge Musik. The post-raid report by Bomber Command's Operational Research Section blamed most of the losses on flak as aircraft were blown over defended areas. 'Fighters achieved comparatively very little success,' it read, 'because the strong winds that scattered the bomber stream proved unfavourable to constant interception by fighters.'[42] If available to the *Nachtjäger* units the report would have caused much amusement as they celebrated in their messes the next day.

The luckiest man to reach the coast was perhaps P/O Farmiloe. His Lancaster had streaked flame from one of its two dead engines all the way across the fighter-infested skies west of Berlin, but not one fighter had come to investigate, perhaps thinking him already doomed. H-Hellzapoppin continued to burn as it descended over the North Sea, its pilot heading for the nearest airfield on the coast and answering a position query from the emergency Darkie watch to guide aircraft in trouble by asking them to merely look up. P/O Farmiloe brought his aircraft into the airfield of Little Snoring at 0215, his bomb aimer at last able to unlock his arms from the starboard rudder pedal.

By then most of the bombers that would be coming back were already down, their crews wearily standing beside their now silent aircraft in the cold night air, glowing cigarettes nervously passed from hand to hand as they waited for the truck to take them to Intelligence before welcome sleep. These airmen reported sixteen combats over Berlin itself. F/Lt J. Woodroffe of 49 Sqn, who bombed a green target indicator at 2232, reported to intelligence staff: 'Many combats were seen. I went out of the way to miss the searchlight area. Many who went through were seen shot down.'[43]

There were countless tales of courage including that of F/Sgt Tom Hall, of 106 Sqn. The raid had been his first and he had had to make an emergency landing at Wing in Buckinghamshire. He told station staff: 'Wanganui flares and the glow of fires was seen on the first bombing run, but the aircraft was south of target, so I made a second run, this time bombing the centre of five flares from 22,000 feet at 2250. The aircraft was extensively damaged by heavy flak and I made the return journey on three engines.'[44] Hall was put up for an immediate DFM. It was announced ten days later. By then the 21-year-old airman was dead, killed on an even more savage raid, that on Nuremberg.

At debriefings up and down the country several shocked crews expressed their dissatisfaction with the High Wycombe planners. P/O A. R. S. Bowman told intelligence officers in the operations block of 463 (RAAF) Sqn at Waddington: 'For a clear night it was thought to be definitely poorly routed, passing cones of searchlights, and also too close to Osnabrück and Magdeburg ... the Master of Ceremonies would have been effective if distortion wasn't so bad, it was useless to us.'[45]

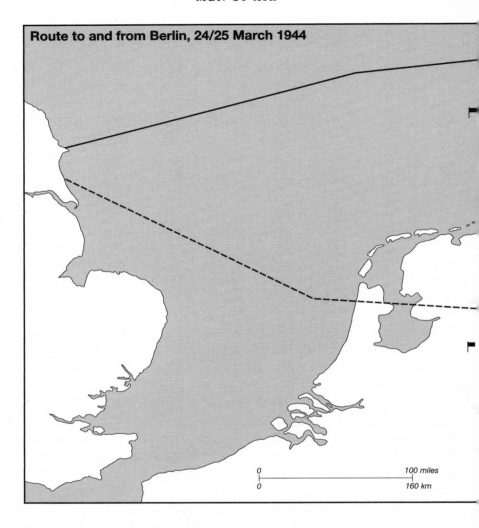

Route to and from Berlin, 24/25 March 1944

100 miles

160 km

Diarist John Hennessey of 49 Sqn recorded the next day:

It was a deadly route for as soon as we crossed the coast of Denmark we ran into a belt of searchlights and saw four kites coned and two were shot down immediately. When we returned to base we found cloud down to the deck and we had to come in on FIDO. The Air Vice Marshal and Air Commodore were at interrogation and we told them in no polite terms what we thought of the route. There was an MC on this raid, his remarks were really quite funny.[46]

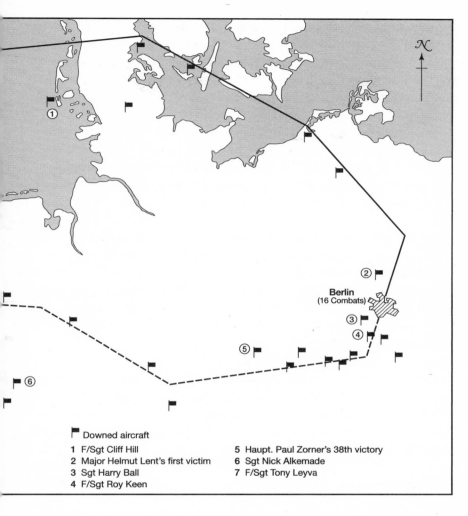

Berlin
(16 Combats)

Downed aircraft
1 F/Sgt Cliff Hill
2 Major Helmut Lent's first victim
3 Sgt Harry Ball
4 F/Sgt Roy Keen
5 Haupt. Paul Zorner's 38th victory
6 Sgt Nick Alkemade
7 F/Sgt Tony Leyva

On the morning after the Berlin raid of 24 March, Bomber Command's Operational Research Section produced this chart showing the position of downed aircraft, using the logs of surviving crews. The real story was that far more aircraft had been lost, 72 in all, the third biggest loss Bomber Command ever suffered on a single raid.

MANY billets displayed rows of empty beds that morning, testimony to the 516 airmen who had not returned. In their lockers lay the touching evidence of their brief lives, half-read books still with their markers, well-thumbed photographs of girlfriends and those last letters they had written just in case they lost the nightly battle with the Luftwaffe. They would now be posted with their effects after the Air Ministry telegrams, labelled 'Priority' in blue, had gone out to their families the next day, saying they were missing from operations. F/Sgt Hill flopped on his bed at Graveley with his own last letter still intact in his locker, where it would remain for the rest of his stressful second tour. He recalled:

> It had been harrowing to write it. I just thanked my parents for bringing me up, that sort of thing. I destroyed it after we were screened. It was later on in life before I realised just how lucky I was to survive two tours and what a great worry my operational flying must have been for my parents. Luck was my middle name.[47]

Of the airmen who had been shot down 133 would become prisoners of war and four would evade to get back to England weeks and months later where they would be expected to continue their tours. Some of those new prisoners of war now had an opportunity to see Berlin at close quarters. Wireless operator Harry Ball, who left Berlin for Dulag Luft by train after his Halifax was shot down by a night fighter, was one of them. He remembers:

> I was taken in a private car to Berlin and walked through the streets in full flying kit. Civilians were shaking their fists. I couldn't see any bomb damage in the area I was in and I couldn't understand that, everything seemed to be operating normally. I remember there were plenty of soldiers going by giving the Nazi salute.[48]

The damage was indeed light for all the effort and courage that had been expended. Most of it was in the south-west of Berlin, which had already been heavily hit and which Harris was at pains to avoid. No factories were destroyed, though several were damaged. A total of 126 small towns and villages to the south-west of Berlin reported bombs. The Operational Research Section calculated, with the few bombing photographs obtained that showed ground detail, that only eighty-seven of the 811 aircraft that set out had bombed within 3 miles of the aiming point.[49] A total of seventy-two aircraft were missing, the third biggest loss Bomber Command would suffer on a single raid in the course of the whole war.

AND so ended the Battle of Berlin. It had cost 492 night bombers and most of the aircrew within those aircraft in 9,111 sorties against the capital. Another 954 aircraft had been badly damaged, of which ninety-five never flew again, raising the total loss for Berlin to 587.[50] In the nineteen other raids in the period of the battle since 18 November another 555 Lancasters and Halifaxes had failed to return as Harris played the constant game of trying to fool the enemy as to his nightly intentions. It was the period of highest loss ever for Bomber Command, the 1,047 bombers plunging over enemy territory and into the North Sea far outshadowing the losses in the four-month Battle of the Ruhr the previous year when 872 bombers had gone down. The equivalent of more than the entire front-line strength of Bomber Command had disappeared.

The Command's heavy bombers would never return to the Reich capital. The closest they would come would be a night raid on Potsdam, in April 1945, though Berlin would continue to gnaw at Harris as a means of ending the war. In the late summer of 1944 he would fruitlessly join with the USAAF's General Jimmy Doolittle in urging a joint daylight attack against the capital by 2,000 RAF and American bombers to panic the German government as their forces retreated headlong through France.[51]

The Battle of Berlin and its accompanying raids had cost the lives of 6,185 aircrew. Death had made its random selections among all types on all squadrons. Its scythe had been unsparing among both the daring and the desperate; the boastful and the bashful; the Valentines and the virgins; the wizard and the wayward; the cruel and the kind; the major and the minor; the ace and the joker; the beardless boy and the handlebar-moustached tyro. All had vanished into the cannon's maw that was Berlin.

At the end of it all Berlin's factories still functioned and, in fact, production increased in 1944 because of plans laid in 1941 that took time to come to fruition. But bombing had placed a ceiling on German war production, which was well below what Germany would have been capable of producing after 1943.[52] The morale of the German people and their capacity for armed resistance had not been fatally weakened. However, it had taken pressure off the Russians, with the need for 88-mm flak guns to defend Berlin causing a shortage in the East, where they were required against fleets of Russian tanks. It also helped to produce a siege mentality among the powerful who lived and worked in Berlin and the depressing worm of an idea that Germany would not now win.

The evidence was in the rubble in the streets – 55 million cubic metres of it, which was to be piled into four enormous hills within Berlin known as *Trümmerberge*, altering the geography of the city for ever. By 1944, 2 million soldiers and civilians were engaged in ground anti-aircraft defence in Germany, a considerable proportion in the Berlin area. As Maria Vassiltchikov of the German Foreign Ministry's Information Department illustrated, many key offices had been forced to relocate outside the capital and the Wilhelmstrasse and Reich Chancellery were smoking testimony to what the night bombers could do

Harris, aware from his experiences as a First World War pilot on the Western Front of what carnage a land campaign could mean, had seen the Battle of Berlin as an alternative to a new Somme-like battle, which he considered might follow an invasion. Because many in the War Cabinet shared those fears his aims – which corresponded with those of Churchill, ultimately responsible for giving Harris his orders – had met little opposition. In fact, the Battle of Berlin had turned into Bomber Command's Passchendaele, a war of attrition in which neither side would yield. It had not cost Germany the war as Harris had predicted. It had ended in a draw with the Luftwaffe.

The Pathfinders commander, Air Marshal Don Bennett, quick to deflect any possible criticism of his own command, claimed in 1944 that Main Force crews, depressed by the losses, had 'baulked at the jump' in the Battle of Berlin. 'There can be no doubt that a very large number of crew failed to carry out their attacks during the Battle of Berlin in their customary determined manner,' he said.[53] Yet on the last raid of the campaign when it would be expected morale would be at its lowest the official Bomber Command analysis the next day made much of the fact that 'many crews who overshot the target turned back to bomb.'[54] No mean achievement to go back again over the hell of Berlin when the brain screeched that sound sense was to drop the load and bank away home.

The truth is if there was any one factor on which the blame could be laid it was the most imponderable. The weather had proved impossible to accurately foretell and then overcome. Night after night cloud cover had made a meteorological mockery of Harris's plans, preventing the Pathfinders seeing their aiming point to lead Main Force into a concentrated attack. It was ironic that on the last night of the campaign forecasting would plumb new depths for ridicule by hurtling those same Pathfinders across the target so fast pursued by the jet stream that there was no chance to find the point of aim.

*

AS the aircrew who had returned from Berlin tussled with their private nightmares in their billets in the dawn of 25 March, others of their colleagues who had lost their individual battles with the Luftwaffe months and years before were involved in their own desperate ordeal. On the very night Bomber Command's heavies were raiding Berlin the long-planned mass breakout by RAF men from Stalag Luft III was taking place. The wide-ranging air raid alert had in fact delayed the escapers, by turning the lights off in their tunnel. But now they were abroad in the forests and boarding trains. Within hours their adventure would create a *Grossfahndung*, involving the diversion of 70,000 German troops, SS and Gestapo and infuriating Hitler. The escapers would need all the luck in the world for what was to follow.

7

The Underground Air War

The POW tunnellers whose makeshift spades lifted the final frozen earth barriers to freedom at Stalag Luft III in the coldest March for thirty years were aware they were literally breaking new ground. There had been escapes before from camps across Germany as downed airmen refused to have their wings clipped and in the course of the war thirty-four would make it home. But this was something different. More than 650 Allied aircrew had been engaged for almost a year in an operation involving the digging of three tunnels with the aim of releasing 220 men at one go to spread confusion throughout Germany.

F/Lt 'Jimmy' James, who had made eight previous escape attempts, remembers the joy as he climbed the ladder to the tunnel exit and with thumping heart took in the beauty of the stars and the 'jolly cold' night air. 'I crawled as quickly as I could into the wood,' he recalls. 'It was a wonderful feeling when I got into the trees to realise I was outside at last, the first time I had got beyond the wire.'[1] In the event, partly because of the Bomber Command raid on Berlin that night, only seventy-nine would get out. What happened to fifty of those would begin a retributive manhunt which lasted for more than twenty years.

The story of what the world came to know as the Great Escape had begun four years before when bomber pilot F/O Graham Hall, who had set up a letter code with his wife Vera in case of capture, was shot down. It simply told her that the next word following a full stop, semi-colon or comma would make up a coded message. She went to MI9 with his first POW communication, from Stalag Luft I, and subsequent letters between the airman and his wife were under military intelligence guidance. Eventually MI9 gathered a number of bomber crews for a top-secret briefing and told them if they were ever taken prisoner to try to make contact with F/O Hall. Within three months a briefed flyer did turn up at his camp and a second two days later. From that moment began a spy network in which scores of prisoners at Stalag Luft I would each send one sentence of a given message made up of carefully chosen letters of the alphabet, in their routine *Kriegsgefangerpost* back to the UK. In his own letter home F/O Hall would link the order in which the alphabetic arrangement and sentences were to be read.[2]

By the winter of 1942/3, as prisoners of war were transferred from camp to camp, the spy network had spread across Germany, supplying information about troop movements, bomb damage, German morale and new Luftwaffe techniques. The system, which employed a five-letter word code known as Bob, reached Sagan's East Compound with the transfer of a POW party, and when 850 prisoners were switched to Sagan's North Compound in April 1943 RAF letter-writing spies went with them. Code intelligence officers were set up in each compound to sift the information.[3]

With the arrival of the charismatic Roger Bushell at Sagan the information and help the POWs were systematically sending to MI9 became a serious two-way exchange. Bushell, a fighter pilot who was captured by the Germans when he crashlanded in France in 1940, had been taken under Gestapo guard to the rapidly expanding Sagan after the latest of his many escape attempts in November 1942. He was aware it was likely he would be shot if he fell into the hands of the Gestapo again. Bushell brushed the danger aside and after his appointment as Big X in Sagan's East Compound that winter resolved that as head of the camp's escaping committee he would create a mass outbreak. He saw the chance to do so as he watched the building of a new North Compound, which the RAF and USAAF joint bombing offensive was making necessary with the arrival of so many Allied airmen in the Reich. Bushell, aware the RAF and Commonwealth Air Force officer prisoners would be moved into this compound, realised the regime and conditions of a new camp would provide the ideal opportunity to build three escape tunnels, Tom, Dick and Harry, to get 220 men away at one go to swamp the German security network.

To learn the layout of the new camp – and its escape possibilities – Bushell's X Organisation would volunteer to help with its building. The Germans, always short of labour, agreed and prisoners' work parties left the East Compound each day and each night returned to supply Bushell and his escape committee with details of the foundations, layout, electrical system and plumbing of the new northern camp. With the transfer of Allied aircrew from East to North Compound in March 1943 construction of the tunnels began.

Now it was time for MI9 to repay in quantity for all the information the letter-spies had been sending back to Britain and requests for escape materials in bulk were relayed to MI9's headquarters via the mail code where they were passed on to a specially set up subsidiary, IS9. Senior military figures were well aware of IS9's clandestine operations. The Chief of the Imperial General Staff, General Sir Alan Brooke, recorded in his private diary as early as October 1942: 'Took lunch in car and went with DMI [Director of Military Intelligence] to see the institution engaged in assisting escapes of our prisoners and of codes to them.' The General added: 'A very well run and interesting organisation under a live wire.'4 The man who had so impressed General Brooke was Clayton Hutton, known as 'Clutty', who specialised in inventing ways of getting contraband into POW camps, beginning with RAF uniform buttons that unscrewed to reveal tiny compasses.

Clayton Hutton, based at Wilton Park in Beaconsfield, Buckinghamshire, on the north-west edge of London, realised the only way to get large quantities of escape materials into Sagan was via the Red Cross parcels and packages from POWs' families at home that the Swiss-based organisation vetted. To do so British Intelligence would be contravening the Geneva Convention and compromising the integrity of the Red Cross, taking an enormous risk with the welfare of prisoners.

Nevertheless, a small team was set up by MI9 to fix special parcels that the Red Cross would unwittingly deliver, under its scheme of providing books and games parcels from prisoners' relatives or charity organisations. There was no lack of opportunity in filtering special parcels into the stream now being dispatched to POW camps. Twice a year a relative of a prisoner of war could deliver a clothing package to the headquarters of the Red Cross at Finsbury Circus in London, and books and games parcels were largely unrestricted. Red Cross leaflets P1/A and P1/B explained what could go in the packages. As the insertion of contraband into the camps by MI9 got underway the *Prisoner of War* magazine, free to the next of kin of all prisoners of war, complained in May of the difficulty of keeping to the previous schedule of dispatching personal parcels to prisoners 'within two or three days of receipt'. By

July the magazine was able to announce 'the delay has now been reduced to approximately eight days, excluding the time spent in the post, before the parcel reaches the prisoner', and the Finsbury Circus centre was dispatching 1,500 parcels a day.[5]

Each packer of the special illegal parcels had a unique mark the prisoners at Sagan were alerted to look out for and as the tunnels pushed forward in the spring and summer of 1943 the steady trickle of escape materials turned into a sizeable store. There were Monopoly sets with real German money inside instead of the play variety, brushes that came apart to reveal contraband including inks for forging documents, sports equipment that hid the same compasses going into uniform buttons, and blankets that when washed revealed pattern marks to cut along and turn them into civilian jackets. On one occasion MI9 even delivered a complete authentic German uniform.[6]

So many contraband parcels were now arriving for named prisoners, occasionally they turned up without the POW being alerted in advance. P/O Al Wallace, a Canadian air gunner from 419 Sqn, got one not long after arriving in Sagan in the summer of 1943, following his enforced bale-out during a raid on Duisburg. He remembers:

> I received a personal parcel and when I opened it I thought: 'What the hell is all this?' It had hair brushes in it and bits of different sports equipment, ping pong bats and so on. I took the handles apart and there was German money. There were also dyes concealed here and there. I handed all that over to the escape organisation.
>
> But as well there was a sweater made out of a form of nylon which could be taken apart to make a strong rope. I gave it to one of my fellow prisoners and he made a hammock out of it because most of the bedboards from the bunks had by that time disappeared to make shoring for the tunnels. For a while we hadn't realised it was an escape parcel. It was just a parcel of odds and ends postmarked London and addressed to Prisoner 1338, Luft III, Sagan, which was me.[7]

The tunnels were rapidly absorbing the camp's supply of bedboards to an alarming degree. The interior space of each tunnel had been determined by the 70 cm by 15 cm of each lateral slat in the tiered bunks and eventually thousands would be used. With them in one year would also vanish 30 of the camp staff's shovels, 69 lamps, 34 chairs, 76 benches, 62 tables, 1,219 knives, 582 forks, 478 spoons and 90 double-tier bunks themselves. The need for material to make escape outfits would also lead to the pilfering of 1,699 blankets, 3,424 towels, 655 palliasses and 1,212 bolsters.[8]

Tom, Dick and Harry were clever and well-constructed tunnels indeed, in what was considered an escape-proof environment by the Germans. Sagan had been carved out of a pine forest in the flat, cold eastern stretches of Greater Germany. By the time the Great Escape was staged it consisted of four vast compounds entirely built on sand, which was the Germans' ace card in deterring escape attempts. Any of the bright yellow sand brought up from a tunnel would be immediately spotted against the grey of the compound surface and the camp would then be searched until the workings were found. The soft, insidious sand, which could bury a tunneller in an instant, was why the bedboards were needed to roof and shore the sides of the three tunnels as they were painstakingly dug beneath what had been the forest floor. The new North Compound was about 300 metres square, its main enclosure consisting of three rows of five blocks, each divided into eighteen rooms. The northernmost blocks were numbered 101 to 106 and the southernmost 119 to 123. The Tom tunnel ran from Block 123 out under the western wire to the woods; the second (Dick) from 122, an inside hut and not likely to be suspected; and the third (Harry) from 104. Harry was planned as the longest and most daringly constructed, designed as it was to run right under the wire of the German administrative headquarters, then on under the side of the main gate to the woods. But the Dick tunnel was the cleverest. It had been built at the side of a washroom sump – which contained visible waste water when in use – by constructing a false removable concrete wall to the well. Every time tunnelling ceased the false wall was replaced and water sloshed back into the sump.

P/O Alan Bryett, a young bomb aimer shot down in a Halifax of 158 Sqn over Berlin in August 1943, arrived in Sagan in October and shortly afterwards found himself in charge of security for the Dick tunnel. He remembers:

When you arrived in prison camp people very quickly put you in touch with fellow-prisoners from your own area and the fighter ace Bob Stanford Tuck, who had gone to the same grammar school as me in Catford some years earlier, came to see me because he knew I knew cousins of his in London.

We chatted for a while then he said, 'Come for coffee tomorrow and I'll introduce you to some people.' In fact, I was introduced to Roger Bushell and all the leaders of the escape organisation. Shortly afterwards I was asked if I would take over security for the Dick tunnel in Hut 122. I didn't find out until about a month later that Bushell was the head of the whole X Organisation.

Each hut had a security man and I was in charge of 122, reporting to S/Ldr Tom Kirby-Green [the deputy head of security for the escape organisation]. Primarily I had to watch the water level in the sump to make sure it was always at a realistic level. If the sump had not been effectively sealed after the tunnel had been used, the foul washing water from the sump would leak into the tunnel. Thus the sump would be empty of water, which would be suspicious to the guards. The leaking water would also damage documents stored in the tunnel.[9]

By the time P/O Bryett took over the Dick tunnel it was being used purely for storage of escape equipment and contraband. The Tom tunnel, always the most vulnerable, positioned under Block 123 closest to the woods, had been discovered by the Germans in September and the decision had been taken to stop tunnelling for a while then put all efforts into Harry. The large USAAF contingent in the North Compound, who had put so much work into constructing the tunnels under the leadership of Lt/Col Albert Clark, were moved into their own compound a week later and never saw the benefit of their hard work.

Bryett remembers:

I was in the room next to the Dick tunnel. The ferrets [roving German guards] came into the camp every day and occasionally one or two would sit on the steps of 122 talking and Russian prisoners would sometimes come into the hut and we would give them cigarettes or chocolate. These things seemed quite insignificant, but were the kind of thing I would eventually report to Kirby-Green. Other prisoners in the hut would report things to me. I was only a junior pilot officer and Kirby-Green, who was a senior squadron leader but a pleasant sort of chap, told me: 'Never feel anything you see around 122 is so insignificant you don't want to make a fool of yourself by reporting it. In fact, you are probably helping to build up a picture.'

We were counted twice a day and while we were out sometimes one of the ferrets would climb into the roof of a hut or get in a gulley under the hut and lie there for twelve hours, listening, so when we came back from *Appell* each morning and evening I had to check the roof and underneath to make sure there was nobody there.[10]

As the escaping season faded into winter the inventive leaders of the various sections in the X Organisation went into overdrive to produce enough documents and sets of clothing to equip more than 220 escapers. The forging section made travel permits, identity cards and *Urlaubscheine* for crossing frontiers; the tailoring section made clothes ranging from German uniforms to foreign-worker overalls; the map department produced compasses and drawings of both the local and wider area.

In mid-January Roger Bushell ordered the Harry tunnel to be reopened just as the colleagues of the men behind the wire prepared to renew the costly onslaught on Berlin in the non-moon period. By then the Harry tunnel had reached a level of technological expertise never before seen in the history of escaping. Its laddered entrance shaft plunged beneath the base of the heating stove in Hut 104 for 30 feet to avoid the seismograph microphones the Germans had buried in the compound to pick up the sound of digging. It then ran due north, gradually rising. Inside there was a well-designed trolley system to carry tunnellers to the face and bring sand back; two halfway houses, Leicester Square and Piccadilly, wide enough for tunnellers to switch trollies; an air pump with pipelines made out of powdered-milk tins; and electric light tapped into the camp supply thanks to a roll of cable purloined from German electricians who were then too frightened to report their loss.

To further expedite Harry's progress towards the wire a home-made generator was installed so that the tunnellers could work during the day when the camp lights were off. It was designed by Lt Nathaniel Flekser, a South African Air Force pilot and former electrical engineer whose companions in his six-bunk room included Jimmy James. Flekser was promised a place in the tunnel for his work and hoped for a home run. 'I decided I would assume the identity of a Dutch electrician who worked in a nearby chemical factory, going back to Holland on leave,' the South African later wrote. 'My plan was to go by train to Amsterdam where I hoped to make contact with friendly Swedish sailors who could smuggle me aboard their cargo ship.'[11] Flekser would take ship back to Britain before the following winter, but not as a result of the tunnel. A camp doctor diagnosed that the severe stomach pains he was experiencing were caused by a duodenal ulcer. He reluctantly agreed with Roger

Bushell to give up his place in the tunnel to someone else and was repatriated via Sweden on a hospital ship in September.

The final selections of who would get a place in the tunnel and in what order were decided in the weeks before the final break-out. More than two-thirds of the 900 men in the North Compound had been making some large or small contribution to the escape attempt and not all could go. There were also some who, because of their language skills and previously demonstrated escape abilities, would have a better chance of making it home. Those selected for early places in the tunnel were to catch trains.

Others, who would travel across country and were known as 'hard-arsers', were in the second batch for the tunnel. They were not expected to make a home run, but by being free for a while would sow confusion among the enemy. F/Lt James Howard was one of those:

> I lived in Room 23 of Hut 104, the actual room where the tunnel began, and that's how I earned my ticket for a place in the tunnel because I lived with the building of it from the word go. I didn't work on the tunnel myself. We just had to put up with the inconvenience of it and co-operate with those opening it up every day and closing it down again. The tension mounted as the weeks went by. The first 100 escapers were selected and the second 100 took part in a lottery to be 'hardarsers'. I was No. 117 so I had a fair chance of getting out.[12]

The Canadian air gunner Al Wallace was also in Hut 104. He says:

> I lived there for about four months. It was a rather difficult room because it was the tunnel room, which I was unaware of when I moved in. Whenever the tunnel was in operation you couldn't get back into the room and it was a difficult situation. I didn't go into the tunnel or even see the tunnel opened. I wasn't in the ballot for the tunnel because I had no desire to escape. I had played my part in the air over Germany and I figured that placed where we were, in what is now Poland, there was only a chance in a million of getting back to Britain.[13]

P/O Ron Heatherington, the sole survivor of his 106 Sqn crew after a Mannheim raid the previous autumn, was one of those who was disappointed in not getting a ticket for the tunnel. He remembered:

About half the people in the North Compound were in the escape organisation and one of the rules was you weren't to disclose to anybody what job you were doing. My main job for the Great Escape was copying maps and I was also stooging, looking out for the sentries. It was decided the fluent German speakers would go out of the tunnel first. They thought another few might get out and everybody involved was given a number and the numbers were put in a hat. They picked out about another hundred numbers, but mine wasn't one of them.[14]

However, F/Lt Ken Rees, shot down towards the end of 1942 on his fifty-sixth operation, was guaranteed a place in the tunnel because of all the work he had put into it. He recalls:

I was a tunneller on Harry more or less right from the start, in fact right after the shaft had been dug. Johnny Bull, who had the bunk opposite me, was a team leader on the tunnel and four of us to start with would work down there. I suppose all told eighteen to twenty were involved in working down there. I never suffered from claustrophobia, but there wasn't much room in the tunnel. It was about 2 feet square. I was just a bit worried in case there was a roof fall. It was pure sand. You did realise that if anything happened the Germans didn't know you were there and they would have had a bit of a job to dig down and get you out.[15]

How to get rid of that telltale yellow sand – 80 tons in the last two months – excavated from Harry and before the final blitz on Dick and Tom, had been one of the biggest headaches for the X Organisation. Then someone had come up with the bright idea of recruiting 150 'penguins' among the prisoners who would take it to a designated safe area, or walk around the compound distributing it in small amounts at a time from bags inside their trousers. Al Wallace was one of the penguins.

We had a little garden outside the hut and I stood in the dug-over garden and twisted my feet until they were below the surface, then pulled the cords of the bags under my pants and released the sand below the grey earth and wiggled it in. The Germans supplied us with rakes and shovels on an honour basis for the garden. It wasn't very successful for growing anything, but it was a wonderful spot to get rid of sand. On another occasion I was fitted up with my sandbags and instructed to go to a show in the theatre late in the afternoon. I was directed to a certain one of the seats made out of Red Cross boxes and under my feet a trap door opened and I pulled the pins and down the sand went into the floor under the theatre. The vast majority of the sand ended up there.[16]

S/Ldr Gordon Carter, shot down on the Leipzig raid of 19 February, was just in time to lend a hand with the escape.

I had arrived in Sagan only a month before and was immediately ushered into the group ensuring security, signalling the approach of the German 'ferrets' who were continually patrolling the compound looking for any untoward activity. We had a signalling system to allow the diggers to keep working until the very last moment.[17]

THE tunnel was pushed forward frantically in March after nineteen key X Organisation figures – including Bob Stanford Tuck – were transferred suddenly and mysteriously to the fourth Stalag Luft III compound of Belaria. In nine days 112 feet were dug and shored, taking Harry immediately past the camp's main gate and under the roadway running alongside the stalag to within a few feet of the 365 feet the POW amateur surveyors estimated would get them into the pine forest. Lt Flekser was in Hut 104 with Roger Bushell as the last few feet were dug. 'There was a muffled shout from below, "three feet to go, two feet". I looked at Roger and marvelled at the complete lack of visible emotion,' he wrote.[18]

The decision was taken to lift the last spadefuls to freedom on the 24th, for the same reasons as Bomber Command planned a major raid – it was a night without a moon. As the bomber boys were boarding their aircraft to hit Berlin that evening the final dates were being applied to forged passes and permits at Sagan and handed over to the hopeful. Bushell set the break-out time for 10 p.m. 'As darkness descended escapers began to drift into 104 and the regular inmates moved out. In all 220 hopeful escapers packed into Hut 104, whose normal complement was 80,' Lt Flekser wrote.[19] Not all of the would-be escapers were young. F/Lt Bernard 'Pop' Green, an air gunner shot down in 1940, was 57 and Major John Dodge, held in the camp because he had been picked up by the Luftwaffe after one of his previous escape attempts, was 50.

Among those packed in the fetid and feverish atmosphere of the escape hut as the freezing weather took a grip on the glinting wire surrounding the compound was F/Lt Denys Street, a 21-year-old bomber pilot from 207 Sqn, and son of the British Permanent Under-Secretary for Air, Sir Arthur Street. He would successfully exit the tunnel. P/O Bryett, also waiting in 104, wouldn't. Alan Bryett remembers:

> We made our way over to Hut 104 individually. The Germans came round about 9 p.m., closed all the shutters and locked the doors at each end, not planning to open them until 6 a.m. as usual. It was an unbelievably tense atmosphere as you waited for your turn to enter the tunnel. It was very crowded as there were more than 200 of us gathered there dressed in various guises. I had identity papers of a French foreign worker and had a dirty white striped shirt, a jacket from a dyed RAF battledress blouse and a pair of army trousers that had been dyed grey. Bushell and all the top people were there and they had the operation taped in a highly efficient way. As you entered the hut you were quietly shown to a bunk and told to wait for the deadline when the escape was to begin. I was told to keep as quiet as a mouse until my turn came. The front people in the escape were in the rooms near the stove where the entrance to the tunnel was.[20]

F/Lt James Howard, who lived in the actual room where the entrance shaft was, also remembers the crush as would-be escapers filtered into Hut 104. 'The atmosphere was very tense, but very upbeat. This was something that had been worked on for so long and it was going to happen. Everybody was very enthusiastic and impatience crept in as we waited our turn.'[21] P/O Bryett recalls: 'When it began we got constant messages from the top people who were along the tunnel waiting to get out. That's when we heard quickly from Bushell that he had discovered the tunnel was 15 feet short of the woods.'[22]

The amateur surveyors had made a mistake and the tunnel was in full view of a watch tower. Fortunately the guards had no reason to look anywhere but into the camp. Among the first to discover the tunnel was short was F/Lt Sydney Dowse. He remembers:

> It was a little bit tense in the tunnel. I was meant to open it up with a couple of other chaps. Johnny Marshall was the first one out and Johnny Bull No. 2. I and Johnny Bull broke the soil to open it and

there was a rush of cold air. It was a terrific moment, but very disappointing when it was realised it was short. We sent a message down the tunnel to tell those in Hut 104 what was happening.[23]

Bushell, who was waiting to go out as No. 4, decided that Bull would dash across to the trees with a rope from the tunnel, then give a tug on it when he could see the ground was clear. Gradually the evacuation of Sagan began, but not at the pace that had been intended. P/O Bryett remembers:

It caused immediate worry and slowed everything up ... there was terrific apprehension because it was obvious the thing was not going as smoothly as anticipated. We also got reports back that condensation was rising from the tunnel in a column because of the heat of all the people below waiting to go. Nobody had thought of that and there was an attempt to disguise it by spreading blankets around the hole so that it didn't go up in a straight line.[24]

Sydney Dowse recalls:

I was right at the front of the queue going out through the Harry tunnel and in fact was No. 3. I had tried to escape before and I suppose the escape organisation thought I had a good chance of getting home. I went out with a Polish officer, Stanislav Krol, who I named Danny. After we got out we went to Sagan station, but there were too many there including Germans and I said to Danny, 'This isn't wise, they might find too many of us on the station,' so we started walking east, travelling mostly at night. There was thick snow on the ground and it was very cold.[25]

P/O Bryett recalls:

As escapers went out you were being constantly moved up by marshals to the rooms nearer the entrance. Eventually all the priority people, who were rail travellers, had already got to Sagan station and were getting away quite satisfactorily, but about midnight an RAF raid on Berlin to the north began and all the lights in the camp went out, which, of course, put out all the lights in the tunnel as they were connected to the camp supply.[26]

Lt Flekser, who had handed all his documents and German money to a fellow South African, Lt Johannes Gouws, listened to the 'drone of aircraft and the thump of falling bombs' in the distance as he tried to get over his disappointment at not joining the escapers. In fact, it saved his life; Lt Gouws was among those shot.[27] Down below escapers were left in darkness, cramped in the confined space fearing being buried alive. The raid further delayed the exit rate as fat lamps were frantically searched for and lit to replace the now useless electric lighting. Slowly more men poked their heads out of the tunnel in response to a tug on the signal rope, then dashed for the trees. The exit rate speeded up as the raid ended and the lights came on again in the tunnel. Searchlights once again began sweeping across the silent camp, frozen in expectation.

F/Lt Howard, still in Hut 104, recalls:

Everybody was very enthusiastic and impatience crept in as we waited our turn. You expected if things had gone without any hitch you would have been out already. We kept hearing of delays, some escapers got stuck. The air raid didn't help when all the lights had to go out in the tunnel. I remember I was surprised to hear then that it stopped operations. I would have thought that if the lights were out this was a better opportunity. Everybody knew more or less where everything was and I would have been much happier to get out when the camp and tunnel lights were out than to wait. However, we knew those who were operating the tunnel knew of possible problems and wouldn't have willingly delayed things.

People waiting in Hut 104 to go were in all kinds of disguises. One chap appeared in a German uniform and caused a bit of a scare because he looked like the genuine article. I was wearing khaki trousers with a doctored long-sleeved jacket. I was going out with a particular friend, Des Symonds, a South African who was in the same room as me and our papers were for agricultural workers.[28]

F/Lt James, who had been a prisoner since 1940, was the thirty-ninth to exit the tunnel. He remembers:

It was very tense in Hut 104 as people waited to enter the tunnel. I had been in the tunnel before, but hadn't helped to dig it as I was on security and dispersal. I had, however, done plenty of tunnel-digging before. The lights were back on in the tunnel at that time, it was about

1.30 a.m and the air raid was over. It wasn't crowded because it was very strictly controlled. You got on a trolley at the bottom of the shaft and each escaper was pulled singly to the first halfway house, then you got on another trolley and the next hauler pulled you to the next halfway house, then you changed onto a final trolley and were pulled to the exit shaft.

I intended to travel with a Greek Air Force officer Sotiris 'Nick' Skanziklas. We planned to travel through Greece to Turkey. Skanziklas was the next one just behind me. When I climbed up the exit ladder and saw the stars above it was certainly a sensation. The air was jolly cold. You pulled on the exit rope and if the man hiding behind a bush in the woods gave an answering tug, it was OK to go. Two tugs meant stop because the guard was walking near by along the wire.

When I got the tug for OK I crawled as quickly as I could into the wood. I was in a group of twelve who had a pass of sorts showing us as workers going on leave from a local woodmill. We walked as a party right round the woods for about 7 or 10 miles to the country station at Tschiebsdorf, south of Sagan. We got there about five in the morning. Our group were the only escapers to use that station. Our leave pass was presented by one chap, Jerzy Mondschein, a Pole speaking fluent German, and we travelled down towards the Czech border, 100 miles by train, to another country station (at Bobenohrsdor), then we split up.[29]

Little by little escapers exiting the tunnel were reducing the crush on the surface in Hut 104. P/O Bryett remembers: 'I was very far back on the list and didn't move until the early hours of the morning. By about 3 a.m. we realised a lot of people, including me, weren't going to get out because it was going so slowly.'[30]

F/Lt Rees recalls: 'I went down the tunnel after about fifty had been pulled through. As an experienced tunneller I was to help pull about twenty-five escapees through and then go out myself.' Rees was going out with Joe Noble as a 'hardarser'.

I was wearing my service trousers and my battledress which I had tried to alter as much as I could. I had tried to dye it by using the black binding from books. It came up a somewhat motley colour. I also had a couple of sweaters underneath and a couple of sweat shirts and a pair of long johns. They were all intended to keep me warm as I and others headed down south to Czechoslovakia, but there were quite a few inches of snow on the ground. We hadn't got a hope in hell, but at the time we were very keen and hopeful.[31]

Not far ahead of F/Lt Rees in the queue was S/Ldr Len Trent, who would receive a VC almost a year after the war for the raid on which he was shot down.* Rees was within feet of the exit when it was discovered by a patrolling guard, who had almost fallen in the hole when he stopped to relieve himself. New Zealander F/Lt Michael Shand, officially the last man out of the tunnel, had just moved among the pine trees and dropped to the snow-covered ground. Trent was halfway out when the guard raised his rifle and aimed at Shand. Trent yelled 'Don't shoot' as the guard let fly with a single shot and missed. Shand got up and made off through the trees.[32]

Rees remembers:

I was approaching the exit shaft when I heard the shot. I realised the tunnel had been discovered and backed up to Leicester Square, the last halfway house. Joe Maul and Clive Saxilby, who were at the exit, came back and after they passed me I followed, trying to kick out some shoring in an attempt to collapse the tunnel behind me as I feared the Germans might fire along the tunnel. Luckily there was a slight bend. Once we had got round that we felt OK.[33]

The rifle crack echoed in the crystal-clear night air across the snow-filled, deathly quiet camp. It was heard by Al Wallace, now in Block 107, who remembers thinking, 'Oh boy, the game is up.' It was also heard by Gordon Carter in Block 112, who immediately knew, 'That's the end of it,' and it was heard by every one of the would-be escapers who had crowded into Hut 104 hours before and still awaited their turn in the tunnel. Alan Bryett realised there was now no chance at all of drinking beer in London within weeks as he had hoped. 'There was panic in the hut because a whole lot of fellows were going to get caught with escape aids,' he says. 'People underground started coming back and I and various

---

* S/Ldr Trent led eleven Venturas of 487 (NZ) Sqn on a daylight raid against an Amsterdam power station in May 1943. All were shot down, but Trent and his navigator survived. His VC was not gazetted until March 1946.

others started little bonfires in the hut to burn the maps, diagrams and disguises.'[34] F/Lt Howard, near by, also recalls the frantic burst of energy in the next few minutes:

> People trying to get escapers into the tunnel suddenly started working in reverse. There was something of a panic, we realised the game was up and we weren't going to get out. I was disappointed, I didn't expect to get very far, but you never know your luck and the prospect of a brief freedom was great.[35]

F/Lt Rees remembers:

> It was pandemonium when I got back up the shaft to Hut 104. People were burning maps and money and eating as much as they could of the rations they had prepared. The Germans were furious when they came rushing in. One of the first in was the *Hundführer*, a guard with a dog. The guard came stamping up and down, but the dog was very happy because the prisoners kept slipping it bits of chocolate. Other Germans poured in with machine guns and Tommy guns and the hut was surrounded while we were marched outside in the snow. We were lined up and 'Rubberneck' [Unter-offizier Karl Griese] called over myself and Joe Noble because we were his arch-enemies. He told us to take our clothes off and we were a bit reluctant in that weather. One of the guards came over and started pulling at us. I pushed him away and up came Rubberneck's revolver. I thought, 'Christ!' At that moment the commandant came out of the hut and yelled something at him and it was lowered, but Noble and I decided we'd better quickly obey and stripped down to our long johns. We were marched off to the cooler where we were held for fourteen days.[36]

F/Lt Howard was luckier. 'The Germans surrounded the hut with machine guns,' he remembers. 'The guards were very shocked, of course, by what had happened and knew some of them were for the high jump. They wanted to send us all to the cooler, but there were so many of us it wasn't big enough, so I and many others were just told by the camp commandant to disperse.'[37]

But for Alan Bryett it meant solitary confinement, which he has never forgotten.

There was no brutality, but we were immediately sent to the cooler, which was very crowded of course, while they searched the rest of the camp. There was intense bloody-mindedness from the Germans that we had been able to do this huge thing and they had been caught with their pants down. Even though there was no chance of my drinking beer in Piccadilly Circus in a fortnight's time I didn't feel my life was being risked unnecessarily because the mere opportunity of helping those very clever fellows who had arrived in the camp ahead of me was recompense itself. They were the super chaps of the RAF and Commonwealth Air Forces and of course as officers it was our duty to escape. The experience of being put in solitary confinement has stayed with me. The cells were only small and you had plenty of time to think. Often when I have a meal today in a strange restaurant I have to get up halfway through to make sure I know where the exit is and how to get out of it.[38]

THE ordeal of those who considered they had been lucky to get out of the tunnel was only just beginning. Apart from three captured at the shaft or in the woods facing it, seventy-six were now abroad in the Reich.

The majority of the escapers were back in captivity within hours. F/Lt James, who had arrived 100 miles south at Boberrohrsdorf railway station before his group of twelve split up, remembers:

Most of us were caught that evening. It was very cold and we decided to go into Hirchsberg West station to try to get a ride further on to the Czech border, but they were looking for us and we got caught in the station. We were taken to the local police station and eight of our group were taken from there in the next few days. We thought they were going back to Sagan, but they were shot.[39]

Obersturmbahnführer Max Wielen, the head of the Breslau SS criminal police in whose area Sagan lay, had quickly upgraded his manhunt known as a *Kriegsfahndung* to a *Grossfahndung*, a national alert, when it was realised just how many prisoners of war had escaped. It meant that not only the SS, but also the armed forces, the Hitler Youth and thousands of civilians were now involved. The Great Escape, planned by prisoners who had been seen as impotent by their Nazi incarcerators, was making its dint in the German war machine. It would eventually involve the diversion of 70,000 German troops, SS and Gestapo.

The 'hardarsers' were among the first to find themselves 'back in the bag', as expected. They had been chilled to the marrow as they stumbled through snowdrifts, their laboured breath bursting in clouds on the freezing air. In the early hours of 28 March those of them in Sagan jail, nineteen in total, were transferred to the civilian jail in Gorlitz, which rapidly filled up with escapers. By the end of 29 March there were thirty-five prisoners of war in the prison.

Of the rail travellers, Roger Bushell and his escaping companion, Lt Bernard Scheidhauer of the Free French Air Force, were the first to be recaptured – early in the morning of 26 March at Saarbrücken. Bushell, also a French speaker, had gone to enormous lengths with his documents and cover story that he and his companion were French businessmen heading for Paris. They passed an exhaustive Gestapo check and then, it is believed, one of the officials delivered a question in English. Scheidhauer, though French, had been speaking English for months and it is thought answered in the same language.

Four more of those escaping by rail had successfully travelled to and from Berlin, but were caught near the Danish border at Flensburg. Another three had reached Küstrin, 60 miles east of Berlin, when they were arrested. Tom Kirby-Green, whom P/O Bryett had found such a pleasant senior officer as he reported the movements of camp 'ferrets' to him, got as far as Hodonin in the south of Czechoslovakia, but was thrown into the prison at Zlin on 28 March. Dennis Cochran, in the same hut as the disappointed Ron Heatherington who didn't get a ticket for the tunnel, was within 4 miles of the Swiss border when he was picked up as a lone traveller.

The fury of Hitler himself was about to descend on the Great Escapers, now languishing in the pitiless cold of Gestapo prisons. They would pay for the refusal of men in air-force blue at camps across Germany to recognise that for them the war was over. The shame of the successful three-man Wooden Horse escape from Sagan's East Compound in October, a mass escape by thirty-two men from Szubin six months before then, which had tested local resources before all were recaptured, and an earlier unsuccessful escape by fifty-two men from Kirchhain, near Finsterwalde, had festered into deep Nazi resentment.

Hitler was at Berchtesgaden with some of the party's most senior figures on the morning of Sunday, 26 March when he was given the Gestapo report into the latest mass break-out. He immediately called a conference with the head of the SS, Reichsführer Himmler; Generalfeldmarschall Wilhelm Keitel, Chief of the High Command; and Goering, who as leader of the Luftwaffe had ultimate responsibility for the escapers. A 'very excited' Hitler ordered: 'They are all to be shot on recapture.' Goering objected, for practical reasons, that it would obviously be murder if all were killed and there might be reprisals among German POWs in Allied hands. 'In that case,' Hitler said, 'more than half of them are to be shot.'[40] Himmler suggested fifty and the cohort of cruelty agreed. Himmler immediately referred it to SS Obergruppenführer Ernst Kaltenbrunner, who issued his 'Sagan Order' the next day. It read in part that after interrogation by the Gestapo 'the recaptured officers are to be taken in the direction of their original camp and shot en route. The shootings will be explained by the fact that the recaptured officers were shot while trying to escape, or because they offered resistance, so that nothing can be proved later.'[41]

Among the first to be executed, on 29 March, were 'Big X' Roger Bushell and his escape companion Lt Scheidhauer. Gestapo man Emil Schultz, hanged in 1948 for his part in the crime, described at his trial in Hamburg what had happened. He said the two prisoners, looking 'very down at heel', were taken from solitary confinement in the prison at Saarbrücken and driven towards Kaiserslautern. A spot not too far away was chosen for the shooting by his boss, Saarbrücken Gestapo chief Dr Leopold Spann, because 'we have to economise on fuel'. Schultz said the car pulled off the road and the two prisoners were allowed to get out to relieve themselves. Schultz and Spann then shot the two prisoners in the back. In his statement to the RAF investigator read out at his trial, Schultz said:

> The smaller one fell face downwards and the taller one [Bushell] on his right side, slowly turning over on his back. He drew up his legs and I could see he was in great pain. He did not speak and I lay down on the grass close to him and taking careful aim shot him through the left side of his head.[42]

Among the last to be killed, merely because he stayed free so long, was Stanislav 'Danny' Krol, who had been one of the first out of the Harry tunnel with Sydney Dowse and had decided with Dowse not to take a train from Sagan station because there were too many escapers there. Instead they had set off on a mammoth trek east across country. Dowse remembers:

We travelled mostly at night. There was thick snow on the ground and it was very cold. After twelve days we came across a barn. I didn't want to go in, but Danny said he wanted to sleep. We went into the barn and dug ourselves into some hay on the right-hand side, but Danny got a bit claustrophobic and wanted to go to the other side. I tried to stop him, but went to join him after about 10 minutes and that's where we were caught. A Hitler Youth had seen us and he went to get some others. We were taken to a prison at Oels, then guards came to take me away. I rushed over to Danny's cage and told him, 'They're taking me off to Berlin and they're sending you back to Sagan.' He said, 'They won't send me back to Sagan, you won't see me again. Don't go without me.' I said: 'I can't do anything, I've got guards with me Eventually I was taken to Sachsenhausen Concentration Camp.[43]

In all, forty-six urns and four boxes containing the remains of the Gestapo victims were returned to Sagan. Among the urns was one for F/Lt James's escaping companion, the Greek officer Sotiris 'Nick' Skanziklas, one of eight in the twelve-strong woodmill party to be executed after being taken from Görlitz prison, east of Dresden. Others showed the names of Tom Kirby-Green and Dennis Cochran. Another bore the name of the well-connected F/Lt Street and was marked Breslau. He was among six men who left Gorlitz under Luftwaffe guard on 6 April. Convinced they were going back to Sagan and keen to get back among his comrades sooner rather than later Mick Shand, the last man out of the Harry tunnel, asked Street to swop places and offered him a square of chocolate in return. Street declined and F/Lt Shand returned to Stalag Luft III shortly afterwards.[44] In the weeks that followed the comrades of the executed fifty were allowed to build a memorial to them outside the wire.

F/Lt Rees remembers:

I had been in the cooler about ten days when I heard that some escapers had been shot. It was shouted across to us from the main camp that forty-three had been shot, then we were told forty-seven and finally fifty. There was a great sense of shock. Once I got back to the main camp I found there was a great feeling of gloom. I was particularly cut up because Johnny Bull, who was shot, was a big friend of mine. I used to look across at his empty bunk. He had a son he had never seen because he had been shot down before the boy had been born and I used to think about that.[45]

P/O Bryett recalls:

The Senior British officer in the camp was told after a few days that captured escapers had been shot. The Germans put a list up in the camp of the dead, then a few days later a few more names went up to make fifty. When I realised that so many of the POWs I knew and had worked with had been shot I was absolutely horrified and deeply shocked. They were some of the bravest men I had ever met and were among the cream of the RAF. They had borne the brunt of flying operations in the early years of the war.[46]

Others of the escapers were kept in various Gestapo prisons and POW camps until the end of the war and four – Jimmy James, Sydney Dowse, W/Cdr Harry 'Wings' Day and Major John Dodge – were sent to Sachsenhausen Concentration Camp under an ominous transfer order that 'to the outside world they are to be considered as escaped and not recaptured'.[47] They decided to tunnel to freedom again. F/Lt James says:

I and Sydney Dowse and a commando colonel, Jack Churchill, tunnelled out of Sachsenhausen together. We had learned by that time that fifty of the Great Escapers had been shot. We read about it in the *Völkischer Beobachter* newspaper and Jack Churchill, who was taken prisoner in July, confirmed it when he was brought in. We decided to go ahead with the tunnel anyway. I don't know if we thought we had nothing else to lose. We were all press-on types and thought, 'To hell with it, let's get out of here if we can.' The SS had told me, 'You can't escape from here, Herr James,' so we thought we would. It was a 100-foot tunnel, but the big problem was security because we were in such a small compound, so only one of us could go down at a time. We also needed to conserve air as no air pump or air holes were possible. Jack Churchill and I leaped up onto a railway and jumped a train, hoping to get to the Baltic. I was free for about two weeks. After we were all recaptured Himmler ordered our execution, but it was commuted to solitary confinement, which went on for five months. It wasn't very nice.[48]

F/Lt Dowse says:

> It was about three weeks after the escape before we arrived at Sachsenhausen and late September when we broke out of there. I said, 'We're going to do a tunnel,' so Jimmy said, 'Where do we start?' I said, 'Under your bed.' He said, 'What's wrong with your bed or somewhere else?' I said, 'Because if you look under your bed there's a knot in the wood and if we get that out we'll get the floorboard up,' so he had no choice. We knew we were in a concentration camp and knew what was happening there. We were aware if we were caught tunnelling out of Sachsenhausen we would be killed. Wings Day told me: 'I forbid you to try to escape,' but I told him, 'You know what you can do with that,' so Jimmy James and I started the tunnel and Wings decided to come with me. Wings and I were trying to get to the Friedrichstrasse Station in Berlin to get a train to Stettin. We hoped to get on a boat from there to Sweden. We were picked up on the station, taken to a Gestapo prison and then taken back to Sachsenhausen ... we were put in the execution block. We saw people being taken out from time to time to be hanged. My cell was on the side that faced out onto the courtyard and I could organise myself to climb up to peer through a window. I could see people being hanged.[49]

Fifteen escapers were returned to Sagan, including F/Lt 'Pop' Green, the oldest man in the tunnel. As Sagan's bitter spring turned to uneasy summer the letter code from Britain revealed what had happened to three of the other escapers, still unaccounted for. In fact, they had made it to England, three of the 220 who had entered Hut 104 that freezing cold night two months before with such high hopes.

Dutchman Bob van der Stok, a flight lieutenant in the RAF, had travelled alone by rail, reaching Dresden by 10 a.m. after exiting the tunnel. He spent all day there, mostly in a cinema, then took a train for Holland where he contacted the Resistance. Three weeks later he made his way to Belgium where he stayed another three weeks, an uncle in Antwerp providing him with funds. Then he made his way by rail across France to Toulouse and finally joined a party being taken across the Pyrenees to Spain on an escape route organised by the French Resistance. He got back to England via Gibraltar and returned to combat flying.

Per Bergsland and Jens Muller, Norwegians serving in the RAF, were lucky enough to find a faster route to freedom. They had made it from the pine woods to Sagan station where they caught a train to Küstrin, near Frankfurt-on-Oder, changed to a Stettin train and arrived in the Baltic port on 27 March. They had a contact address from Bushell – supplied in the letter code from IS9 – which turned out to be a seamen's brothel. There they met Swedish sailors who hid them in a locker on board their vessel. A German patrol searched the ship the day before it sailed, one of the Germans almost poking Bergsland's eye out as he felt around in the locker in the dark. The ship sailed the next morning and the two Norwegians reached Stockholm on 30 March and reported to the British consul. They were flown back to England within days for debriefing by MI9.[50]

A report prepared by the Air Ministry in the wake of the cold-blooded shooting of the escapers including that of the son of a member of the Air Council, came to the conclusion: 'A great deal more escape intelligence should have been supplied by IS9, especially about contacts in occupied countries, routes, frontiers, ports and shipping.' The report remained on the secret list for nearly forty years.[51]

By mid-April 1944 the full, dreadful story of the executions by Gestapo men, also under orders to cover them up, was blown. A representative of the Swiss Red Cross had visited Stalag Luft III and given a report to Sir Anthony Eden's Foreign Office in London. Eden rose in the House of Commons on 19 May and told the world of 'these cold-blooded acts of butchery' and promised that the perpetrators would be 'tracked down to the last man'.[52]

That tracking down took place by way of a nineteen-man RAF investigation team who began work at the war's end. Fourteen Germans were hanged in Hamelin in 1948 for their part in the executions. The last sentence was handed down in 1968. It was on Fritz Schmidt, head of Kiel Gestapo in 1944, who was accused of ordering the execution of the four men arrested near Flensburg. He was jailed for two years.[53]

At Sagan itself – where Luftwaffe notices were being displayed from April warning: 'Escape is no longer a sport' and even MI9 in its coded messages had freed officers of the duty to flee – life sank back to what passed for normal in the limbo-like existence of the prisoner of war. Prisoners still attended lectures on every subject from banking to basket-making, hung their washing outside their huts on summer Sundays and watched performances by amateur actors at the camp theatre. Life so reverted to the Sagan routine that despite all the new warnings and certain dangers the indomitable spirits of Stalag Luft III began a new tunnel, beneath the theatre itself. It ran from a trap under the twelfth row of the theatre and was codenamed George.* By July the tunnel was creeping towards the wire. That telltale yellow sand, which had needed a masterpiece of organisation to hide as it was gradually unearthed from the other three tunnels, was being spread under the floor.

To assist in its dispersal there were new prisoners in Sagan. Some had arrived as surviving Great Escapers were being returned to the camp. They were the result of the most disastrous operation ever mounted by Harris, his crews being shot down on another freezing night over the snow-covered Reich while some of the escapers were still at large.

* George was not used for an escape and was abandoned when Sagan was evacuated on January 1945, as the Russian Army approached.

8

Massacre in the Moonlight

The name of Nuremberg had long stood out on the target list of Bomber Command as a place worth special attention. It contained large Siemens and MAN factories, and produced tanks, armoured cars, diesel engines and a range of electrical goods required by Germany's armed services. More than 200,000 of its 495,000 population were busily engaged in fulfilling those needs. It was also an important communications and administrative centre. For the planners at High Wycombe and their Whitehall masters it had an added attraction. It was dear to the Nazi heart because of the Teutonic sound-and-light spectacle of the rallies held before the war, which had so chilled the free world.

There were other targets Harris could have chosen. At the beginning of March he had come under further pressure to obey the Pointblank Directive in which both the USAAF and RAF Bomber Command were asked to give priority to targets concerned with the German aircraft industry. There was now a new diktat listing six towns or cities considered vital to the Luftwaffe, beginning with Schweinfurt, which allegedly produced 40 per cent of all Germany's ball bearings, although the Reich Armaments Minister Albert Speer had dispersed production following USAAF raids in 1943. The other five in order were Leipzig, Brunswick, Regensburg, Gotha and Augsburg.[1] However, Harris knew that if his crews could not accurately concentrate their bombs on a large target like Berlin under the harsh winter conditions Europe was now suffering, they were unlikely to successfully attack such small targets as those on the list. Bomber Command had already been to Leipzig and Schweinfurt the previous month, so Harris may well have considered he had temporarily fulfilled his Pointblank obligation. After the blood-letting of the Berlin raid six days earlier the more southerly towns and cities of Germany became more likely to be chosen as the night's target. The allure of Nuremberg among those south German targets was compelling.

As an area target Nuremberg had so far escaped the full might of Bomber Command and the heavies had not bombed it for seven months. The last time they had visited it, on 27 August 1943, was only four days after a Berlin raid in which 7.9 per cent of the force – fifty-six bombers – had been lost, the greatest loss of aircraft in any night up to that period. Memories of those losses were fresh in the minds of some crews on the 27th and although PFF accurately marked the aiming point, creepback developed, which the master bomber was unable to halt, and most bombing fell in open country to the south-west. On that raid thirty-three aircraft had been lost, 4.9 per cent of the 674-strong force.

It was ironic, therefore, that the new nemesis of Nuremberg for Bomber Command would follow that of another Berlin raid a few days before, which had proved the costliest by far of the battle. The seeds of the retribution lay in the facts that it necessitated a long return flight of 1,600 miles, which would lay the bombers open to the searing cannon of the *Nachtjäger* for at least five hours of that journey; and, inevitably, in the weather and its forecasting, which had proved so disastrously inexact in the latest Berlin operation.

The preparations for the attack on Nuremberg began, as with all other raids, in the underground operations room of Bomber Command's headquarters at High Wycombe at the early conference into target possibilities the C-in-C liked to call 'Morning Prayers'. Here Harris was told that the possibility of fog, which had prevented his command operating in strength the previous night, had abated. His crews had now been rested for three nights following a big attack on Essen with a surprisingly low percentage loss of 1.3 per cent. There was one telling reason why their rest should continue. It was now the moon period. The moon was one-quarter through its cycle and there would be a half moon at its maximum height an hour before sunset. It would not set until the early hours of the next morning, 31 March.[2]

Harris would not normally consider sending his crews out in moon-light to a target three times further into German-held territory than the Ruhr, but he was on the very cusp of handing his command over to Eisenhower for pre-invasion needs. 1 April was the date by which Harris had somewhat over-enthusiastically promised the Air Ministry four months before that his Lancaster force would be able to produce 'a state of devastation in which surrender is inevitable.'[3] The nights of 30 or 31 March would be his last chance to strike a blow at a German industrial target before that crucial date. The early weather reports showed cloud was likely to cover any target in the north yet leave clear areas in the approaching track, which would give the night-fighter aces ample opportunity of increasing their scores in the moonlight.

However, there was a cold front that had been moving slowly south for days and now covered northern France and southern Germany, where lay industrial Nuremberg, still virtually a virgin target for Bomber Command. The front's leading, southerly edge would most probably contain cloud to shield his bombers, yet it was forecast that Nuremberg itself would likely be clear. A late take-off would probably allow Harris's bombers to fly out under this cloud, attack Nuremberg in the last light of the moon and return in darkness after the moon had set. The Met report indicated a strong tail wind to speed the bombers over Germany. It was too tempting to resist. Others, such as Harris's deputy, Sir Robert Saundby, expressed doubt about such a long flight in the moon period that seemed so uncertain.[4] Harris, who had gambled so often before, demurred and began another metaphorical shake of the dice in the game he had been playing with his opposite numbers in Germany since February 1942.

THE crews who would live or die as a result of that decision were alerted early to this new maximum effort. F/Sgt Don Gray was a new skipper on 50 Sqn. He had more than 1,000 hours of experience as a navigation school staff pilot and after many applications had finally been posted for training at an OTU. He remembers:

> By the time we finished Lancaster Finishing School Bomber Command was losing crews in the Berlin raids and we were sent straight to 50 Sqn at Skellingthorpe without any leave.
>
> Skellingthorpe was considered an excellent operational posting, because it was right on the edge of Lincoln and the bus terminus was actually outside the camp gates. But when we arrived on 18 March it seemed very empty as although there was room for two Lancaster squadrons only one was there at that time. My crew and I were directed to an empty Nissen hut on the opposite side of the road to the main camp, in the woods. It contained enough beds for about four crews,

but we were the only ones in it. We were given a fairly frosty interview by the squadron commander, W/Cdr Anthony Heward, and told not to leave camp for fourteen days. I think we were expected to be on hand to fly cross-countries if there were no operations. Due to our isolated living quarters and limited free time we were unable to get to know anybody, aircrew or ground staff.

I was only on the station for twelve days, during which I did four operations and I found it rather depressing, particularly as we had had no furlough for many weeks. The atmosphere at Skellingthorpe was a complete contrast to what I'd found in the previous three years of my RAF service.

Despite what the wing commander had ordered I did get into Lincoln, though. The night before I got the chop a couple of the crew had gone into the city when my name came over the tannoy to report for a flying exercise. I got onto the wing commander and told him some of my crew were missing and he blew his top. He told me to go round all the watering holes in Lincoln until I found them, bring them back and wheel them up in front of him the next morning. I went round the watering holes all right, but I didn't find them. It so happened that a friend of mine from Civvy Street, now a staff pilot at Cranwell, had turned up at the camp to see me that night so he and I had a good time and he was able to stay in our Nissen hut. The next morning it was a maximum effort for Nuremberg and the CO was too busy for disciplinary interviews. I thought, 'At least this isn't Berlin and it might be an easy one.'[5]

As crews were alerted for their long flight to southern Germany the final details were being made at High Wycombe to the flight plan. It was unusual because most of the outward route over enemy territory consisted of one long leg, 265 miles in length, from Charleroi in Belgium to Fulda, north of Schweinfurt. The main aim in any routing was to avoid the flak defences of cities, apart from the inevitable ring around the target itself. It would take the stream between two night-fighter assembly beacons, Ida, near Bonn, and Otto, north of Frankfurt. But there were twenty-one such beacons, the locations of which were well known to Bomber Command, and it was difficult to avoid them all. The major flaw in this route was that although the lack of dog-legs meant less time over enemy territory its arrow-straight precision gave the German controllers ample time to get their night fighters into the stream.

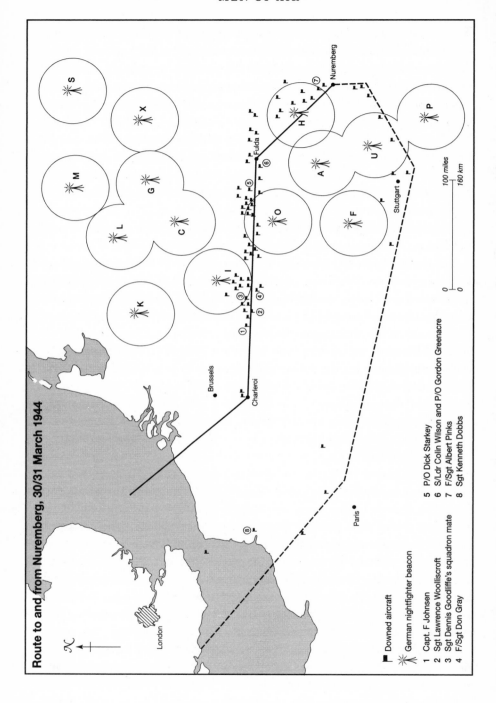

Route to and from Nuremberg, 30/31 March 1944

London

Paris

Brussels

Charleroi

Fulda

Stuttgart

Nuremberg

S
X
M
L
G
C
K
I
O
F
A
U
H
P

100 miles
160 km

■ Downed aircraft

✳ German nightfighter beacon

1 Capt. F. Johnsen
2 Sgt Lawrence Woolliscroft
3 Sgt Dennis Goodliffe's squadron mate
4 F/Sgt Don Gray
5 P/O Dick Starkey
6 S/Ldr Colin Wilson and P/O Gordon Greenacre
7 F/Sgt Albert Pinks
8 Sgt Kenneth Dobbs

The route's success was now entirely dependent on there being cloud cover and it would shock many when unveiled in briefing rooms. There had been long legs before, notably the Berlin raid of 29 December, four months before, when the stream had flown one course from mid-North Sea all the way to the Leipzig area, turning north-east for the short haul to Berlin. On that occasion the German controller had been confused by spoof raids on Magdeburg and Leipzig. The *Nachtjäger* had not caught up with the bombers until they were over Berlin and the chop rate was only 2.8 per cent, remarkably low for a Berlin raid. It is possible such a low loss against highly efficient night-fighter units had been at the back of the planners' minds when the long leg was drawn. If there was cloud again to hide the bombers such a daring, unbroken route might succeed once more, this time in southern Germany.

But the prospect of cloud cover – the primary excuse for such a long leg – was fast disappearing. A Mosquito of 1409 Flight at Wyton had flown over the North Sea shortly before noon to check the weather and had discovered scattered cloud, though the navigator forecast that 'over Continent convection cloud is expected to break up appreciably'.[6] A second 'Pampas' flight then flew an arc over the Ruhr and Belgium to assess the weather for the Nuremberg force as it began its long leg. The crew found their Mosquito left a long vapour trail at 25,000 feet-plus and below them at 10,000 feet was light cloud, which would probably disappear in the cold night air.[7] The bombers were now likely to stand out clearly in the moonlight. The later report also forecast that Nuremberg itself, where clear conditions were needed, was in fact likely to see large amounts of stratocumulus cloud.

The disastrous development was handed to Harris's deputy, Sir Robert Saundby, shortly before 5 p.m. Sir Robert wrote to the historian Martin Middlebrook in 1971 about that crucial weather report and Middlebrook printed the letter in his excellent account of the operation. It read: 'I can say that in view of the met. report and other conditions, everyone, including myself, expected the C-in-C to cancel. We were most surprised when he did not. I thought perhaps there was some top-secret political reason for the raid – something too top secret for even me to know but now I do not think that was so.'[8]

Crews, too, thought the raid might be scrubbed, as icy gusts swept across bleak tarmac and found gaps in Nissen huts. A prospect of another night off was tempting; 30 March was a Thursday and, then as now, Friday and Saturday were the big nights out in Britain's cities, when airmen particularly liked to visit the dance halls and pubs to meet the girls fresh from shop counter and factory bench. But there was always the prospect of a few pints of wallop and the flicks mid-week. Some among the aircrew of 1 and 5 Groups based north and south of Lincoln had planned to see the Bob Hope film *Let's Face It* at the Regal during the moon period. Friday would provide even greater delights – a 'Grand Dance' was advertised at the County Assembly Rooms, Lincoln, with the Marina No. 1 Dance Orchestra. If they couldn't afford the 3s 6d entrance fee, there was always the two-bob hop at Robey's Sports Club on Canwick Road with the popular Norman Applewhite and his band.[9]

At Lissett in 4 Group's area, P/O Joe Hitchman, whose first operation had been to Berlin on 20 January, was looking forward to a few days far away from flak and fighter.

> I and my crew were supposed to be going on leave that day and we had actually got to the main gate when we were recalled. My flight commander, S/Ldr Jones, shared G-George with us and when we got to briefing we found we had been temporarily assigned an aircraft new to 158 Sqn, F. That aircraft went on to do 128 operations as 'Friday the 13th', but S/Ldr Jones was shot down that night in G. We didn't particularly want to go as we weren't supposed to because we were due leave.[10]

Sgt Kenneth Dobbs, the wireless operator whose 78 Sqn aircraft had been so badly shot up over Berlin and had then found himself transferred as a 'spare bod' to 158 Sqn, also discovered he was on the battle order at the last minute. He remembers:

> I hadn't been detailed to fly and was going home. I went up to the flight office just to see what was going on and F/O Harvey the deputy signals leader came up to me and said, 'We're a wireless op short for F/Sgt Brice's crew, his w/op's gone sick.' I said, 'I'll go,' because I had thirty trips to do for a tour and I wasn't getting them done very quickly. I met F/O Harvey again in hospital in Germany; he was shot down on Nuremberg too.[11]

P/O Dick Starkey of 106 Sqn volunteered to go to Nuremberg at the behest of his crew. 'We had been stood down because it looked as if four crews on the squadron would finish their tours at the same time and they wanted to stagger us,' he remembers. 'The crew asked me to see if the flight commander would let us go and after some talking he agreed and said one of the other crews would be stood down.'[12]

The maximum effort order touched all squadrons in Bomber Command except 617, the elite unit that had breached the Ruhr dams the previous May. Some were able to put up more aircraft than others, but none more than 101 Sqn, which operated the special Lancasters packed with jamming equipment codenamed 'Airborne Cigar'. The ABC aircraft would be needed to block night-fighter reception through-out the five waves of the attack and 101 Sqn had twenty-six aircraft ready to be interspersed throughout the stream.

Australian F/Sgt Graham Boytell was one of those who had lately been posted to the squadron as a special operator of the ABC equipment, as the jamming role was stepped up in the technological battle for supremacy between Bomber Command and the Luftwaffe. The special operators' work was highly secret and the selection process was rich in drama. Boytell remembers:

I was doing wireless operator training at Dumfries when I was called out on parade and told I had been posted and had to leave at 4 p.m. I and another wireless operator were duly loaded onto a covered truck and taken to Dumfries railway station with no indication of where we were headed. At the station we were told to board an empty carriage, which carried the placard RAF ONLY. During the journey we stopped at various stations at which various aircrew people would enter until eventually there were fifteen people in this special carriage. As each entered he was asked, 'Where are we going?' to which each answered he didn't know or what for. To make things even more strange the group now consisted not only of wireless operators, but gunners, bomb aimers and navigators. There were no pilots so there was no possibility of us making up a crew.

Eventually the train arrived at Leeds and our party of three Can-adians, eleven RAF and one Australian (myself) were put in covered trucks and taken to RAF Lindholme, a conversion unit. Once more we asked, 'What are we here for?', but the Lindholme personnel told us, 'We don't know, we were just told to expect a group of odd bods.' We then moved to RAF Hemswell (a Lancaster Finishing School) where we asked the same questions and got the same answers, but we were told we had to log ten hours' flying in Lancasters.

Within a short time we were moved, again by covered truck, to another RAF station where we were taken to an isolated building and told, 'You are now on an operational squadron, 101, at Ludford Magna.' We were further advised the job we were doing was highly secret, we mustn't tell anyone what we would be doing, even the crew we were flying with would have no idea of what the job entailed. 'They are not permitted to even ask you and of course you cannot tell them,' we were told. 'In fact, the station commander, G/Cptn King, doesn't know and cannot ask you.' We had apparently all been picked for the job because we had learned to speak German at school, a fact learned by the air force by a questionnaire sent to RAF stations about a month before.

In a few weeks at Ludford we were taught how to operate our equipment with the necessary precision to become combat ABC operators and jam the R/T communications between the German radar stations and their associated night fighters. I was never asked by anyone what my job entailed. This high level of secrecy had its advantages. It created an air of importance, which elevated our status on the station and meant we were always given what we requested with no questions asked. The batch of fifteen special operators I was in completed the necessary complement to bring the squadron up to full strength. Prior to our arrival the squadron only had about eight special operators. Of the fifteen of us who came to Ludford that day only five survived.[13]

In fact, some of them would be shot down on the Nuremberg raid as F/Sgt Boytell made his maiden operational flight.

The crews who were called to briefing in the early evening of 30 March were told spoof raids would be mounted by Mosquitos on Aachen and Cologne, to keep the German fighters in the Ruhr area as the stream flew on, and later on Kassel, which it was hoped would make the German controller think there had been a course change and send his fighters to Berlin. The latter would work in part because some fighters were sent to the capital, but by that time more than 200 were already in the stream shooting down bombers as a beacon to others and the main effort would continue in routing fighters along the correctly guessed track and into southern Germany. In fact, the Luftwaffe would have twenty-three of its twenty-eight *Nachtjäger Gruppen* in the air before the bombers had even crossed into enemy air space.

Some crews made shocked comments as they saw the route outlined in bleak briefing rooms. Sgt Russell Margerison, the mid-upper gunner on 625 Sqn at hastily constructed Kelstern, who had seen a bomber apparently shot down with one shell on the Berlin raid six days before, remembers: 'On the map we could see there was a very long unbroken leg to the target, far too long without a turn. There were a lot of groans and whistles of derision about it and it was a moonlit night as well.'[14]

THE bombers began to take off for Nuremberg shortly after 9 p.m. A separate force of the older marks of Halifax also rumbled away for a mining operation near Heligoland, Windowing furiously as it crossed the North Sea in the hope of drawing off the northern-based enemy fighters. After them came faster Mosquitos making the spoof raids. Fifty-five Mosquito fighters and four American also soared into the sky at various times to carry out Intruder operations and begin Serrate patrols to lock onto the impulses of the *Nachtjägers'* Lichtenstein radar in the hope of turning those who preyed on the bombers into victims.

Among the bomber squadrons, the ones based in Yorkshire and Durham had further to fly than those further south and took off first, so the last of the Nuremberg-bound squadrons weren't airborne until an hour and a half after the first. F/Sgt Jack Gagg on 166 Sqn in 1 Group north of Lincoln was supposed to be in the middle of the stream, but left so late he was at the rear. He remembers:

It was our fifth operation. I flew ED905* on my first few raids, and we warmed up its engines at dispersal and ran each one up to full power, but I had a magneto drop on one and it was spitting and spluttering. The ground crew came out and changed all the plugs, but that didn't fix it, then they changed the magneto and it was still giving problems. The wing commander came up and said: 'There's a spare aircraft, switch over to that.' We got out and went to the spare aircraft, DV367, but it all took time and by the time we were ready the rest of the squadron had been airborne for forty-five minutes. As I taxied out, the wing commander called up and said we were too late, we would never

---

* ED905 became one of the thirty-five Lancasters that would complete 100 operations or more. It had been delivered to 103 Sqn in May 1943, where it was flown by the crew of F/Lt Douglas Finlay (see the author's previous work *Bomber Boys*), transferred to 166 Sqn, then eventually to 550 Sqn where it carried the name 'Press on Regardless'.

catch up with Main Force and asked me what I wanted to do. I asked the crew what they thought and they all wanted to go, so we went. Nobody liked to scrub after getting so far.[15]

As F/Sgt Gagg took off, aircraft at the head of the stream were already experiencing problems. A total of fifty-two aircraft had to return early from various causes including oxygen failure, though three of them that had already crossed the enemy coast were able to bomb targets of opportunity. F/Sgt Gray was among the first away from Skellingthorpe before a Lancaster burst a tyre as it hurtled along for take-off and blocked the flarepath, forcing four more aircraft to wait and be diverted to a different runway. Gray remembers:

> To gain height you had to fly nearly to Wales then back over the aerodrome and we set course over Yarmouth. As we approached the enemy coast the rear gunner, Sgt Douglas Maughan, started experiencing trouble with his oxygen supply, but there was no way I was going to turn back, not with the squadron commander we had and I'd put up a black with him already the previous night. So we carried on and the wireless operator took the rear gunner a spare helmet and oxygen mask. The wireless op was going backwards and forwards trying to help him, but he said he couldn't do anything with him.[16]

The stream was now 68 miles long, structured to hit Nuremberg with a seventeen-minute storm of bombs. It was about to lose its tight concentration. The direction of the wind had changed from north-west to almost due west and several assigned Windfinders on the route had picked this up, but few of their broadcasts had reached their groups, giving a distorted picture, the wind speed alone differing by 44 mph. The rebroadcast winds for the stream to use were therefore wrong, not recognising the true realignment and a lessened strength of the wind, and it caused the stream to gradually drift north. It was a fatal development.

The German controller at the underground headquarters of the 3rd Fighter Division at Deelen airfield, near Arnhem, had correctly decided that the mining force heading across the North Sea was a diversion and the real threat came from the second, larger force of bombers, which had crossed the British coast over Norfolk and was apparently heading for central or southern Germany. Four fighter divisions, NJGs 1, 3, 4 and 6, together with elements of two others, were now ordered to assemble at beacon Ida and those who couldn't make it on time were told to go to beacon Otto, north of Frankfurt.[17]

The first spoof raid by Mosquitoes dropping target indicators and bombs now took place on Aachen, but the controller wasn't fooled because the *Nachtjägers*' path to Ida took them across the track of the bombers and some picked up emissions on their SN-2 radar sets shortly after midnight. The first bombers now began to fall, many picked off by tracerless Schräge Musik, the explosions in the night sky later being described by some inexperienced crews lucky enough to return as the scarecrow rockets intelligence officers had told them about. One Lancaster of 101 Sqn was shot down by another British bomber in the confusion.

Squadron flight engineer Sgt Dennis Goodliffe saw his fellow crew lost.

A Lancaster was on the port beam about 200 to 300 feet above us. Suddenly another bomber, I'm told it was a Halifax, drifted across between us and its mid-upper gunner opened fire on the Lancaster pouring fire into it from the front right back to the tail and hitting everybody below that line. I found out later the aircraft was from our squadron, skippered by P/O Adamson. The mid-upper gunner, Sgt Don Brinkhurst, was the only one unhurt. He got out of his turret, helped the special operator out of his seat and they both agreed to go down on Don's chute. I think the operator's chute was damaged. Don and he baled out together, but the operator slipped out of Don's arms and was killed. Don walked home and several weeks later appeared in the sergeant's mess.[18]

The 156 Sqn Pathfinder aircraft of Australian W/O John Murphy in which Sgt Lawrence Woolliscroft was the wireless operator was among the first to go down in the first part of the long leg. It was caught near Holzweiler by Oberleutnant Gunter Koberich flying a Schräge Musik equipped Ju88 of II/NJG2 at Quakenbrück. Oberfeldwebel Walter Heidenreich, the radar operator, later recorded:

Just before Aachen I got an SN-2 contact at a distance of about five kilometres. I remember quite clearly that this blip on my radar had a strange, unusual shape ... We worked ourselves literally metre by metre closer but we didn't sight him until we flew into a patch of clearer sky where, to our amazement, the strange blip resolved itself as two planes flying in close formation.[19]

The first Lancaster was in fact the aircraft of Murphy's Norwegian friend on 156 Sqn, Captain F. Johnsen, RNAF. Koberich fired at the left-hand plane from 250 feet away and set the left wing ablaze. 'We peeled off to the right and a few seconds later were sitting under the second machine. Strange as it may seem it continued flying in the same direction. We acted quickly and our slanting cannons spoke again,' Heidenreich wrote.[20] Both Lancasters still flew on the same course, now ablaze. The Luftwaffe crew didn't see anyone bale out.

Sgt Woolliscroft, the sole survivor of fifteen men, remembers:

The Australian rear gunner, W/O George Wood, had seen the other Lancaster and we headed their way and kept station with them. We could see by reading the fuselage letters in the moonlight it was someone from our squadron, but we didn't know who. We had flown alongside before and called it 'going hand in hand'. We were flying at 24,000 feet and as most attacks occurred between 15,000 and 20,000 feet we thought we were safe there, but someone called on the intercom, 'Bandits to starboard.'

I was in the astrodome taking a sextant shot for the Canadian navigator, F/O Jack Toppings, and sure enough there was an aircraft just below us. We thought at first he was going to ignore us, so we shoved our height up a little further. However, he started firing from the rear, missing us, and the navigator pulled at my clothing and told me to put my chute on. I had just put my chute on one hook of my chest harness when we exploded. The night fighter's cannon must have hit the bombs. I came to to find I was falling at speed with my chute pack half attached. It was absolute terror. It was obvious I wasn't going to survive and I thought, 'How will my family find out about this?' I decided to close my eyes and just pray. I thought, 'I'm going to hit the ground then I shan't know anything.' I like to think that what happened then was due to praying. I had pulled the ripcord without realising it and found myself falling sideways with the chute above. Because I was sideways on I saw another parachute above me. I landed in some trees and was being dragged along the top, so released myself from the chute and fell about 10 feet to the ground.

I thought I'd broken my ankle. I lay on the floor for a while. I was very shocked and felt very alone. I felt myself all over very carefully and realised that I was still alive and able to stand up. I had never thought for one minute that I would survive. I thank God for it. I got on my knees and prayed and prayed that I would see the person who was in the other chute, but I didn't. I now think he was probably dead in the chute or the chute was empty. I thought I would be killed by the Germans, I think because we had been told at Upwood that airmen were being killed by civilians. We were terrified to be caught. After a long while I heard voices and found I was on the side of a hill in some trees. I crawled down and saw woodmen chopping timber.

Sgt Woolliscroft would be on the run for four days.[21] His Lancaster had been shot down just before the Rhine was reached, near Bonn.

F/Sgt Gray's aircraft from 50 Sqn was attacked shortly afterwards beyond the Rhine and it was this particular stretch of the long leg all the way to the turning point above Schweinfurt that became the graveyard for most of the fifty-nine bombers downed in one hour from Charleroi to Fulda. The night fighters were circling the Ida radio beacon just as the second of the night's spoof raids opened with Mosquitos dropping target indicators and bombs on Cologne to the north. The bombers were meant to fly miles to the south of this as they skirted the defences between Cologne and Coblenz in the 20-mile-wide corridor known as the Cologne Gap. In fact, the errors in rebroadcast winds meant they were now north of the corridor heading straight for the orbiting *Nachtjäger*.

Five minutes after the Cologne spoof opened the unsuspecting crews of 700 heavy bombers charged straight into the assembly of Zahme Sau and Wilde Sau night fighters, just as surely as the 600 cavalrymen of the Light Brigade had blundered into the Russian cannon at Balaclava ninety years before, and just as surely, they were cut down. The midnight massacre by the waiting fighter pilots, who usually had to search fruitlessly for their prey across hundreds of miles of sky, now began in such spectacular fashion that it gave rise to the false rumours, which persisted for many years after the war, that the Germans knew the route in advance.

The night fighters could hardly miss their victims. To add to contrails above, a thin sheet of cloud now appeared thousands of feet below in the moonlight. Sgt Goodliffe, on his fourth operation, remembers: 'We soon realised what we were up against. You could see aircraft outlined on the cloud below like bugs on a sheet and I quickly started seeing air-to-air combats and bombers starting to go down followed by flashes of light under the cloud as they crashed. I logged twenty-three on that route before I stopped counting.'[22]

Sgt Kenneth Dobbs, who had found himself on the battle order at the last minute, recalls:

> On the long leg from Charleroi I could see through my small wireless operator's window several aircraft going down. Nobody said anything, but there was certainly more activity that night than on any other raid I'd seen. There wasn't usually a deal of talking when you were flying, you just got on with your job and I was listening on the set.[23]

Sgt Russell Margerison got a grandstand view of the action in the mid-upper turret of his 625 Sqn Lancaster. He remembers:

> We could see aircraft getting a pasting all around us. We had just turned onto the beginning of the long leg at Charleroi and the half moon clearly showed up the condensation trails of our aircraft. I saw a blossoming reddish glow on our port side as the first bomber fell. Within fifteen minutes string after string of fighter flares were illuminating our course. Red and green tracer was criss-crossing the sky and I reported a Halifax going down on the port side, then the rear gunner saw a Lancaster going down behind. Immediately afterwards I watched a Lancaster near by as its wing folded up at right angles and it toppled over. Another bomber skidded below us, on fire. At that point we decided to stop logging the downed aircraft, it was too demoralising. There seemed to be no part of the sky where an aircraft wasn't falling. The rear gunner and I counted fifteen bombers go down. Yet in the whole time no one in our aircraft actually saw a fighter.[24]

P/O Hitchman, the 158 Sqn pilot, remembers:

> I have never been so tired in my life as I was that night. We were logging combats almost all the way to the target and back. I was weaving all the way and corkscrewing as the gunners saw fighters. We saw so many aircraft shot down the navigator logged about twenty until eventually I said, 'For Christ's sake, lads, don't report kites shot

down, just keep your eyes open for fighters,' so we didn't log any more.'[25]

F/Sgt Gray, whose rear gunner was suffering from poor oxygen supply, was attacked near the Rhine town of Sinzig, between Bonn and Coblenz. He recalls:

I started to see fighter flares going down in front and burning aircraft falling. I could see it was going to be a right do and I suggested to the flight engineer, who was only a young lad, it was his job to go back and see what he could do for the rear gunner. At that moment the mid-upper gunner shouted 'Corkscrew port' and started firing his guns like mad. I corkscrewed away and the gunner told me the fighter had gone. I straightened up and the wireless operator came forward and told me that the engineer was also now unconscious apparently through oxygen failure. I thought, 'I'll have to go down to 10,000 feet, below oxygen height,' and was just trimming for the descent when there was a bang and the Australian bomb aimer, F/Sgt George Wallis, said, 'We've been hit.' I looked across and the starboard wing was ablaze. I could see we were in a right pickle. I tried to feather a blazing engine, but I could see the wing was starting to go and I ordered, 'Bale out.'

The Australian navigator, F/Sgt Campbell, went flying past me and I was trying to hold on to the thing. I thought if I could close the petrol tank levers on the engineer's side I might cut down the flames. I picked up a chest parachute while I was there and put it on, then went back to my seat. There was a sudden *whoof* and a bright light, then everything was black. I thought I was dead, but something was hitting me in the face. By some light in the distance I could see it was the parachute pack, so I pulled the ripcord. It was very quiet and I thought then I must still be in the aircraft. My arms were hanging down by my head so I pulled them down and they shot up again. Then I looked at the parachute open above my feet and I realised I was hanging upside down.

I had slipped out of the harness and it was tangled round my ankles and I was coming down head first. By God, I panicked then. It was lucky I was wearing the old-type green canvas flying boots without the centre zip. They were very tight, unlike the brown suede type, and it was like pulling a pair of wellingtons on and off. I'm sure I would have just slipped out of my boots if I'd been wearing the zipped type. I thought about trying to bend myself like a trapeze artist and trying to grab the harness, but I had an Irvin jacket on and knew I wouldn't manage it. Instead I kept very still.

Within a few moments there was a bump, a branch struck my face and I had hit the ground in a forest. I saved breaking my neck because it had been a snowy winter and the ground was soft in the wood. I tried to move my limbs and when I moved both legs the parachute harness came off. I think now that as I stood up to release my seat straps to go to the engineer's position I also turned the quick-release buckle on my parachute harness which I would normally do at the end of a flight, so that I could carry my harness out. When the chute opened the harness opened up, went through my legs and tightened up round my ankles. I just wasn't meant to be killed that night.

In the first few minutes on the ground I couldn't straighten my neck properly and one leg hurt badly. I thought, 'This is a pickle, it'll take me at least three months to get back home and start flying again.' I started to walk westward and almost immediately came onto a road. I realised if I had landed on that I would have broken my neck. I climbed a fence and went across a field into a forest then found myself on a path with benches by the side like a beauty spot. I saw a train and made for it, but I was very groggy and tried to sleep. It was very cold and I think shock was setting in, so I set off down the road again and realised there were houses either side. I felt all-in but thought I could perhaps jump a train so carried on. A train went by a level crossing at the bottom and suddenly four torches flashed out of the gloom. Four old chaps on Home Guard duty armed with rifles came over and I put my hands up. I think they were more worried than I was, but they took me to the police station in Linz, south of Bonn.[26]

F/Sgt Gray's navigator, Alan Campbell, later recorded:

Upon the order 'Abandon aircraft' I clipped on my parachute, leaving the navigator's compartment for the bomb aimer's compartment. On passing the observation windows to the right of the pilot's seat it occurred to me that with luck the opportunity to observe an engine fire at night would never occur again, so I stood up and looked out. The starboard inner engine was certainly ablaze, a long tongue of flame, blue and changing to yellow, streamed from the cowling over the wing reaching almost to the tail of the aircraft, a truly astonishing sight. I quickly dropped down on all fours and crawled the few remaining feet to the top of the steps leading into the bomb aimer's compartment.

In the dim light I could see the bomb aimer was very actively trying to remove the bundles of tinsel and forged German food coupons etc. from the top of the escape hatch. Sighting me he commenced throwing them up to me and quickly cleared the hatch. The time was passing and I was very conscious of that engine and the 500-gallon fuel tank behind it. He was having trouble though, the hatch refused to open and at about the same time he gave a hopeless, arms-outstretched sigh of failure there was a *whoompf* and I felt myself propelled forward and down the steps. The landing was not soft. I had a sensation of pressure, flame, general disorientation and then nothing. My eyes opened ... quiet, not a sound, no sense of motion. I was on my back and could see stars above me. I was not sure I was clear of the aircraft, but pulled the parachute handle anyway. Wonderful! The chute opened with a jerk. I gingerly tugged on the straps and felt the webbing was tight, looked up and in the moonlight could see that glorious great canopy billowing above me. I looked down, below and in front was the top of another parachute. [Probably F/Sgt Gray's.] Good, someone else was out.

After only a few moments Campbell hit the ground and got to his feet, moving off after disentangling the harness. But a figure appeared in front of him.

It seemed to me that it must be a German farmer armed with a pitchfork. Hands above head I explained in perfect English I was the navigator of the Lancaster, the remains of which could be seen burning not far away. The figure advanced silently, placed a hand on my shoulder and said, 'Don't panic, Al, it's me, George.' It was George Wallis our bomb aimer, who explained he had escaped through the shattered Perspex after the explosion. Together we commenced our journey.[27]

They were captured two days later and eventually discovered four of their crewmates had been killed when the bomber exploded.

*

THE special operators in the first of the ABC Lancasters in the front two waves of the stream had detected the night fighters heading for beacon Ida some time before as they peered into their cathode ray tubes covering the whole of the German *Nachtjäger* frequencies from 38 to 43 megacycles. Blips on the cathode ray tube meant there was a transmission. They listened in and then jammed it, on one of the three transmitters they carried, sending out a high-pitched noise like bells being rung out of sequence. Then they searched for another transmission with their other five receivers to repeat the process. As the killing began over beacon Ida and beyond the special operators found it difficult to keep up.

The RAF radio station at Kingsdown in Kent, which listened into the night-fighter traffic, discovered the Germans used nine plain-language channels and two Morse channels on the Nuremberg raid. At the height of the air battle the running commentary was heard at Kingsdown on sixteen separate channels, of which ABC jamming was heard on eleven, but because the jamming had been spread so thinly and so many powerful German transmitters were in use the commentary still came through clearly. Kingsdown was also able to chart what a disaster the operation had become in the hour after midnight as Luftwaffe pilots continually called in their successes to base.[28]

In an attempt to fool the German controller one last time the third spoof of the night took place as the bulk of the bombers flew on past Ida. A small force of Mosquitos flying above the stream flew off at a tangent, north-east to Kassel, dropping target indicators along the way, then TIs and bombs on Kassel itself. Some fighters were dispatched to the Berlin area in case the tangential raid was mounted there, but it was by now easy to tell that the real direction of Main Force was towards Fulda by the burning pyres of crashed aircraft.

P/O Dick Starkey's Lancaster was shot down near Königsberg, not far from Fulda. He remembers:

> Under almost a full moon the bombers started making condensation trails and we thought, 'This is like a daylight raid.' We got to the turning point and started going on the long leg and the combats began. It was hell upon earth then. The combats were all over the place. I saw about thirty go down. I didn't know whether to alter course and go a few miles north, but I kept doing banking searches (weaving) and it happened.

Nobody saw the night fighter, it came from the left side underneath. What happened then took about fifteen seconds. The night fighter let fly and bullets went between my legs and I could see tracer flashing past the Perspex. The port wing was on fire with the port engines, so I gave the order to bale out. The bomb aimer got his parachute out of the rack and said, 'Bomb aimer going,' but the rear gunner reported, 'I can't get out,' because I had had to feather the port engine and that supplied the power to his turret. By this time the wing was a mass of flames. The engineer, Johnny Harris, handed me my chest parachute pack and I managed to get one of the two hooks of the pack attached. The controls of the aircraft were loose and we were going down and I had to resign myself to the fact that that was it. I was sure it was over. I felt helpless, it was all a mass of flames, the bombs were still on board and I was sitting on the Cookie. Then suddenly I had a sensation of being forced up with my neck down. I came to to find myself in the sky. I must have been blasted through the canopy by the exploding petrol and bombs. It had taken only that quarter of a minute.

I felt the harness, but it was on the side without a connection and I thought, 'I'm coming down without a parachute.' I felt the other side of the harness, saw it was fastened and hung on like grim death. I looked up and above me the parachute canopy was full of small holes. It could have been bits of the exploding aircraft that went through. Because it was silk it hadn't kept burning. I had no idea what height I was or how fast I was coming down. My flying boots had been jerked off and I was bleeding from the face. I was terrified that I might be killed on impact and the next thing I hit the ground with a terrible bump, which knocked all the breath out of me.

I could hear the rest of the aircraft flying over and I tried to stand up, but I fell over and thought, 'The Germans are using traps,' because my foot collapsed. I tried again then realised my foot was at an angle to my leg, so the ankle was broken. My neck and back were also very painful. I lost consciousness and a little later some people came along with a torch and found me, taking me to the burgomaster's house in the village of Königsberg. I felt like the cat with nine lives. I could have been killed by the night fighter's bullets or by the explosion or because my chute wasn't properly clipped on. A lot of villagers came to see me, mostly women. They didn't seem to be mad at me, they seemed more motherly. I was only 21. They were more curious than anything.[29]

P/O Starkey had been shot down by the Luftwaffe ace Oberleutnant Martin Becker of I/NJG6. He had employed his favourite tactic of approaching from the starboard rear, pulling up the nose then opening fire at the same time, immediately afterwards pushing on the rudder pedals to go right or left. This had killed the wireless operator George Walker and mid-upper gunner Jock Jameson immediately. The bomb aimer, Sgt Wally Paris, who baled out, was the only other crew member to survive.*

Becker claimed seven victories that night, and a third of the aircraft shot down fell to eight Luftwaffe *Experten*, many of the novice crews who made up most of the night-fighter arm being unable to position onto a bomber and hold on long enough to down it. Major Martin Drewes of III/NJG1 shot down two with Schräge Musik, including the 97 Sqn Lancaster in which the expert F/Lt Richard Trevor-Roper was the rear gunner. Trevor-Roper had won a DFC on the Dams Raid the previous May in Guy Gibson's crew.

The depleted and battered stream of bombers that P/O Starkey heard continuing to Nuremberg now reached the final turning point and altered course through nearly 90 degrees for the target. The bombing was due to open at 0110 and sure enough at that time bombs could be seen exploding, though there appeared to be no target indicators. A few minutes later red and green TIs were seen going down in the clear air and approximately 120 Main Force aircraft unloaded in the next few minutes, their relieved pilots diving away after the photoflash. But this wasn't Nuremberg, it was Schweinfurt, 55 miles too early. The incorrect winds rebroadcast to Main Force had taken them north and the bearing and distance from the turn to Schweinfurt were approximately the same as they would have been from the right turning point to Nuremberg.[30] Schweinfurt, which Harris had been reluctant to attack because it was difficult to find, was being bombed after all and three of the town's ball-bearing factories were damaged.

Nearly all of the Main Force survivors in fact went on to Nuremberg,

---

* Sgt Paris thought he was the sole survivor until P/O Starkey traced him in 2002. At approximately the same time P/O Starkey also found out, when he related the details of his own ejection from the aircraft to the Irvin Parachute Company, that his escape was even more remarkable. The company told him that not only was his chute held by one clip, he must also have put the pack on upside down. When P/O Starkey hit the forest floor he left an impression of his body 2½ inches deep.

but ironically the correct target – which had been chosen because it was forecast to be clear of cloud when the outward leg wasn't – was covered in cloud more than 10,000 feet thick. The exact reverse of what had been desired when the raid was planned had happened. It was another indication of how difficult it was for Harris to launch a successful long-distance operation amid all the imponderables and why Bomber Command had to take part in area attacks rather than attempt precision strikes if it was to hurt the enemy sufficiently.

The Pathfinders' planned visual attack, the Newhaven method, had had to be hurriedly changed to an emergency skymarking, or Wanganui, raid. The parachute-held flares were quickly blown across the target and the Pathfinder aircraft that did unload red and green target indicators watched them drop into the cloud and vanish. Some Pathfinders had been led astray by the wrong rebroadcast winds. No master bomber had been laid on to guide – one of the most serious errors of the Nuremberg raid – and it meant Main Force arrived to find a target so badly lit it was nothing like many of the experienced crews had seen before. There were two groups of skymarkers, one 10 miles to the east, and most crews bombed this instead of Nuremberg. Further creepback meant most of the bomb loads that were actually carried as far as Nuremberg went down in open country; few hit the middle of Nuremberg itself. There was no setting ablaze of the city centre as planned and not a single bomb fell on the important MAN and Siemens plants. However, another ten aircraft fell to night fighters.

One of them was the 578 Sqn Halifax of F/Sgt Albert Pinks, who had only arrived from conversion unit six days before and had not even done a second-dickey raid. He was among the nine crews for whom the Nuremberg raid was their first trip. Despite evasive action Pinks would have had little chance against the expert he came up against, Helmut Lent, *Kommodore* of NJG3. Lent had taken off in his Bf110 late from Stade near Hamburg and arrived north of Nuremberg just as the stream was turning in to the last leg to the target. He shot down Pinks's Halifax at 0121, as the bombing raid was coming to an end, 10 miles north of the aiming point, a railway goods depot near Nuremberg railway station.

The correspondent Werner Kark, who had flown with Lent on the Berlin raid six days before, was again in Lent's crew and wrote about the action in the *Oberdonau Zeitung* the next day. He described how when called to cockpit readiness his unit had thought it was a red herring because 'When was the last time the British had come in bright moonlight and clear visibility?' They had then flown east and seen how

the torches of aircraft going down in flames and the flickering flashes in the sky mark the bitter aerial combats between our fighters and their enemies ... the fires from the crashed bombers illuminate a thin covering of cloud. The flames of burning machines below it light up blood-red. Around us it is as bright as day. Two, three, four combats have flared up very close to us. A fighter is just diving steeply down on its prey. To our starboard streams of tracer flash past our wings, and above us we can make out the sharp outline of a Halifax swathed in flame from tail unit to cockpit. On our port side a bomber explodes in whirling fragments.

Then they had come across the aircraft later identified as Pinks's, Lent's sole victory of the night. Kark wrote:

Our foe seems to be overcome with fear. He is twisting and turning for his life in this inferno. But the *Oberstleutnant* doesn't let the victim off the hook. We follow him into a dive, pull up with him. Go over on to the left wing, then the right one, so that everything in the cabin that is not fastened down floats up, ghost-like. Our target comes into our sights for a fraction of a second. Our pilot fires a long burst. Blood-red flashes streak from the barrels of our cannon. The shells hit his starboard wing, tear it off. For an instant wreckage fills the air, and then the bomber goes down vertically and hits the ground. There is a ball of fire on the earth, a thick black cloud of smoke from the explosion.[31]

There were no survivors.

The skipper of another 578 Sqn aircraft would be awarded a posthumous VC. P/O Cyril Barton pressed on to Nuremberg with his bombs even though attacks by two night fighters put an engine out of action, destroyed the communications equipment and left him with no working turrets. The navigator, bomb aimer and wireless operator in the front of the aircraft baled out in the confusion. Barton turned for home after bombing Nuremberg and without navigation aids eventually crashed in the yard of a coal mine at Ryhope, Co. Durham, killing himself and a miner going to work, but saving the remaining three members of his crew.[32]

The 101 Sqn special operator, F/Sgt Graham Boytell, flying with an experienced crew, had been somewhat bemused by the baptism of fire on his first operation. He says:

The flight to the target was uneventful as far as I was concerned. I was kept busy jamming, but the rest of the crew felt there were far more aircraft being shot down than usual. We bombed without incident, but just afterwards the rear gunner saw a Ju88 approaching our tail. When the fighter got to within 200 yards the gunner called for a corkscrew starboard and opened fire, but only one of his four guns was working and it only fired one shot. The guns were all frozen solid in the minus 40° temperature. The fighter made two more attacks, which we managed to thwart before he realised we were awake. We all heard a loud bang through the encounter, but there was no evidence of damage. The most difficult feeling for me throughout all this was utter helplessness. I wanted to get behind a gun myself.[33]

F/Sgt Boytell's operational innocence would irritate his CO when he returned to Ludford Magna.

THE 661 bombers still flying after the furious onslaught by the Luftwaffe faced a new enemy as they turned for home. The tail wind that had proved so deceptive on the outward route was now a stiff head wind and the navigation problems that had caused so many to bomb Schweinfurt in error drove some into the Stuttgart flak. Cloud cover, so desired but lacking on the outward leg, was also now evident. Night fighters were much less of a problem, both because of the more difficult interception conditions and because they had got low on fuel after following the stream for so long and had to land, though a few went hunting again after refuelling and rearming. Oblt Martin Becker, who was one of them, was then vectored onto a Halifax of 429 Sqn, which he dispatched over Luxembourg. He was awarded the Knight's Cross for downing seven bombers in one night.

Sgt Dobbs's 158 Sqn Halifax was virtually on the last lap when it was caught by Hauptmann Ernst-Wilhelm Modrow of I/NJG1 near Caumont in the Pas-de-Calais. He remembers:

We were hit by flak over the target. I remember the pilot saying he was having a bit of difficulty with the controls, so as we were a bit off course we decided to head for the emergency aerodrome at Manston. We were only about 20 miles off the French coast and at between 12,000 and 15,000 feet when a fighter, which I later found out was a Heinkel 219, came in from the port and strafed straight along the side of the aircraft. I remember seeing the flashes. I think some of the crew were shot. The Halifax made a turn then went into a dive. I tried to roll over onto a couple of steps next to me as my parachute was in a stowage across the way, but I didn't get to it because I passed out. A chap on the ground told me later the aircraft exploded in mid-air. I've no idea what happened to me. I came round in a truck being driven to hospital in Lille with German soldiers on either side. I had a broken leg, broken ribs and head injuries and cannon shell injuries to a thumb. Apparently I came down in the rear of the aircraft and a Frenchman pulled me out when it hit the ground. I met him later and he told me I was in the rear. As the wireless operator's position in the Halifax was in the front I can't understand how I got there at all. The rest of the crew were dead in the aircraft, except one other who did bale out apparently, but he was dead when they found him. It might have been the rear gunner because he had the best chance of escape.[34]

The Lancaster of mid-upper gunner Russell Margerison was nearly added to the total of fifteen aircraft shot down on the way home. He remembers:

We were attacked after we left the target and turned north of Stuttgart for the long leg towards Paris. The rear gunner called a corkscrew, then as we resumed straight and level flight I saw a single-engined fighter coming in from starboard up. I called a corkscrew to starboard and we lost him for five minutes, then white tracer flashed above us. We still couldn't see the fighter. The pilot announced he was going to corkscrew continuously for the next hour and we did.

We had no further trouble, but the corkscrewing used up so much fuel the pilot asked each crew member whether we should bale out before trying to cross the Channel. We decided to try to get home and before we crossed the English coast the pilot was calling up 'Darkie' for somewhere to get in. We eventually got a response from Silverstone, then as we approached we were told we couldn't land. We found out later a Lanc had crashed on their runway. We were diverted to Bovington in Hertfordshire, but we got down to about 500 feet without reaching the airfield so the pilot said, 'I'll have to put her down,' and got us all to assume crash positions. I looked out and all I could see was trees, but he made a brilliant wheels-down landing in a small field. We went through a hedge and a country lane, through another hedge where we left part of a wing and rumbled across a field of the Duke of Bedford's estate at Little Chalfont. The police and Home Guard came out and we were given breakfast by locals. A wagon came for us from the USAAF base at Bovington and they gave us a meal there and then they took us to King's Cross Station to get back to Kelstern.[35]

Not everyone who flew on the Nuremberg raid found it a horrendous experience. Most of the Pathfinders at the head of the stream were through the Cologne Gap before the night fighters arrived. Sgt Dick Raymond, the 19-year-old Pathfinder flight engineer on 83 Sqn who had survived the ground explosion of his Lancaster months before, says:

As far as our crew was concerned it was just another trip. We didn't see anything untoward, it was an uneventful night, but when we got back aircraft were being diverted. We didn't have the best possible wireless operator and he didn't receive the diversion signal from base. We were trying to get in at Wyton in a snowstorm and the skipper called 'Overshoot'. I bunged the throttles through the gate and the skipper pushed the stick forward to build up speed and his seat collapsed. He found he was looking at nothing but his flying instruments. How the heck we got out of it I don't know. He just had to go round by feel.

The pilot always claimed we overshot at a speed so low for the Lanc it should have caused it to stall. Then we got a rollicking for landing at base when we shouldn't have done. We considered ourselves extremely lucky to be back on the ground. We were one of the few crews debriefed at Wyton. No aircraft were lost from our squadron, but so many landed away from base we didn't know who was missing and who wasn't. It wasn't until the next morning we heard about the losses. We couldn't understand how the heck we didn't run into any trouble ourselves.[36]

One of the luckiest skippers of the night was P/O Jack Gagg, whose operation had begun so badly at Kirmington when his assigned aircraft developed engine trouble. Taking off forty-five minutes late possibly saved his life, four of the 166 Sqn crews who left on time failing to return. He remembers:

> Instead of climbing up to 20,000 feet I kept low, making a gradual ascent because I thought it would give me a better airspeed. We went across Germany at about 10,000 feet. Just south of Bonn we started to see a lot of vapour trails. It was a very clear night and very cold. The fighters had followed these trails and knocked down a lot of aircraft, but because we were so late I think by the time we got there they were on the ground refuelling. The same happened on the return journey. We didn't have a shot fired at us.
>
> What we did see were a lot of what we thought were 'scarecrow' shells ahead on the way out, but what we didn't realise was these were exploding bombers. On the way back the rear gunner called me up, again near the Bonn area, and told me to look down. He said he thought someone had dropped a load of incendiaries all over the place, but afterwards I realised it was Lancasters shot down on the way out and still burning. When we got back to base and went into debriefing we found out what had happened. Some crews were so upset they were crying at the debriefing tables. They had been so badly knocked about and were glad to get home.[37]

P/O Hitchman returned late to 158 Sqn's aerodrome at Lissett. He recalls:

> Because we had used so much fuel in corkscrewing we couldn't get back to base and had to land at Odiham. We'd been in the air seven hours and thirty minutes. We didn't go to bed and got back to Lissett at about 10 or 11 a.m. The flight commander asked me before we went to debriefing what it had been like and I said I thought at least fifty had been shot down. He told me off and said I shouldn't be claiming as many missing as that. Then someone else landed and he asked that pilot what it had been like. 'Piece of cake,' he said. 'I didn't see a thing.' He thought he had just seen spoof flares. I told him that if he hadn't realised they were aircraft going down in flames he wouldn't be here in a fortnight and he wasn't.[38]

Sgt Margerison didn't find out the true scale of the Nuremberg disaster until he arrived at King's Cross.

As we walked up the ramp I could see the *Daily Express* placard saying '96 Down'. We were staggered. We had with us all the machine guns we had taken out of the Lanc and all our flying equipment and we piled them up on a trolley on the platform. There wasn't a train until 5 p.m., so we told a porter, 'Look after that lot,' then two or three of the crew went in the pub and the rest of us went to the cinema. We didn't have any money so they let us in for nothing. People were coming up to us and shaking our hands and saying, 'God bless you, lads,' and, 'You're doing a good job.' When we got back to Kelstern we got a brand-new aircraft that we had for the rest of our trips.[39]

Diarist John Hennessey of 49 Sqn, who had so disparaged the Berlin raid to senior officers six days before, returned from Nuremberg with only eight operations of his tour to go. He wrote in his diary that day: 'The greatest mistake the RAF has made; for we went to do the attack in moonlight. Fighters intercepted us as soon as we crossed the enemy coast and kites were being shot down all around us ... 96 aircraft were missing from this operation – the greatest number yet lost in a single operation.'[40]

The deepest shock was being felt on 101 Sqn. They had suffered the highest loss of all. Flight engineer Dennis Goodliffe remembers:

When we got back I spoke to engineers who hadn't completed their logs because they were so sure they were going to get the chop. After we got down and saw who had been chalked in on the operations board we realised seven aircraft were missing. It was dreadful as aircrew began looking at each other in amazement. We hung around in the debriefing room for some time to see if anyone else turned up, but they didn't ... That morning the breakfast tables were almost empty in the sergeants' mess. The cook came round and asked us all to move to make up a few full tables so that it would look respectable. Within 48 hours we were back on almost full complement as new crews were drafted in.[41]

The special operator Graham Boytell, whose operational experience had begun only hours before, now found himself on the receiving end of some of that Ludford Magna shock.

On return to base all the crews were discussing the large numbers of aircraft shot down and the station commander, G/Cptn King, called our crew into his office and asked each crewman what he thought about the raid. I didn't think he would ask me as security about my job was so tight. I didn't know how to answer without divulging any secrets and I finally said, 'Nothing unusual, sir,' this being my first op. He jumped on me, accusing me of going to sleep on the job. I felt I had been shot down myself and from then on whenever Groupy called us in after a raid and questioned me I always gave him the standard answer: 'About what I would have expected for that kind of target, sir.' He always accepted it.[42]

MORALE among the bomber boys was now at rock bottom. It had been the very worst seven days for the Command. The Berlin raid of 24 March had claimed seventy-two bombers and after final calculations in the dawn of 31 March it was known another ninety-five had disappeared. That figure of aircraft lost to the Command would rise to 105 after counting crashes in England. A total of seventy had battle damage, a few so severe they would be scrapped and cannibalised for spare parts. One of the Mosquito intruders also failed to return. F/O Osborn and his navigator, F/O George Ingham, a married father of two, from Manchester, had taken off to patrol the Münster area. Their failure to return to 21 Sqn brought the toll for the night to 106. In one night more aircrew had died than in the whole of the Battle of Britain. Many of the messes of Bomber Command now echoed with loss. P/O Gagg remembers: 'We used to complain sometimes about Harris and call him Butcher Harris for sending us so often because in March, for instance, I operated on 15 March to Stuttgart, then again on the 18th to Frankfurt and, of course, there was Nuremberg at the end.'[43]

Many of the young Lincolnshire airmen who had set out on 30 March with high hopes of dancing with the local girls at the big dance in Lincoln's County Assembly Rooms were now lying in shattered airframes littered across Germany. The shock wave of those losses went right through the Command from High Wycombe all the way to the training bases.

Sgt Frank Etherington, a 21-year-old flight engineer, was in the final stages of instruction before going on to an HCU and a successful tour, when he heard about how many Nuremberg had claimed.

We didn't think much about Bomber Command's losses when we were training until that day in late March. A few of us were sitting on our beds in the billet at St Athan when over the tannoy we heard that ninety-six were missing on Nuremberg. We gave each other sickly smiles as if it didn't really matter, but I thought, 'This is bloody awful, there's a war going on out there I didn't know about.' That's the effect it had on me. Before the beginning of my tour I got a bit apprehensive. If the truth be known you rather hoped the war would be over before you started. A lot of people including me were in it for the stripes and the brevet to attract the girls.[44]

On the ground in Germany the scale of the Luftwaffe's victory was evident in the numbers of aircrew still trying to evade. Sgt Woolliscroft, who had been so terrified of falling into the hands of vengeful civilians, hid among trees after being startled by woodmen near Holzweiler, south of Bonn, where he landed. 'I then started walking at night and hiding during the day,' he remembers. 'I knew from base intelligence that there were POW camps near there and my object was to get to one of those because I would be treated as a prisoner.' Eventually after four days the brave but shocked wireless operator, who had completed forty-two operations, was so exhausted by trying to make his way across the wooded landscape he decided to risk giving himself up.

I lay down and a large civilian carrying an axe and a shotgun came by. I stood up and said the first thing that came into my head which was, '*Ich bin Romanski.*' At first I really thought he believed I was a Romanian ally because he turned away, then he turned back with gun raised.

I was taken to the local police station and not badly treated. I was given a cup of tea and a loaf with a chunk of meat in it. I started to chew away, but collapsed. I suppose it was the terror of what would come next, but they were decent people. I was taken for interrogation at another police station where because I would only give name, rank and number the interrogator, who spoke perfect English, said he refused to believe I was shot down a few days before. I just shook my head and repeated name, rank and number. Eventually I was transferred to Dulag Luft then to a POW camp in eastern Germany.[45]

P/O Starkey, brought to earth near Königsberg, found himself in a cattle wagon within days, being taken with nine others shot down that night to the interrogation centre near Frankfurt. 'From the train I could see wrecked bombers in the fields, about five or six,' he remembers. 'We looked at each other and realised a lot had been lost.'[46]

Like schoolboys in England during the Battle of Britain, those in Germany underneath the combats in the night went out the next day to look for the downed aircraft. Sometimes they were unprepared for what they found. Heinrich Dietz was a 14-year-old in Ober-Moos, near Fulda where the 7 Sqn Lancaster of 38-year-old S/Ldr Colin Wilson, the oldest man to die on the Nuremberg raid, was shot down. Heinrich had been woken in the night by a bang, which also woke his mother. They thought it was a falling bough of a tree that a neighbour had started felling the day before. As morning arrived the teenager heard that a bomber had come down and went to look for it with others, in the nearby Nieder-Moos area.* He later related:

On the way a policeman stopped us and asked us what we wanted. As we explained our plan, he said, 'What do you want there? you have a crash in Ober-Moos yourself!' So we turned round ... the whole crash site was covered with body parts and aircraft debris. The bomber must have exploded in the air. The only complete body was lying in the small forest, Am Trieschwald, about 400 metres away. In his fall tree branches had torn skin from his face. People who had been there before us told us Polish people had taken a gold watch from the man, who I later learned was named Fuller†. To the left of the spot in the forest where Fuller was lying was an engine of the bomber.

Within minutes young Heinrich found himself conscripted into the 'ugly work' of taking the remains away.[47]

In the days following Nuremberg the inquest began into what had gone wrong and would continue among surviving crews for many years to come. In his post-war memoirs Harris would ignore the catastrophe, though in a letter to the head of the Air Historical Branch long after the war he would describe it as 'the one real disaster, and we were lucky not to have had a dozen'.[48]

---

* The Halifax of P/O Gordon Greenacre of 76 Sqn was shot down in the Nieder-Moos district, one of four 76 Sqn aircraft lost on the raid.
† Sgt Frank Fuller was the 20-year-old rear gunner in S/Ldr Wilson's doomed crew.

This was true and Harris's gambles had often paid off. But it does seem that the urgency for one last area-bombing maximum-effort strike before handing his force over to Eisenhower obscured his judgement. There was too much reliance on cloud to cover the stream, though – after all the irritating overcast on Berlin that winter – it's not surprising that the subliminal thought was for cloud rather than not. But in the light of the late weather forecast Harris should have called the raid off, as his trusted deputy thought he should – particularly after the losses on Berlin six nights before. It was, after all, the error for which Harris's predecessor Sir Richard Pierse had eventually been sacked by Portal, mounting a maximum-effort raid to Berlin in November 1941 in the wrong weather conditions, which had caused a 12.5 per cent loss.[49]

Then there were problems with the route. To feed the force through the Cologne Gap south of Ida, which allowed every *Nachtjäger Gruppe* in the west to converge if the direction of route was guessed right, was a risk too great, and to organise a spoof raid on Cologne just five minutes before the leading elements of the bomber force were due to cross the Cologne Gap was likely to compound any problems caused by lack of cloud cover. Harris was a clever and resourceful commander, but this disaster was more important than something to be dismissed as one error when he got everything else right. Diarist John Hennessey was correct: 'The greatest mistake the RAF has made.'

Most of Bomber Command did not operate for the rest of the moon period and many crews were sent on leave. Hennessey himself was able to see his wife and baby son in Bexleyheath, returning to fly in a more moderately sized 341-bomber attack on Aachen on 11 April which proved to be the most accurate raid of the war on the German city, causing widespread damage and fires in the old town area. It would perhaps have been some satisfaction to Hennessey to witness this impact on the enemy's economy after the costly shambles of Nuremberg, but he didn't have the opportunity. He and his crew were shot down over Belgium on the way by Oberleutnant Heinz Wolfgang Schnaufer of Stab IV/NJG1, the fifty-second claim of the man who would end the war as the leading German night-fighter ace with 125 victories. Hennessey died just as the worst was over and the bombing war entered a new phase, which would see losses per raid fall to an average of 2.2 per cent in the shorter pre-invasion targets.

SPRING

9

Making a Mark

It was never the same after Nuremberg. Bomber Command's operation planners would not again devote the night to one stream of aircraft attacking a single target. Those now halfway through their tours on squadrons or counting off the last few operations were left with the memory of that terrible winter campaign, which had claimed the lives or freedom of 2,256 of their fellows in January, 1,529 in February, and 1,880 in March.

Unknown to them, however, the Luftwaffe would now start to go into steady decline as the USAAF's bomber gunners and fighter pilots shot it out of the sky in daylight and Bomber Command's 100 Group Serrate Mosquitos stalked the *Nachtjäger* in darkness. In fact, 100 Group's countermeasures to Luftwaffe night-fighter technology would dramatically improve from April and by the war's end the group had largely strangled the German night-fighter arm, employing thirteen squadrons equipped with Halifax, Stirling, Fortress, Liberator, Wellington, Mosquito, Beaufighter and Lightning aircraft under the command of Air Vice Marshal Edward Addison, a technocrat himself, specialising in electronics and signals.

As the attrition among Bomber Command's squadrons declined and the efficiency of aircraft production improved, Harris was able to call on an average of 1,000 heavy bombers a night from early April, and eventually many more, to light the way for D-Day and the ruin of the Reich. The sacrifices of the Battle of Berlin and beyond had made way at last for the dawn of hope on the airfields of eastern England. Among the biggest changes of the month, as the deadly winds of winter made way for the warm zephyrs of spring and the prospects of invasion, was the development of a new low-level marking technique by the leader of 617 Sqn, known as the Dambusters by an unusually awestruck press because of its success the previous May. It would lead to 5 Group becoming a virtually independent force, a scheme dear to Harris's heart.

The splitting away of 5 Group did not please No. 8 (PFF) Group's leader, Don Bennett. He did not believe in low-level marking because of the difficulties of map-reading at high speed and minimum height and told Harris exactly that in a phone call when asked about so marking Berlin. 'Within half an hour I had a message to report personally to the C-in-C,' Bennett recorded. He was received by an 'obviously peeved' Harris and was given 'a frigid and formal notification that I was immediately to send 83 and 97 Sqns (Lancasters) back to their parent 5 Group, together with one Mosquito squadron, and that in future 5 Group would adopt the method which I refused to accept.'[1] In fact, the rivalry that now ensued between Bennett's high-level Pathfinders and the low-level experts in Sir Ralph Cochrane's 5 Group would lead to increasing efficiency, not less. The fact that in future there were in effect two Pathfinder forces also made it easier to mount two important raids at the same time to confuse the controller of the deadly Zahme Sau *Gruppen*.

FEW could claim to have single-handedly made a change for the better in the bombing war, but W/Cdr Leonard Cheshire could. He was serving as station commander at the heavy conversion unit at Marston Moor in October 1943 when he asked for the second time to lead 617 Sqn. The first time had been in July 1943 after Guy Gibson, who had formed the squadron, left, but Cheshire was told he had been pipped by George Holden.[2] Holden was now dead, leading one of the five crews from the squadron lost in a calamitous raid on the Dortmund–Ems Canal in September. Cheshire, already well known to the public as the author of *Bomber Pilot* – published in 1941, but a seller throughout the war – and a man with two DSOs and a DFC, dropped a rank from group captain to take over 617 Sqn. The serendipity of the right man of courage in the right place at the right time was about to improve the marking of German and pre-invasion French targets to such a degree that it would win Cheshire the VC and make a marked change in the progress of the night air war.

Cheshire had seen the need for marking targets at low level as far back as his days as a novice Whitley pilot, bombing bridges in the Battle of

France. 'I started putting up papers to that effect while still on 102 Sqn,' he remembered in a post-war interview. 'They were quite well received by the CO, but they didn't get any further.'³ Cheshire's low-level creed would now go a great deal further following a precision attack 5 Group mounted on an aircraft works at Toulouse on 5 April. Cheshire had flown a Mosquito for the first time only six days before, but was able to dive accurately to 500 feet to drop his flares on the well-defended target. Two 617 Sqn Lancasters dropped further precise markers on his flares and the subsequent bombing by ordinary crews of 5 Group, who had not undergone any special training, was near perfect. Harris was now convinced of the efficacy of low-level marking and rapidly told Cochrane, who had badgered for almost a year for his group to mount its own operations; he could now operate as an independent force using his own marking tehniques. 617 Sqn was provided with two Mosquitos, then after Mosquito-borne Cheshire and his squadron's Lancasters demonstrated the success of the low-level marking method again with an attack on the small, but key, Luftwaffe signals depot at St Cyr next to the gardens of Versailles he received another two and crews were named to fly them. All four Mosquitos were used to successfully mark rail yards for the bombers at Juvisy, south of Paris, on 18 April and at La Chapelle, north of the French capital, on the 20th.⁴

The method now needed to be tested on a bigger, municipal target. Harris chose the small town of Brunswick, one of the six towns or cities vital to the Luftwaffe he had been asked to give priority to in the refinement of the Pointblank Directive in March, but which he was reluctant to raid after the disappointment of Berlin because he didn't think his crews could hit them successfully. The two Pathfinder squadrons, 97 and 83, which had been moved to help set up 8 Group, had been moved back to 5 Group bases on the 18th and some of their crews had flown on the Juvisy raid to see what low-level marking could achieve.⁵ The move had been the usual wartime scramble, the rear party of 97 Sqn still arriving at Coningsby from Bourn as the Brunswick briefing was being laid on. The attack on Brunswick would involve the whole of 5 Group, a total of more than 250 Lancasters. At the same time, to divide the enemy's defensive capability, nearly 600 aircraft would be going to Düsseldorf and another 181 bombers would be hitting the Laon rail yards. It was the third time in a week Bomber Command had dispatched 1,100 aircraft in one night.⁶

Sgt Ken Hulton, the 57 Sqn flight engineer coned over Berlin on his fourth operation a month before, was now an experienced member of aircrew with six more operations behind him. Called to briefing for Brunswick in the dark at East Kirkby he recorded in his diary later: 'We were told it was the first time new cluster-burst incendiaries were being tried out – containers bursting at 100 feet and incendiaries spreading out plus burning oil and creosote. We were also told it was the first time low-level marking would be used over a heavily defended German city.'[7]

Brunswick had not been attacked since 14 January when thirty-eight of the 500 aircraft that set out had been lost and it was hoped the heavy tonnage of the all-Lancaster force would strike a severe blow in a short raid starting just after 0200. But at Bardney, where WAAF Dorothy Mason was courting 9 Sqn flight engineer Cliff Williams, only three aircraft had got away when P/O G. Maule in WS-C swung on take-off half an hour before midnight. The undercarriage of the bomber collapsed and it crashed at the edge of the main runway and caught fire. The crew, unhurt, ran for shelter as the fire threatened the bomb load, which contained the new incendiary bombs, known as J-types. LACW Mason remembers:

> There were a lot of aircraft behind it waiting to go and my boyfriend was in one of them, watching the fire. An officer dashed into the teleprinter office where I was working and we were all ordered to run towards the village of Bucknell. I was trying to get on my bike, but I was told, 'Leave the bloody thing and run.' The officer ran to the airmen's billets to get the men up and I went to the WAAFs' billets to help to wake the WAAFs. All the WAAFs were ordered out, but many of them didn't want to leave their beds, they had to be persuaded. When we got a couple of miles away we got the all clear. By that time the aircraft had exploded. I found out later my boyfriend and his crew had been ordered from their aircraft to a shelter.[8]

SPLITTING Bomber Command's effort between two targets went exactly as planned for the Brunswick-bound aircraft. The German controller dedicated his effort into the Düsseldorf stream – night fighters and flak shooting down twenty-nine aircraft – and virtually ignoring the Brunswick force. Cheshire and his fellow-Mosquito markers dropped their flares accurately, but a problem with the plain-language VHF radio sets now surfaced that would have a dreadful effect when it was repeated on a small-target raid at Mailly-le-Camp ten days later. The newly transferred 97 Sqn had sent fifteen of its Pathfinder crews to back up the 617 Sqn flares. Twenty minutes from the target the cloud cleared and it was decided to carry out a visual (Newhaven) attack, but the adjutant later recorded in the operational record book:

> As the target approached ten-tenths high cirrus and very poor visibility was encountered. The flare leader therefore decided on emergency Wanganui (skymarkers), but the orders were not generally received by VHF and either not received in time by W/T (in Morse code) or misunderstood and some slight confusion in illumination resulted. Two concentrations of bombing were seen approximately 3 miles apart, one in the old town area and the other more dispersed south and south-west.

Almost as an afterthought the adjutant added: 'J-type incendiaries seen to be very effective.'[9]

The dissipation of bombing meant the effectiveness of the new marking technique on a German city target could not be properly judged. The J-type incendiary, described by Harris in his post-war memoirs as 'a kind of flamethrower', would also prove disappointing in the long term. It had been demonstrated in front of Harris on a purpose-built wooden structure at High Wycombe in August 1943 where the unit's fire brigade had succeeded in soaking the C-in-C instead of putting out the fire, but did not arrive in quantity for another six months. 'We tried out the J bomb ten times on operations and conclusively proved that ton for ton it was just half as effective as the 4lb incendiary,' Harris would later record, dismissing the device in a diatribe against general 'bungling' bomb production as 'a weapon which looked well on paper and was put into production without regard for the opinion or needs of the people who were going to use it'.*[10] On the plus side, as assessments were made of the Brunswick raid, the losses had been extremely light, only four Lancasters going down, a rate of 1.5 per cent, which crews hadn't seen for a long time over the Fatherland. Ironically, one of the missing was

---

* The J-type incendiary bomb wasn't the only weapon Bomber Command had problems with. As demand exceeded supply, American high explosive bombs and some dating back to the First World War had to be used, one wartime German report concluding that eighteen of every 100 HE bombs dropped by the RAF failed to explode.[11]

one of the few 9 Sqn aircraft that had managed to get away from Bardney before the runway was blocked. WS-O, piloted by New Zealander F/Sgt W. R. Lauder, was hit by flak shortly after bombing and only he and three others of the crew survived.

TWO days later Cheshire and the three other Mosquito crews of his private marker force tried again, on Munich, and this time it was a complete vindication of his methods. It was Cheshire's own suggestion that he be allowed to try out his technique on Munich, during a meeting with Cochrane and Harris.[12] However, it was just beyond the Mosquitos' range from 617 Sqn's airfield at Woodhall Spa. Cheshire asked for overload petrol tanks to be fitted, making it clear the operation could not be safely carried out without them. 'Unfortunately this statement was not taken seriously and no drop tanks were provided,' he wrote just after the raid.[13] Instead a plan was devised for the four marker Mosquitos to fly down to Manston, Kent, the closest possible take-off point for Munich, to park them at the runway threshold and then have their tanks topped to the last drop. A direct route was planned to the Bavarian capital, climbing in the short hop across the Channel, then flying southeast between Paris, Strasbourg and Augsburg and passing close to the main Bomber Command target for the night of Karlsruhe. It would allow less than twenty minutes' reserve of fuel in which to successfully find and mark the target, yet have sufficient in the tanks for the return journey. Any problems with navigation or weather en route could well wipe this out. Cheshire wrote somewhat caustically in his post-raid notes: 'This meant that no allowance could be made for the leaders arriving late on the target, so that the attack as well as the safety of the leaders themselves was seriously jeopardized.'[14] As the four Mosquito crews walked to the crew room at Woodhall Spa before take-off for Manston, Cheshire pointed out it was a beautiful sunset. One of his pilots, S/Ldr David Shannon, who had distinguished himself on the Dams Raid, retorted: 'I'm not interested in beautiful sunsets. I'm only interested in beautiful sunrises.'[15]

The four Mosquitos climbed out above Manston for Munich just before midnight. Their colleagues in 617 Sqn's Lancasters had already been airborne for hours and now thundered deeper into enemy territory, heading for an eventual turn over Lake Annecy, with six of the squadron's aircraft continuing over the Alps, dropping Window in a spoof for Milan, where they set air raid sirens wailing by unloading flares and target indicators. The Mosquitos found themselves flying above unbroken cloud and Cheshire called up Shannon for a check as they crossed the Rhine. Instead he heard the voice of S/Ldr Micky Martin, another of the orginal Dambusters and the man Cheshire credited with teaching him about low flying, now serving with 100 Group as an Intruder pilot. 'What the hell are you doing?' asked Cheshire. 'Sticking my neck out for you types,' answered Martin, who was strafing a German night-fighter airfield.[16]

It was not long after this that the clouds parted and exactly on time the four Mosquitos arrived over Munich in moonlight and clear visibility. The flare force provided by 83 and 97 Sqns was already over the target as planned and the early illuminators straddled the city. Fighters were few, but Munich's feared searchlight defences, described as 'intensely active', weaved, then formed cones across the target as the red bursts of accurate, predicted heavy flak stained the sky.[17] Cheshire wrote immediately afterwards: 'The town (*sic*) was heavily defended by guns and a vast number of searchlights and as the Mosquitos went in they could see the Lancasters way up above illuminated in the cones and ploughing steadfastly through the thick concentration of flak.'[18]

Cheshire pushed forward on the control column of his Mosquito and pointed the nose of his aircraft at his aiming point, a white building near the main railway station. His altimeter, which had registered 10,000 feet, unwound rapidly and the aircraft began to judder with the speed of his power dive. It took courage of a special kind not to flinch momentarily from the streaks of light flak – meant specifically for him now – which at first arced lazily upwards, but as they neared, zipped and buzzed, finally cracking past the tailplane of the light wooden machine. Then, as the white structure almost filled Cheshire's windscreen, the red spot-fire indicators tumbled from the Mosquito bomb bay and the aircraft flattened out and hurtled over the rooftops of Munich. As the CO climbed away he dropped a wing and looked back over his shoulder to see the red flame blooming exactly on target.

The other three Mosquitos were called in to mark and the rest of the 83 and 97 Sqn Lancasters came in to release their flares, the skipper of one of them, F/Lt Robert Eggins, reporting back at Coningsby hours later: 'Red spot fires seen in the marshalling yards ... heard W/Cdr Cheshire say markers were excellent.'[19] In his post-war private papers Cheshire wrote: 'The spearhead that the squadron [617] provided gave the RAF the opportunity they had waited for so long – an unmistakeable and accurate marker – and they were quick to make the most of the moment. The bombing that followed was remarkably concentrated and far in advance of any bombing of a major German target achieved in the past.'[20]

S/Ldr Les Munro, another of the few remaining Dams Raid pilots still serving on 617 Sqn, had been appointed to call in the other 234 Lancasters of 5 Group to bomb once the target had been accurately marked. The New Zealander remembers:

I was the bombing leader. Cheshire's markers appeared on time and were backed up by Dave Shannon and Terry Kearns [a fellow New Zealander]. F/Lt Gerry Fawke's markers failed to release, but as it turned out it didn't matter. Cheshire confirmed that the markers were on target and requested me to back them up which I did with six red spot fires and eight J-type clusters from 18,500 feet. That they were on target was later confirmed by an aiming-point photo.*

On ascertaining that these adequately backed up the initial marking by the Mosquitos Cheshire gave me the OK to instruct the main Lancaster force to bomb. This they did with excellent results, causing substantial damage to the city for the first time in the war. My part in the operation completed I turned for home and as we flew away from Munich the sky behind was all lit up as a result of the mass of fires. One point of interest to me was that as we were leaving I saw the silhouette of a Wellington† bomber a couple of thousand feet above us flying in the opposite direction. On reporting this at debriefing we were advised that the Germans had several Wellingtons, which they used to infiltrate our streams and attack the bombers.[21]

F/O Nicky Ross, another 617 Sqn skipper, coming to the end of his third tour, was a backer-up in the operation. 'As we left the target there was a terrific explosion at 0210,' he remembers. 'We could see the fires beginning and it was obviously going to be a very successful raid. At debriefing there was no doubt it had been a success.'[22] In fact, the raid –

* Cheshire was so impressed by the accuracy of Munro's bombs he kept the aiming-point photograph in his private papers.
† It is known the Luftwaffe had been interested in using decoy aircraft for some time and KG 200, a unit tasked specifically with flying captured or rebuilt Allied aircraft, had been formed on 10 February 1944.

by only one Bomber Command group – had been such a triumph, as Cheshire later remarked: 'We did something like twenty times the damage that the entire Bomber Command and the USAAF had done over a period of a year.'[23]

Ute Vallance was a 22-year-old student who was being held in Munich's Stadelheim prison in early 1944 on treason charges. It was the same jail where Sophie Scholl and other student members of the resistance group, the White Rose, were guillotined in 1943 for distributing leaflets saying the Nazi Party was destroying the German people, handing them out because as Sophie Scholl remarked at her trial: 'Somebody, after all, had to make a start.' In a post-war autobiography Fräulein Vallance described what it was like to hear bomb after bomb falling on Munich. She had woken to hear explosions and was led from her cell into a passage with other women prisoners after the jail's chapel and store houses were hit.

> Bombs came whistling down one after the other as if without a pause. The backs of the prisoners were bent as in prayer. The tremor of the explosions shook the air with such force that we were pushed backwards and forwards in one continuous rocking movement. The ear-splitting whine of the bombs coming down, the blasts of the detonations, the fierce crackling of burning wood, the roar of the aeroplanes and the scream of the prisoners – everything merged into one whole. It was inferno ... Oh let the bombs come down, let them come! They symbolized justice, the great revenge coming from the sky. What would it matter if we die, the guards would die with us.[24]

A total of eleven Lancasters were shot down on the Munich operation, including one from 617 Sqn, and one each from the recently transferred 83 and 97 Sqns. The Lancaster of Sgt Dick Raymond, the teen-aged flight engineer who had survived his bomber blowing up on the ground before a Berlin raid, nearly became a second for 83 Sqn. Raymond says:

> We had just started our bombing run at about 21,000 feet when we were coned. It was the first time it had happened to us and it was frightening. Ken Lane our pilot did some violent corkscrewing with the bombs still on board and I can remember our rear gunner screaming, 'For Christ's sake get rid of the bombs.' Ken told our bomb

aimer Don Cope to jettison them and he opened the bomb doors, but I can still hear the bomb aimer, who came from Ashton-under-Lyne, saying in his strong accent, 'Ee, I can't, the jettison bars are stuck.'

In front of me was a manual jettison toggle which dropped the bomb carriers as well, and without any instructions from anybody I pulled it harder than anything I've pulled in my life and we got rid of the bombs. Eventually we got out of the searchlights, but by then we had two engines on fire from flak that had been firing up the beams. I pushed the Graviner of one and managed to put the fire out and feathered the engine, then operated the Graviner on the other. I think in panic I switched off the wrong fuel cock and we finished up with just one engine. I quickly put it back on again and we were back to two engines, fortunately one on each side and we had at least one inboard engine that worked the hydraulic pumps. We headed for home on a direct course, all the time losing height.[25]

Navigator F/Sgt Bob Burns, a recent addition to 106 Sqn, was over Munich in his sixth operation in just over two weeks, most of them long trips. He remembers:

There was a fair bit of milling around before we were called in to bomb. This could have been quite worrying, though I didn't see any aircraft going down, but a few nights before when 5 Group was trying out this kind of attack at Tours we were kept an hour over the target milling around while the markers identified the AP – so as to minimise French civilian casualties.

We suffered slight flak damage ourselves over Munich. I always went into the front of the aircraft over a target and could see the buildings on fire below. By the time we left, Karlsruhe, which the Main Force had gone to, was also already on fire and we could see the fires very clearly for about half an hour as we headed towards them. Then we had to pass fairly close by as we went home. Because of double summer time it was daylight as we crossed France and we went down on the deck for about half an hour to reach the coast. The amazing thing was that looking out I could see another half a dozen Lancasters flying virtually alongside us, all on track and all with the same idea of hedge-hopping.

We were very concerned about fighters and at rooftop level there would have been no means of escape, but of course it did take us below German radar, which was the idea. Everybody at the front was looking out for obstacles. We climbed a bit to about 6,000 feet over the North Sea. The fuel situation was fairly desperate and we, like a lot of crews, lobbed down at any airfield we could find. Some went into Ford on the south coast and we went into Thorney Island. After landing, two engines cut out for lack of fuel while we were taxiing to dispersal. It was a very close-run thing.[26]

The 83 Sqn Lancaster of Sgt Raymond also made it home by the narrowest of margins. He remembers:

We had to lose all excess weight to lighten the aircraft and dumped all our guns and even the toilet. We used maximum engine revs of 2,850 and nine boost – neither of which you were supposed to use for more than an hour – and just kept them to try to maintain some height, but we were losing it gradually. We eventually came out over Le Havre in broad daylight at 3,000 or 4,000 feet and they took no notice of us. We decided to get in at the first airfield we could see as we were so short of fuel and it turned out to be a base used by American fighters at Lashenden in Kent. We did a split-arse turn and normal approach and luckily the wheels came down and the flaps operated, so we knew the hydraulic lines hadn't been hit and the pilot did a perfect landing on this metal-strip runway on two engines. The Yanks weren't very pleased because they had been about to take off and there was this Lancaster right in the middle of their runway. It was towed away and the pilot later counted more than fifty flak holes in it.

Ken Lane was given an immediate DFC for a brilliant bit of flying and a few weeks later I was called in front of the adjutant who said, 'Sgt Raymond, you've got immediate promotion to flight sergeant and if you smarten yourself up you might be a warrant officer one day.' But the reason I was so dishevelled was I was still suffering from the effects of being blown up. There was great hunks cut out of my hair because of the bits blown into my head and my jacket was ripped and blood-stained. I'd tried to wash the blood out, but the stores said it was still serviceable. I didn't like to go into the details of why I looked so scruffy.[27]

From 97 Sqn, too, a Lancaster crew was lucky to return. P/O R. Lasham later told intelligence officers:

My flares dropped right over the middle of the town and a concentrated mass of fires was burning round several well-placed markers as the aircraft left the area. Seven holes in the wings are believed to be from incendiaries falling through over the target at 0153. The fuel pipe to the port outer was severed, the engine being feathered. Return was made on three engines due to the damage and landing made at Tangmere.[28]

It had been a long and tiring trip for the Lancaster crews of more than nine hours, but the chatter at debriefing tables was mainly about what a success the operation had been after the disappointment of Brunswick two days before. One 97 Sqn pilot F/O John Smith, told intelligence officers: 'My gunners report fire and smoke from 150 miles away and consider the raid the best ever seen.'[29]

The operation was indeed one of the most successful of the war and achieved far greater results than that launched on Karlsruhe the same night by a much greater force of bombers – 637 from all groups except Cochrane's. The target had been marked by the traditional Pathfinder methods of Don Bennett's 8 Group and cloud over the target and a strong wind had caused PFF to drop their TIs too far to the north, most bombs then falling outside the city. A total of 100 bombers are thought to have hit Mannheim in error. Yet in the Munich operation more than 90 per cent of the Lancasters' bomb loads had dropped in the city centre. The city that had spawned the National Socialist Party never fully recovered for the rest of the war. The wisdom of Cheshire's low-level marking technique on a major city had been positively proved at last and would be used to great effect on small targets in the coming weeks. On 617 Sqn itself crews needed no convincing about how effective a commander they had. F/O Ross says: 'Cheshire was the absolute supreme. He was the complete gentleman and a wonderful aviator who put Gibson in the shade. Gibson was the great Dams Raid leader, there's no doubt about that. Cheshire was an inspiration to all his aircrew, you had every confidence in him.'[30]

The citation for Cheshire's later Victoria Cross would in part read: 'What he did in the Munich operation was typical of the careful planning, brilliant execution and contempt for danger which has established for W/Cdr Cheshire a reputation second to none in Bomber Command.'

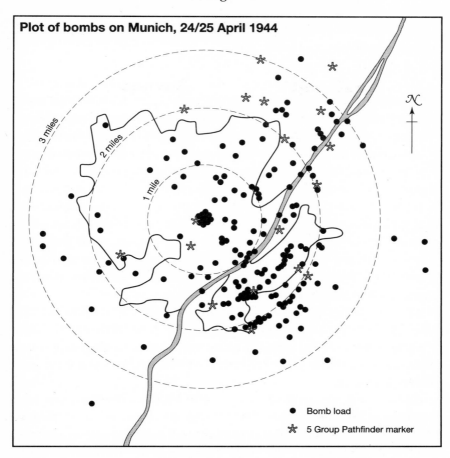

Plot of bombs on Munich, 24/25 April 1944

● Bomb load
✳ 5 Group Pathfinder marker

Cheshire would not receive the VC from the King until the European war had ended. It would be awarded on the same day as another Bomber Command flyer received his own Victoria Cross. F/Sgt Norman Jackson's amazing act of bravery came on the Schweinfurt operation two days after Munich.

But this was an operation Cheshire's boys would not take part in. S/Ldr Munro, one of Cheshire's flight commanders, remembers:

> The day after 617 carried out the Munich operation the squadron was advised we would not be operating until further notice and were to undertake specific training of an exacting nature. Not only Cheshire but all the senior pilots were quite upset about being taken off operations, although we were not told at the time that the training we were

to undertake was related to the D-Day landings and the opening of the Second Front.[31]

THE task of low-level marking for the coming Schweinfurt operation was now handed on to 627 Sqn, which had been transferred with its Mosquitos from the 8 Group airfield of Oakington to Woodhall Spa on 15 April, where they were quickly initiated into the Cheshire technique. The move had not been without problems. Some of the squadron's Mosquitos had been adapted to carry a 4,000-lb Cookie. This would not be required if they were to be employed purely as marker aircraft and they were quickly exchanged at Upwood for 2,000-lb flare carriers. The other problem was the shock of leaving the permanent brick buildings of an airfield laid out in the pre-war expansion period for the hastily constructed Nissen huts of an aerodrome built with enthusiastic austerity under wartime conditions. Woodhall Spa was a small airfield, suitable for only one heavy bomber squadron, not the usual two, which was why it had been chosen for the security-sensitive 617, and the aircrew of 627 Sqn found themselves in sleeping accommodation at a dispersed site one mile from the airfield. The NCO aircrew took meals in their mess. The officers did better.

Cheshire was an enlightened CO, who believed his flyers deserved the ultimate from their country for risking their lives. While heading 76 Sqn at Linton-on-Ouse the previous spring, Cheshire had had a nearby stately home, Beningborough Hall, requisitioned as a billet for his NCO aircrew. As the new commander of 617 Sqn he had acted again when 617 moved from Coningsby to Woodhall Spa in January 1944, taking over the luxurious, half-timbered Petwood Hotel in the village as the officers' mess. The officers of 627 Sqn now also took their meals there in wood-panelled splendour.[32]

Where a Bomber Command airman was posted for his tour was a matter of luck almost as great as that of survival itself. The fortunate would find themselves on pre-war stations such as Scampton, Binbrook or Driffield, with all the facilities permanency provided, from purpose-built shower blocks to sports fields, gymnasiums and cinemas. The majority would have to put up with wartime chill and squalor where the corrugated iron of a crowded Nissen hut across muddy fields was home and sanitation was often inadequate. The officers of 617 Sqn were aware how lucky they were.

F/O Don Cheney, who joined the squadron at the beginning of April 1944, remembers the Petwood Hotel's 'fine large dining room, sitting room, separate bar, billiards room and a beautiful patio at the rear where one could sit and bask in the sun on fine days'. Officers shared two to a room and mornings of operations began with a gentle tap on the door by a smiling WAAF, presenting steaming cups of tea and biscuits.[33] It contrasted with the Nissen huts Cheney had previously been used to at wartime-constructed East Kirkby where he had flown Berlin raids with 630 Sqn. And it was distinctly different to the conditions experienced by, for instance, 10 Sqn flight engineer Sgt Frank Jones, who found himself in a service hospital with dysentery for six weeks following the 24 March Berlin raid in which he had flown through an avenue of fighter flares. While he was away his crew were shot down. Jones says:

> My life was saved by the lack of hygiene on an RAF base. In the sergeants' mess at Melbourne we had ablutions and showers, but on the domestic site about a mile and a half away across ploughed fields we had bucket-type toilets for the huts, which were supposed to be emptied every day. They weren't and I learned while I was in hospital that some senior NCO ground staff had just come back from the Middle East and one of them might have been carrying dysentery. I was the unlucky one to get it in the insanitary conditions.[34]

Sgt Jones found himself 'doing odd jobs for the flight engineer's section' as D-Day came and went, then joined a crew on 76 Sqn. It meant he didn't finish the tour he started on 15 February until the end of October.

THE well-catered-for officers of 627 Sqn carried the considerable hopes of the Air Ministry as they prepared to take off in their Mosquitos to mark Schweinfurt on 26 April. The main Bomber Command effort that night was to Essen, where nearly 500 bombers from all groups except Cochrane's would be led by the Pathfinders of Don Bennett, who had pressed for considerably better marking techniques than on Karlsruhe two nights before. Another 200 or so Halifaxes would be bombing a French railway target, making a total of 1,060 sorties for the night. But it was Schweinfurt and 5 Group's new low-level target marking where Air Ministry hopes were pinned.

As far back as July 1943 the Ministry of Economic Warfare had persuaded Air Commodore Sidney Bufton, the Director of Bomber

Operations reporting to Air Marshal Sir Norman Bottomley, the Deputy Chief of the Air Staff, that eradicating Germany's principal means of ball-bearing production housed in five specific factories in Schweinfurt would rapidly bring German industry to a halt. Subsequent daylight attacks by the US Eighth Air Force in August and October had cost the USAAF a lot more than Schweinfurt, but again in November the MEW asked that a raid on the town be given the utmost priority.[35]

The idea of attacking what he considered to be a panacea target was anathema to Harris, who believed Germany would only be beaten when all its industry lay in ruins in all its towns and cities. He wrote to Bottomley as the year drew to a close pointing out that Schweinfurt was 'extremely small and difficult to find. It is heavily defended, including smoke screens. In these circumstances it might need up to six or seven full-scale attacks before a satisfactory result was secured on the town as a whole.' In conclusion Harris said: 'If Schweinfurt is as important as it is alleged to be, it is pre-eminently a job for the US Bomber Command rather than for us.' There was also the small matter that Germany got much of its ball-bearing stock from Sweden, which was also supplying Britain, BOAC making regular runs to the neutral country to pick up supplies.[36]

The answer, on 14 January, was that Harris should attack Schweinfurt 'on the first opportunity when weather and other conditions allow and that you continue to attack it until it is destroyed'. There then followed the instruction, which later became an amendment to the Pointblank Directive, that after Schweinfurt 'high priority must also be given to the destruction of those towns associated with the assembly of fighter aircraft, particularly Leipzig, Brunswick, Gotha and Augsburg'.[37] To support the USAAF's Big Week of concentrated raids Harris had then attacked Schweinfurt on the night of 24 February. Weather conditions were almost perfect, but of the 734 aircraft dispatched only seven aircraft of the first wave and fifteen of the second brought back bomb-release photographs showing them to be over the target. Harris was apparently right. Schweinfurt, in a valley with smoke pots set in the hills, was no easy target to locate, mark and attack at night.

The USAAF, however, still held it in its sights. Only two weeks before W/Cdr Adrian Warburton, considered the greatest reconnaissance pilot of the war, had died in a mission to photograph Schweinfurt's Luftwaffe defences on behalf of the USAAF, flying from Mount Farm in a P-38, the day before an assault by the US 1st Air Division. But the Air Ministry were keen for Harris's boys to try again, despite Harris's belief, later proved correct, that the Germans had diversified ball-bearing production since the accurate American raid of the previous October. Now, to placate the Air Ministry once more, 5 Group with its new low-level marking technique was told to have a go.

Remarkably, the plan repeated some of the mistakes made in the Nuremberg raid a month before. There was a new moon and the bombers would fly an unbroken leg, not as long as that from Charleroi to Fulda on 30 March, but one that would still stretch more than 130 miles from Troyes south of Paris to Strasbourg, then into the target. This time the loss rate would be 9.3 per cent, 106 Sqn losing five of its Lancasters. Norman Jackson, about to win the VC, was the flight engineer in one of them.

The 215 Lancasters took off from the 5 Group airfields around 2130 and headed east across the North Sea. F/Sgt Jackson's Canadian skipper, F/O Fred Mifflin, was one of the first off from Metheringham on the penultimate raid of their tour. P/O Cyril Bishop, whose navigator, F/Sgt Bob Burns, knew Jackson slightly, took off five minutes later. Burns and Jackson would meet again, in a German hospital. Navigators of the 5 Group Lancasters quickly realised as they entered enemy territory that the weather briefing of broken, medium stratocumulus cloud was wrong, as were the forecast winds. In fact, they found no cloud and a head wind of 45 mph.

The *Nachtjäger* came across the stream in the moonlight as it entered the long easterly leg south of Paris. Combats then followed all the way into the target. A yellow target indicator was meant to be dropped southwest of Schweinfurt, four minutes before the attack was due to open at 0200, as a datum point for the marking force and half of the bombers, loaded with 30-lb incendiaries to set the city on fire. The bombers, Force A, would then pass over the target to draw flak away from the marker aircraft, turn to port and approach the target downwind. It was hoped that by then twenty-four red spot fires would be burning around the aiming point north of the river, dropped by 627 Sqn's marker Mosquitos. Five minutes after Force A attacked at 21,000 feet, the other half of the bombers, Force B, was to come in from the north on its bombing run 5,000 feet below.

Flare-dropping illuminators provided by 83 and 97 Squadrons would light up the target in advance for the Mosquitos. In fact, the unexpectedly strong head wind, harrying by the night fighters, and Schweinfurt's usual effective smokescreen spoiled much of the attack. Bomber Command's Operational Research Section later concluded: 'The flares were late and scattered. The first spot fires fell south of the river and were followed by others still further off the mark. The master bomber made every effort to redeem the situation, by instructing aircraft to overshoot the green markers, but he was poorly received and the attack became concentrated to the south of the target area.'[38] Yet again, the VHF radio sets that had caused problems on the Brunswick raid four days before were preventing accurate communication, at least one flare-dropping crew reporting back at base that Channel B was jammed.

Fourteen fewer bombers arrived over Schweinfurt than had started the leg from Troyes, many of them victims of the often unseen Schräge Musik. P/O J. A. Jones, a shocked skipper on 49 Sqn, which lost three of its aircraft, reported at debriefing: 'The latter half of the long leg before Stuttgart was alive with fighters.'[39] Another seven, including two lost by collision, would go down before the night was through as night fighters now engaged the bombers over Schweinfurt itself.

It was here, over the city, that F/Sgt Jackson became such a hero. His 106 Sqn Lancaster, O-Orange, had just bombed from 21,500 feet in Force A when a night fighter attacked and the starboard inner, the nearest engine to Jackson's position as flight engineer, caught fire. Without hesitation Jackson stuffed a fire extinguisher in his Mae West life jacket, pulled his parachute ripcord so that crew members could hold onto the rigging lines and crawled out through the hatch in the top of the canopy to fight the blaze. 'It was my duty,' he said. He held onto the air intake at the side of the aircraft, which was travelling at between 140 and 160 knots, fired the extinguisher at the engine and got the flames under control.

But the night fighter attacked again and the whole aircraft was shaking and jumping, he said. He couldn't let go because the bomb aimer [F/Sgt F. L. Higgins] and navigator [F/Sgt M. H. Toft] were still hanging onto his chute rigging lines. Finally he was hit in the legs by the night fighter's bullets and fell off the wing and his crewmates let go. He came down rapidly with burning holes in his chute 'getting bigger all the time'. 'I watched it burning about me,' he said. Bushes broke his fall. He stumbled and crawled to a farmhouse where the male owner harangued him, but two young women inside pushed the man aside. They turned out to be nurses from the local hospital and they attended to burns around Jackson's eyes and on his arms. The surviving members of his crew turned up in the local area soon afterwards. He spent ten months in hospital during which the night-fighter pilot who shot him down came to see him.[40]

The 106 Sqn aircraft of F/Sgt Bob Burns was shot down over Schweinfurt at approximately the same time. He says:

It was lunacy really to penetrate deep into Germany in moonlight, as it had been to Munich two nights before. The Germans put all these smoke pots out which gave a smokescreen over the whole place. I went up to the cockpit to have a look at the target on the bomb run and it was full of smoke, but it was blowing all over that night, the Germans hadn't been terribly successful, and the fires could be seen in between.

Night fighters had sussed out our bombing course and laid a path of two rows of flares. It was just like flying down a runway. I had returned to the navigator's station and we were just coming off the bombing run when we were attacked by a Ju88. The Canadian rear gunner, Sgt Bill Stevens, a former printer and known on the squadron as 'Eagle Eye', called a corkscrew then fired at the exact moment the Ju88* fired. Both aircraft went down in the exchange of fire.[41] Our aircraft came down about 15 miles from Schweinfurt, but the night fighter actually crashed on the outskirts. We were hit underneath in the bomb bay, and in the engines. I felt the banging of the cannon shells under me. There was no indication of fire within the aircraft, but we got the order to bale out. It was standard practice for the navigator to go out through the front hatch, but on our squadron we were told the navigator should go out through the back door. That saved my life. I struggled towards the back, picked up my chute and clipped it on.

The plane was by then going down in a steep dive. By the time I got close to the door it was already open and the wireless operator and the mid-upper gunner were lying on the floor near it, pinned by the G force. I then found myself also pinned down. At that moment the aircraft exploded and I was thrown out in mid-air. I think it broke in

---

* The pilot of the Ju88 was Walter Bornscheen, the CO of Hitler's own transport squadron (*Führerkurrierstaffel*), who had taken off with two other of his pilots to engage in combat over Schweinfurt apparently on a whim. When Hitler heard Bornscheen had been shot down he banned his personal pilots from taking part in such combats again.

two just where I was because afterwards a piece of aluminium the size of an envelope was taken from my thigh. I pulled the ripcord and could see the aircraft going down in an arc to one side of me, then very soon afterwards I hit the ground. The bomb aimer, Jack Pickstone, was the only other one to get out. His position, of course, was right over the front hatch.

I was bleeding badly on the ground, but I put a field dressing on and made off to try to find a train. We were always told to try to get a train out of the area of the crash, but this was very bad intelligence because German trains were very heavily guarded whereas ours were not. I could hear trains in the distance and was walking for about two hours. I was in a marshalling yard and suddenly all the lights came on like at a football match today and I found I was looking at the wrong end of about a hundred rifles.

The Wehrmacht officer tried to question me, but I didn't speak German and he didn't speak English, so they took me in a car to a little village hospital where I was for four or five days and that's where they took the piece of aluminium out of me. I was badly cut at an angle close up to the groin and I found out fifty years later it was a hair's breadth from the main artery. I had a lot of stitches in my leg, but when they came to take me to Dulag Luft I had to walk a mile or two to the railway station then right across Schweinfurt, then 3 or 4 miles at the other end of the journey to Dulag Luft. My leg was in a right state.

I was fed on nothing but black bread and soup at Dulag Luft and the idea of first aid there was either a brown ointment or white powder and the bandages were simply crepe paper. After about ten days of this with my leg being dreadfully painful and now all the colours of the rainbow I kicked up a fuss and was taken to the Medical Inspection room. There the fresh air from the open window made me faint because I had been all this time in an overheated cell, with very high temperatures.

I think the medical orderly then realised my wound was far worse than they had admitted and I was taken to some sort of medical quarters they had. I had told them nothing at interrogation and they kept me a night on my own there and then another interrogator came in who spoke perfect Oxford English and said I really must co-operate or they would send me back to the cells. I had had a decent meal by that time, I had slept in a decent bed, washed and had had a shave for the first time, so I thought well if I have to be moved back, so be it.

But the next day they moved me out to a POW hospital at Mein-ingen near Frankfurt. I had known Norman Jackson by sight on the squadron and he was in there. He came along to see me and started talking to me at the side of my bed, but I didn't recognise him at first because his face was very red from the fire. He also had his hands heavily bandaged across his chest. He was talking to me for quite a while before I realised I knew him.

He told me he had been shot down on Schweinfurt but didn't tell me what he had done that night. We felt a bit of kinship because we were squadron-mates. I never saw him again. I was there for three or four months before being sent to Stalag Luft VII at Bankau and he was in hospital for about nine months.

I didn't find out what had happened to the rest of my crew until I got back home at the end of the war. The wireless operator and the mid-upper gunner had both had their chutes on when I saw them in the aircraft, but they went down with it. When I went back to Schwein-furt in 2001 I met two ladies, a schoolteacher and one of her pupils, who had seen the plane crash in a field by a copse near the village of Schraudenbach.

They said the bodies were in the two parts of the plane. The wireless operator and the mid-upper gunner were in one part and the pilot and flight engineer were so badly burned up in another part that they buried the two in one grave.* The rear gunner was thrown out, I think on impact, and they were surprised because to them he looked as though he was sleeping.[42]

THE attack had not been a good beginning for 627 Sqn's record as low-level markers, though at debriefing the five marker crews thought they had marked successfully in the smoke over the target. All had cour-

---

*Villagers at Schraudenbach testify that their pastor, Hochw. Hernn Oswald Franz, defied a decree by Hitler that Allied aircrew were not to have a Christian burial by burying the five dead crew members from the Lancaster in the village churchyard. Several hundred people from the village are said to have turned out for the funeral and bedecked the grave with flowers. A photograph of the decorated grave was handed to W/O Burns when he visited the village many years later. The pastor was taken away to a concentration camp, but survived the war and returned to his ministry in the village.

ageously dived from 5,000 feet to a minimum of 400 feet to drop their red spot fires, one reporting he 'saw church steeple through smoke screen – judged it to be town centre'. Sadly, the church was on the south side of the river away from the ball-bearing plants.[43] However, later reconnaissance showed damage to all five ball-bearing factories, though it was not known how much was due to the USAAF raid of two weeks before. The raid had also diverted the night-fighter forces from the much larger Essen operation, which was judged an accurate attack, and only seven aircraft were lost.

Harris had now fulfilled his Schweinfurt obligation to the Air Ministry and apparently proved his point, that the ball-bearing factories could not be hit successfully at night. There were bigger aims about to be considered. Eisenhower, or more specifically his airman deputy, Air Chief Marshal Sir Arthur Tedder, needed Harris's full-time commitment to pre-invasion targets. The next few weeks would prove to be an outstandingly successful period for Bomber Command, which would crucially affect the lives of every soldier facing the Nazi divisions. Harris's old lags would bottle up the Germans in Normandy and starve them of tanks, ammunition and the routine necessaries to make war by cutting off their lines of communication. The Command was about to make a contribution to the Normandy battle plan that would prove vital to victory.

IO

Escape Lines in the Railway Desert

The Transportation Plan, which would be judged to be one of Bomber Command's greatest achievements, had no greater critic than the very head of the force itself. In the run-up to D-Day Harris had fought bitterly to retain authority over his squadrons and continue his assault on Germany's material base. Any cessation would give the Germans time to make good what damage Bomber Command had already inflicted, he argued. The head of the US Eighth Air Force, Carl Spaatz, felt the same, that the war could be won by bombing alone and he was best able to decide where the bombing should take place.

Harris was also unsure that his airmen could strike small targets such as marshalling yards successfully. In January he had written to Portal among others accepting that 'Overlord must now presumably be regarded as an inescapable commitment', but stressing that his bombers were not suitable for cutting railway communications at key points.[1] In his immediate post-war book, *Bomber Offensive*, he wrote: 'All previous experience had gone to show that the RAF's heavy bombers, with their futile .303 defensive armament, could not operate by day in face of serious opposition, and could not hit small targets by night except when the opposition was negligible and the weather and light exceptionally good.'[2]

Three months before D-Day Harris was also claiming that bombing railway targets would cost thousands of French lives at a time when French goodwill was so needed, a point that also worried Harris's boss Portal, Churchill and even Eisenhower. There was some justification for concern. It was greatly satisfying in early March to hear from the French

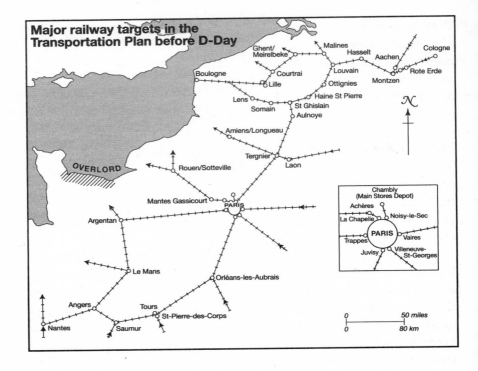

Major railway targets in the
Transportation Plan before D-Day

Resistance that the 263 aircraft of Bomber Command, which on the 6th
had dropped 1,258 tons of bombs on the railway centre of Trappes,
south-west of Paris, had put it out of action for days, but later intelligence
revealed that sixty Frenchmen had been killed[3] and another such raid on
marshalling yards at Lille a little over a month later caused 456 civilian
deaths.

In France itself several bishops expressed fears of bombing as D-Day
inevitably approached, appealing to the higher clergy of the British
Empire and the United States to intervene to 'ensure the greatest possible
diminution in the horrors of aerial bombardment'. Air Marshal Vallin,
commander of French air forces in Britain, replied in a radio broadcast
to France in mid-May that he regretted the appeal had not 'been made
earlier and addressed to others. It was in 1940 that the first French
cathedrals were destroyed by fire and materials manufactured beyond
the Rhine.'[4]

The worries of Frenchmen apart it was clear to the military in Britain
there was a need to switch the might of Bomber Command to sealing
off Normandy both before and after the invasion. The Transportation

Plan was designed to create what was later described at Bomber Command headquarters as a railway desert.[5] Its prime mover was a zoology professor, Solly Zuckerman, Tedder's former scientific adviser in Italy, where the problems of invasion had already been tested. Zuckerman was part of the Allied Expeditionary Force Bombing Committee and the committee's plan was firstly for bombing to reduce the capacity of the French and Belgian railway system to carry traffic and then, as D-Day neared, for both Harris's and Spaatz's forces to join with the Second Tactical Air Force and Ninth USAAF in a tactical phase, hitting railway and road junctions, bridges and rolling stock to paralyse movement of the German Army to the invasion area and within it. A list was prepared of seventy-five targets comprising the major railway servicing and repair centres in northern France and Belgium.

It was a compelling argument that the winners of the Transportation Plan would ultimately be the winners of the invasion. If the Germans were able to constantly resupply their armies they would be able to fling the invaders back into the sea. The material and men they would need to achieve that would be immense. For instance, at Trappes alone six Wehrmacht trains a day went through before Bomber Command started attacking it. But Harris, focused on area bombing where the results could be clearly seen and against panacea targets per se, was still unconvinced. He wrote to America's Assistant Secretary for Air, a close friend, at the end of March: 'Our worst headache has been a panacea plan devised by a civilian professor whose peacetime forte is the study of the sexual aberrations of the higher apes.'[6]

After the success of the 6 March Trappes raid, however, Portal had been won over to the efficacy of bombing marshalling yards, and the low French casualties, at that time at least, helped to convert Eisenhower. Churchill and his Cabinet were also eventually convinced and it became useless for Harris to protest further. On 15 April Tedder gave him a scaled-down list of thirty-seven railway targets, where it was thought French casualties would not exceed 150 each time, and told him to get on with it.[7] The list included Villeneuve-St Georges, Aulnoye, Lens, Rouen, Orléans and La Chapelle, but not Lille. Yet again Harris demonstrated his great strength. Given his task he went to it with a will to make it a success. By D-Day Bomber Command – despite Harris's initial reluctance – had dropped 54,589 tons of bombs on transportation targets.[8] The USAAF had been handed more targets – forty-five – but were slower to act. Just one had been bombed by the end of April and by D-Day it had dropped only 11,648 tons of bombs on twenty-three targets.

Harris had several tools to make the campaign a success. Oboe, so vital in the Battle of the Ruhr a year before, was able to be used once more to mark targets, as they were within its limited range affected by the curvature of the earth. The role of the master bomber also now became the norm rather than the exception and several master bombers would lose their lives that spring and summer as they circled aiming points during attacks to achieve the right concentration in a small area. And as April advanced Cheshire and his low-level marker crews convinced Harris he now had the means to find and hit a small target. In fact, remarkably, the average bombing error by 5 Group in the next few months would be 380 yards, compared to 680 yards on an Oboe-led attack.[9]

THE crews who had survived Nuremberg were not slow to appreciate that their chances of seeing old age had been dramatically improved by not being asked to go back to Germany so often. The expected lower chop rate wasn't lost on Bomber Command headquarters either. It had already notified all squadrons in late March – causing 'considerable resentment' as the war diarist of 431 (RCAF) Sqn noted[10] – that trips to French and Belgium targets would now be counted as only a third of an op, making an average tour length at this time thirty-three operations, not the previous thirty. The edict would cause a near mutiny in early May after savage losses on the French target of Mailly-le-Camp. However there was a hidden benefit to raiding occupied countries – the likelihood of successfully evading capture after bale-out went up considerably.

Harry Fisher was one of those shot down as the transportation campaign gathered pace, but whom the Resistance eventually got back to Britain. P/O Fisher, a wireless operator on 218 Sqn, had completed eighteen operations of his tour on Stirlings by the autumn of 1943, then a football injury put him in hospital for three weeks. By the time he recovered his crew had finished their tour with another wireless operator. P/O Fisher remembers:

I was crewed up with a crew who had lost their pilot and wireless operator and we were sent back to HCU at Stradishall where we got our new pilot, W/Cdr Cecil Poulter. He had flown ops on Whitleys early in the war and now dropped a rank to squadron leader to get back on operations. He was 28, which seemed quite old to the rest of us. I was 23.[11]

In the afternoon of 22 April the crew were called to briefing at Woolfox Lodge for an attack by 181 aircraft on locomotive sheds and marshalling yards at Laon, in northern France. Stirlings made up forty-eight aircraft of the mixed bomber force and it would be the last major bombing raid of the war by the aircraft, which had been withdrawn from operations over Germany in November 1943 because their low operational height made them particularly easy prey for both flak and fighter. It would also be the first and last operational flight for the new crew of the now Squadron Leader Poulter.

Laon had been attacked a month before, but the master bomber called a halt after only half the force had unloaded because 50 per cent of their bombs had been scattered up to 2 miles from the target and there were worries of heavy civilian casualties. On this second occasion there were two master bombers controlling a two-wave attack and one of them paid the ultimate price in ensuring there was no repetition of previous errors. W/Cdr Alan Cousens of 635 Sqn was killed with the rest of the Lancaster crew except the pilot P/O D. Courtney, who evaded. Crews of 160 aircraft later claimed to have bombed their target, inflicting much damage, but another eight aircraft were lost, three of them Stirlings.

Harry Fisher remembers:

After what I had been through during earlier operations over Germany in 1943, Laon was not considered to be one of the more difficult of operations. How wrong this turned out to be. We had left the target after bombing when I heard both gunners engaging a fighter. Then the next thing was the port inner engine was on fire and I think this was the result of an attack by another fighter.*

I went up into the astrodome and could see flames from the engine blazing back and fuel running down the wing. Then the port outer

---

* S/Ldr Poulter's Stirling III, HA-M, was shot down by Oberleutnant Dietrich Schmidt of III/NJG1 and crashed at 0026 between the villages of Hautefontaine (Oise) and Vivieres (Aisne), 11 miles south-west of Soissons. Oblt Schmidt also shot down another Stirling, of 90 Sqn, that night in which all the crew were killed.

caught fire and we were obviously in a pretty bad way. There was no way to put the fires out, we were losing height and the pilot gave the order to bale out. I moved to the forward escape hatch and it was already open. The navigator had gone, the bomb aimer had gone, the flight engineer was just beside me and as I looked up the pilot, who was in his seat, gave me a couple of pats on the shoulder and out I went, followed immediately by the engineer. The rear gunner had gone out of his rear turret, but unknown to me the mid-upper gunner had been hit and didn't get out. Both he and the pilot died in the aircraft. I had only known S/Ldr Poulter about six weeks. He had been very keen to get back on operations I believe, after so long at a desk job.

I have no recollection of pulling the ripcord, so I may have blacked out after leaving the aircraft. I came to floating down and my neck was quite sore as if with whiplash, so I mustn't have been braced properly when the chute opened. I landed in a field near the village of Vic-sur-Aisne, between Compiègne and Soissons. I was feeling very shocked and alone. My watch showed it was twenty minutes after midnight. I got my parachute and Mae West off and hid it in some long grass and started following a railway line until I came to a cottage. I rapped on the door and tried to explain who I was but the occupants were obviously scared and told me to go away. I followed the railway to another cottage and tried again. This time a young couple took me in. They bathed some scratches on my face and gave me a meal, but I couldn't eat it. I was nauseous with nerves. They told me to lie down, then a short time later, while it was still dark, took me to another house where I was told to change out of my uniform into civilian clothes. It was quite a thought – I knew I was then entering different territory. I was taken to another farm where I met up with the Canadian bomb aimer, Archie McPhee.

The two of us were taken from the farmhouse and hidden in a mushroom cave for the best part of 10 days, then we were taken in a farmcart, hiding under straw, down to the village of Vic-sur-Aisne. Through the straw we could see Germans on guard at the railway crossing. It was amazing. We were taken to the house in the village that belonged to the Resistance chief in that area and we were interrogated by him, all in French, which wasn't too easy. He asked various questions about places in the UK and we still had our dog tags. At that time the Germans were dressing in RAF uniforms and knocking on doors late at night to infiltrate escape lines, but he was obviously satisfied we were genuine.

We were then taken to another farm where we remained some time and eventually the farmer's wife took us by train to her mother's house in Paris so that we could be guided by the official Underground. There were a lot of Germans around and after a little time we were moved to a nurse's house where we stayed about two weeks and were able to visit her clinic where we actually listened to the BBC from London and got up-to-date information about the war. It was quite amazing, because up to then we didn't have a clue what was happening. Things really started to move once the official Underground got involved and I met up with our flight engineer Harry Bossick there.

Towards the end of May, armed with bogus identity cards supplied by the Underground – mine stated I was 75 per cent disabled and unable to speak (I only had schoolboy French) – we were taken by a girl from the Underground movement, along with a few others, on a twenty-hour train journey to Toulouse. Included in this group was the flight engineer. We had been given train tickets and told to follow the girl, who was only a little bit older than myself. We were warned that on no account were we to approach her or speak to her. The idea, of course, was that if we got caught we would probably get away with it, but if she got caught she would be shot or worse as they tried to get information from her. The idea of the escape line was everybody worked in cells, everybody didn't know everything so if they were tortured there was only so much information they could give.

We changed at Toulouse to a train for Pau, taking us through Lourdes to the Spanish frontier. We arrived at Pau after curfew and I was given a pass by a guard on the station, allowing me out after dark, so I was able to follow the girl to the safe house in Pau. We were later taken by car up into the snow line of the Pyrenees where we met our Basque guides. The French Underground paid these Basques to take RAF men across the border, but they weren't very reliable. There were quite a number of aircrew together with some Jewish refugees. We broke up into smaller groups and our bomb aimer Archie McPhee went with another group. The Basques left us in the mountains for a whole night on 4 June, pointing to a valley, which they said was in Spain. Apparently we were right on the frontier. We decided to bed down for a bit as we were exhausted and hadn't had much to eat.

We set off just before the dawn, then heard rifle shots, presumably aimed above our heads. We looked round and there were three German soldiers about 100 yards away pointing their rifles at us. They must have been lying low, just watching us and I think we were actually in Spain, but we wouldn't have stood a chance. Four us were captured – myself, Harry Bossick, a Lancaster pilot and an American in the USAAF.

It was a dreadful feeling, almost indescribable, to think I was almost there and then find freedom snatched away from me. Archie McPhee, who was behind our group, managed to evade the Germans and got into Spain, then made his way home via Gibraltar. We were taken down the mountain to a village on the French side and put in a cell. We told them we should be in a POW camp, but of course we were in civvies. I heard the door rattling and a German officer appeared. He was a very smart-looking guy with highly polished jackboots and as we got to our feet he asked: 'Who's the English officer, here?' Although I'm Scottish I said, 'I am.' He said in first-class English: 'Stand to attention when you speak to a German officer.'

We were taken to another room and asked various questions about our base, aircraft and target and then the punch line was, 'Who helped you?' I gave him the usual, 'Geneva Convention, I am only required to give you my name, rank and number.' Then he tried the others with no greater success and stood back and looked at us. I can remember his exact words, almost as if they came from an American movie. They were: 'Huh, so you won't talk. Well, it's not my job, but we've ways and means of making you talk.' We were taken back to Pau to Gestapo headquarters, but in effect nothing bad really happened to us. We were given a reasonable meal and then taken back to Toulouse.

We were under guard on the train to Toulouse, but a Luftwaffe officer came into the compartment and asked who we were. I said: 'Royal Air Force,' and he gave each of us a cigarette and said, 'Good luck.' It was a surprising show of kindness. We were then thrown into a civilian prison in Toulouse under German guard.[12]

Harry Fisher's adventures would continue as the Allies held their newly achieved beachhead, then pushed through Normandy and prepared to invade the south of France as well.

THE first phase of the Transportation Plan continued throughout April, May and into the first days of June before D-Day itself. For every target in the invasion lodgement area, two more were attacked outside to fool the Germans as to where the troops might eventually land, though as any attack on any section of the SNCF Région Nord affected the smooth running of the rest, every operation was effective. Often aircraft of a single group operated independently or with one other, Oboe Mosquitos usually guiding them to their target of railway maintenance depots and marshalling yards. Several targets would be hit in one night.

For civilians who lived near airfields or those RAF personnel whose jobs kept them on the ground it seemed the skies were never still as aircraft pounded the circuit on air tests or took off for what was for most erks or WAAFs a destination unknown. Sometimes the dangers aircrew faced were brought into their own lives. LACW Marian Smith was a 22-year-old MT driver on 166 Squadron at Kirmington, who regularly took crews out to their aircraft in a 30 cwt truck or the purpose-built crew bus. The previous September she had married a sergeant fitter on A Flight and, because in wartime there were no married quarters, they were allowed to live in a cottage just off the base.

On the night of 10 April 908 aircraft of different groups were split between five transportation targets. The raid by an intended force of 132 Lancasters of 1 Group on the rail yards at Aulnoye was short of eighteen aircraft because of an incident at Kirmington. Marian Smith remembers:

> At about eleven at night the planes were taking off when a tyre of one of them burst as it was travelling along the runway. Apparently the undercarriage of the plane collapsed and a wing went down. The fully bombed-up Lancaster caught fire, fortunately the crew managed to get out, but the aircraft exploded.
>
> My husband and I had just gone to bed in our cottage on the borders of the airfield when we heard the explosion and the next thing the ceiling fell in on us. There was plaster and distemper and all kinds of things coming down. My husband pulled the bedclothes over my head to protect me, but neither of us was hurt. We knew something had gone, it was such a terrific explosion, but there was nothing we could do and we were on duty the next morning so we went back to sleep.[13]

Only four Lancasters had taken off when the aircraft of P/O D. C. Gibbons swung badly after travelling two-thirds along the runway, one undercarriage leg collapsing in a shower of sparks. The Lancaster burst into flames and a member of ground crew saw the aircrew evacuate the aircraft unhurt and run past him like a swarm of bees, shouting 'the bombs, the bombs'. The bomb load exploded and the remaining seventeen aircraft had to head back to their dispersals. The squadron aircraft that had already left for Aulnoye were diverted to North Killingholme on return. 'There were big holes all over the runway the following morning and everybody on the station had to lend a hand to get them filled in,' LACW Smith remembers. 'Lorries came from all over the place carrying rubble and materials, the holes were filled and the squadron was able to operate again the following night.'[14]

Drivers such as LACW Smith were often the last female face crews would ever see as they were driven out to their aircraft. The young WAAF, who remembered her name being written on many bombs going to Germany, would remain on the squadron until the end of 1944. She recalls:

Those of us on duty would stand by the NAAFI hut to watch the take-off and count the bombers out. We would then wait for them to come back. The saddest thing was counting them in on return. Sometimes it was a really long time before they returned and all too often fewer came back than went out. We used to watch them come in one by one. So many were lost, it upsets me to think of them now. I would pick crews up from their dispersal and they were usually a lot noisier coming back than when they went out. They would give me all the chocolate they had left from their flying rations. It really struck home when a crew didn't return because we knew all the aircrew. They were only lads, most of the crews were in their early twenties and some younger than that. We lost 921 aircrew in two years from Kirmington.

At one time it had been standard practice that when an aircraft landed after an op a WAAF driver had to drive a Standard van with a male corporal in the back pointing the aircraft to its dispersal from the end of the runway by means of a board with red and green lights on reading Stop and Go. LACW Smith had often found herself as the van driver. 'These kites were revving their engines right behind me as they followed and in bad weather, in the dark with poor visibility I often managed to park the aircraft in a turnip field rather than its dispersal. The little van was so tiny compared to the aircraft behind,' she remembers. But there was the occasional treat. 'I did have one or two trips in a kite,' she says.

'My husband made sure I only flew in a plane he was responsible for and he came too. Going for such a trip in a bomber on an air test was strictly forbidden and I should have been in deep trouble if caught, but I never was, fortunately.'[15]

THE Transportation Plan was proving a bigger success than even the D-Day planners had hoped as the Wehrmacht, Luftwaffe and Kriegs-marine in western France were slowly choked of supplies. Bombing accuracy was such that civilian casualties were low – only fourteen being killed in the Aulnoye raid of 10 April – though by the caprice of war, communities in Belgium tended to suffer more, 171 dying in an attack on Malines on 1 May, which destroyed more than 1,300 buildings, and forty-eight civilians being killed in an attack on Ghent nine days later.[16]

Occasionally efforts to avoid civilian casualties could increase problems for Bomber Command as aircraft orbited small targets until the master bomber was satisfied that nearby houses would not be hit. A particular case was that of the 5 Group raid on the Tours marshalling yards on 19 May, where both the marking and bombing force were ordered to carry out their tasks with particular care. The 61 Sqn Lancaster of bomb aimer F/Sgt 'Pat' Patfield was nearly lost in the mêlée.

> I was about to give the order 'Bomb doors open' when there was a hell of a crash and a shout of 'Christ' from the pilot and the aircraft vibrated like a mad thing. I brought the target back into the cross wires and released the bombs and the pilot [P/O Ron Auckland] informed us we had been hit by another Lancaster, but were flying reasonably well on three engines.
>
> In the cockpit I could see the port outer propeller bent backwards and the wing itself from that engine to the tip had been ripped open. The Perspex top of the cabin just above the pilot's head was also broken. He told us that the aircraft which hit us was flying in almost the opposite direction and had just skimmed over us. Another foot or so and there would have been an awful big bang.[17]

The aircraft eventually made it back to England for an emergency landing at an airfield near Exeter and the pilot was awarded an immediate DFC.

A rapid paralysis was spreading over the rail network of Normandy and the web of lines leading to it. W/O Geoffrey Haworth took part in another successful Loire valley raid three days after the Tours operation, on the station and railway repair workshops at Orléans, a night in which 1,023 Bomber Command aircraft were engaged on six targets, including big efforts on two German ones, the cities of Dortmund and Brunswick.

Like Cecil Poulter W/O Haworth was another who had spent a long time trying to get onto an operational station as D-Day approached, only to be shot down on his first raid. He had joined the RAF in July 1940 at the height of the Battle of Britain, qualified as a pilot eleven months later but spent the next two years as an instructor, eventually reaching an operational training unit where he was crewed up, then becoming incapacitated by illness. He was finally matched with another, headless crew in April 1944 and they reported to their first operational squadron – 77, at Full Sutton, near York – on 18 May. They were shot down four days later in an old Halifax V.

W/O Haworth remembers:

We took off about midnight and it was only two hours to the target. We bombed, turned west for about 20 miles with no problems and were almost due to turn north for home when there was a deafening noise and bullets and shells were exploding inside and outside the aircraft for four or five seconds. I started to weave and called the crew to ask, 'Where is it?' The rear gunner replied he couldn't see it and there was no reply from the mid-upper. The flight engineer was in shouting range behind me despite the engine noise and I asked him to check on the mid-upper. I continued weaving and trying to contact the rest of the crew on intercom. The only reply I got was from the rear gunner. The flight engineer reappeared, making a thumbs-down sign and pointing in the direction of the mid-upper gunner and wireless operator.

About two minutes later we got another long burst, the controls went floppy and the aircraft went into a dive. Up to then I had hoped to fight off or evade the fighter and return. I shouted to the flight engineer to bale out and to tell the others. He would pass them on the way to the front escape hatch. The flight engineer remembered the drill and spent a few valuable seconds getting my parachute, I would never have found it in the dark. I then had difficulty clipping it on – not enough hands with all the other activities. I continued trying to get control. The rear gunner, whose turret had been put out of action, appeared alongside me and I shouted to him to bale out and to tell the navigator and the air bomber whom he would pass. At some stage we got a third burst of fire.

Each crew position had an emergency signal light and I started to tap out 'P', the code for parachute. I had had no direct contact through-out with the navigator, air bomber, mid-upper gunner or the wireless operator ... I could see the light reflecting below so knew it was working. By now the whole affair must have been going on for eight to ten minutes. We were still diving and I knew we must be near the ground so I stopped signalling and made a dash. The escape hatch should have been jettisoned when the first man went out. In fact, it was still there, but ajar. I lifted it and could see ground features. It seemed too low to count to five, so I pulled the ripcord as I fell out. There was a bit of a tug as the parachute caught on the tailplane, then everything was quiet except for a gentle flapping sound. I looked up and saw a bite out of the parachute. That was the last I knew for some hours.

Only two other members of the crew had survived: the rear gunner Sgt Jack Taylor and the navigator Sgt Chuck Hale.* The flight engineer, 19-year-old Sgt Reg Rose, who had looked for and found the pilot's parachute, was among the dead, thought to have been killed in the third attack. The aircraft crashed at Séris, 14 miles north-east of Blois and was the only one of the 128 aircraft that had set out for Orléans not to return.

W/O Haworth's heavy impact with the earth in his damaged parachute fractured his spine and several ribs. By the time he regained consciousness it was daylight. He recalls:

Two larks were singing overhead. I was sure larks were English birds and that we must have got back. There was a farmstead 100 yards away though and it didn't look English. I managed to stand but with difficulty. I moved towards the farm and three or four men came to meet me and put me to bed in a barn. There were many visitors, handshakes and even kisses. I can't remember how long afterwards, but I was told that because of the spinal injury they could not hide me and the SS arrived, who behaved very correctly.

---

* Sgt Hale's escape from death proved short. He was being transported through France as a POW when the German convoy he was in was shot up by Allied aircraft and he died of his injuries in Tours on 22 June.

In fact, W/O Haworth was later told, he could not be taken to a local Resistance camp where other RAF evaders were hiding out, because a collaborator knew where he was.

W/O Haworth was taken to hospital in Orléans, then placed in the local jail. As he was taken through the local streets he was treated as a hero – one woman put a sweet in his mouth as he passed by. When several days later he and his rear gunner Sgt Taylor arrived at Frankfurt railway station on the way to the Dulag Luft interrogation centre at Oberursel, his reception was very different. The party of ten prisoners of war found themselves waiting on the platform for the local train to the centre, 'surrounded by a crowd of locals who were clearly very hostile'.

W/O Haworth remembers:

An elderly man, big, fat and bullet-headed, was whipping up fury. He knew all the English four-letter words and used them loudly. The group grew to forty or fifty and you could feel the crowd hysteria rising and those few minutes taught me how frightening and uncontrollable it can be. The four or five guards would have done nothing. I fixed my eyes on the elderly man. The other POWs said afterwards they too had fixed one person. There was an elderly lady at the back sobbing her eyes out, whether for us or them I don't know. It seemed to go on a long time, but probably for only two or three minutes before they dispersed. We decided afterwards they were waiting to get the train from the next platform. It was whistled out and that may have turned the scales.

Instead of being taken by train to Oberursel, the badly injured W/O Haworth was now marched there. 'I would not have made it without the help of Jack Taylor and two USAAF NCOs,' he says. He knew better than most aircrew what to expect when he arrived. All aircrew were shown a film during training, warning of the methods of interrogation at Dulag Luft and the dangers of giving away even an apparently trivial piece of information. 'As an instructor I had seen it many times. It proved surprisingly accurate,' W/O Haworth remembers. Within half an hour after arrival,

as about thirty POWs waited in a stiflingly hot room, a *Feldwebel* came in. He ranted for about ten minutes, his theme being that Germany had fought for five years and suffered tremendous losses. They were not going to be thwarted now just because a few prisoners would not talk. We could forget the Geneva Convention. We could forget the film we had seen, which they knew all about. We must answer every question. If not we would be handed over to the Gestapo.

Looking back, I and most other POWs had no important information to give. The Germans knew it and it was a ploy to make us tell the few things we did know, such as squadron, where stationed, any new equipment, how many planes and so on. I suppose the accumulation of a lot of apparently trivial information can give a picture of RAF general strategy.

The day before D-Day W/O Haworth's interrogation began with him refusing to answer anything but name, rank and number to a young officer who eventually revealed all he knew about the RAF pilot's squadron. The conversation then took a bizarre turn.

I used the expression, 'We must agree to differ.' He had not heard this before and could not understand how we could agree, if we differed. We spent some time discussing the niceties of the English language. I suppose I was the fifth man he had seen that day and the fifty-fifth that summer and it was a relief from boredom to brush up his idiomatic English.[18]

A few days later W/O Haworth, as uncooperative as the vast majority of RAF and Commonwealth Air Force flyers proved to the German interrogators, was moved to prison camp at Bankau, then to the POW hospital at Lamsdorf and eventually was repatriated in January, 1945, making a full recovery from his injuries.

THE approach of D-Day produced a tension in Britain as keen as the trepidation on the other side of the Channel. The oily, grumbling, nocturnal chains of British and US Army convoys snaking and grating through ill-lit country roads, heading for the holding camps and embarkation areas on England's southern edge, sounded a clear signal that the dawn of liberation was coming. Newspapers showed pictures of families holidaying at home in London, bathing in the river at Richmond and 'other Thames-side spas' as they obeyed the injunction not to travel by train, thus freeing the railways for important invasion material.[19] London was eerily empty of the American troops who had flooded the capital with khaki in the past few months, handing out candy to East End urchins and chatting up the office girls. It was no secret where they had gone, to wait like the rest of Britain.

There was little else to do than speculate about the invasion date, now being generally called by the American term D-Day, and the newspapers joined in. 'July is D-Date' ran the headline in one newspaper in early June, merely because American authorities had happened to suggest that £140 million would be needed to feed and clothe the liberated population between July and December.[20]

The phlegmatic young aircrew of Bomber Command, who had just learned they had established a new record for their force in May by dropping a total of 37,000 tons of bombs, waited in the dark to play their part in the great event. Meanwhile, the warmer weather and lighter nights took them further afield from their bomber bases than usual. Those who had access to a motorbike or car visited pubs in sleepy villages with ancient churches, built when an earlier invasion was the talking point. F/Sgt Cliff Hill, the Cheshire-born rear gunner, who had found the introduction to his Pathfinder tour on 35 Sqn so unnerving with the Berlin raid of 24 March, was one of those now exploring the Huntingdonshire countryside round his base of Graveley.

He remembered:

Bill Lloyd our flight engineer, who came from Sale, bought a Raleigh three-wheeler car on leave from someone who had gone missing. He picked me up at the end of a leave at my home in Macclesfield and we had just left the town when he told me he had never driven before. We had a lot of fun in that car. Bill called it Sweetpea. We used to get five of us in it. We were having a drink one time in the Graveley Arms near Graveley with a Welsh navigator and two WAAFs when we decided to go to a dance at Buckden. It was 9 p.m. when we set off, a bit late, so Bill put a move on. He got it up to 55 mph and it went off the road at a bend. It turned over twice. I found myself in a field and thought I was unconscious as I couldn't see a thing, then I realised one of the WAAFs had landed on my head. Fortunately we had crashed right outside Station Sick Quarters. We got patched up in double-quick time, apart from Bill, who was in hospital for a few days, but Sweetpea was a write-off.[21]

On the afternoon of 2 June F/Sgt Hill and his Canadian skipper, F/O Harold Hoover, visited their injured flight engineer in the sick bay. They had just been briefed for a return to the marshalling yards of Trappes, south-west of Paris, which had been attacked by more than 200 bombers in two waves only two days before with the small loss of four Lancasters from what was described as 'slight fighter opposition'.[22] The briefing was carried out by their squadron commander, W/Cdr Pat Daniels, who would in fact be the master bomber for the raid. 'The MO didn't let us linger too long,' F/Sgt Hill later recorded. 'I remember us chuckling at Bill's plight and saying, "See you tomorrow." He replied: "Mind you don't get the chop."'[23]

It was a warning that was almost prophetic. This time the Luftwaffe would be up in force and the Trappes raid would exact the heaviest toll of the Transportation Plan targets. Sixteen aircraft (12.5 per cent) were shot down in the moonlight when night fighters, drawn by the exploding bombs and burning railway buildings, fell on the bombers as the force headed for home. It was mainly 4 Group that would put up the 128 aircraft taking part and a single squadron in that group, 158, would lose five of the Halifaxes it dispatched. Another would be so badly damaged it would not fly again.

F/O Bob Farnbank was the 22-year-old navigator in one of the lost aircraft, skippered by F/O George Dalton. He says:

We were briefed to fly from base to Goole then Beachy Head at 2,000 feet and our height for bombing was very low for heavy aircraft. The CO told us at briefing: 'Sorry about this, but the target has to be obliterated.' We had been told earlier in the day that we might be going to a German target and funnily enough I didn't want to go on the op to the French target. It wasn't premonition, I just wanted to go on the German one. We were quite happy to fly down the UK at 2,000 feet, though, because we thought we would wake everybody up. It was a beautiful evening with a moon. Practically all my operations were on railway yards in France. Most of the operations were carried out at 13,000–14,000 feet, but I think basically we were asked to go in at low level at Trappes because it had to be knocked out, so many trains were going through that would have been important for reinforcing Normandy.[24]

H-hour for the attack to open was 0050, with the Oboe Mosquito marker due for release eight minutes before to allow W/Cdr Daniels time to assess its accuracy and drop his own yellow target indicators. F/O Hoover's crew, with a flight lieutenant aboard as temporary flight engineer, was one of the two backer-up crews to his markers. F/Sgt Hill recorded:

> We arrived over the target exactly on time and it was so clear you could see the ground, and the marshalling yards were identified visually. We went in at 9,000 feet and dropped our white target indicators plumb onto the master bomber's yellows which our bomb aimer, Jack Mossop, said were framed in his bombsight and bang on the marshalling yards. Our bombs, a 4,000-lb Cookie and two 1,000-lb HEs dropped simultaneously with our TIs, produced a large explosion with heavy smoke. The Main Force came in and Pat Daniels could be heard clearly instructing them to bomb on the yellows and later to new arrivals to bomb the centre of the conflagrations. The fires were concentrated and the bombing was accurate apart from the odd fringe merchant. Daniels could be heard urging the latecomers to get stuck in.[25]

The twenty-three aircraft of 158 Sqn were all due to bomb within five minutes of the Main Force attack opening eight minutes after the Oboe target indicator. 'The Master Bomber was heard by most crews, but there was a good deal of talking back which interfered with the reception of his instructions,' the adjutant's staff would later report in the squadron's operational record book.[26] In fact, High Wycombe staff were currently examining the problem of backchat over targets following a barrage of imprecations over Mailly-le-Camp as crews helplessly orbited, watching their fellows cut down by fighters.

The tonnage of bombs released on the four marshalling yards of Trappes was a little over half the 872 tons dropped two nights before and around a third of that on the first raid of 6 March, but it caused great damage, tossing locomotives in the air as French families safe in their houses half a mile away listened with satisfaction. Not one civilian life was lost. Before the Transportation Plan began 4,000 wagons were sorted in the Trappes yards every 24 hours. In the 2 June attack an ammunition train, loaded in Cologne, blew up. Also wrecked by Bomber Command's attack was a train-load of staff cars, three wagons of radio sets, two wagons of aeroplane propellers and a mobile radar unit. It totally disrupted the main rail service between Paris and the west.[27]

Edouard Robert, the deputy stationmaster, later told the British war correspondent J. D. S. Allan:

After the first raid the Germans collected every person for miles and forced them to work on repairs. They did the same after the second. But after the third they gave it up as a bad job. Your bombers had simply suffocated the yards. And do not forget that every train averaged 200 kilometres a day. After Trappes many of the tanks had to go to the front on their own tracks and many of them wore out.'[28]

The bombers returning from the spectacularly successful raid on Trappes were seven minutes away from the target when the first of the night fighters attacked. From the rear turret the marshalling yards could be seen well ablaze as they receded. F/Sgt Hill later wrote:

As the navigator gave Hoov a course for base we began what was just forty-five minutes flying time to the coast and I poured myself a coffee and bit into my chocolate, then the quietness of the night erupted. Combats began taking place port and starboard ahead and astern, tracer rippled across the sky and bombers began to go down.

I traversed my turret, searching in every direction. It was a bright night and we were sitting ducks. Hoov's voice came over, 'Watch out for fighters, gunners. Jesus, there's more combats than you can shake a stick at up front.' We all fell silent as the longest half-hour of our lives played out. Two Halifaxes went down behind, dead astern. I didn't have time to watch their downward path. I rotated the turret from side to side, glad for once that the front Perspex had been removed. I was aware of the Halifaxes' demise, a crimson flash lighting up the sky.

Another Halifax way over on the starboard quarter was fighting a furious battle with a blur, which looked like a Messerschmitt 110, flashes from his cannons and subsequent flames from the Halifax indicated they were in trouble. The rear gunner was still firing when they blew up, pieces falling everywhere. I felt cold with fear as I stood up, backside propped against the turret doors enabling me to see below as far as possible. I could see for miles.

It was at this moment I spotted him, sitting there on the port quarter down, a black blur on the darker side of the sky, a single-engined fighter, possibly an FW190. I shouted, 'Fighter, corkscrew port, go,' and Hoov responded immediately, diving down, turning tightly into the attack. I had just time for a short burst before I was pinned to the side of the turret by the force of gravity. The fighter flashed above me and I heard the guns of the mid-upper gunner, Jock, firing. I'd seen a brief flicker from the fighter's cannons and sweat poured down my face.

The flight engineer called in that the fighter had sheered off and the Lancaster regained an even keel.

Fifteen minutes from the coast F/Sgt Hill saw another Halifax flying a parallel path to port, firing from its rear turret to an unseen attacker coming in on a course that would meet that of F/O Hoover's aircraft. He recalled:

> I opened fire at a spot where I guessed the fighter to be, aiming so that it converged with the rear gunner's fire from the Halifax. I could now make out a dark shape, an Me109, I thought. Our mid-upper gunner fired a similar burst. He disappeared underneath. I don't know whether any of us hit him, the combined firepower could have frightened him off, or more likely he was short of fuel. I hoped the Halifax crew appreciated they had been helped out by a Lancaster. There was great friendly rivalry.[29]

It was at this time that a night fighter picked up the outline of F/O Farnbank's aircraft half an hour into the Halifax's return journey. He says:

> Shut away in the nose the navigator doesn't know what's happening, but the gunners warned us there was a night fighter and we were hit midships. The German broke away, but there was a small fire that the flight engineer put out with an extinguisher, then we were hit hard in a second attack. We were too low to corkscrew. The pilot called out that we had lost the elevator control, so we couldn't maintain height. He ordered a bale-out and there was no waste of time in doing it, the entire crew were able to get out. The bomb aimer was by the escape hatch and went out before me and I followed immediately. I don't even know how rapidly the aircraft was going down, the bale-out was absolutely instant.
>
> I landed right by a hawthorn hedge and the parachute draped itself all over it, so there was no way I could hide it. I had come down near

a road and was actually walking down the road when I saw German lorried troops approaching. During my aircrew training we took part in field exercises with the army in which they showed us camouflage techniques and what it meant to be perfectly still. I dived into a ditch face down and remembered all I had been taught, lying as still as a mole until they drove by. I was in a state of shock, but my training paid off and I was able to assess what action needed to be taken. I had come down not far from Evreux in Normandy and decided to head for Spain. As a navigator I knew the stars, so I got the Pole Star behind me and started walking south. On either the first or second night down I came face to face with a gendarme on the edge of a town. He just turned away. I headed south for about eight nights in all, contacting farms along the way at each dawn for food and shelter then moving off again at dusk. I was always given help, but I would take no names or addresses in case I was caught and tortured.

My family had had an Air Ministry telegram the day after the Trappes raid saying I was missing and later the Red Cross wrote to them saying there was no further news, but my mother was convinced I was still alive. She was a bit fey and within a few days of my being shot down she told my father she had met me coming up the stairs at home in uniform and telling her I was all right.

One morning as I called at a farmhouse I was told the invasion had taken place about four days before, so I decided to retrace my steps in the direction of the Allied armies. Walking north I found myself in a wood surrounded by numerous enemy lorries. It was quite surprising. I thought it best to continue walking straight ahead and I wasn't stopped.[30]

F/O Farnbank's evasion would go on throughout July and August and his story continues in the break-out from Normandy.

At Lissett, near Bridlington, the crews of 158 Sqn who had made it home waited in vain for their absent colleagues to turn up. One of the six aircraft missing was eventually reported as having landed at an aerodrome near Bournemouth. Its Australian pilot, P/O B. D. Bancroft, had brought it back with a huge hole in the floor centre section, torn away by a Ju88's cannon fire. Three of the crew were missing, the skipper reporting: 'The wireless operator, mid-upper gunner and flight engineer either baled out or fell out. The aircraft was extensively damaged, all instruments and hydraulics being rendered u/s. The remainder of the crew fought several fires and eventually by steering by the North Star I landed at Hurn.'*³¹

There was some bitterness, however. Another Australian pilot, F/Sgt R. J. Chilcott, who had been fired on by a single-engined aircraft, complained at debriefing: 'H-8 was considered far too early to start the attack. This presumably enables fighters to start in early and also to drop dummy markers. Yellows were seen approximately 20 miles south-west of the target.'³² Eighteen members of the squadron were by now dead, six were prisoners of war and fourteen were evading.

Air gunner Cliff Hill had returned at 0233 to the concrete of Graveley. 'As we climbed out of the aircraft Les the navigator said quietly to me, "Cliff have you taken your caffeine?" I said, "No, I didn't need it, why?" He asked, "Can I have it?" I replied, "Why, you'll be awake all night." He smiled: "Someone's waiting for me."'³³

THE Transportation Plan continued in the days and weeks after D-Day, keeping the German Army sealed up in the battle front and short of reinforcements and supplies. As the Allied forces took a foothold in Normandy, then consolidated in June, it was obvious the Transportation Plan had proved crucial, with the lion's share of operations being carried out by Harris's men. Twenty-two of the thirty-seven targets handed to Bomber Command were now in Category A, meaning that no further attacks would be necessary until the Germans were able – if able – to carry out vital repairs; the other fifteen were in Category B, severely damaged but still possessing a number of installations that would require further assaults. None of Harris's targets were in Category C, showing little or no damage.³⁴

Professor Zuckerman, whom Harris had so disparaged, wrote in his diary as the campaign drew to an end:

The amazing thing is that Harris, who was even more resistant than the Americans to the idea of AEAF domination, has in fact thrown himself whole-heartedly into the battle, has improved his bombing performance enormously, and has contributed more to the dislocation of enemy communications etc, than any of the rest ... The Americans, on the other hand, are terrified lest they be asked and never offer.

* The pilot's instrument panel from this aircraft was salvaged and is displayed at the Australian War Memorial museum in Canberra.

What the battle in the West gets from them is what is left over from pre-planned operations against oil, the aircraft industry and ball bearings.[35]

The cost to Bomber Command throughout the Transportation Campaign from early March to early June had been light – the 2 June Trappes raid notwithstanding – only 203 aircraft missing out of 8,795 dispatched. For the young men who crewed the bombers there was now indeed new hope as the loss rate fell overall, but occasionally there would be a target in the run-up to D-Day where the losses for a small force would be as bad as if not comparatively worse than anything that had come before. To the men of 1 Group and 5 Group the German Panzer base at Mailly-le-Camp exacted a price in percentage terms almost as great as Nuremberg had on the Command as a whole.

II

Training and Terror

The RAF was approaching its peak in personnel of 1,185,833 as the world waited for D-Day. Bomber Command, which made up so large a part of the air force, also gathered strength as the winter attrition made way for the balmy days of spring, targets closer to home and an excess of aircrew, who now saw hopes of finishing a tour. In fact – somewhat confidently – as the invasion approached the numbers of aircrew under training had already started to decline. The Minister of National Defence for Air Mr C. G. Dover announced on 16 February that the British Commonwealth Air Training Plan had now reached its objective and the number of courses were being reduced and some training schools closed.[1] Before the war was over the CATP would have trained a total of 131,553 aircrew, by far the greatest proportion in Canada.*

There were now other demands for manpower, however. The first Bevin Boys – drafted at random and usually unwilling to hew coal rather than be a prospective hero in the fighting services – started work on 14 February.[3] The army was also likely to be short of men as it battled through Normandy and, in fact, some Bomber Command squadrons saw a bleeding-off of non-essential personnel in the middle of 1944 to replace losses by the army. There would be a manpower crisis in Nor-

* Of that number, which also included aircrew for Fighter, Coastal and Transport Command, 72,835 were Canadians, 42,110 were from Britain including other nationalities serving with the RAF, 9,606 were Australians and 7,002 were from New Zealand.[2]

244

mandy in July and pressure was being put on Harris to release more of his aircrew for other duties or at least force them all to do a second tour. The Secretary of State for Air Sir Archibald Sinclair replied in the spring of 1944 to a memorandum by the Air Member for Personnel of the Air Council, noting the 'serious situation' that '2,000 aircrew and this number increasing by 200 or more a month are now idling ... We have something equivalent to manpower of two divisions locked up in our deferred lists.' The memorandum was dated 9 April – 24 hours after the losses of the Nuremberg raid were revealed, which shows scant appreciation of what it meant to serve as aircrew in Bomber Command.[4] In fact, 2,000 non-flyers were transferred to the navy and army in May, 1,500 from the RAF Regiment.[5] Harris's battle to protect his old lags would go on throughout the summer.

The RAF's peak strength meant 80,000 in air force blue in Lincolnshire alone – approximately 13 per cent of the county's total population. Bomber Command's Lincolnshire airfields covered 30,000 acres of countryside. It wasn't just the men who flew who boosted trade for local businesses and favourite pubs such as the Wheatsheaf in Louth or the White Hart in Gainsborough, and competed for girls at village hops or large dance halls such as the Gliderdome in Boston, the county also accommodated a host of construction workers, many from Southern Ireland, who were needed to build those airfields.

By far the great majority of the aerodromes they created were operational bomber stations, but not all. Some were operational training units or heavy conversion units as aircrew took the last step before venturing into enemy territory. The scenes the local civilian population witnessed at those aerodromes were often as dramatic as at the operational field down the road. Approximately 10 per cent of Bomber Command aircrew killed during the war were lost in training. The RAF non-operational base at Sandtoft in North Lincolnshire was a prime example of how dangerous flying could be, even out of the firing line. The station opened as 1667 Heavy Conversion Unit on 14 February to finish the training of fifteen heavy bomber crews a week before they were dispatched to the operational squadrons of 1 Group, which operated Lancasters. However, crews were expected to complete their training on Halifaxes as every Lancaster was needed for the front line of the air war. The Halifaxes supplied to the new base, and to all other heavy conversion units of Bomber Command, were operationally expired and showed all the stresses and strains of any aircraft that had regularly corkscrewed in the night skies above Germany as the Luftwaffe shot holes in its airframe and engines. It wasn't long before those stresses reached breaking point at Sandtoft.

Within three weeks of the station opening a crew on circuits and bumps, by which landing practice was known, were all killed with their instructor when their Halifax went into an inexplicable spin. During the rest of March three more Halifaxes crashed, killing another twelve novice aircrew. In April the station adjutant recorded another four crashes, including a Wellington from an operational training unit at Gaydon that came down on Sandtoft's railway sidings and burst into flames. In May three further aircraft were lost, killing two airmen, and four more Halifaxes were damaged in various incidents including undercarriage collapse in two cases, where the Halifax Mk II demonstrated its alarming and often fatal tendency to swing violently to starboard or port in the last stages before take-off.

Notwithstanding a section dance in the NAAFI on the 5th, where aircrew were able to meet newly arrived WAAFs, morale on what was after all a non-operational station began to suffer, the medical officer recording 248 aircrew reporting sick in May, compared to 182 ground personnel. It was at this point that Sandtoft began to be called 'Prangtoft' by Bomber Command aircrew, a nickname that stuck over the next two months as the statistics of random mortality figured in mess gossip throughout the lexicon of 1 Group aerodromes.[6]

F/Lt Peter Johnson, who had won the DFC at the end of his own 101 Sqn bomber tour in 1943, was one of the flying instructors at Sandtoft at that time. He remembers: 'We had these operationally tired Halifaxes and the maintenance had been bad. A big problem was coolant leaks, which usually led to engine failure. Most of the training was on circuits of the airfield, which meant the aircraft were flying at around 1,000 feet, so nine times out of ten an engine failure at that height meant a crash.'[7]

Sgt Jim Lord, a pilot in the final stages of his training at Sandtoft before joining 550 Sqn at North Killingholme, where he would be commissioned and win the DFC, figured in the May accident statistics at 1667 HCU. Lord says:

The airfield at Sandtoft was littered with damaged Halifaxes when we got there. We as a crew thought, 'What have we come to?' We quickly found out. Most aircraft at OTUs and HCUs were clapped out and this was the case with a Halifax V we took on a night cross-country from Sandtoft. En route we had to feather two engines because they were giving trouble. We were descending all the time and decided to go into Halfpenny Green [near Wolverhampton] and they told us they could land a four-engined aircraft. By that time we only had the starboard outer feathered. As soon as we got onto final approach they gave us a red signal not to land. The flight engineer opened the throttles to overshoot and we hit a tree as we climbed, leaving a big hole in the starboard mainplane. It took us another twenty minutes to get back to the circuit height.

I had the crew in their crash positions with their parachutes on and we managed to stagger round the circuit again, then as we came in again I got another red. They didn't tell us why we kept getting reds and I thought, 'Sod this,' and came in and landed at the side of the strip. An aircraft had just crashed on the runway, which is why we kept getting the red warning. I landed with brakes on and applied them even more so when I saw how short Halfpenny Green was. I could see the control tower heading towards me through the windscreen and we finally stopped about 10 feet in front of it. It was one of the most dramatic landings I made in my flying career. One thing about the Halifax V was that once you were down you stayed down. I think that aircraft would have required a change of all four engines before it could fly again.

Within a couple of days Sgt Lord found further problems with a Sandtoft aircraft. He remembers:

We were down to do a practice bombing detail and the starboard outer of the Halifax I was given was absolutely streaming glycol. I refused to take it and the officer in charge of night flying ordered me to. I asked him if he was coming with me and he said, 'No.' What then happened was we swung as we tried to take off, so I taxied the aircraft back. They found the tyres were showing slippage beyond the allowable creep marks on the rims and we retired to bed. The next morning I was hauled before the CO and given a right rollocking. He implied that because we'd made such a song and dance about the aircraft we'd invented something. He threatened to send me off the course if there was a similar incident. In those days I had a system whereby whether I was being commended or rollocked I didn't say a word and that's what I did then. I just kept quiet and I never told the crew.[8]

The miles of concrete and grey, air-force-regulation buildings now stretching across the one-time farmland of eastern England, and the men who came to use them, were changing England's agricultural and social landscape for ever. Perhaps the greatest impact of all was the influx of Americans who had first come over to build the bases of the Eighth Air Force and were now populating those airfields or waiting for the rallying call to Normandy. A total of 426,000 US airmen were stationed in Norfolk and Suffolk in 1944, where their aerodromes were no more than an average of 8 miles apart.[9] By the spring there were so many USAAF men in Suffolk every sixth person was an American.

A special booklet, printed by the British Information Services in Washington, had been in circulation for a year giving tips about the blackout, ration books and queuing, and suggesting GIs, who were paid an average of 10 shillings (50p) a day, shouldn't ask for oranges at the village grocers – they were restricted to children under 5. They were also told all women from 18 to 45 now had to register for labour of national importance and that meant a range of tasks from working on the railway to cleaning windows. It didn't tell them that they could expect to see a lot of women taking part in the air war, 180,339 WAAFs serving at the time.[10]

THAT spring the country was coiled and tense, bursting to hear the news that the cork was out of the bottle and the armies were going ashore in France. The Transportation Plan meant that the German armies were contained in the lodgement area with supplies dwindling to a trickle and no way out. Now Bomber Command was called on to smash the Panzer battalions that might try to burst through by road and rutted field to the beaches. The first of such operations fell to Cheshire's low-level markers to guide. The gremlins that had made VHF reception such a problem for the heavies when 5 Group's marker Mosquitos had operated over Brunswick and Schweinfurt just days before would return with a vengeance and cause the loss of forty-two Lancasters, 11.6 per cent of the 360 aircraft involved, as the night fighters picked their targets among the bomber crews helplessly orbiting, waiting for instructions to bomb.

The plan to attack the Panzer barracks and training ground at Mailly-le-Camp, 80 miles east of Paris, was thanks to the courage of a member of the French Resistance, Raymond Basset, who had entered the camp through the main entrance weeks before, waving a false French police warrant card supplied by the Special Operations Executive. He then had several conversations with a German officer about camp security and committed to memory the layout of the Panzer base he saw in charts and plans scattered around the Wehrmacht office.[11]

The operation was planned by 5 Group, whose experts were particularly well informed because of M. Basset's bravery, to produce a bombing pattern that would eradicate the camp and the major part of the 21st Panzer Division, which was in training there, together with the extensive repair and replacement facilities. Because the target was so small the attack would have to be carried out in moonlight. Leonard Cheshire was told about the operation after he and his fellow 617 Sqn aircrew returned from the week's leave they had been granted following the Munich operation. In papers he compiled after the war he said: 'The plan, which was hurriedly made because orders were not received until late in the day, was designed to achieve tactical surprise and speed.'[12] The order of attack was timed to the minute. In fact, H-Hour was 0001, one minute after all soldiers were traditionally supposed to have booked in at the guardroom, so that the barracks would be full with 5,000 troops as the three Oboe Mosquitos arrived to drop their green TIs as a guide for Cheshire and his three other low-level markers.

Apart from the heavies of 5 Group, squadrons of Air Vice Marshal Sir Edward Rice's 1 Group were also being called on and because such a large force was involved in so small a target the bombing was planned to be in two sequences, the first between H+5 and H+11 on Cheshire's red spot fires in the south-eastern part of the three barrack blocks, the second nine minutes afterwards on a marker in the north-western block.[13] This was a period when group commanders were anxious to follow Harris's long-felt ambition and 5 Group's lead, to operate as independent forces, and AVM Rice had formed a Special Duty Flight only a month before, which it was hoped would eventually rival Cheshire's low-level markers. The six-crew-strong flight would mark the tank-repair shops with two squadrons of Lancasters briefed to bomb those alone in the interim between the two attacks.[14]

As on the successful Munich operation of two weeks earlier, as well as Cheshire controlling the markers, there would be a Main Force controller – in this case the 83 Sqn CO W/Cdr Laurence Deane. A deputy had also been appointed, S/Ldr Neville Sparks, one of Deane's flight commanders. The Lancasters would be waiting, orbiting a datum point near Châlons-en-Champagne marked by two 627 Sqn yellow TIs at the same time as the Oboe green TIs went down over Mailly.

Once Cheshire was satisfied with his own and S/Ldr Dave Shannon's

Mosquito marking, the 173 Lancasters of 5 Group would be called in by Deane and they would approach at between 6,000 and 8,000 feet from the assembly point and each unload their Cookies and 500-lb high explosive bombs to smash the barracks to matchwood and the messes and MT buildings to red dust. By H+11 Cheshire's second pair of Mosquitos, piloted by F/Lt Dave Kearns and F/Lt Gerry Fawke, would begin marking the western part of the target, Main Force being ordered to cease bombing in the nine-minute interim so that the wooden Mosquitos would not be blown to pieces by blast. Bomber Command would be laying on other raids to divert the night fighters, some over the Luftwaffe fields themselves, such as one at Montdidier near Amiens, which would be attacked by eighty-four Lancasters of 8 Group.[15]

There were four possible problems. The first that of the *Nachtjäger* itself, operating under a three-quarter moon. I/NJG5 had ten Bf110s and Me410s on its base at St Dizier, less than 25 miles to the east of Mailly-le-Camp; I/NJG4, a mixed unit of twenty Bf110s and Ju88s could be called from Florennes, Belgium; II/NJG4 had fifteen Bf110s and Do217s at Coulommiers, 55 miles west of the camp; and III/NJG4 at Juvincourt was similarly equipped and a particular ace operated from there, Hauptmann Helmut Bergmann, who already had twenty-eight night victories. At Athies-sous-Laon, 90 miles to the north of Mailly, III/NJG4 had another sixteen night fighters, III/NJG5 also had twenty and III/NJG1 had eleven Me Bf110s. It was here that the ace Major Martin Drewes, who had shot down two on the Nuremberg raid, was now based. Both he and Bergmann would add in spectacular fashion to their scores before the night was through.

The second possible ingredient for disaster was the yellow datum markers – later replenished – north of Mailly, which aircraft would orbit, waiting to be called in. They would be a clear point for any night fighters in the vicinity to head for. The planners at 5 Group liked datum markers, employing them for their time and distance bombing technique from a fixed point, although High Wycombe were phasing out similar route markers by this time precisely because they attracted night fighters.

The third potential problem was the nine-minute delay between bombing the south-east aiming point and the north-west. If fighters were already active they would catch 1 Group, tasked with the second target, as they came in. And the fourth possibility for carnage was a communication fault – as VHF had proved so uncertain on the Brunswick and Schweinfurt raids – causing a hold-up in the heavies receiving

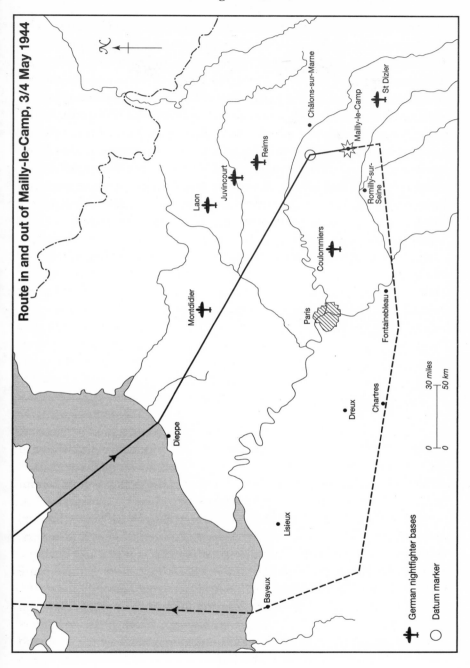

Route in and out of Mailly-le-Camp, 3/4 May 1944

Châlons-sur-Marne

St Dizier

Mailly-le-Camp

Reims

Juvincourt

Laon

Romilly-sur-Seine

Coulommiers

Montdidier

Paris

Fontainebleau

Dreux

Chartres

30 miles

50 km

Dieppe

Lisieux

Bayeux

German nightfighter bases

○ Datum marker

the master bomber's instructions. In fact, 5 Group had decided that the instructions would be passed to Main Force from its controller, W/Cdr Deane, by W/T in Morse through his radio operator and not by the VHF method.[16]

The crews of 1 and 5 Group who found themselves listed for operations as they checked in to flight offices on the morning of 3 May were relieved to find at briefing it was another short-haul French target. True, it was in moonlight and they were being asked to bomb at between 6,000 and 8,000 feet – little room for manoeuvre if they were attacked by a night fighter – but it didn't have the dangers of flying over the Reich and looked like another routine trip. The pity was it would only count as a third of an operation because of the new edict about non-German objectives.

Flight engineer Dennis Goodliffe remembers the briefing at Ludford Magna.

We were advised that the target would be marked by 617 Sqn as visual identification was necessary due to the compactness of the target and the close proximity of the village and civilian population. Our squadron was in the second wave and we had been told we would be required to circle a yellow ground marker and then await instructions from the master bomber to come in and bomb.[17]

Sgt Ken Hulton, the 57 Sqn flight engineer, remembers from diary notes made at the time: 'We were told at briefing that German officers would have a passing-out parade at Mailly-le-Camp the next day and we would be making sure it didn't happen.'[18]

At Waddington, just south of Lincoln, where the RAAF squadrons 463 and 467 were based, Australian P/O Albert Berryman didn't even have time to unpack before finding himself on the battle order and off to briefing. Berryman, a 29-year-old married man, who had arrived at the base that very day with his crew, found himself down for a second-dickey trip with the experienced 467 Sqn skipper F/Lt D. J. Conway.[19] One of 467 Sqn's aircraft was a veteran, having successfully seen crews through their tours on 83 Sqn as Q-Queenie. Now recoded as PO-S* she would be making her ninety-seventh trip that night and would

---

* The aircraft, R5868, is now on display in the RAF Museum at Hendon.

eventually make 144 in all. The other RAAF heavy bomber squadron, 460, based at Binbrook, north-east of Lincoln, was putting up seventeen crews and another of its aircraft had been lent to 101 Sqn at nearby Ludford Magna for the raid.

At the 5 Group airfield of Fiskerton, W/Cdr Malcolm Crocker was operating for the first time in his new role as the CO of 49 Sqn, after being transferred from 630 Sqn, which he had formed as a squadron leader at the very end of 1943. Several of his aircrew would report horrendous experiences over Mailly.

On 101 Sqn twenty aircraft had been readied for operations. Sgt Goodliffe, who had eaten breakfast in a virtually empty sergeants' mess the morning after the Nuremberg operation had claimed seven of the squadrons' crews, was now about to see the Grim Reaper take another five from Ludford Magna. Goodliffe says:

Anyone who did Nuremberg and Mailly-le-Camp rates Mailly as the worst of the two. Ops made you quite superstitious. For instance, we all used to smoke Players No. 3, which came into the sergeants' mess in 100-cigarette boxes and on the afternoon of the Mailly-le-Camp raid three of us engineers, myself, a Canadian called Tom McDonald and Stan Rodway, whose 21st birthday it was, went to get some from the sergeants' mess bar. We were told they were coming in the next day and would we like some put aside. Tom and I wouldn't do it because we thought it tempted fate to assume we would be there to collect. Only Stan Rodway said, 'Put me down for some.'

Later as we waited to take off I remember I was wrestling on the grass with Stan, whose aircraft A-Able was parked at the next dispersal to ours. My skipper told me to cut it out as I would start to sweat and that could freeze at altitude. The worst time was waiting to go on an op after you'd been dropped off at the aircraft. My skipper used to have to go for what he called a nervous pee every five minutes. We used to sit in the ground crew's igloo hut playing cards with them to try to pass the time. But as soon as you got the aircraft off the ground you had no more bother, you just got on with your job. Concentration was required to watch the airspeed, watch the gauges and watch the fuel state at the same time and keep a log with a tiny pinpoint of light from the lamp on the engineer's panel.[20]

THE double wave of bombers set windows shaking as they climbed over blacked-out Britain, crossing the coast at Beachy Head still reaching for altitude until hitting the French coast 10 miles north of Dieppe at 12,000 feet. From here they started a gradual descent to the assembly point 200 miles away. The visibility was so good under the three-quarter moon in a cloudless sky crews could clearly see other bombers flying near by. And it was at Compiègne, only 100 miles from the coast, that the first of the night fighters – who had been on standby since the Luftwaffe listening service had heard so many bomber radio sets being tested earlier in the day – found them. The element of surprise had already been lost, before they reached the deadly yellow markers at Châlons-sur-Marne.

The later inquest into the raid by Bomber Command's Operational Research Section would read: 'At first the enemy lost more heavily than did the bombers, losing three, probably four fighters, before turning south near Epernay. Then the unfortunate delay before the main force received their instructions resulted in a concentration of aircraft over the datum point in the bright moonlight, presenting fighters with great opportunities of wholesale interceptions.'[21] The first two of the possible ingredients for disaster, a large force of night fighters in contact and the glowing yellow datum markers inexorably drawing both bombers and night fighters together, were creating a devil's concoction that would leave a bitter memory among the survivors of the raid for years to come.

W/Cdr Cheshire's two red spot fires had fallen accurately on the south-east aiming point at thirty seconds past midnight and had been added to by S/Ldr David Shannon's markers just over five minutes later.[22] P/O A. Drinkhall of 83 Sqn then backed up the already burning red spot fires slightly to the south on Cheshire's instructions, his photoflash clearly showing the lines of barrack buildings and camp roadways.[23] Cheshire now pressed his R/T button to ask W/Cdr Deane's wireless operator to tap out the Morse signal for the first wave of 5 Group aircraft to bomb. It soon became clear, however, that Deane's instructions were not being received by the majority of his force, though as one bombed, some others from the first wave who had seen the bombs going down joined in. Several burning bombers started to plummet towards the camp and surrounding villages. Skippers had been told at briefing to make a circuit to port of the assembly point if there was any delay in being called in to bomb, but in the confusion, amid the streams of light flak coming up and night-fighter and bomber tracer criss-crossing the sky, bombers were now arriving from all directions in a hurry to bomb and get away.

Flight engineer Sgt Cliff Williams, the boyfriend of LACW Dorothy Mason at Bardney, was among the first to reach the datum point, in the 9 Sqn crew of Australian F/O James Hancock. He remembers:

We were flying in to bomb at 5,000 feet, very low level. When we reached Mailly the Germans already had a few fighters up, but we were circling so long the Luftwaffe gathered. As we finally ran up to the aiming point I saw another bomber coming straight for us on the opposite heading and shouted a warning to our skipper. He put the nose down and the other pilot pulled his up. I heard the noise of the other aircraft's engines roaring across the top of us, it was so near. It was so fortunate that both pilots did the right thing in each case. A couple of feet up or down for either aircraft and we would all have had it. In fact, when we got back Jim told me, 'I was at a stage where I didn't know whether to go up or down, he was so close.'

We continued on the bomb run, dropped our load, then there was a huge explosion and most of the windscreen was blown through. I and the pilot were both looking forward when it went in a *whoof*. There was an explosion of sound as the slipstream whipped in. The pilot thought it had been an attack by an unseen fighter. Maps were whirling round in the cockpit in the freezing wind and we still had to make our way home. All the way to the coast we could still see aircraft being shot down. It was obvious the losses were going to be terrific. For-tunately we weren't hit again and we were very glad to get back to Bardney.[24]

Sgt Ken Hulton was also in that first wave. He remembers:

We were circling for twenty minutes to half an hour before we were called in to bomb. I saw the night fighters shoot down three aircraft in that time. The navigator was informed one was going down, then he was told, 'There's another one, navigator.' Our skipper said, 'Come on, concentrate on this, never mind what's happening elsewhere.' We stuck to the pattern, we were told to orbit and we did. It was pretty nerve-racking, watching out for our own aircraft as well as the other bombers coming in.[25]

Many of those who survived Mailly-le-Camp did so by using their own initiative. Sgt Alf Ridpath, wireless operator in the 49 Sqn crew of P/O Alan Edgar, says:

We were supposed to orbit this yellow marker, but we could see it was going to attract night fighters so we cleared off about 20 miles to the south and orbited there waiting to be called in. While I was there I looked through my window by the set and started to see aircraft going down. You could see some falling away after being hit in an engine or a wing and others just exploded immediately with a vivid flash. I went up in the astrodome at one point and aircraft were going down on the four points of the compass. I counted fourteen aircraft lost in total. It was like daylight under that moon. I was horrified at what I saw. On the set as we waited for instructions all I could hear was a crackling mixed up with this jazz music. There was terrible indiscipline over the air as well. You could hear a lot of Australian and Canadian voices demanding to know why they couldn't go in and bomb. Finally I think our pilot got instructions over the R/T from aircraft to aircraft and went in with his bomb load. The target was well hit, but it was obvious the planning was a total cock-up.[26]

The rush to bomb by the first wave was the stuff of collision nightmares. F/Lt J. F. Adams of 49 Sqn, who bombed at 0017, towards the end of the initial attack, later reported: 'The congestion over the target was ridiculous to a degree of suicide. As we bombed, eight aircraft were seen within 200 yards of us.'[27] In fact, only one-third of 5 Group had bombed by 0016, five minutes after the first attack on the south-eastern aiming point was due to cease. However, Cheshire could see the bombing was accurate and in his post-raid debriefing Deane said the 'No. 1 marker' ordered it to continue.[28]

As the first wave of destruction passed Deane then followed instructions from Cheshire to order a halt to bombing. The plan had been that the second, westerly aiming point would be marked at this time, without the Mosquitos being hit, but in fact Cheshire said in post-raid papers that as 'the bombing never ceased' and bombs were now going down over the entire target he ordered his Mosquito crews to re-mark the original aiming point, 'although the new markers were hardly distinguishable through the smoke'.[29]

W/Cdr Deane reported back at Coningsby that he by 'W/T and R/T ordered cease bombing at 0014' and 'by red star cartridge at 0016'. The second pair of markers completed their work by 0025 and the bombers of 1 Group that had arrived over the assembly point some minutes before and were orbiting, constantly under attack by night fighters, were ordered in. It was now that the greatest chaos ensued as most bomber radio sets again failed to pick up the master bomber's instructions. 'From the many H/F transmissions it was obvious that all had not received message, so repeated continuously on H/F (0029–0033 hours),' Deane reported.[30] The transmissions the master bomber was talking about were the imprecations filling the airwaves, from pilots desperate to escape the carnage over the assembly point and be allowed to bomb.

Rear gunner Sgt Gordon Wallace was on his third operation in the 101 Sqn crew of P/O Tom Welsby. He remembered:

Mailly-le-Camp was undoubtedly the most nerve-racking raid of our tour. We had been briefed for what we considered a routine French trip for which we would be credited one-third of an operation, but approaching the target in the second wave we could see aircraft being shot down. Normally on an operation there was radio silence, but this time we could hear the markers talking to one another as we approached. We couldn't understand why the target wasn't being marked. We were circling round a yellow flare and from the rear turret the sight of aircraft being hit has stayed with me. We heard one crew going down screaming.

One Commonwealth pilot on our squadron called up twice: 'Hello, master bomber, can we come in and bomb?' and both times the reply came back, 'No, do not bomb, continue circling.' He asked again and this time the reply came: 'No, continue circling, what would the Germans think of the RAF?' The pilot replied: 'F— the RAF, we're coming in.' He bombed at the same time as ourselves. We could see the light flak coming up. We were only at 7,000 feet, but luckily we weren't attacked by a night fighter. We were the last back at Ludford Magna, twelve minutes after the preceeding aircraft and had been chalked up as missing. There was the odd remark by crews that it only counted as a third of an operation.[31]

P/O Jack Gagg, the pilot who escaped the night-fighter carnage on the Nuremberg raid because of a late take-off, was among the twenty-four skippers from 166 Sqn, the largest force of any squadron that night, who took part in the Mailly-le-Camp raid.

> It was bright moonlight and I could see all these aircraft circling and I thought, 'Not for me, we're too vulnerable here.' I went round once and could see the fighters coming in and attacking aircraft. In fact, an aircraft went down quite close to us and of course at about 5,000 feet there was very little chance of getting out, so I told the crew, 'I'm going to circle on my own further out, I'll still be able to hear the master bomber when he calls us in.' It was about half an hour, in fact, before we bombed. The night fighters were still attacking, but most of the damage had already been done. We hit the target OK. My bomb aimer was very good, he had been at Oxford before the war and I always said he was too clever to be a pilot.[32]

The 101 Sqn crew in which Sgt Goodliffe was the flight engineer were also experienced enough not to orbit the deadly datum point. He remembers:

> As we approached the target I could see that the Lancasters already orbiting the yellow ground marker under the moon were being shot down at an alarming rate and the degree of brightness from the markers below, coupled with the moonlight, was enough for me to read the identification letters of the bombers. I suggested to the pilot, Ken Fillingham, that we hold off, as to enter the orbit was virtual suicide. Ken, who was only 19 like me, then called upon our navigator, Stan Licquorish, who was 32, to come to the cockpit and advise. He looked out at the massacre and said, 'My God, heads will roll for this – dog-leg north three minutes.' As we turned north I counted the remains of thirteen Lancasters go down after exploding. They had been attacked after their bombs were fused as they were in the target area.
>
> The delay in calling in the second wave to bomb gave the fighters free range in a shooting gallery. A number of pilots who were being attacked while orbiting the marker were shouting things to the master bomber such as, 'Pull your finger out, we're dying out here.' We did hear one Australian pilot, under fighter attack and trying to listen to evasive action from his gunners, call out to those shouting abuse to 'Shut up and give my gunners a chance.'[33]

F/Sgt Roy Ollerhead was a 626 Sqn navigator at Wickenby, an airfield that would show seven empty dispersals in the morning, the night fighters claiming three Lancasters from 626 and four from 12 Sqn, which shared the base. His crew was one of those knowledgeable enough to give the yellow marker a wide berth. He remembers:

> It was our tenth operation and we were in the last wave. It was disastrous as the night fighters had arrived in the clear moonlight and before we got there the crew could see planes going down. It was one of the few occasions I didn't turn my light off in the navigator's position and go and see what was happening. I usually did do that over the target, but I could hear from other members of the crew that aircraft were going down. There was also a lot of Canadian bad language we could hear over the airwaves. Our skipper, F/Lt Ray Ravenhill, decided we would make our own circuit quite a way away and we could see all the night-fighter attacks going on.[34]

F/Lt Ravenhill would later report at Wickenby: 'The assembly point was marked 20 minutes before the main force arrived with the result that enemy aircraft were just orbiting round the markers and shot down Lancasters as they wanted.'[35]

Surely there can have been few more cruelly colourful nights over occupied France that spring than this one – the heavy bombers, their huge fins, fuselages and wings defined in the moonlight, circling the yellow datum markers to the thunder of many Merlins, then one by one exploding in a red flash turning to orange as burning petrol tanks melted away from the plunging wreckage and painted obscenely gaudy trails through the sky. Within sight of those still desperately orbiting, waiting for intelligible instructions, the target glowed with pulsating life, bursting into fresh red flame as the first crews unloaded their high explosive amid the white, green and yellow streams of light flak arcing across the arena.

W/Cdr Deane, who had criss-crossed the target at 2,000 feet at great risk, amid bursting bombs and exploding flak as his Lancaster 'did everything except stand upright', reported later: 'Reception of Channel C HF was very bad owing to British broadcast being on the same frequency apparently.'[36] In fact, most crews reported hearing an *American* broadcast drowning out the master bomber's messages, 550 Sqn skipper F/Sgt D. M. Salmon reporting when back safely at North Killingholme:

'One didn't know whether to go in and bomb or stay "Deep in the Heart of Texas".'[37] However, Deane's deputy, S/Ldr Neville Sparks, could see orbiting aircraft were not apparently receiving the master bomber's instructions and had sent out his own order to bomb, on VHF at 0033.[38] By that time Major Martin Drewes of III/NJG1 had arrived in the area, had shot down two Lancasters and would shoot down three more before 0050.[39] The other ace flying that night, Hptmn Helmut Bergmann, of III/NJG4, shot down six bombers within twenty-nine minutes, beginning at 0010 as 5 Group orbited the assembly point. He received the Knight's Cross on 9 June 1944 and was shot down and killed less than a month later by a Mosquito intruder.[40]

As aircraft of 1 Group in the second wave picked up the deputy master bomber's instructions and turned south to begin their bombing runs they were joined by others who realised the second attack was now on, including some crews of 5 Group, yet to bomb, who had wisely stayed away from the datum marker that had claimed so many of their colleagues. The result was a mêlée, which even exceeded that of the attack on the first markers. The operational record book of 550 Sqn later summed up: 'When the order to bomb was finally given the rush, to quote W/O J. M. Knox [a Canadian bomb aimer] in 'D', was like the starting gate at the Derby.'[41]

Dennis Goodliffe says: 'The dog-leg we made I am sure saved our lives. We had a clear run through the target and bombed. The 4,000-pounders going off below gave us quite a buffeting as we were so low.'[42] Roy Ollerhead remembers: 'We could hear the master bomber's instructions ordering us to go in and bomb, but barely so because we were a bit too far away I think. Anyway we went in and bombed and didn't get any flak, so weren't damaged. We were straight in and out.'[43]

Those Cookies were having a devastating effect on the 21st Panzer Group. In all 1,500 tons of bombs were dropped with great accuracy. A report after the raid by 21st Panzer's commander said bombs hit 114 barrack buildings and 47 transport sheds and ammunition buildings. A total of 102 vehicles, including 43 tanks were destroyed, 218 German soldiers – most of them Panzer NCOs – were killed and 156 wounded. Nearly all the casualties died from bomb splinters or blast collapsing the lungs, but some were buried alive when Cookies exploding near by caused their slit trenches to collapse and a few drowned when the camp water tower was holed and the deluge rapidly filled their narrow earth shelter.[44] Ironically it was the final attack, between 0026 and 0034 hours, which caused the greatest destruction and some casualties occurred because soldiers used the short break in the bombing to try to recover weapons and gear and were then caught in the open by the new deluge of bombs.[45] There were no French casualties in the nearby village through bombing, but some civilians were killed when a shot-down Lancaster fell on a house.

One of the aircraft badly damaged over Mailly was that of P/O Ted Ball, of 49 Sqn. He was meant to bomb in the first wave with the rest of 5 Group, but in fact dropped his Cookie at 0031, the time of the second, because he had orbited the datum point for thirty minutes, unable to receive radio signals. Eventually P/O Ball began his run-in. His rear gunner, Sgt Ron Eeles, remembered:

> There was a blinding pink red flash along the port side of the aircraft followed immediately by the pilot saying (not shouting): 'Christ, put on chutes, chaps.' Within a second of this the plane was hit again by flak along the fuselage. There was a sizzling sound in the intercom and it went dead. The pink red glow on the port side persisted and I assumed we were on fire.
>
> I was disconnecting my electric suit plug and leaving my flying helmet on the seat when I now come to the point that has always mystified me and to this day I still think of it at times . . . I had a vision of my mother's face outside of the turret and she was saying, 'Jump son, jump.'[46]

Sgt Eeles got to the rear door despite the fact that the fuselage was full of smoke and the aircraft apparently out of control. There the mid-upper gunner was already going out and Sgt Eeles followed. In fact, P/O Ball managed to bring his aircraft home with great difficulty, later reporting that he had been hit by flak on the point of bombing and had to jettison, the intercom then going dead after the order to put on chutes, possibly because of a fighter attack.* 'The engineer, Sgt Eric Wardman, saw the enemy aircraft on the starboard quarter up,' he said at debriefing. 'I continued violent turns down to zero feet. The starboard outer engine was feathered due to being on fire and the port outer was only giving half power.'[47]

* The apparent apparition probably did save Sgt Eeles's life. P/O Ball and his crew were killed bombing a V-weapon site on 8 July, believed shot down by another Lancaster.

Another 49 Sqn skipper, the New Zealander P/O Bill Green, had one of the most harrowing experiences over the Panzer camp, reporting cryptically at Fiskerton: 'While on bombing run aircraft ahead blew up and ours sustained damage to Perspex nose and windscreen. Log and chart blew away. Harassed by fighters from target ... homed on Gee from French coast.'[48] The fighters, in fact, pursued most of the bombers out of the target, shooting down several as they put the nose down to gain speed for the beckoning coastline.

By now four of the 101 Sqn aircraft had been lost and another fell on that homeward leg. Only the rear gunner survived and his escape was remarkable. Sgt Jack Worsfold heard his skipper F/Lt John Keard call 'bale out' after a night fighter set the starboard engine and fuselage on fire and reached for his parachute in its tray behind him to find it in shreds. Again the night fighter attacked and the aircraft exploded. The 19-year-old gunner found himself trapped in the tail, upside down, then somersaulting. Something hit him hard in the ribs and he passed out. He woke up in a smouldering gorse bush near Troyes with a broken thigh, rib fractures and a broken finger. He discovered later that the tail section of the Lancaster, with him inside, had fallen 1½ miles, hit some high-tension wires and bounced onto a tree before coming to ground, tipping him out.[49]

As the bombers orbited Mailly, then flew away pursued by the night fighters, Frenchmen on the ground watched the torment. One of them was André Guillet, a 23-year-old father of two girls, who had been sent to work in Germany the summer before for the Service du Travail Obligatoire. He had escaped and was now in hiding at Donnemarie-Dontilly, between Mailly-le-Camp and Paris, working with the Resistance. He remembers:

> Every night Allied aircraft were flying over my village. They were on their way to bomb German military targets. But on the night of 3/4 May 1944, unlike the other nights, the aircraft were moving round in the sky. They were shot at by both the German anti-aircraft defences and the German night fighters. My parents, my wife and I had gone out to watch what was happening. It was between midnight and 1 a.m. when a flash split the darkness. My mother told me: 'They have just launched a rocket.' I answered: 'No, the aircraft is on fire.' I had already seen such an event in Germany.
>
> The aircraft candled and began to fall. At approximately 3,000 feet

the front of the aircraft exploded and fell in a small grove 60 feet from the road and 160 feet from the nearest house. Our house was 1,600 feet from it. My father and I immediately went to the place where the aircraft had crashed. It was still burning. Shortly afterwards German soldiers came in a van from the castle in the village, where they were stationed, and ordered us to leave.

The day after, my wife and I went near the spot. We could see the turret of the aircraft had fallen into a field about 1,000 feet from the rest of the aircraft. Near it lay the body of an airman who must have been thrown out. He was sitting with his parachute still fastened up and had made a hole in the ground. The tail of the aircraft was intact about 2,000 feet away. The other six members of the crew had died in the burning aircraft.

Hiding behind bushes we watched the Germans bury the body of the Allied airman after taking off his boots and putting on gloves to raise the body. They gave the town council the job of burying the remains of the other six airmen in the cemetery of Donnemarie-en-Montois. I had made a frame into which the English and French flags were drawn with the comment: 'Glory to the Allied Airmen.' Women from the village put flowers on the grave. When the Germans found out they dug up the bodies and had them transferred to the cemetery in the village of Dontilly where they have lain to this day. I had found a watch in the remnants of the front of the aircraft. On the back of it the name Baskerville* was written. I also found a cigarette case. I gave these objects to the families of the aircrew when the war was over.[50]

ONLY 312 aircraft returned from Mailly of the 362 that had set out, eight had come back early with various faults, but now more than forty lay as scrap in France, a stunning loss rate. Among them was the 83 Sqn aircraft of the deputy master bomber, S/Ldr Neville Sparks, shot down on the way back near Orbais in the Marne region. Sparks and most of the crew evaded and were home within weeks. P/O Berryman, the newcomer on 467 Sqn, also returned safely to base, though his tour was short. He was killed attacking a V1 site at Prouville on 24 June. The

---

* The watch belonged to Canadian bomb aimer P/O Norman George Baskerville, 24, of Toronto. He died with the rest of the crew of P/O Cyril Bell, of 207 Sqn, shot down by a night fighter. Bell's flight engineer, Sgt Raymond Dance, was just 18.

squadron had only lost one aircraft at Mailly, but there was some rancour from returning crews at what they had experienced. P/O J. W. McManus, who had flown the squadron's veteran S-Sugar many times, told intelligence officers: 'The target tactics were definitely considered most unnecessary. Aircraft should be timed to bomb within five minutes of zero, thus eliminating the odd half an hour of orbit which causes these unnecessary losses. Consider one third of operations most unjust.'[51] His fellow skipper, P/O H. W. Coulson, put it more succinctly: 'If this is a third of a trip I'm verging on LMF.'[52]

However, it was another of the Australian squadrons, 460 at Binbrook, that suffered the most, losing five of the seventeen crews it sent and the other aircraft lent to 101 Sqn; 101 Sqn lost four aircraft and five crews. Only five men, including Sgt Worsfold, survived that night of those seventy-four highly trained aircrew flying in 460 Sqn or 101 Sqn. The very first aircraft to have been shot down on the raid was the Lancaster in which the flight engineer was Stan Rodway, who had been wrestling with Sgt Goodliffe at dispersal before take-off. The bomb aimer was the only survivor from the crash.

Dennis Goodliffe remembers:

When we got back we realised four of our aircraft had gone. I and Tom McDonald came back, but Stan Rodway's aircraft, SR-A, was shot down to the west of Reims. As I walked back to my bed with my head down, thinking about the good friends I had lost, I passed an engineer officer. He shouted after me, 'Don't you normally salute when you see an officer?' I told him that when he got to the Flights he'd realise why nobody was seeing much that morning.[53]

Within days 5 Group's operational record book had been compiled for the raid and it stressed that not only had RT communication been badly interrupted by a station 'broadcasting American news', but that 'the W/T transmitter in the leader's aircraft was at least 30 kilocycles off frequency'.[54]

Leonard Cheshire had been appalled by the sight of so many bombers going down in vivid orange fire around him. In a wide-ranging interview for the Imperial War Museum sound archives in 1987 Cheshire himself brought up the subject of Mailly-le-Camp. 'All worked well until just after dropping the marker and confirming it was accurate,' he said, presumably referring to the first marker.

I looked up and saw two aircraft shot down before they had even reached the target. I knew that meant the Luftwaffe was up in force, it was bright moonlight and our aircraft didn't have a chance, so I immediately gave the order – rightly or wrongly – to abandon the attack and go home and it didn't get through on VHF. I got all my other aircraft to try and get through. I tried W/T ... I never got that message through.[55]

Dennis Goodliffe can confirm Cheshire's anguish. He says:

I met him at a reunion for survivors after the war and he told me he questioned the whole operation before taking off for Mailly-le-Camp. It was such a tight corner trying to avoid damage to French property and civilians. The target itself was so small it had to be done visually and that caused the delay. He also wasn't happy about using the yellow marker and the raid being carried out in bright moonlight ... He told me it was the worst twenty minutes of his life trying to get the master bomber to call off the raid when he saw so many going down, but could not get through to him.[56]

It was obvious nothing like it could be allowed to occur again and when 5 Group was called on eight days later to attack another large military camp, at Bourg Leopold in Belgium, and once more a yellow datum marker was used, the raid was quickly abandoned by the master bomber after only half the 190-strong force had bombed because of difficulty in marking the target in hazy conditions. Some crews still had problems with their radio sets, however, F/O T. P. Jupp of 83 Sqn later reporting: 'VHF reception was very poor, high pitched – particularly on Channel B.'[57] And as it was the raid did last long enough for a few night fighters to appear, shooting down the Lancaster of the Australian 467 Sqn CO, John Balmer, on his bombing run, killing him on the last trip of his second tour.

Sgt Alf Ridpath was in one of the 49 Sqn aircraft on the operation, his third since Mailly-le-Camp. Two nights before he had taken part in a small 5 Group raid to an aircraft-engine factory near Paris in which five of the fifty-six aircraft were lost and his own aircraft had been attacked by a fighter as he tried to write down a Morse message, 'pencils and rubbers flying up to the ceiling', in the corkscrew as he listened to 'the rattle of machine-gun fire like hailstones on a tin roof'. Approaching the

Dutch coast they had been attacked and escaped again, Sgt Ridpath 'instinctively ducking even though I knew it didn't do any good'.

He remembers:

Bourg Leopold we thought was going to be a cake walk, it was only a short trip of two and three-quarter hours. We had been ordered not to bomb and were on our way home with the bombs and almost at the point where you think it's safe to get the Thermos flask out. The navigator had just taken a fix as we approached the Dutch coast and immediately there was a crash, bang, wallop as this fighter attacked from below. A cannon shell went right through the rear gunner's parachute stowed behind him, another burst the Elsan toilet and there was chemical fluid all over the floor. The pilot, P/O Alan Edgar, immediately put the aircraft into a dive, we opened the bomb doors and we let the bombs go. I think the night fighter thought the bombs were us going in and that's why he didn't come back. The gunners never saw the fighter so I think it must have been Schräge Musik. The aircraft was in a terrible state, there were dozens of holes in it. All aileron control had been lost and the aircraft kept pitching up, then diving, like a bucking bronco.

It took the pilot, the flight engineer George Bedford and the bomb aimer Alan Millard on the controls together to try to get it level. The pilot had his leg round the control column trying to hold it back. They got a rope round the column eventually. There was surplus oil on fire in the fuselage. I stamped on the flames in my flying boots and the mid-upper gunner, Johnny Watters, came out of his turret and beat it out with his gloves. I didn't think we would make it home and I don't think the pilot did. We had a vote about whether to bale out. The pilot said he thought it was best if we abandoned the aircraft. I said, 'We're over the North Sea and I can't swim, I vote to stay.' We all decided to stay because we realised the pilot would have had no chance at all to hold the aircraft after we had jumped. I radioed base to tell them what a mess we were in and we were told to try to make our way to Woodbridge.* The pilot told us to get to our crash stations as we

---

* RAF Woodbridge in Suffolk had been specially constructed to save bomber crews returning in trouble, often without hydraulic power to operate flaps or brakes. Its runway was 3,000 yards long (compared to the average 2,000) and 250 yards wide (80 normally) with 500 yards of grass undershoot and 1,000 yards of grass overshoot. During intensive raiding periods the verges were often littered with crashed aircraft, hurriedly pushed aside. In 1944 alone 2,424 Allied aircraft had cause to use it.

approached Woodbridge and we got in OK. The aircraft was riddled, it was like a colander, but none of us had got so much as a scratch in the attack. It wasn't until we landed that I noticed the terrible smell from the Elsan.

We left the aircraft at Woodbridge. It was later rebuilt and went to 619 Sqn. We asked to come home on the train, but we were told to wait for an aircraft to pick us up. We got a 48-hour pass at base and when we got back to Fiskerton there was a brand-new aircraft that had just been delivered, designated EA-A, like the other.

The pilot was awarded an immediate DFC, but the trip still only counted as a third of an operation. 'There was nearly a revolution about that,' Sgt Ridpath remembers. 'I heard one aircrew complaining that you had to get killed three times for it to count as a trip.'[58]

In fact, a change was already on the way. The commanders of 1 and 5 Groups, the two Lincolnshire-based forces that had been so mauled at Mailly-le-Camp, had expressed 'strong views' to Bomber Command headquarters at High Wycombe about how resentful crews were about the third-of-an-op edict and the views of all the group heads had been sought. Harris's deputy, Air Marshal Sir Robert Saundby, wrote to the group chiefs in May:

> There is evidently real feeling among Lancaster and Halifax III crews that as they carry the weight of attack on Germany they should be allowed to offset this by counting full marks for operations against more lightly defended areas. This is not an unreasonable view ... we can now count on summer outputs from training organizations so that the crew prospects are very much better than they were two months ago and the ruling as to the third of a sortie may, therefore, be said to have achieved its purpose.

He suggested that the operational tour for Lancaster and Halifax III crews go back to thirty. But at the same time he put forward the view that the tours of Stirling and Halifax II and V crews, which did not operate over Germany, be raised to forty.[59]

What had looked like a burgeoning mutiny on some squadrons was now over.

12

Return to the Reich

In the midst of the propaganda and hyperbole newspapers could often put their finger on changes in the air war. The day after the attrition by night fighters at Mailly-le-Camp had been woefully calculated, the *Daily Mail* reported: 'In switching his fighters to the defence of the invasion targets in France the enemy has obviously decided on the RAF main bomber forces staying out of Reich territory while the Moon is up.'[1]

As the moon waned it would be time to return to Germany again, to keep the Luftwaffe on the defensive and remove any belief that the Reich was safe while the invasion beckoned and that its hammered industry could be replenished. Tactically it was necessary to raid Germany whenever possible to stop the Luftwaffe high command shifting *Nachtjäger* units from Luftflotte Reich to Luftflotte 3, covering France. But it was known the price of raiding the Reich would always be high, partly because of the longer time required over enemy territory. Operations on three German cities over two nights in May cost a total of sixty Lancasters.

The largest single force was reserved for Duisburg on 21 May, a town that hadn't been raided for a year. Harris sent 510 Lancasters. Flight engineer Sgt Tom Howie was on his way to the target with the rest of his 460 Sqn crew in the anonymity of the night when the rear gunner's turret light came on at 22,000 feet, advertising the aircraft to any searching night fighter. He remembers:

We could see the light shining in the fuselage, but couldn't raise the rear gunner on the intercom, so the skipper asked the wireless operator to go back and get it turned off. The wireless operator reported the turret was turned onto the beam and he couldn't get in, so the pilot told him to take the fire axe and hack his way into the turret to put the light out. The wireless operator hacked his way in and got the light out. He could see the gunner slumped over the guns and thought he was dead from oxygen failure.

The wireless operator needed to get back to the astrodome to search the sky for fighters and I was busy chucking out Window. I was surrounded by it, there were so many packets I could hardly move. After we'd bombed and descended below oxygen height a voice came on the intercom. It was the rear gunner asking: 'Are we at the target yet?' It was like hearing a ghost. We pulled him out of his turret and one hand, which he had left exposed, was like white plasticine. A coupling had come loose on his oxygen hose, but he must have just been getting a trickle of oxygen, which kept him alive.[2]

Much of Duisburg had escaped damage. It was within Oboe range, but the target was cloud-covered and the Pathfinders' red target indicators that followed the Oboe-directed TIs soon disappeared. W/Cdr Malcolm Crocker, who believed in leading 49 Sqn from the front, reported at debriefing: 'Widely scattered red TIs seen disappearing immediately into cloud. No skymarkers, making identification of target impossible. The poorest show ever seen'; and he added 'heavy fighter opposition'.[3] The fighters had indeed been active, claiming most of the twenty-nine Lancasters lost.

One of them was that of Sgt Russell Margerison, the 625 Sqn gunner, who had found the London public so grateful after his crashlanding coming back from Nuremberg.

We had turned early onto the target and this put us ahead of the bomber stream and we were on our return home at 23,000 feet. We had gone through a lot of heavy flak, then it was quiet. The pilot had just been told by the navigator it was half an hour to the coast when a stream of tracer came from our port side up. I heard the sound of heavy cannon and it was pouring straight through. It was a pitch-black night and it was obvious a fighter had been vectored onto us. He must have seen us at the last second, nearly crashing into us and had opened fire and broken away. The two port engines were on fire and we were in a tremendous dive, the centrifugal force meant you couldn't move. Someone was shouting, 'Pull the bugger out.'

From my mid-upper turret I could see strips of metal peeling off the tailplane and careering away exposing the framework. The pilot and engineer did manage to level the aircraft out enough for five of us to bale out. When I climbed down from my turret and leaned against the side of the fuselage it was like a blow torch inside. I couldn't see through the flames to the front at all. I never put my chute in its stowage. I just used to drop it on the floor below my turret and after a trip it was usually somewhere at the back of the aircraft. On this occasion it was exactly where I left it and as I picked it up, flames were licking around it. The rear gunner had opened the back door and gone, but I couldn't clip my chute on. I leaned against the fuselage and thought, 'You've had it, this is it'; but then I roused myself and had one last go and found the clips. I got to the back door, knelt down and was sucked out by the slipstream. I pulled the ripcord, then as I hung beneath the chute I heard the German fighter coming closer and I thought he was going to hit me, but he flew away. I think he was just having a look at the Lancaster. I must have been suffering from lack of oxygen because I was convinced I was going up instead of down. I watched the aircraft curl round as it went down and crash.

Neither the pilot nor the engineer got out. The wireless operator, who was one of the three to go through the front hatch, told me later he had seen the two of them with their arms around the control column pulling as hard as they could to keep the Lanc reasonably straight to enable everybody else to get out.

It took about a quarter of an hour for me to come down. I landed in the middle of a Belgian cornfield. I released my harness, then as I was hidden in the corn decided to inflate my Mae West, wrap myself up in the chute and get some sleep. At dawn I knocked on the door of a farmhouse nearby. I told the farmer I wanted a drink and he slammed the door, but he came back with some ersatz coffee and slammed the door again. I started walking and got onto a cobbled road. Whenever I heard someone coming I jumped in the ditch, then by mid-afternoon I came across two women talking. One thought the invasion had started and said, 'Boy, you've arrived.' I told her I was on my own but the invasion force was coming soon. As I was talking to her a farmer came along with a cartload of logs and motioned for me to get under the pile. That night I was put in touch with the Underground and met

Dick Reeves the wireless operator. We were in the care of the Resistance for ten or eleven weeks, but eventually a bunch of us were betrayed
and put in the hands of German military intelligence in Antwerp.[4]

Later Sgt Margerison was taken to prison camp at Bankau.

HARRIS, who had fought so hard to continue his assault on Germany's
economy while the major plan – quite rightly as events would soon
prove – was to use his force for pre-invasion targeting, sent 361 Lancasters back to the Ruhr again the next night with a raid on Dortmund
and dispatched another 225 to Brunswick. He had already argued
strongly that any cessation in ruining the Reich would give the Germans
time to make good what damage Bomber Command had already achieved. Dortmund, subjected to the heaviest raid of the war on 4 May the
previous year, notwithstanding the earlier 1,000-bomber operations, was
a classic example, he believed, and since Bomber Command had visited
it in force its industrial capacity had increased. Brunswick (which had
provided Cheshire with his first opportunity of low-level marking on a
German city on 22 April but with disappointing results because of poor
visibility and communication problems between the bomber controllers)
was being visited again to give 5 Group another chance. Other sizeable
Transportation Plan raids were being made on Le Mans and Orléans.

Many of Harris's crews, who had welcomed the shorter hauls in May
to France and Belgium, now feared that the no-moon period would
mean a new period of attrition over Germany before the invasion,
whenever that might come. Occasionally an airman would have a premonition that this would be his last flight, going through the preparations
for operating on that last day and eventually courageously taking off,
knowing there would be no return, but still being willing to go and face
the inevitable.

F/O Douglas Hudson, a navigator who won the DFC flying with 100
Sqn from Grimsby, saw it happen twice, the second time before the
Dortmund raid. F/O Hudson was on his second operational tour in the
first half of 1944. His first tour had ended in August 1940, when his
Blenheim had to crashland in Tunisia after running short of fuel en route
to Malta. He had then spent more than two years slowly starving in
three successive Vichy French POW camps in North Africa – including
Laghouat in the Sahara desert – his salvation being the Red Cross parcels
that reached the camps throughout his incarceration. He was liberated

as a result of the Allied landings in Algiers in November 1942.

He remembers that the first time someone in his presence admitted knowing they were doomed was as officers queued in the mess at Grimsby for afternoon tea.

> This navigator* had just come back from leave and looked so ill. One or two of the guys said it was nice to see him back again and he said in passing he knew the next operation he went on he wouldn't be returning from. He said, 'I know we're not coming back,' and sure enough within a day or two he and his crew were lost.
>
> Then another time we were about to go to the crew bus on a lovely late spring evening and I could hear a blackbird singing. I remarked to another navigator it was a beautiful evening and he said, 'It's a bloody awful evening, I know we're not coming back.' I think I said something like, 'Come off it, old boy, I'll see you for the bacon and eggs when we return,' but I didn't see him at breakfast and he hadn't in fact returned.† Sometimes you could see the fear in someone's eyes in the crew bus and often they were the ones who didn't come back. I also used to find that often a married man would go missing on his first operation back from leave.[5]

The aircraft of the 100 Sqn navigator was one of two from the squadron lost on the Dortmund raid, which claimed eighteen aircraft in all, 4.8 per cent, most of them falling to night fighters. The engineer in another aircraft lost, from 166 Sqn, was aged 45. Sgt Cyril Webb thus became one of the oldest airmen to be killed in Bomber Command in 1944. His was an unusual crew, the two air gunners who died with him were both Belgians serving in the RAF.[6] The raid they died on, like the one the night before, had mixed success, most of the attack falling in south-eastern Dortmund. The smaller Brunswick raid lost fewer aircraft, thirteen, but the percentage loss rate was higher, 5.5.

Nights over Germany or its approaches in an RAF bomber were still

---

* F/O Edward Bashi, a 26-year-old Iraqi, was killed with all but one of the crew of P/O William Bell on the Friedrichshafen raid of 27 April, their aircraft coming down near Vittel in France.
† This is likely to have been F/O A. T. Sparks, navigator in the crew of F/Lt J. C. Kennedy, RCAF, who took off for Dortmund at 1944 on 23 May. Their aircraft was coned between Bonn and Cologne and set on fire by flak. The whole crew baled out from around 15,000 feet and survived to become POWs.

a gamble against the odds in which even the most experienced airman could see his tour end tragically in seconds. F/Sgt Dick Raymond was a case in point. Few had a more eventful tour than the teenaged flight engineer. He had survived his Lancaster blowing up on his airfield way back in November, a near crashlanding on the Nuremberg raid, and then being coned over Munich in April. He remembers:

We were hit by a night fighter with Schräge Musik over Holland on the way in. I was in the nose chucking out Window when the rear gunner called out 'Fighter' and at the same time we were hit, bang. The next minute the whole aircraft was on fire, the intercom had gone and I ripped the escape hatch open and as those hatches did, it jammed in the entrance. In my panic I got it free and out I went. There's no question of lying on your back to pull the ripcord or anything like that, you just pulled it as quick as possible. I remember feeling the blast as the aircraft blew up and I thought, 'God I'm the only one out.' I was to have been best man at the skipper's wedding on the Saturday and the first thought that went through my mind was, 'I've missed the blooming wedding.' I didn't know if I was over land or sea, but that was what I was concerned about.

Fortunately I was over land and came down soon afterwards in a field. I desperately tried to bury my parachute as per instructions, breaking my finger nails, when some Dutch people came along. Much later I learned they dug it up again to make underclothes. They took care of me, offering me black bread and goat's milk – the last thing I wanted having fallen out of the sky. The next day they called a doctor who put me on the back of his motorcycle and took me across the dykes to his house. I almost enjoyed it, it was a beautiful May morning and his family came to meet me. One of his daughters I still meet today. He looked me over and I was just sprained and bruised. He explained that the Germans knew where I was and they couldn't do anything else for me other than treating me as a friend. Then this German arrived, stuck a gun in my ribs and told me, 'Don't try to escape,' and took me to the nearest police station. Who should be there but Ken Lane, my skipper. He had been wearing a seat-type chute and was blown out when the aircraft exploded and came to in his chute.

We were taken to hospital at Groningen where we met our Canadian wireless operator Stanley Aspinall, who had been quite seriously injured. I imagine he and the bomb aimer had just had time to clip their chutes on when the aircraft exploded. Ken and I then went by rail to Amsterdam and somewhere along the line Don Cope our bomb aimer joined us. The train ground to a halt during the journey and we got strafed by the Americans. The Dutch people dived out but this German guard with us cocked his rifle and said, 'This is not war,' and made us sit there. Fortunately the fighters only peppered the engine. We eventually got to Amsterdam and were put in solitary confinement for a week or ten days in the city jail. We were then taken from Amsterdam main railway station, where the Dutch were giving us V signs, to a place on the Dutch–German border.

This was the first time we saw a bit of brutality because our bomb aimer wanted a pee and they wouldn't let him go to the door and he eventually peed himself all over the floor. The guard hit him on the head with his rifle. We were then taken down the Rhine through Cologne to Frankfurt and arrived in the early hours of the morning just after the Allies had bombed the place. We didn't get a very good reception, the civilians would have had us if the guards hadn't formed a ring around us. They were trying to hit us with umbrellas and calling us baby killers and *Schweinehunds*. We then got another train to Dulag Luft. There were so many aircrew turning up at that time we were rushed through and we were sent to Stalag Luft VII at Bankau in no time. We arrived on the morning of D-Day. Bankau was new then and my POW number was 47.[7]

The navigator and both gunners in W/O Lane's aircraft had not survived the fighter attack and explosion, but Sgt Raymond was able to keep his appointment to be best man at his skipper's wedding when they came back from prison camp. W/O Lane was Sgt Raymond's best man five years later.

The operations to Dortmund and Brunswick were Harris's last major raids on German industrial targets until late July due to commitments in Normandy. As with Dortmund the results in Brunswick were a disappointment. It had been covered by cloud, which 5 Group's low-level marking technique couldn't cope with any better than Bennett's Pathfinders had.

However, Harris could look back on the spring with some satisfaction as the period of softening up the Germans in their homeland and containing them in Normandy prior to the invasion entered its final days.

From 1 April to 5 June 24,060 sorties were flown by Bomber Command from which 525, aircraft were lost. It made an average of 2.2 per cent. In the previous period of four and a half months covering the Battle of Berlin and Nuremberg 29,449 sorties were flown, from which 1,117 aircraft were lost, 3.8 per cent.[8] Notwithstanding the dreadful toll on some squadrons of operations such as Mailly-le-Camp, Trappes and Schweinfurt, the average percentage loss compared to the start of the year was now approaching half.

Bomber Command was winning the night war against the Luftwaffe. Harris had an average of 1,000 heavy bombers available every day at this time; the Luftwaffe had approximately the same number of night fighters – on paper. In fact, the Transportation Plan attacks cutting off supplies of spares, the presence of Mosquito intruders over Luftwaffe bases and the attacks on German industry had combined to reduce the nightly availability to approximately 400 aircraft and crews.[9] Many of those were in the homeland, defending German cities. When the invasion came they would not be in the skies to threaten the airborne troops, the landing craft or the bombers and fighters laying waste to the enemy defences as had been feared. The sacrifices of Bomber Command over the winter and spring had not been for naught. Now the stage was set for the greatest military enterprise of the century and the men of Bomber Command were about to be called on to play a vital role.

SUMMER

13

The Longest Night

The dawn of a new age that D-Day promised was heralded by Bomber Command in the night. As the invasion fleet set sail in darkness Bomber Command flew 1,211 sorties – the greatest total yet – in support, bombing German gun batteries and troop emplacements facing the five Normandy beaches and beyond. The crews took off, unaware that the invasion was on, many being shocked as they returned over the Channel to see beneath them the greatest armada ever to set forth. The 5,267 tons of bombs the crews had dropped in two hours had been meant to stun the German troops facing this invasion, but the most important facet in the D-Day plan did not involve weaponry. It was the deception plan Fortitude, in which the Allies had played on the paranoia engendered by defence strategy and persuaded the Germans that the main invasion would indeed be in the logistically easier Pas-de-Calais, as they believed.

Of the bombers out that night 110 had been taking part in operations designed to convince the Wehrmacht that the real invasion forces would make a landfall between Boulogne and Le Havre. It succeeded so well Hitler and OKW kept the main elements of the Fifteenth Army, with its much-needed armour, in the Pas-de-Calais until late July. Two virtual convoys, codenamed 'Taxable' and 'Glimmer' were created by forces of aircraft dropping Window at precise intervals and places across the Channel while the real Overlord convoy was masked by a screen of twenty radar-jamming Stirlings and Flying Fortresses. Other bombers had already destroyed the six long-range reporting stations south of Boulogne and fifteen others in the area were made unserviceable, leaving large stretches of the Channel coast devoid of radar cover. For long periods of the night of 5/6 June only 5 per cent of the radar cover in north-west France was in operation.[1]

The key players in the Taxable plan were the precision flyers of 617 Sqn, dropping a dense screen of Window that advanced slowly across the Channel to simulate a large convoy setting out from Littlehampton towards the French coast north of Le Havre. They had been practising since the beginning of May, the Lancaster crews flying no other operations. Among the 617 Sqn skippers was the Dams Raid veteran S/Ldr Les Munro, who had the squadron commander, W/Cdr Leonard Cheshire, flying as his co-pilot in Taxable. S/Ldr Munro says:

> When we eventually found we did not have an attacking role on D-Day it disappointed most of us and although Cheshire never expressed his personal feelings I am sure he was less than thrilled at not seeing any action. Each plane carried thirteen or fourteen crew as it had been decided that because of the repetitive and tedious nature of the operation and the need to maintain the utmost accuracy – any deviation could possibly show up on the German radar and arouse suspicions – all crew positions would be duplicated. In my case I flew the first spell and Cheshire, who was on board as my second pilot, flew the second, making a total of two hours before the next wave of eight aircraft took over. It required intense concentration not only on the outward and inward legs, but at the turns at the end of each oblong circuit. It was not hazardous however.

The next day there was no doubt though about how important and successful Operation Taxable had been. Munro says:

> I have always considered the operation to be in one sense among the most important the squadron carried out in my time – not because of bad weather, nor because of any threat of enemy action and not measured by any visual result, but because of the very exacting requirements to which we had to fly and navigate. There was absolutely no latitude for deviation from ground speed, compass bearings, rate of turn and timing. Navigators played a major role in adherence to all those factors.[2]

The Glimmer convoy, appearing on German radar screens as moving from Folkestone to Boulogne, was in fact six Stirlings of 218 Sqn, each carrying three navigators. Other Stirlings dropped Ruperts – dummy paratroopers – near Yvetot, north of Le Havre, to give the impression of an airborne landing north of the Seine in the area of Fifteenth Army, as part of operations codenamed Titanic. Several more Stirlings and Halifaxes in the Titanic plan dropped Window and noise-making Ruperts south of the American parachute-drop zones.

To prevent the German night-fighter force discovering the ruse of ghost convoys and fake paratrooper landings the twenty-four Lancasters of 101 Sqn were called on to play their part in the deception plan with the three ABC transmitters each aircraft had to drown German *Nachtjäger* frequencies. They flew a repeated course establishing a jamming screen between Hastings and Amiens and dropping Window to simulate a Main Force bombing stream. Luftwaffe night fighters took off to engage the non-existent stream and three 101 Sqn aircraft were fired on, but the actual force of D-Day bombers attacking strongpoints in Normandy and the aircraft towing gliders were largely unaffected by night fighters. The contribution of 101 Sqn had been one of the most vital to the success of D-Day.[3]

F/Sgt Graham Boytell, the ABC operator whose baptism of fire had been the Nuremberg operation, recalls:

On the night of 5/6 June we flew from dusk to dawn from the Channel coast to a point near Paris and back, repeating the route many times. We were at 26,000 feet because we didn't have any bombs and we special operators were briefed to keep the radio band we worked on fully jammed all night. We just switched on the transmitters and left them on. In fact it was rather a boring night for an ABC operator, but at about 4 a.m. we saw the gliders going into France. Afterwards it gave us a good feeling to say we took part in D-Day.[4]

Sgt Peter Kaye was another 101 Sqn special operator taking part in the deception. He remembers:

At briefing we were told there would be no single or twin-engined aircraft of ours operating that night and the gunnery leader made a point of saying, 'Any you see you are expected to destroy.' Over northern France the rear gunner spotted a twin-engined aircraft coming in directly astern and opened fire. Then the aircraft seemed to break off into the moon path and the mid-upper started firing, but was told to stop by the rear gunner as he realised it was a Mossie. The other aircraft didn't open fire and we weren't damaged. We reported it at debriefing and rather expected to get a rocket later if a Mosquito reported being fired at by a Lancaster, but we heard nothing more about it.[5]

In fact, Bomber Command's operations over the Reich, keeping a large part of the *Nachtjäger* strength on the nightly front line of Germany's cities, helped to ensure the Luftwaffe was hardly in evidence on D-Day. During the first 24 hours of the campaign only thirty-six Luftwaffe aircraft were seen.[6] This alone was a considerable contribution by Bomber Command to the success of the invasion. Fighters in force over the beaches would have turned each of them into a killing ground, far greater than that of the 3,000-plus loss on the toughest landing point, Omaha.

The 101 Sqn information that all twin-engined aircraft seen over Normandy would be Luftwaffe was clearly wrong and there were forty-nine Mosquito sorties on D-Day, supporting ground operations. F/Lt Robert Bray, a pilot on 105 Sqn, flying from Bourn on his second tour, was not alone in making two trips to Normandy on D-Day. He remembers:

We had a vague idea something was happening because there was an obvious build-up, but I don't think we were told until an hour or so before take-off what it was all about. We took off in the early hours of 6 June to make one trip to the French coast to mark a gun emplacement at Longues near Cherbourg for seventy-one heavy bombers. I remember my flares were three TI reds and one TI green from 18,000 feet and the zero hour was 0420.

We then came back and took off again, after refuelling and bombing up, for Coutances where we were Oboe-marking a road junction for 100 heavies. Halfway down the run-in at 22,000 feet I looked back and was startled to see an aircraft very close behind on the same track and height. My immediate thought was it was a night fighter, but it turned out to be another 105 Sqn aircraft also using Oboe Mk III multi-channel tracking. It was quite a relief. I don't remember it as particularly exhausting, doing the two trips within a short period. From East Anglia to the French coast and back wasn't more than an hour and a bit in a Mossie and including the time for loading up again the whole thing wouldn't take more than five hours. It was thrilling to take part in D-Day, but the full impact wasn't felt until it all came out on the news the following day. That's when it was exciting and you knew you were at the beginning of something big. When we were making the trips they were just another job.[7]

Ten days later F/Lt Bray finished his second tour, having flown a total of eighty-six ops.

Wireless operator Sgt Alf Ridpath, whose pilot had received an immediate DFC after bringing home his badly shot-up Lancaster from Bourg Leopold, bombed the gun emplacements at La Pernelle shortly before the troops landed. La Pernelle was one of only two targets attacked in clear visibility as high, cold winds brought cloud over the Channel coast. 'We had no idea at briefing that the coastal battery we were to attack was as part of D-Day,' he remembers. 'Over the Channel I was looking at the Fishpond radar set for fighters and it was full of "grass", covered in blips. I kept banging it, wondering what was the matter with the thing, then I peered out and I called up, 'Oh my God, look down there.' We all looked out and could see this great armada coming across.'[8]

The sight of so many craft, mighty and minnow, ploughing their way across the grey, foam-flecked sea was a sight never to be forgotten by the crews of Bomber Command out that momentous night. Each yard, each spray-spun mile eastward was another marker in the journey of hope that the airmen of Bomber Command had begun in the first winter of 1943 when *they* were the Second Front, the battered standard bearers for the sailors and soldiers who would shortly begin unlocking the Nazi seals to Europe.

Flight engineer W/O Ken Hulton, who like Sgt Ridpath had seen the carnage over Mailly-le-Camp, also bombed La Pernelle and experienced the same exultation at seeing the dawn of a free France. He recalls:

It was only when we got over the Channel and saw the wake of so many ships to starboard and to port Halifaxes towing gliders that we realised the Second Front had opened. The sky was full of aircraft. What a sight – it was very exciting to see. The whole crew was thrilled, something was moving at last towards the end. There was both heavy and light flak coming up over the target, but we didn't have any trouble and we were there and back in four and a half hours.

Immediately after D-Day W/O Hulton's crew were transferred to 97 Sqn, 5 Group's Pathfinders, where they would have to fly a double tour. 'We were given ten days' leave. Father knew what I was doing, but not a word to mother,' he says.[9] His combat career, which had begun on 57 Sqn in March, would continue into February 1945, when he completed his fifty-fifth operation.

One of those in a glider tow plane was another flight engineer who would notch up fifty-seven operations. W/O Ron Brown was coming to the end of his first tour, on Stirlings at 218 Sqn, when D-Day broke and he was due to marry. He had already postponed his wedding once after seeing his best friend, Jock Lamond, shot down by a German night fighter during an OTU exercise, three weeks before Lamond was due to wed. W/O Brown remembers:

I was supposed to be his best man three weeks later and I had to write one of the most difficult letters ever to his fiancée. He was to be my best man for my wedding too. This situation made me have second thoughts to marry. It seemed unfair to subject my wife to the uncertainty of any future together, so we deferred our wedding to when my tour was coming to an end, 6 June 1944. All the arrangements were fixed, my crew were all coming to my home, the cake was made, the reception organised and the vicar had been informed. Then, out of the blue three days before, all hell was let loose, furloughs were cancelled, we were allowed no phone calls and no mail was being accepted. But fortunately I spoke to my very sympathetic CO and he told my mother I wouldn't be coming home for the wedding and it would have to be postponed.

At short notice on 5 June our crew was detailed to fly a Stirling over to Cottesmore and without ever seeing a glider before we were ordered to tow one to Normandy full of US troops. They were desperately short of aircraft and three Stirlings were sent from 218 Sqn. It was a fantastic sight to see two rows of gliders with tow aircraft lined up in a row on each side of the runway. We didn't let the GIs know we'd never done it before. In the early hours of 6 June, only a short time before I should have been walking up the aisle with my bride Connie, we were releasing a glider of very courageous troops. I well recall looking down at the dropping area and seeing gliders upside down and smashed up. We thought, 'My goodness aren't we fortunate going back to base?' When we got back to Woolfox Lodge our Stirling was refuelled and bombed up and another crew went on an operation in it to support the invasion forces and were shot down. I did thirty-four trips in all on my first tour and got married eventually on 29 June.[10]

F/Sgt Roy Ollerhead, the 626 Sqn navigator who had survived Mailly-le-Camp, bombed the coastal batteries at St Martin-de-Varreville and found that keenness wasn't appreciated on every occasion by the RAF.

The markers were very near and we bombed on target. I didn't have a chance to get up and go to look myself because there was very little time as there were several tight turns to get out of the area. We all had to come out via the Cherbourg Peninsula because there were other aircraft coming in. We didn't know it was D-Day of course, we were just told to come back south and west of Jersey and head for Southampton.

The bomb aimer Ken Vaughan reported flak in front of us and the skipper queried my course, he thought we were heading towards Jersey. However, the bomb aimer said it appeared to come from a flak ship. The skipper said: 'Right, I'll dive. All of you get your guns to give it him.' Even the bomb aimer, who had never fired a shot in anger, had to get in the front turret and the skipper tilted the aircraft so the mid-upper gunner could aim at it and for the first time we let everything go. As we pulled out the rear gunner reported the ship was in flames.

We thought this was all pretty good and back at Wickenby after our skipper had given the details about the target to an intelligence officer I said: 'What about the flak ship?' The skipper gave me such a dirty look and when we told the intelligence officer, he said: 'You shouldn't have done it. You put the aircraft in a dangerous position.' There was no mention of us perhaps saving other aircraft and I thought it was rather unjust. The skipper gave me a bit of a rollocking afterwards for speaking up.[11]

P/O Jack Gagg, the 166 Sqn pilot, was on the same target.

We attacked in the early morning in low cloud. There was quite a lot of flak, but we couldn't see what we were bombing, we were aiming at the Pathfinder markers because it was ten-tenths cloud below. We didn't know it was D-Day, but as we went back over the Channel the navigator had the H2S set on and he called me up to say: 'There's spots all over it.' About halfway across the Channel the cloud cleared and there was the invasion fleet below. When we got back to base there was a great buzz at debriefing. We sat outside for a while listening to what was happening instead of going to bed, but there wasn't a lot of information at that time and it was after we'd been to bed we really found out what had happened.[12]

S/Ldr Charles Owen, a pilot with 97 Sqn, who had begun an operational career the previous November that would lead to a DSO and a DFC, kept a diary at this time, filling in the details of each operation within hours. The night of 5/6 June found him bombing a gun battery at St Pierre-du-Mont, not far from Utah Beach. Safely back at Coningsby, he wrote:

> We thought the briefing sounded a little odd for this trip and sure enough when we broke cloud over the French coast the Channel was full of ships. The army had pulled its finger out at last and D-Day was on. We bombed at 0500 just as it was getting light and had a grandstand view of the Americans running in on the beach. First-class prang on the battery but saw Jimmy Carter shot down by a Ju88 over the target. Marvellous sight coming back as the sun came up – we on the way back and the Americans on the way out. Landed back in time for breakfast, but very disappointed that there was nothing on the 8 o'clock news.[13]

In fact, two aircraft from 97 Sqn were lost in the attack, first W/Cdr Edward James Carter's Z-Zebra went down, then that of a Norwegian crew. Nobody survived from either aircraft, but the loss rate for the night's operations had been remarkably low thanks to the deceptions – only eleven bombers in all.

Cpl Victor Jones of the 9th Field Ambulance, RAMC, saw one of the British bombers ditch as his landing craft approached Sword Beach just before dawn. 'The plane dropped down between our ship and the one next to us, obviously avoiding us, to crash in the sea behind. I can still see the face of the rear gunner looking at us, but no one survived the crash ... That is still my most poignant memory of D-Day.'[14] This was a Halifax of 578 Sqn, the only bomber known to have come down in that part of the Channel that night, and, in fact, some of the crew had already escaped. Sgt Bill Middleton was the flight engineer and he survived to find himself heading for the invasion beaches in a landing craft. The aircraft was hit at 0437 while on the run-in to a gun battery at Montfleury, possibly by a bomb from an aircraft that had just been seen above. As flame spurted out of a hole in the port wing 'like a blow lamp' the pilot, S/Ldr Geoff Watson, tried to put out the fire by diving as he headed for the Channel, but the flames spread under the trailing edge of the wing. 'The skipper suddenly told us to bale out,' Sgt Middleton remembered. 'I clipped my chute on and picked up my dinghy in its pack and went down to the escape hatch in the bomb-aimer's position.' The navigator, bomb aimer and wireless operator had already gone and as he struggled to get through the hatch with his parachute pack and dinghy Sgt Middleton, a non-swimmer, remembered a friend on the squadron telling him only a few days before that if you had to bale out over the sea you were as good as dead. He dropped through and immediately pulled the ripcord.

> For a fleeting second I thought the parachute had caught fire and then it opened with a crack and a jerk which caused the dinghy pack to come away from my harness and disappear towards the water. As I looked down I was surprised to see the waves and realized that the aircraft must have been very low when I left it. It was the burning plane reflected in the silk chute that had made me think it was on fire. I remember thinking the pilot would have no chance. The next minute I was in the water and waves were breaking over my head.

The half-inflated chute dragged him through the sea at speed as he desperately tried to reach the quick-release box. Eventually he did so, the chute blew away and Sgt Middleton sank like a stone. He came up again and again only to be buried by succeeding waves. 'During one of these immersions I saw a light and realized it was the torch that switched on when hitting the water,' he remembered. 'I grabbed it from its pocket and held it above my head shouting, whenever I broke the surface, "Help, Help." There was no one to hear me, but it gave me hope somehow.'

As Sgt Middleton thought of the devastation his parents would feel when they heard of his death, he suddenly saw a ship coming towards him. He bumped against the vessel's side and lost consciousness. He came to in daylight, lying wrapped in a blanket and was told he was on a tank landing craft, heading for the invasion beaches. He had been saved – even though invasion craft had been told not to pick up anyone from the water – because the rocket barge the LCT had been towing had sprung a leak and when it hove to the crew had seen the chute blowing along and then the torch flashing.

Sgt Middleton remembered:

> The engines started and we were heading for the beach at full speed. Vehicles and men were off-loaded rapidly and soon we were heading back to England. Having thanked them again for pulling me out of the "drink" I was transferred to another boat and after some food and another night's sleep I was transferred again, to a submarine chaser, and taken to Bognor Regis.[15]

Sgt Middleton discovered that remarkably the bomb aimer, F/O Paddy Hefferman, and the wireless operator, F/O Bert Onions, had also survived, being scooped from the water by a French destroyer. The bodies of the pilot and of the rear gunner, F/O Sidney Turner, were never found. After fourteen days leave the survivors went back to 578 Sqn where they then had to complete their tour with another crew.

AS the bombers landed back at their bases after bombing the gun emplacements the big guns of Admiral Ramsay's invasion fleet opened up to further impress the German defenders before the troops went ashore. The Americans began landing on Omaha and Utah from 0630 and the first units of British I and XXX Corps stormed Gold, Juno and Sword beaches one hour later. The British official history of the campaign reads:

> Never has any coast suffered what a tortured strip of French coast suffered that morning; both naval and air bombardment were unparalleled. Along the whole 50 mile front the land was rocked by successive explosions as the shells of ships' guns tore holes in fortifications and tons of bombs rained on them from the skies ... The soldiers borne forward to attack were thrilled by the spectacle of Allied power that was displayed around them on every hand.[16]

The BBC, which kept spirits alive in Occupied Europe, launched a new service on 6 June, *War Report*, in which correspondents on the front line recorded events as they were happening on specially built portable machines. It ran on a daily basis until the end of the European conflict and among the first voices the public heard as they gathered in their spartan living rooms, leaning in anticipation towards the comforting heavy permanence of the static-laden family radio set on the evening of D-Day, was that of Air Commodore W. Helmore. He had been aboard a medium bomber tasked with destroying a Normandy railway bridge before the troops went in and his recording brought the fear of night operations to the family hearth and gave the Home Front some conception of what husbands, brothers and sons in the RAF were suffering. Helmore reported nervously:

> We're just going in to drop our bombs. It's a very tense moment – just the dawn of the moment when our troops are going in on the French beaches. I've seen them with my own eyes, practically in the act of touching down on the beaches. I feel it's a great privilege to be here. I'll be glad to get home all the same. Never mind, we're just getting ready to go in and bomb and I'd better shut up. Hold it! My God, there's some bloody nasty flak around this place – very nasty flak, blast it![17]

The onslaught continued that night, 1,065 Bomber Command aircraft going out to drop 3,488 tons of bombs on rail and road communication lines to prevent the Wehrmacht bringing up reinforcements, especially tanks. The key to D-Day as Rommel correctly saw was armour to throw the invaders back into the sea within 24 hours before air power could take over, but the only tanks Rommel had under his direct control on the morning of 6 June were those of the 21st Panzer Division, which had been heavily knocked about by Harris's men at Mailly-le-Camp. On 15 May the Enigma machine decoding centre at Bletchley Park had forwarded to SHAEF the contents of a message from the German Seventh Army saying, 'The remaining elements of 21 Panzer Division ... have arrived.'[18]

It was later learned from intelligence on the ground that the division turned up south of Caen from the west. Rommel's absence from the battle front for his wife's birthday on 6 June and bungled communications led to delays. When finally ordered to attack the British 3rd Division front late on D-Day only one bridge in Caen could be found intact. 21st Panzer came into action far too late and lost 50 tanks on D-Day, mostly to the Allied DD tanks, which had floated ashore. Only one other Panzer division could be got into place in Normandy on 6 June – the 12th SS

Panzer Division held at Lisieux. It was pounded from the air when it finally got permission from OKW to move on the afternoon of 6 June and remained on the eastern side of the city. Meanwhile, further waves of Allied infantry and tanks were pouring ashore well into the late evening.

F/O Douglas Hudson, of 100 Sqn, who had heard fellow navigators forecast they were for the chop, saw the second tour he had begun in bleak January come to an end on D-Day with an operation in his crew's much-respected Lancaster R-Roger on the important Normandy road junction at Vire. Hudson remembers:

> We got airborne about 10 p.m. and because of double-summer time it was still daylight as we went over the Channel. We could see this huge armada of ships going across. When we got back our tour was over. The anti-climax was such that instead of going into town and living it up we did the very opposite. I was as miserable as could be. I think it was because the invasion had started and things were really happening at last.
>
> I was talking to the pilot the next day as we watched the squadron aircraft take off for another raid and I said, 'Are you thinking what I'm thinking?' He said, 'I'm game to carry on if you are,' so we consulted the rest of the crew and they agreed. We decided we would ask the squadron commander if we could go on if we could have R-Roger back and he was delighted, after all we were an experienced crew. The following day the MO, Doc Marshall, told me, 'You'll carry on over my dead body. I've quashed it. You don't realise as a crew how sick you are.' We hadn't realised what a strain we were under and that we needed a rest before being ready for operations again; we had started thinking it couldn't happen to us. In fact, 100 Sqn lost six Lancasters that month.[19]

As some tours ended others began and navigator F/Sgt Vic Farmer found himself preparing for his first operation on D-Day at North Killingholme, home to 550 Sqn. It was to the marshalling yards at Achères, north-east of Paris, part of the later stages of the Transportation Plan that included putting a ring around Paris, so that no rail movement could be made in or out. He says:

> We had been on the station about fourteen days and knew something was coming up. Our pilot, 'Skip' Thomas, had already flown overnight

on 6 June as a second dickey for experience, bombing guns on the French coast, but not having been to a briefing at that time we didn't know it was D-Day until it was announced on the radio. There was tremendous euphoria and we were very keen to take part. We were briefed in the evening of D-Day and we were told the target was marshalling yards on the outskirts of Paris. We took off at twenty-five minutes after midnight. As newcomers to the job we were listed as one of the last to attack. We were instructed, as we later always were with French targets, to be very careful about where we placed our bombs. I think there were about 100 aircraft on the target. The flak wasn't too bad and of course we knew, as it was just after D-Day, there was a very good reason for going to this place. We did get a break in the cloud cover and dropped our bombs. Three nights later we went back to Achères again.[20]

Australian F/Sgt Harry Stack, bomb aimer in F/Sgt Farmer's crew, says of that first trip: 'It was my most memorable operation. As we came home we could see all the troops and barges and what looked like hundreds of ships coming out from behind the Isle of Wight and heading towards France.'[21] The crew's tour would be rapid in the intense raiding period supporting the troops ashore, their final operation being barely three and a half months later.

Some were disappointed to find they were not to take part in operations on D-Day. F/O Jim Wright, the navigator who had nearly lost his badly frostbitten arm after a Berlin raid in the winter, had just been transferred with his crew from 630 Sqn to 97 Sqn and reported for briefing at Coningsby. Wright remembers:

Our Australian wireless operator, Harvey Glasby, was quite upset when at the last minute the CO called us to one side and said he was sorry that he did not need us to go – he had enough aircraft and crews to meet the commitment. Harvey grumbled that he had come a long way from Toowoomba, Queensland, and what was he to tell the grand-children? – that he was here and did not go on what was obviously an historic day. He threatened to steal a ride. On 30 July, when our crew was not scheduled to fly, he joined F/Lt Hugh Baker's crew as a second wireless operator in a total crew of nine on a daylight operation to attack enemy strong points in the Normandy battle zone. The aircraft crashed south-east of St Lô and seven of the crew including Harvey were killed ... I wonder if Harvey was really needed on that trip or whether he went for the ride.[22]

Those from the Commonwealth felt keenly they had come a long way to see D-Day and wanted to make a difference. F/Sgt Stack got a pass from North Killingholme and decided to view liberation at first hand.

Just after the D-Day landings I went to Dover trying to get a lift over to France to see what it was like on the ground over there. Looking for a place to sleep I found all the Salvation Army hostels had been knocked down or blown away. I was having a drink in a pub and the chap next to me said, 'Come and stop at my place for the night, my son is in Burma.' He took me home to meet his wife and she gave me her son's room in the attic.[23]

There was little time to reflect in the days following the invasion as Bomber Command was called on again and again to back up the troops, but S/Ldr Munro snatched a few minutes to fill in his log book about Operation Taxable. He did it with some irony.

My personal frustration at not having an attacking role on D-Day found an outlet when I entered the description of the operation in my log book the next day. It read: 'Ops. The creation of a tactical surprise to support the landing of troops on the opening of a Second Front. The most hazardous, difficult and most dangerous operation ever undertaken in the history of air warfare, involved flying within at least 9 miles of the enemy coast without fighter cover and in conditions of bright moonlight and at a height of not more than 3,000 feet at which the aircraft was open to attack by the deadliest of weapons – light flak. Believed successful.'
    Come the end of the month when the adjutant Harry Humphries left all the pilots' log books on the CO's desk to sign, instead of leaving mine open at the pages showing the monthly summary as was the normal practice he left it open at the page showing the op of 6 June and put it on top of the pile so that Leonard Cheshire couldn't miss reading my entry. At the side of my greatly exaggerated description of Operation Taxable he wrote: 'Certified that S/Ldr Munro is still in possession of most of his faculties after completing the operation described on this page.'[24]

There were few people in Britain to whom D-Day meant more than the members of 346 and 347 Squadrons in 4 Group. They were the two heavy bomber squadrons of the Free French Air Force formed at Elvington near York in May and they were about to start bombing French targets to help liberate their country. They attacked many Normandy targets in June including Maisy and St Lô and in July Caen, the day after losing their first Halifax setting off for the Mimoyecques V-weapons site. Most of the aircrew were older than their equivalents in the RAF and all had stories to tell about how they had reached England.

Leonce Vaysse escaped from German-held territory in Tunisia via Algeria and Morocco to Liverpool, and would be posted to Elvington as a flight engineer before the year was out. He was in training on 6 June at RAF Locking in Somerset, looking forward to wearing the RAF flight engineer's brevet with the equivalent French flying badge of a propeller inside a cog. He remembers:

> Woken at five in the morning we were gathered on the main platform to be solemnly told about the Normandy landings and the French flag was hoisted up the great mast. On 14 July the small town of Weston-super-Mare was declared a 'French city' by the Lord Mayor and the Frenchmen were invited to the town hall. Each of us received a book published in honour of the Lord Mayor and advertising the resort's attractions.[25]

In Germany the news of D-Day was slower in coming – officially. P/O Alan Bryett, whose hopes of getting back to Britain from Stalag Luft III had been dashed when the Great Escapers were discovered, remembers:

> We knew something was up on the night before D-Day because on our secret radio we heard at the end of the news a series of coded messages, obviously for the Resistance. You sometimes heard one or two, but this time there were about twenty. For three days the Germans didn't give anything away, then on 9 June we were told the Allies had landed in France, but were being pushed back into the sea.[26]

Grete Paquin, an academic in the Lower Saxony university town of Göttingen, kept a diary during the war. She wrote on 8 June:

> Tuesday (D-Day) was like every other day in the office. Our senses are so toughened, we did not know anything, we did not sense anything

... then I tried to use the telephone, but it did not work. I went across the yard to another institute, no telephoning. When I returned a student came from the town and cried: 'Invasion, invasion!' We stopped work.[27]

BOMBER Command's contribution to the Battle of Normandy continued on a nightly basis for more than a week as the Oboe-led heavies attacked railway and road targets to prevent German reinforcements reaching the front line. Aerodromes fringing the fire zone were also attacked by hundreds of Lancasters and Halifaxes to prevent the airlifting of supplies. On a raid on the railway target of Cambrai on the night of 12 June, a Canadian mid-upper gunner from 419 Sqn, P/O Andrew Mynarski, won a posthumous VC for trying to rescue the trapped rear gunner of his Halifax, setting his clothing and parachute on fire as a result and plunging from the aircraft as a human torch.

As the troops moved forward, overrunning strong points and gun emplacements, there was also an opportunity to assess what damage Bomber Command had achieved on the night before the invasion. The results had been mixed, the cloud cover on all but two gun emplacements saving many from total destruction. A British officer, Major 'Andy' Anderson of the Ministry of Home Security, collated information about each one and sent the results back to Bomber Command headquarters at High Wycombe. At St Martin-de-Varreville, for instance, he reported 'an excellent crater pattern' and at Montfleury overlooking Juno Beach the 'ammunition store and other buildings had been destroyed by bombing'. But the Maisy battery – in the gap between Utah and Omaha – 'remained in action until 10 June' even though there had been a 'good concentration around the aiming point' and was eventually silenced by US warships.[28] Cratering of the beaches, allowing shelter to troops pinned down by enemy fire particularly at Omaha – would also have likely reduced army casualties, but Bomber Command was not asked to do this.

It might have seemed to the bomber boys attacking communication targets in the week following D-Day that they could look forward to night after night of the same, but then the air war took a lurch in a direction unthinkable only weeks before – Bomber Command went back to a tactic it had not dared to try regularly since the early days of the war, raiding in daylight. Harris was reluctant to mount the operation and feared a decimation of his crews in their inadequately armed Lancasters, but the target – the E-boat flotilla at Le Havre – was considered too vital to miss and a squadron was available with a new weapon that it was considered would achieve previously unheard of results.

The threat of E-boat torpedos had been a constant worry to the invasion force and the waves following in subsequent days. The small, fast craft had achieved a spectacular success on 28 April while the US 4th Infantry Division was in training for Utah Beach, killing 749 GIs off Slapton Sands by sinking two landing craft. But on D-Day itself and those following few Allied vessels had been sunk by torpedo. Now it was necessary to make sure that the E-boat flotilla holed up in the concrete pens of Le Havre could not put to sea again.

Two days after D-Day 617 Sqn had tried out the new Tallboy bomb designed by Barnes Wallis, whose previous ballistic breakthrough had achieved such success in the Dams Raid of just over a year before. The 12,000-lb Tallboy was totally different from the blast bombs the RAF had been using until that time. At best the 4,000-lb Cookie was nothing more than a thin-cased dustbin that could not be aimed with accuracy. Two or three bolted together at least allowed more explosive in one place, but at an even greater cost to bomb-aiming. The Tallboy, by comparison, was dynamically perfect with a very high terminal velocity, which allowed it to be properly aimed to drill through strong structures such as concrete and explode beneath. The Dambusters squadron had dropped it from 10,000 feet to great effect on a railway tunnel at Saumur in the Loire valley and it had neatly blocked the line to Normandy, preventing the Germans rapidly bringing up Panzer reinforcements from the south.

F/O Don Cheney, the young Canadian pilot on 617 Sqn, remembers the puzzlement of most of his comrades when they first saw the Tallboys a few days before the invasion. He recorded:

> A convoy of large, flatbed lorries arrived at the squadron, each loaded with long, tapering shapes carefully covered by heavy canvas. All hands followed the lorries in great haste and excitement, thinking that we were receiving a squadron of 'knocked down' Spitfires intended to provide us with fighter cover during daylight operations. Not so! To our amazement the largest, most aerodynamic projectiles we had ever seen or even imagined were quickly unloaded and stowed in the bomb dump.[29]

S/Ldr Les Munro was now asked to lead the skilled pilots of 617 Sqn, their bomb bays loaded with Tallboys, against the E-boat pens at Le Havre on 14 June. Their Tallboy-laden Lancasters would follow Leonard Cheshire's marking by Mosquito in which he dived from 11,000 feet to 5,000 feet to drop his spot fires amid the boiling bursts of black, red-centred flak. In all 221 Lancasters of four groups went in in a two-wave attack, the first wave during the early evening and the second at dusk. But it was 617 Sqn and its Tallboy-carrying Lancasters that began the wave of destruction, the shock waves of the Tallboys puffing out in a visible ring across the target as the bombs drilled underground and exploded. Munro says:

> I have always had a sense of pride in leading the Lancasters of the squadron in formation in the attack. As far as I was aware there was no consensus of concern among crews because it was a daylight op, and we had a fighter escort. Certainly in my case the responsibility of leading the Lancaster formation on an as accurate as possible bombing run outweighed any fear factor. I had a job to do and there was no room for fear.
>
> There was scattered flak over Le Havre, not concentrated in one spot in spite of the Lancs being bunched in formation. We bombed at 18,000 feet, which could account for the flak being somewhat scattered. I was conscious of the flak bursts, but did not allow them to distract me from the job in hand and I'm sure that the other pilots felt the same.[30]

It was the first operation of Sgt Ken Down, a flight engineer on 550 Sqn at North Killingholme.

> All our training had been for night operations, so we were very surprised when we were woken up early for a day raid. We wondered what was going on. When we went into briefing there was some sort of apologetic remark about this being Bomber Command's first daylight raid for some time, but 'never mind' it would be good experience. In fact, we were thinking the losses might be quite high. Nobody expressed it, but you thought it was likely to be a bit dodgy.
>
> Just before the target there was a lot of flak coming up to port as we cruised along and I thought, 'I'm glad we're not going there,' then immediately afterwards the navigator told the pilot, 'Turn onto 242,'

so we were straight into it. But oddly enough we sailed right through without being hit. Going in to the target, when I saw 617 Sqn's bombs explode it was as if the whole surface erupted. We hadn't been told anything at briefing about the Tallboy bombs, but when I saw them go in it was obvious this was something special. We went in to bomb ourselves then were away back over the sea without problems.[31]

Sgt Tony McKernan, a wireless operator on the squadron, had begun his tour with an Aachen raid ten days before and by now was used to spending '90 per cent of every op standing on the step with my head and shoulders in the astrodome' looking out for fighters. He saw Leonard Cheshire open the attack at Le Havre. 'Cheshire marked the pens from a very low level, he dived through the most horrifying concentration of flak, and plonked a red marker slap on the roof of the U-boat pens,' he recorded later. 'We were approached by two Me110s on a recce, luckily nobody fired and the 110s were seen off by a box of four Spits, a lovely sight.'[32]

The next day 617 Sqn led nearly 300 aircraft of Main Force on a similar attack on Boulogne harbour, this time without fighter cover, and went in 10,000 feet lower. Les Munro's aircraft was damaged by flak, but notably only one aircraft from Main Force was lost from each operation. The quickly called raid severely curtailed the social arrangements of 101 Sqn. Engineer Dennis Goodliffe remembers: 'The flight engineer leader at 101 Sqn, Jim Smith, had invited lots of aircrew from Ludford to his wedding on 15 June, but when he came out of church there was no one there. We had all been confined to camp to take part in the squadron's first daylight operation that day, on the Boulogne E-boat pens.'[33]

The day-raids experiment Harris feared had turned out to be a great success. Harris wrote just after the war:

> There could be no more convincing demonstration of the effectiveness of air power than these two operations. Within 24 hours, at wholly negligible cost to our forces, the enemy lost all power of seriously disrupting the passage of convoys to Normandy. At Le Havre very nearly every ship in the dock, more than 60 all told, were sunk or damaged and at Boulogne 28 vessels were sunk and many others damaged.[34]

Daylight operations would now become a constant alternative for Bomber Command, virtually doubling its strength in an instant as aircraft could be used for two operations in one 24-hour period. As a new threat loomed that summer the ability to strike in daylight would become essential.

14

Squashing the Doodlebug

The blustery weather over the Continent and at Britain's airfields that had threatened the invasion itself had deteriorated even further by mid-June and Bomber Command's bases were socked in for three days from the 18th. Aircrew for the most part took the opportunity to visit the cinema to see the newsreels of the milestone they had helped to reach, in what was hoped was the beginning of the end. The historic footage had been showing for days, *The Cinema* magazine reporting as early as 7 June: 'The first newsreel rushes of the Invasion arrived in London early yesterday. Well over 100 frontline cameramen had shot 1,000,000 feet.'[1]

There was no shortage of cinemas to choose from in Britain, a total of 4,800 picture houses offering some relief from the blackout in cities, towns and villages. Cinema-going had grown exponentially in wartime, up from between 18 and 19 million tickets sold every week at the start of the war to eventually reach 30 million by the end, and a trip to the flicks had proved so popular many town watch committees had removed the ban on Sunday opening. To cope with demand 361 English-language films were made in 1944.

The cinemas ranged from the humble village flea pits to plush entertainment centres such as the Odeon, Leicester Square, which Commonwealth airmen with a weekend pass liked to frequent. Elegance and size wasn't just confined to London, however. Bolton Odeon, built in 1937, could seat 2,534.[2] Virtually everyone in wartime Britain was captivated by film, even the Prime Minister. Diarists such as the Chief of the Imperial General Staff, General Sir Alan Brooke, regularly complained about Chequers dinners being extended into the early hours by Churchill's insistence that his guests watch the latest Hollywood epic in his private cinema.[3]

That week, as rain bounced off the pavements and the country reflected on the successes of D-Day two weeks before, aircrew from 5 Group south of Lincoln and 1 Group to the north flocked into the city to see the newsreels and catch the latest flick. They crammed the city's Savoy cinema, wet battledresses steaming in the heat, to see Spencer Tracy and Irene Dunne in *A Guy Named Joe*. Some took in the matinée, then sank a few pints and nipped across to the Astoria ballroom and paid the week-night rate of 1s 6d (8p) in the hope of meeting a young woman who might be suitably grateful for their efforts in French skies.[4]

Further south, in 3 Group's area where the RAF competed with the USAAF for the favours of local girls, Cambridge was having its Holidays at Home week, a government incentive to stop families jamming the railways, with a local variety show and signs of stalls and rides being erected for the fair on Midsummer Common. Cambridge itself was busy with the chocolate and khaki uniforms of American flyers and the *Cambridge Daily News* was now printing baseball results, the New York Yankees ending a losing run by beating the Washington Senators.[5] The Yanks had even made an impression at nearby New-market where the American-owned Hycilla had won the Oaks on 16 June at 8 to 1.

In York, the target for 4 Group and the more southerly based squadrons of the Canadian 6 Group, various fund-raising events were being held for Salute the Soldier Week, arranged long before the soldiers' spectacular success across the Channel, but the big attraction for airmen was to catch Constance Bennett in *Sin Town* at the Clifton before the week was over and the programme changed. Some of the more adventurous Canadians made it to Leeds where the City Varieties music hall, being advertised as 'Now One of Leeds' Leading Places of Entertainment', was competing with London's Windmill Theatre by presenting *It's Time To Tease*, starring Doreen and her retinue of eight glorious models.[6]

For those able to wangle a 48-hour pass and travel to London there was a range of theatrical entertainment on offer, not just the statuesque tableaux at the Windmill. *Arsenic and Old Lace* was in its second year and *Blithe Spirit* in its third. The young Richard Burton, soon to train as an RAF navigator himself, was making his stage debut at the Westminster in the Emlyn Williams play *The Druid's Rest*. But it was the revue *Sweet and Lower* with the hilarious Hermione Gingold that was attracting aircrew out for a laugh.

THERE was now a new edge to cinema and theatre-going in London, however, and as airmen and others queued for seats in the rain they kept an eye on the skies. The *Vergeltungswaffe* (retaliation weapon) onslaught, long threatened by Goebbels, had begun on 13 June and within three days 647 of the V1s had arrived, killing 499 people and injuring 2,000. A rapidly resupplied stream was now reaching the capital, one hospital, St Mary Abbots in Kensington, having to be evacuated it was so badly damaged. Civilians out shopping in Battersea, Streatham, Wandsworth and Putney were killed.

It was as the stood-down Commonwealth crews of Bomber Command headed for London on 18 June that Hitler's new weapon struck its most savage blow, hitting the packed Guards Chapel in Birdcage Walk as the congregation rose to sing a hymn and killing fifty-eight civilians and sixty-three service personnel.[7] Dr Reginald Jones, Director of Intelligence to the Air Staff, who had been influential in the decision to bomb the V-weapons research establishment at Peenemünde the previous August, was in his office near by at MI5's headquarters on Broadway. He heard the explosion, realised what it was, and arrived to see Birdcage Walk a sea of fresh leaves, stripped from the trees.

The V1, 25 feet long, with a wingspan less than 18 feet and powered by a pulse-jet motor to carry the one-ton warhead, was a secret known to only a few in Britain until that second week of June. The Peenemünde raid had been launched to wreck production of the V2 rocket, which carried a quarter less explosive. Subsequent reconnaissance of Peenemünde had shown an unusual, stubby aircraft and later a launching ramp the same shape as strange 'ski' sites, which had been spotted in the Pas-de-Calais. A prototype Peenemünde V1 crashing in Sweden in May had provided British Intelligence with all the information they needed about the new weapon, including the fact that it had a range of about 150 miles, putting those 'ski' sites in northern France well within range of London.[8]

At first the V1s, which dived to their target when their carefully measured fuel ran out, were called P-Planes (for pilotless) by a puzzled press, then Buzzbombs and finally the American term Doodlebug caught on. The campaign would continue day and night for three months. There were signs of desperation by a populace that had become weary of war. Londoners headed by train out of the capital, the Post Office registering 1,110,000 changes of address in London between July and September 1944. Questions were asked in the House about stampedes at Paddington. Mothers and children were officially offered evacuation again, as at the start of the war.[9]

The Home Secretary Herbert Morrison was so worried he suggested strategy in France should be altered so that the only objective would be to clear the north coast and its V-weapon sites at once.[10] Incidents such as the capricious carnage in Aldwych in June after a V1 exploded outside Bush House, sucking all the leaves from the trees and office girls through the windows of the BBC building, leaving their remains hanging from those same trees, led Churchill to consider retaliating with gas and chemical weapons, not for the first time.[11] This may have been because intelligence reports had shown the Germans had originally planned the V1 – and possibly the V2 – to carry the means of spreading poison gas or some other chemical weapon. It is known the German Army carried out gas warfare exercises on the Lüneburger Heide on 15 June 1944 and in July efforts were made to supply the German population with gas masks.[12] Churchill, impetuous and irate, also ordered a scheme to be studied for the obliteration, one by one, of 100 German towns of medium population. Professionals in the RAF persuaded him that none of these methods would work.[13]

Instead of employing gas or retaliatory bombing the Air Ministry turned to the fighter boys to shoot down those airborne V1s that the coastal batteries had failed to destroy, Balloon Command to set up a barrier on London's southern and eastern approaches to catch others and the bombers of both the RAF and USAAF to take out the V1 and V2 launch sites in France. Eventually the USAAF would be assigned the 'ski' launch pads and Harris's men the storage depots to either blast them to pieces with their heavier bomb loads or churn up the surrounding infrastructure to such a degree the sites were effectively isolated. The fact that Bomber Command had proved it could now operate in daylight on short-haul targets without severe loss and that elements of it had demonstrated an aptitude for eradicating small targets with small forces made it prime material for use against the V-weapons.

Like so many others it was not a diversification that sat well with Harris, or indeed with Lt General James Doolittle, now heading the US Eighth Air Force in Britain. They argued it would be better to stage a mass attack on Berlin, using 1,200 US aircraft by day and 800 RAF by night, rather than trying to knock out small targets in bad weather.[14] In fact, the Americans set aside 200 aircraft for 'Crossbow' targets, as the whole campaign was now called, and went ahead with their Berlin raid on 21 June. But Harris was ordered to make his heavies available for V-weapons targets as well as supporting the land war now stalled before Caen and joining the American-led campaign against the enemy's oil supply. During the next two months Crossbow would take 50 per cent of the resources of Bomber Command and in all 3,000 Allied aircrew would lose their lives on Crossbow operations.[15] The V-weapon campaign called for attacks by day and by night.

Australian F/Sgt Harry Stack, the 550 Sqn bomb aimer, made a night attack against a V1 site at Flers near Caen on 25 June which proved the most memorably nerve-racking trip of his tour. He says:

It was our eighth operation and we weren't that concerned as we had been there before just after D-Day and it was considered a nice short trip. We thought it would be a piece of cake as we had been to the Ruhr twice and a few other targets such as Le Havre and into southern France. We thought, 'One more op to completion of the tour.'

We were in our regular T-Tommy, which had painted on its side a kangaroo throwing bombs out of its pouch. A full Aussie crew had finished their tour in that aircraft. We crossed the coast near Beachy Head and I fused the bombs, made sure the bomb sight was adjusted correctly for the target and set about finding our position on H2S and plotting our course to assist the navigator. I also needed to find an identical wind as we got closer to the target to set on the bomb sight. It was a good night for flying with just enough cloud around to be able to disappear into if attacked by night fighters. There were about 200 Lancs and Halifaxes in the loose formation that we flew in and as we crossed the French coast the searchlights appeared.

The Germans always had six or seven big blue searchlights gliding across the sky. If a plane was unlucky enough to be caught by one of these beams and held for only a few seconds a battery of searchlights would be thrown up to envelop the aircraft. At the same time the flak battery would open up and there was little time to get away from it all and avoid being shot down. What our skipper used to do was, as a beam of the searchlights came towards another aircraft, he would slip through the beam and then give the other aircraft a wide berth to avoid being affected by the glare.

As we cruised towards the target this night our luck didn't hold and we were coned, probably because we were still learning. I was working at my position when the full glare of the searchlights hit us and night instantly turned into day. Even with night-vision goggles it was almost impossible to see. My first thought was to get into my turret above and fire the twin Brownings to try to put out the searchlights or watch for night fighters closing in for the kill. The skipper had gone into evasive action as soon as the lights hit us. The heavy aircraft complete with its full bomb load was put into a headlong dive, twisting and turning, then climbing and turning to the opposite side, hoping to avoid heavy flak, light flak, anything that was thrown at us. This diving and climbing put an enormous amount of extra G [gravity] on the plane. I found myself anchored to the floor with maps and pencils floating in the air. It was with great difficulty that I made it to the guns at all and put them on to fire. I found I could hardly see anything. By this time we were running up on the target and it was time to get a sighting and get the bombs away, so clawing my way out of the turret again and setting on the bomb sight the latest wind the nav and I had found I got the bomb doors open and commenced my run on the target, the searchlights still on us.

We lost one engine on the run-in, but the skip feathered it very quickly with the help of the engineer. PFF had marked the target, so it was a case of quick corrections to course and bombs away. I said, 'Keep her steady, Skip, for the photo,' then it was close the bomb-bay doors and 'Let's get the hell out of here.' As soon as the bomb doors closed the skipper threw T-Tommy on its side. Boy, were we glad to get out of those searchlights.

As we came into North Killingholme that morning, gliding in with the sun just rising and the wheat fields around the drome dotted with poppies so lovely and red I couldn't help but feel what a wonderful world it was. I couldn't get out of the kite quick enough to give the ground a great big kiss and say to myself, 'You beaut.' A few weeks later we came back off leave to find that T-Tommy had gone missing.[16]

During the first few weeks of the V-weapons campaign the unusually wet summer weather gave the enemy the advantage and operation after operation was scrubbed at short notice. The V1 could be launched whatever the atmospheric conditions and on 2 July, as many as 161

Doodlebugs were logged as crossing the south coast at the standard height and speed of 2,500 feet and 340 mph.[17] As the distance was pre-set, double agents were now being used to falsely report that most were landing north of London. It caused the Germans to load less fuel, which meant many arrived in the Kent countryside rather than the capital. The deception could have unfortunate consequences, however. On 30 June thirty-two youngsters and adults were killed by a V1 on a children's home, one mile from Churchill's country residence of Chartwell.[18]

Day after day Bomber Command crews were briefed at short notice to take off for a V-site only to have it cancelled immediately afterwards. On 6 July, for instance, the adjutant of 467 (RAAF) Sqn reported: 'Once again ops on, then scrubbed. This is now five days out of six that similar conditions have prevailed. All aircrew are naturally "fed up" and the inevitable happens – a hectic time at the local or something similar.'[19] The Australians had a reputation second to none of letting their hair down and the pubs of Waddington and nearby Lincoln rang to the sound of Aussie anthems at that time.

The fevered atmosphere didn't just apply to aircrew. It was also an irritating time for Harris and his commanders as the Air Ministry made one plan then another. The RAF official history noted ten years later:

> Their criticism of the Directorate of Bomber Operations at the Air Ministry, it must be admitted, had point. This directorate constantly changed the targets which the bomber commanders were called upon to attack. Thus between 15th June and 15th July, large sites, supply sites, storage depots and factories in Germany were all at one time or another given overriding priority, and this at a time when there was no direct evidence that some of the targets listed as storage depots were in fact depots at all.[20]

It was an entirely different war from the winter campaign where operations were laid on as part of a master plan. That summer flexibility and frustration went together. Sgt Frank Jones, the 10 Sqn flight engineer who had gone down with dysentery after the 24 March Berlin raid because of the insanitary conditions at Melbourne, had now been transferred to 76 Sqn where he joined a freshman crew and was able to see at first hand how the bombing war he had known had changed beyond all recognition. His first operation at Holme-on-Spalding-Moor was on 4 July to the V1 site of St Martin-l'Hortier in daylight.

It had been four months since my last trip and then it was all night ops. Flying daylight operations that summer was certainly an education. It meant you could see aircraft being hit and the crews struggling to get out. Two or three might get out then it would start to go down. Often it would go down for a long way before exploding. That summer when we were doing daylights we would sometimes get a stand-down until midnight. We would get back to camp and in bed for about a quarter to twelve, be asleep about an hour, then the service police would come round telling you there was a briefing at 6 or 6.30 a.m. Very often we would be out by our aircraft by 7 a.m. and there would be some mist and we would be there till lunchtime before we took off. They would just bring us a drink out in between.[21]

Attacks on V-weapon sites were carried out by small forces, usually operating at the same time as others. The need for accurate bombing was more important than ever and master bombers were widely used to control the attacks. Several were shot down as they orbited the target area, S/Ldr Ian Bazalgette winning a posthumous VC for accurately marking the flying-bomb site at Trossy-St Maxim on 4 August while his aircraft was a mass of flames. F/Sgt Robert Gill was an experienced air gunner on the Pathfinder 35 Sqn and had been operating since the previous May, in fact taking part in the raid on Peenemünde. On 23 June he was mid-upper gunner in the aircraft of a 22-year-old master bomber in a night attack on a flying-bomb site at Coubronne.

After we had left the target and were over the enemy coast someone in the crew said they thought they could see explosions over the target, so the pilot said, 'I'll go back and see what's going on.' He must have thought there were still aircraft over it. The master bomber was supposed to get there first and circle until the raid was over. I was absolutely alarmed when I realised what he was doing, I thought he was mad. We were probably the only aircraft over Belgium, sitting ducks.

We were on our way back from the target the second time about ten minutes later when we were hit from underneath by a fighter with Schräge Musik. I heard the thump, thump, thump of cannon shells, then the aircraft was alight in the wing and fuselage. The ammunition was going off and I lost my eyebrows and eyelashes and some hair and skin was burned, but it didn't leave a scar. I went down to the fuselage door and kicked it, but I couldn't get it open so I went forward over the main spar and through the open hatch at the front. Just after I left I saw the flash as the aircraft exploded and the wreckage came down at Nieuwpoort, just across the river from Dunkirk. The pilot and rear gunner were still on board.

I landed in a field surrounded by barbed wire and as I got through the wire onto a road, everywhere I looked there were signs for mines. It was a heavily defended area and a soldier on the road saw me. I was taken to some sort of bunker and into a room where a corporal was standing in front of a picture of Adolf Hitler. I remember he pointed to it and said: 'That man will spill his last drop of blood for Germany,' so it showed how he had been educated. After the war I saw the intelligence report on our crash and it said, 'We are at a loss to know what this aircraft was doing over Belgium at this time.'[22]

The tactical change by Bomber Command wasn't lost on the Luftwaffe and it was only a matter of time before they would be able to assemble as a large force of bombers crossed the French coast for a V-weapon site. That chance came on the night of 7/8 July when 208 5 Group Lancasters and thirteen Mosquitos went to bomb a huge storage dump in a series of caves and tunnels at St Leu-d'Esserent, north of Paris, where the Germans had sent forth as many as thirty-four train-loads of flying bombs in a 24-hour period. The day before two new Australian skippers had arrived with their crews at Waddington to join 467 Sqn – P/O Philip Ryan and F/O D. J. Reynolds. The squadron already had two skippers named Ryan and Reynolds and the adjutant noted in the squadron diary it would mean 'programmes will become involved' as a result.

Bomber Command had attacked the site only three nights before, losing thirteen, including two crews from 106 Sqn and two from 57 Sqn. The second raid was directed onto the mouths of the tunnels and the approach roads, blocking access to the flying bombs stored there, and was a success, but the night fighters caught the bombers over the target and as they headed homeward. A total of twenty-five Lancasters and two Mosquitos were shot down, a shocking 14 per cent. From Metheringham 106 Sqn had only been able to send sixteen Lancasters and lost five of them to add to the two already missing. At East Kirkby another three dispersals of 57 Sqn were empty the next morning and 630 Sqn, which shared the base, lost its highly decorated commanding officer, South African born W/Cdr Bill Deas. The problem of two skippers with the same names as others was a problem no more on 467 Sqn – P/O Philip Ryan and F/Lt Robert Reynolds both failed to return.

A month later Bomber Command went back again, dividing 742 aircraft between the St Leu-d'Esserent site and another storage facility in the Fôret de Nieppe. The cost this time was minimal, only two aircraft being lost. One was a Halifax from 433 (RCAF) Sqn, which suffered an engine failure on final approach, coming down in the village square of Skipton-on-Swale near the base in the middle of the afternoon, killing the pilot, the flight engineer and a child who was unable to get out of the way.

The operation was the first with his own crew for F/O Wilbur Pierce, who had lately joined the squadron, and he also suffered severe engine trouble. He remembers:

> New crews get the oldest aircraft and we did! Entering the vicinity of the target we lost all the oil in the port outer. It meant we were unable to feather the propeller. With it windmilling we turned back and the bearings melted. The prop was wildly vibrating, so I pressed the control column firmly to and fro to break the prop off. It finally flew away. The vibration broke the fuel line somewhere and when we switched tanks the two starboard engines cut. We got them back in a hurry, but dropped like a stone for a minute. Then another engine overheated, the temperature soared and the oil pressure plummeted but we kept it on. We were now back over England with a full bomb load of nine 1,000-lb bombs and four 500-lb. We had to land and told Church Broughton. The tower refused because of the bomb load, but I told them to clear the runway I was coming in because I had no choice. I made a beautiful landing and two of the engines of the Halifax had to be replaced.[23]

The next night F/O Pierce was given a brand-new Halifax for another operation over France. It blew up the following day while being refuelled at Skipton-on-Swale, killing two ground crew.

Bomber Command was now winning the war against the V-weapons, but sometimes it was at great cost. The Germans had originally intended to launch 6,000 bombs a day from sixty-four sites, delivering the equivalent tonnage of 1,000 RAF bombers every 24 hours. Bombing of factories in Germany and railway yards in France had ensured there was no chance of Germany ever reaching that total and now Bomber

Dornier Do217 about to take off to engage British bombers. The Do217 was one of the
t German night fighters to be equipped with the deadly *Schräge Musik* upward-firing
non.

e result of tracerless *Schräge Musik*: a bomber explodes. This official picture was printed
he *Daily Express*, in April 1944, with the claim it was a German 'Scarecrow' shell, which
RAF told aircrew were fired to simulate doomed aircraft. In fact there were no
arecrow' shells, only exploding bombers.

The dawn of 31 January 1944 in a typical Berlin street hours after approximately 2,000 tor of bombs had fallen on the Reich capital in less than fifteen minutes. It was the third raid the city in four nights.

omb aimer crouches over his sight in the nose of a Lancaster, his head surrounded by the
w of a burning German city as he prepares to release his load.

e devastation in the centre of Munich after the highly accurate raid of 24 April in which
Dambuster pilot S/Ldr Les Munro acted as master bomber for the main force. The raid
only the Frauenkirche still standing in the heart of the city amid a sea of rubble.

Bombs from higher-flying Lancasters have hit this Halifax over a V-weapon site in France
July 1944, removing part of its tailplane. Bombs from other aircraft were a constant fear f
crews over a target.

There were dangers even without meeting the enemy for Bomber Command airmen, ten
percent of whom died in training. This Lancaster of 35 Sqn crashed on take-off at Gravel
in July. It was the favoured aircraft of F/Lt Harold Hoover, who returned from leave to f
his much-loved C-Charlie wrecked.

Doodlebug, from one of the V-weapon sites Bomber Command battled to wipe out in the summer of 1944, arrives near Drury Lane in mid-July.

The raid on the Panzer training base at Mailly-le-Camp cost forty-two Lancasters, 11.6 per cent of the force which set out, but the camp was wrecked. *Above*: the repair sheds and billets of the 21st Panzer Group before the attack; and *below*, afterwards.

 Nazi hierarchy forced inmates of local concentration camps to dispose of unexploded
bs after bombing attacks. Here such prisoners are seen digging in the rubble after the
y raid on Bremen in August 1944.

Stuttgart was devastated in three heavy raids in July, particularly the night of 25/26, in wh
the centre of the old city southwest of the main station, as shown here, was virtually
destroyed.

The three raids also left their mark on the RAF. Pictured is the Halifax of F/Lt Jim Weav
of 102 Sqn shot up by a nightfighter on the way back from the first operation of 24/25 Ju
The aircraft is leaning to port because of a bullet-ridden tyre, which caused it to groundl
on landing.

Command's strikes at the sites themselves meant that between the middle of June and the end of August the average was ninety-five bombs a day.[24]

The last operation to a flying-bomb site was on 28 August, to Wemars/Cappel near Amiens. F/O Jim Lord, who had found his final training at Sandtoft so hazardous in May, had made several such trips that summer and was on the raid, which claimed a fellow 550 Sqn crew.

Trips to V1 launching sites were short, but they were often fairly low-level. The sites were well defended usually and no trip was a piece of cake, although we didn't see any fighters. On most daylight raids, whether to airfields or V-weapon sites we were subjected to predicted flak. My policy was to change course a degree or two so that the flak came where I would have been. I then resumed normal course. On the Wemars/Cappel raid I saw a Lancaster* going down. There was no fire at the time though it was definitely going down. In fact, although I didn't know it, it was being flown by P/O Beeson whose crew had joined 550 Sqn at more or less the same time as us. I didn't see anyone baling out myself. When we got back I discovered Beeson's name was missing.[25]

IT was known there was an even greater threat to London than the V1: the V2 rocket. Following the successful attack on the experimental works at Peenemünde, development and storage had been diversified and rocket storage and firing sites were identified in northern France at Mimoy-ecques, Watten, Siracourt and Wizernes. In fact, only Wizernes and Watten were designed for the rocket, though all were bombed.[26] Marquise-Mimoyecques was later found to be the site of a no less terrifying weapon, the V3. It was intended that there would be twenty-five of these enormous guns, each 400 feet long, set in inclined shafts in a hillside, with which the Germans intended to fire a rocket-assisted 6-inch projectile to London at a rate of one a minute.

* This aircraft had just bombed the launching site when it received a direct hit from a flak battery. The Lancaster went down and exploded, the pieces then hitting the ground. P/O Beeson and three members of his crew escaped by parachute, but the wireless operator Sgt J. K. Northgate, and the two gunners, Sgts H. S. Picton and J. A. Trayhorn, were killed, the last fatalities in Bomber Command's ten-week Doodlebug campaign.

It was for these targets 617 Sqn was particularly employed under Leonard Cheshire in the early summer of 1944. No squadron made a greater contribution to the V-weapons campaign than 617. In fact, the 12,000-lb Tallboy bomb the squadron could now carry had been designed by Barnes Wallis for the very purpose of destroying the concrete-encased V2 rocket sites. Wallis had been requested to attend a meeting at the Air Ministry as far back as July 1943, to be told there that the Germans were building rockets and a special high-penetration bomb would be needed to answer the threat.[27]

Before 617 Sqn were called in, the Wizernes site had been bombed up to ten times by USAAF B-24s and B-17s carrying nothing heavier than 2,000-lb bombs, which had created little lasting damage. On 24 June two Mosquitos of 617 Sqn marked the domed bunker of the complex near St Omer, with its 4 miles of tunnels that 1,300 Todt Organisation German and French workmen and male and female Russian prisoners of war had laboured over for months. Sixteen of the squadron's Lancasters followed, several scoring hits with their Tallboys.

It was the penultimate operation of F/O Nicky Ross, who had joined the Dambuster squadron the previous October, at the end of his second tour. He remembers:

It was the most dangerous trip I had yet was just a short flight of less than three hours over the French coast. I was the lead aircraft in a loose gaggle of three. The Lancaster on our port side was showing a couple of engines on fire and the boy on the starboard side got a direct hit from flak, his starboard wing was shot off and he went right down.* We saw some parachutes opening. My mid-upper gunner said, 'Jesus Christ, we're next.' Well, it just didn't happen. My guardian angel must have been on duty, but it was rather a tough one.

Flak was always worrying. My ground crew disowned me one time when I returned 'their' Lanc from Essen with seventy-three holes in the airframe. Flak was always present in and around the target area and was most frightening. I found it to be much better than a packet of All Bran. I found German night fighters to be all chicken. My top-

---

* F/Lt John Edward DFC in G-George of 617 Sqn crashed 7 miles south-west of St Omer, the squadron's first loss for exactly two months. The 29-year-old Devonshire pilot and three others of his crew of eight, which included three gunners, were killed, and one died later from his injuries.

class gunners advised me of any sightings and I would at once start bobbing and weaving. The night fighters were then aware they had been spotted and sheared off.[28]

A return by 617 Sqn on 17 July had a more lasting effect on Wizernes. Three of the squadron's 6-ton Tallboy bombs exploded next to the tunnels, one in the mouth of the complex and another just under the dome, causing the hillside to collapse and covering up the two rocket shafts. General Walter Dornberger ordered the site to be abandoned.

The day after the first Wizernes attack W/Cdr Cheshire marked the Siracourt site for his squadron, diving from 7,000 feet to 500 feet in an Eighth Air Force Mustang, which had only arrived at Woodhall Spa that afternoon and which Cheshire had not flown before. As Cheshire orbited the target after calling in the rest of the squadron and its Tallboys he saw one 'direct hit which penetrated the roof of the building and caused a large explosion and one hit by the western wall of the building which blew the wall in'.[29]

On 25 July the squadron dropped Tallboys on Watten, unloading on target in heavy predicted flak. F/O Don Cheney's Lancaster, a borrowed one while his own was being checked over, was so damaged by flak one engine was knocked out and the hydraulic system so severely damaged that the gun turrets wouldn't work and the bomb doors couldn't be closed. 'During our attack the aircraft was awash with leaking hydraulic fluid,' F/O Cheney later recorded. There was also 'a cloud of blue, acrid-smelling cordite smoke from the bursting flak shells exploding so close that we could feel the plane shudder and plainly hear the "boom" of the exploding shells.' In the confusion the mid-upper gunner baled out. F/O Cheney managed to keep control of the aircraft and turned for home.

A small piece of the Perspex above the cockpit had been blown out and there seemed to be a lot of holes, large and small, throughout the aircraft. Thank God, however, there was no fire and none of the remaining crew were injured. As we neared the coast of France more flak came up. We took such evasive action as we could with so much of our 'laundry' hanging out. Fortunately the flak bursts drifted past harmlessly out of range and we began a steady descent in order to increase airspeed and get out of enemy territory as soon as possible. Jim Rosher, the flight engineer, perched on his jump seat to my right, tapped me on the shoulder, smiled and pointed above my head. There, not more than 15 feet above us and sliding gently to port, was the most beautiful Spitfire I have ever seen.

The Spitfire slid back and forth above and below the crippled bomber until much of the Channel had been crossed, eventually perching off the starboard wingtip for five minutes, its pilot 'grinning and giving us the thumbs up, then with a saluting gesture he peeled off to starboard and was gone'.

F/O Cheney made it back to Woodhall Spa, but had to use the emergency compressed-air device to blow down and lock the under-carriage as he had no hydraulic fuel left to activate it. The aircraft, P-Peter, made a safe landing, but because it had nearly a thousand holes in its airframe was later broken up for spares. He found himself apologising to P-Peter's regular pilot, whose aircraft he had been given while he was on leave and 'it also cost me a good few at the mess bar in order to assuage his crew'.[30] Days later news reached the squadron that his mid-upper gunner was a prisoner of war.

On each occasion of the attacks on Watten, Mimoyecques, Siracourt and Wizernes by 617 Sqn, Lancasters of other groups followed and by the time the four sites were overrun by troops in September 7,469 tons of bombs had been dropped on them.[31] Not one V2 rocket was fired from France and the Marquise-Mimoyecques V3 site was so churned up by bombing and the projectile proved so unstable in flight the project was abandoned.

Cheshire's last operational flight in Europe was to the Mimoyecques complex on 6 July where he marked at low level in his Mustang. Six days later he was stood down and so ended a remarkable operational career over Germany and the occupied countries, which had begun on Whitleys in 1940 and finished on a US-built single-seat aircraft. He had completed 100 operations and two months later was told he had been recommended for the VC. Released from operations with him were the three original Dams Raid pilots still flying with the squadron: Les Munro, Dave Shannon and Joe McCarthy. They missed the all-ranks dance four days later, which the whole base had been looking forward to.[32]

THE campaign against the much-vaunted V-weapons by fighter, guns, balloons and bomber brought a diminishing return for Germany and of the 1,124 flying bombs launched between 16 August and 5 September only 17 per cent fell in the target area. Out of ninety-seven V1s reported approaching the United Kingdom on the night of 27/28 August, eighty-seven were destroyed. The Germans were eventually reduced to launching a few V1s from aircraft and when the V2 campaign began in September it was from Holland.[33] On 7 September Duncan Sandys, who headed the Crossbow sub-committee of the War Cabinet, announced 'the Battle for London was over' and blackout restrictions were eased to a 'dim out'. Between 15 June and 15 July, the most threatening time, 2,579 V1s arrived in England, of which 1,280 fell inside the London area.[34] On average each Doodlebug, produced and fired with great effort by Germany, killed only one person in Britain, Churchill announcing to the House on 6 July – using somewhat out-of-date figures – that 2,754 flying bombs had been launched so far for 2,752 deaths.[35]

The biggest enemy to Harris that summer had not been the Germans but the weather. On 1 August, for instance, of 719 Bomber Command aircraft sent to bomb six sites and a depot in a forest, only seventy-four reached their targets. Yet during a brief spell of improved conditions between 3 and 6 August 15,000 tons of bombs went down in twelve successful attacks.[36]

Much had been learned by Bomber Command because of the need to mark and hit small objectives. It was hoped this knowledge could be employed effectively when the time came for the command to return to targets in Germany on release from Eisenhower's needs. On 11 July, for instance, a Lancaster of 582 Sqn had been fitted with Oboe equipment and when it released its bombs on the V1 site of Gapennes so did other Lancasters flying in formation, allowing a great tonnage to be dropped on just one Oboe signal. It became one of Bomber Command's most precise methods of bombing in cloud. In this period, too, Bomber Command began to use the G-H navigational aid, which was a combination of Gee and Oboe, and could be used by up to 100 aircraft at a time to hit a pinpointed small target.

The new Bomber Command support force 100 Group by now consisted of nine full squadrons. Not only were they employed in offensive Ranger patrols, particularly over enemy night-fighter airfields, and Serrate patrols, whereby RAF Mosquitos closed in on the Lichtenstein transmissions of Luftwaffe night fighters and shot them down in great numbers, they were also used to jam enemy radar with radio countermeasures or spy on the Luftwaffe with airborne recording machines and cameras, which copied the wavelengths of German search equipment and then took such information home for the boffins to counteract.

F/O Harry Reed was a 100 Group pilot flying a 169 Sqn Serrate-equipped Mosquito. He remembers:

> The first aircraft I shot down was an Me110 on 28 June. The target that night was Metz and I was asked to patrol the Mucke beacon. My navigator, F/O Stuart Watts, got a Serrate contact, which gave direction, but didn't tell you the distance. As you got closer you hopefully converted this into an AI contact, which gave you height, direction and distance, and on this occasion I made a very easy interception. It was quite a light night and identification was relatively easy. The poor devil didn't know what hit him. I positioned underneath the Me110, pulled back on the stick as I fired and he exploded and went down in a spiral dive, then there was a glow on the ground commensurate with him having gone in.[37]

IN this most intensive span of bomber operations crews were often grateful for a couple of soggy days, which meant a respite off the station. Those due leave and able to travel to London found a friendlier atmosphere in which total strangers, facing a common danger, were apt to burst into animated conversation. There were also fewer queues, now that one-eighth of the population had left, and more food to go round.

The Australian bomb aimer Harry Stack got a few days leave that summer and decided to explore again a country bursting with verdant splendour in the daily showers and wild flowers springing forth from the fringes of one-time meadows now turned to the plough.

> We were always made very welcome by the English. They went out of their way to give us all the help they could. I went on leave with Jamey Curtis, our rear gunner from Regina, Saskatchewan and the youngest member of our crew. We stopped off at Oxford to look around and found everything booked out for the night. The publican at a hostelry called the George made up a bed for us in the lounge after all the patrons had left. They woke us in the morning before people started to clear the mess from the night before. Yes we were treated very well in England, not a complaint anywhere.[38]

But others found pub landlords weren't always so accommodating with boisterous airmen. W/O Cliff Hill, the 35 Sqn rear gunner, remembered:

Most of the crew were having a drink in the Cross Keys in St Neots when Jack Mossop the bomb aimer said he could drink three pints in a minute. Amazingly he did it, then Hoover the pilot slapped him on the back and said, 'Well done!' That was it. Jack threw up all over the landlord's new carpets. We were asked to leave and Hoove and Mossop felt obliged to offer to pay for the carpets being cleaned, but the landlord wouldn't accept it.[39]

It was a moment in time to seize life with both hands and enjoy it while it lasted. Just after the invasion Bomber Command had matched the Americans in their daylight campaign against Germany's oil supplies by attacking at night. No targets were more steadfastly guarded and the sight of stricken bombers flaming red and orange against the blackness became etched on the minds of aircrew as they were called to deny the enemy his resources of fuel in the most heavily defended area of the Reich outside Berlin, the Ruhr. Now several operations were being mounted in one night as the groups fought their individual wars. For the unlucky it meant their group received what looked like the undivided attention of the enemy. One target alone would cost more than a quarter of the Lancaster force dispatched to it by 5 Group.

15

Throttling the Luftwaffe

The oil campaign was designed to bring the Nazi war machine grinding to a halt by starving it of the fuel its aircraft, tanks and trucks gobbled up so greedily in training and battle, and even more so in retreat. That it succeeded was evidenced in the late summer, autumn and winter by the declining quality of Luftwaffe aircrew for lack of fuel to train them properly and by the hose-carrying Panzer troops of Germany's last push in the Ardennes, whose only hope of continuing to keep their huge Tiger armour running was by siphoning from the tanks of captured US trucks. Next to the Transportation Plan of Normandy, which had starved the German Army of supplies, bottled it up for annihilation and even prevented material for the flying bombs arriving, it was probably the single most important campaign Bomber Command fought that summer. Denying the Germans their oil would eventually be the war winner.

But Harris didn't see it that way. Only a week after D-Day the Deputy Supreme Allied Commander, Air Chief Marshal Sir Arthur Tedder, handed him the targets of ten synthetic oil plants situated in the Ruhr and ordered him to stop them functioning. Harris resisted the plan from the start. His most telling arguments were that such a campaign would have to be carried out at night because his poorly armed bombers would have so far to fly; nocturnal operations would inevitably mean inaccuracy; and that such a campaign would inevitably drag into the winter, when poor weather would give the Germans a respite to repair the damaged plants. 'It was only by a conjunction of circumstances which amounted to a miracle that we were able to keep up the attack during those winter months and so disappoint the enemy's confident expectations,' he wrote in his post-war memoirs.[1]

Harris judged it as another panacea plan in the long list of cure-all targets, such as Schweinfurt's ball-bearing plants. But the game rapidly changed. In June Germany still had the vast Romanian oil fields; by August they had been overrun by the Russians. 'This contributed a great deal, as did the loss at about the same time of the refineries in Poland, towards the success of the offensive against the enemy's oil,' Harris wrote two years later.[2] However, in June, Harris contended, 'what the Allied strategists did was to bet on an outsider and it happened to win the race'.[3] Harris, the ultimate good soldier, having been given his orders now did his utmost to make them work. He was aware he would be sending his crews against targets that Germany would defend to the last. Such desperate defence rapidly became obvious to the airmen themselves as they conducted a campaign against oil installations in Germany by night while their comrades in the USAAF suffered equally, continuing the offensive they had begun in May, in bombing their own selected oil installations by day.

The first of such targets allotted to Bomber Command was Gelsenkirchen on 12 June in which more than 300 aircraft bombed the Nordstern synthetic oil plant with great accuracy on Oboe, ending its production of 1,000 tons of aviation fuel a day for several weeks. The price was seventeen Lancasters, 6.1 per cent, a rate some way beyond the supportable for Bomber Command. Many of them were shot down by Schräge Musik, the sight of flaming, falling wreckage appearing suddenly in the sky still being explained away by intelligence officers at debriefings as 'scarecrow' shells. The aircraft of F/Lt Len Isaacson, a Canadian rear gunner on 166 Sqn, nearly became a Schräge Musik victim leaving Gelsenkirchen. He recalls:

I was searching in the dark for any enemy night fighters who might be following us. Suddenly I heard cannons barking loudly and saw lights flashing directly below. We took evasive action and that was it. Even with the noise of the Lancaster motors and the wind and with my helmet on and earphones covering my ears I very clearly heard the loud barking of the cannons. That fighter had to be very close to us and out of sight. At base the pilot told me he saw tracers streaking up in front of him at a steep angle. I wondered how a night fighter could be so very close under our Lanc and yet be able to fire upwards at a 70 degree angle. I completed my tour of thirty-five operations on 30 August still wondering, 'What the hell was that?'[4]

W/O Ralph Laurie, an Australian ABC operator on 101 Sqn, experienced a nightmare return from Gelsenkirchen, his twelfth trip. He remembers:

On the target our tailplane was hit by flak, which punched a hole the size of a football in the aircraft, jamming the wires running to those controls on the port side, so that we had a 12 to 13 degree list. As we were leaving the target one of the port engines was knocked out. The flight engineer clipped on a fifteen-minute oxygen bottle and went down to the tail to try to correct the list manually. Unfortunately he pulled the wrong wire and our list developed smartly to about 23 degrees. Then the other port engine developed problems and had to be feathered. Naturally our speed fell considerably. We dropped out of the bomber stream and approached the French coast at 7 a.m. at a very low height. I could see clearly into the back gardens of French villagers, but somehow we escaped being attacked by German fighters and were not even shot at by the coastal defences.

Over the Channel the pilot, Tom Welsby, put the plane down low so that we just cleared the water and no hostile could shoot at our belly. In this way we slowly made our way back and the White Cliffs of Dover were a very welcome sight. It was generally agreed we should try to make it to base at Ludford Magna, but because of the big list to port Tom had to land the plane on one wheel there while we all took up crash positions. It was a cheering sight to see the ambulance racing down the runway on one side of the aircraft while the fire brigade followed on the other, but Tom made a perfect landing, the plane gradually settling on both wheels as it slowed. When we arrived at the debriefing room we saw the board showed us as missing. We asked the padre for an extra shot of rum in our coffee.[5]

The price of hitting Gelsenkirchen had been heavy, but it was the next raid, on 16 June, which really proved how costly the oil campaign was going to be. The route to the synthetic oil plant at Sterkrade took the 300-plus mixed force of Lancasters and Halifaxes near a German night-fighter beacon. The result was twenty-one bombers shot down by fighters and another ten by flak over the target. The Halifax losses amounted to 13.6 per cent of those on the raid, 77 Sqn at Full Sutton losing almost a third of the twenty-three Mk IIIs it had sent. The Canadian 6 Group particularly suffered: 431 Sqn at Croft – where crews had complained so bitterly about the third-of-an-op edict in March and where early-morning physical training introduced for aircrew was now causing new resentment – lost a quarter of the sixteen Halifaxes it dispatched.[6]

F/Sgt Vic Farmer, the 550 Sqn navigator whose tour had begun with a briefing on D-Day itself, took part in the raid.

It was our second operation over Germany and our second to the Ruhr, we had been to Gelsenkirchen four days before. It was the sixth trip of our tour so as a comparatively new operational crew we were in the last wave to attack. I didn't see aircraft going down myself because I never looked out of the aircraft on any raid. I felt that if I saw flak or whatever it might affect my concentration, so I kept myself well curtained off.

We got back to base OK, had the usual meal after debriefing, then went off to our Nissen hut, but it wasn't long before our sleep was disturbed when the belongings of Neilson's crew, who had shared our sleeping quarters, were collected as they hadn't returned. This was an experienced crew over halfway through their tour. They were a fine group of people, who had advised us about operations.* It was quite traumatic for us. We asked ourselves, 'If they couldn't make it what chance do we have?' Not much sleep then followed as we looked at all those empty spaces.[7]

Sgt Ken Down, the 550 Sqn flight engineer whose tour had begun with the daylight raid on Le Havre two days before, now found himself in the more familiar environment of the night over Sterkrade, but there were more alarming surprises in store for the inexperienced crew. He remembers:

Going in to Sterkrade I could see the flak exploding. It seemed to come up very, very slowly then *whoosh!* it had gone by. I saw two aircraft hit by flak and go down with a long stream of flame. There was no

---

* F/O Donald Neilson, 27, had come from Argentina to volunteer for the RCAF. He and his entire crew, including a Canadian second-dickey pilot W/O J. K. Murray, were killed when their Lancaster was shot down near Achterberg in Holland.

sign of anyone baling out and in fact one aircraft exploded in the air. We didn't see any night fighters, but on the way back we ran into a severe electrical storm. It was very weird. The window frames outside the cockpit had lines of little sparks following each other round and the wingtips were just the same. It was quite frightening. The whole thing lasted about twenty minutes to half an hour as we lost height. We didn't have a clue what it was. We were afraid the electricity we could see would explode the fuel and at the same time the aircraft was being buffeted by the turbulence. It affected the compass and the navigator was tearing his hair out trying to work out where we were.

It meant we made landfall at Southwold instead of Mablethorpe. By the time we got back to North Killingholme we were quite short of fuel, not an unusual occurrence as they would sacrifice fuel for bomb load. When we got down we were told at debriefing they had been about to switch the runway lights off, they thought we were missing. We also found out from the Met people that what we had seen was St Elmo's fire.[8]

The cost of the oil campaign so far had indeed been disproportionate, but it was a double strike on 21 June that proved the most costly of all. Sir Ralph Cochrane had hoped his 5 Group could demonstrate the effectiveness of their low-level marking technique once more and had split his force, sending 124 Lancasters to Scholven-Buer and 133 to Wesseling. Both oil plants in fact turned out to be covered by thick low cloud and Mosquitos were unable to mark at low level, 8 Group Pathfinder aircraft using Oboe-directed skymarkers on Scholven-Buer and the 133 Lancasters bombing Wesseling on H2S. Neither target was seriously damaged.[9] For the first time a Mandrel screen had been mounted by 199 Sqn of 100 Group for the Sterkrade operation of five days before – aircraft, each carrying up to eight jamming transmitters, provided a barrier against German radar from which the bombers suddenly emerged. On 21 June, however, there was no Mandrel screen to divert the attention of the German controller as the two forces crossed the Dutch coast together, then split south of Rotterdam, and the *Nachtjäger* made contact in force. A total of forty-five Lancasters were lost, most falling to night fighters, though the flak was intense at both targets. Two German *Gruppen* alone, I and II/NJG1, destroyed twenty machines, one pilot downing five.[10] 'The enemy controllers plotted our bombers from The Hague and concentrated almost all their fighters on the southern Wesseling force,' the post-raid inquest at Bomber Command headquarters read. 'The brightness of the moonless sky – it was midsummer night – was undoubtedly the chief cause of the unusual measure of success obtained by the fighters.'[11]

S/Ldr Charles Owen, the 97 Sqn Pathfinder pilot who had seen his squadron commander shot down on D-Day, helped to back up the target marking at Scholven-Buer and recorded in his diary the next day:

> The Ruhr again and no one very enthusiastic about it. Ten-tenths low cloud at the target, but the place was stinking with flak and we weren't sorry to come away. Moon came up on the way home and the Jerry fighters enjoyed themselves, even following us halfway across the sea, which we thought rather against the rules. Not at all a nice trip and a lot of chaps missing.[12]

In fact, eight Lancasters were lost from the Scholven-Buer raid, but the missing from the Wesseling element amounted to thirty Lancasters shot down by fighters and another seven falling to flak. A total of 27.8 per cent of the 133 bombers dispatched failed to return, a disaster for the squadrons of 5 Group in the Wesseling force. The twice-decorated CO of 49 Sqn, W/Cdr Malcolm Crocker, was among those lost. He had taken a BBC correspondent with him, Kent Stevenson, who had hoped to do a broadcast for *War Report*. All were killed when the aircraft was shot down near Jülich/Mersch. Another five 49 Sqn aircraft also failed to return to Fiskerton, five vanished from 207 Sqn at Spilsby, six were missing from 57 Sqn – one down in the sea off East Anglia – and another six from 630 Sqn, which W/Cdr Crocker had formed the previous December. 57 and 630 Sqns shared the aerodrome of East Kirkby and the gaps were obvious the next day. But the scene at Dunholme Lodge in the dawn was the most dismal as the rain pattered down. There were six empty dispersals of 619 Sqn and another six of 44 Sqn, which shared the field.

F/Lt Gerry Mitchell was one of the luckier skippers on 44 Sqn who got back from Wesseling. He remembers:

> 44 Sqn sent out twelve Lancasters and six came back. We could see the searchlights flicking about and were just about to release our bombs when we were coned. The flak that came up was so close I could smell cordite. If I hear a plate dropped today I hate it, the sound is so close

to that of the flak I heard that night. I just pushed the stick forward to get out of the searchlights and came down from 18,000 feet to 3,000 feet. I think the airspeed was about 300 mph when I pulled out. You could do that with a Lanc, it was such a wonderful aircraft. The searchlights hadn't followed me at all thank goodness, so we went round again and dropped our bombs and beat it off home.[13]

Another 44 Sqn aircraft had made it back to Dunholme Lodge, but in a severely damaged state and with four crew missing. Mid-upper gunner F/Sgt Albert Bracegirdle was one of those crewmen, on the seventeenth trip of his second tour, which had begun with the Berlin operation of 15 February. He remembers:

We were meant to bomb at 0130 in the morning, but at 0130 we could see nothing. It was just a blank sky except lots of flak flying around. Eventually at 17,000 feet I saw a green marker, not the red spot TI, so I called the navigator and the pilot said: 'Give me a course.' Then, bump, we got hit in the tailplane and starboard wing. We didn't know if it was flak or a fighter. The pilot said: 'I can't hold it, prepare to abandon aircraft.' We had a second-dickey pilot on board and eventually the pilot said: 'Abandon aircraft, we're going down.' Four of us baled out. I was the first to the rear door. I fastened it back on the clip and the wireless operator followed me, then the nav and the second dickey. The wireless operator hit the tailplane and ended up having his leg amputated in Germany and was repatriated the following March.

I was scared stiff when I went out. There was lots of flak flying around and we were still in the target area. I don't remember a thing after leaving the plane. I had my hand on the ripcord handle, but how I pulled the ripcord I don't know. We were 3½ miles up without oxygen. The next thing I knew I came to in a wood as dawn was breaking ... I'd got lots of cuts on my face. I think the chute had hit me as it opened. I managed to stagger onto a cart track and at the end of the track I saw a house. I was shocked, covered in blood and had had nothing to eat or drink. I had wrenched my ankle and decided there was only one thing to do and that was to seek help.

I knocked at the door and a child aged about 10 answered. He indicated to me he was the only one in and would get help. The next I knew the Luftwaffe arrived. They took me to jail in the village of

Jülich, where a young fellow with a big, red swastika armband said: 'You have to take me to find your parachute.' We started walking up the road and another German pick-up truck came along with two RAF men in the back. They were two men from our squadron, a chap called Sargeant and a chap called Such.*

The Germans took all three of us to a German officers' training camp. We were there until the next day and could hear the trainees singing and bawling all night. Then they took us by train to Mönchengladbach where we were put on a trolley bus to a Luftwaffe camp nearby. It came off its wires at one point and we had to get off. A crowd gathered round when they saw us. They were getting very agitated and threatened to lynch us, so the Luftwaffe guard fixed bayonets and formed a circle round us until they could get us up to the camp. We were there two nights. In the meantime the wireless operator from our crew [F/Lt Radaway] arrived. He couldn't walk and was in a wheelchair. After two days they took us down to the train station to go to the Luftwaffe interrogation centre at Dulag Luft. I met the nav at Dulag Luft, but I never saw the second-dickey pilot again. We'd only just met him before we took off. He'd only had two hours of ops and was a prisoner of war already.

Our aircraft had flown on instead of crashing I discovered, so they couldn't put an aircraft to our crew. We were in solitary confinement for a week and each day the Germans would take us out to interrogate us. At first the interrogators were very amenable. They got the cigars out and offered me a drink, both of which I declined. It was all designed to soften me up and each day it got nastier and nastier. Then when they got fed-up of hearing the same name, rank and number every time, they finally said: 'We can't find your aircraft,† so you're going to be shot as a spy.' It was just mental torture. Every two or three days

---

* Sgt F. J. Such and Australian W/O A. J. Sargeant, the flight engineer and navigator of New Zealander P/O Russell Wood's Lancaster. The bomb aimer was Canadian and the wireless operator American. It is thought the crew was the only one lost in the war made up of airmen from Britain, the three Commonwealth air forces and the USAAF.[14]

† After F/Sgt Bracegirdle and the others baled out, the pilot, S/Ldr Steve Cockbain, managed to get the badly damaged aircraft back under control at 8,000 feet and brought it home with the rear gunner, the flight engineer and the bomb aimer still on board. Pressmen photographed them by the badly shot-up plane the next day. S/Ldr Cockbain finished his second tour, but was killed as an instructor in January 1945.

they would shove across these big forms, which they claimed had to
be filled in for the Red Cross, but I was just giving name, rank and
number. Finally when they realised that I wasn't going to tell them
anything they said: 'We know already.' Then they told me who the
flight commanders were on my squadron, the station commander and
the medical officer. They knew more about the station than I did and
I had been there six months. I don't know whether they had any spies
in Britain. I would have thought a lot of the information came from
aircrew who were scared to death.[15]

Two aircraft from 101 Sqn, which carried extra aerials to transmit
from its ABC equipment, were shot down on the Wesseling operation,
one of them that of P/O Gerry Hingley, who was coming towards the end
of a dramatic tour which included buckling the fuselage of a Lancaster in
a high-speed stall after being bracketed by German artillery. He wrote
after the war:

The night we were shot down was a massacre. I lost two engines
over the target, I rarely seemed to come home with all my motors.
We were briefed to come back at the silly height of 5,000 feet and
a few minutes from the coast a fighter got us. I couldn't do anything
except order a bale-out ... I left the seat at 500 feet when all control
had gone. The bomb aimer was dying on his couch, so they pushed
him out having pulled his chute. He came down OK, but bled to
death, his left leg hanging by one ham string ... I broke my back
on the way out, probably those damned aerials ... I hit the ground
damn hard after bouncing against a bridge, which pushed my ribs
into my left lung.[16]

P/O Hingley was in hospital for weeks with a broken thigh and chest
injuries.

The threatened lynching that F/Sgt Bracegirdle experienced in Mönchengladbach was now a growing trend as the tide so obviously turned
for Germany. There had been incidents in 1943 of aircrew disappearing
after their parachutes had been seen to open and in early 1944 of others
seen hanging from lamp standards by newly downed airmen. By and
large if an airman was found by Luftwaffe, Wehrmacht or Kriegsmarine
personnel he was safe. However, on 27 May 1944 in a front-page editorial
in Nazi Party newspapers the Reich Propaganda Minister Josef Goebbels

had declared it was a German serviceman's duty to allow downed airmen to be killed by the mob. He wrote:

> It seems to us hardly possible and tolerable to use German police and soldiers against German people when they treat murderers of children as they deserve. Fighter and bomber pilots who are shot down are not to be protected against the fury of the people. I expect from all police officers that they will refuse to lend their protection against these gangster types. Authorities acting against the popular sentiment will have to answer to me.[17]

So now the German police were being threatened that if they accorded downed airmen the protection due under the Geneva Convention Germany had signed they faced punishment. Goebbels's words found fertile ground among those who had lost homes and family members in the terrible destruction of Germany's cities, which Hitler and the Nazi Party had caused by their policies. Himmler's secret police were able to foment that need for revenge. From now until the end of the war the Gestapo and civilians themselves would kill perhaps hundreds of Allied aircrew. It will never be known how many died in this way.

A pilot from the Coningsby-based 83 Sqn, shot down on the Wesseling raid of 21 June, was among those who was so treated by the Gestapo. The crew of F/Lt Ronald Walker, 21, were on the last trip of their forty-five-operation Pathfinder tour when they were caught by a night fighter near the Belgian/Dutch border on the way to Wesseling. The aircraft exploded and F/Lt Walker was blown unconscious through the canopy, his seat-type parachute automatically opening and bringing him safely to earth, though the rest of the crew, who had all been recommended for gallantry medals, were killed. F/Lt Walker made contact with the Dutch Resistance and was eventually in hiding in a house in Tilburg. He shared it with two evaders shot down on the Sterkrade operation: 23-year-old Canadian navigator F/O Roy Carter, whose aircraft had been among the four lost from 431 Sqn, and Australian F/O Jack Nott, 26, who had been the bomb aimer in one of the 77 Sqn Halifaxes shot down. On 9 July seven Gestapo men arrived at the building, pushed the three men into the courtyard and shot them. A neighbour in the house next door witnessed the Gestapo machine-gun the wounded men to finish them off. The woman hiding them, Jacoba Pulskens, was ordered to cover the bodies with a sheet and instead spread a clean, ironed Dutch flag* over the corpses before being taken away to a concentration camp. She was gassed at Ravensbrück seven months later, one of the estimated 2,000 escape network members who died in Occupied Europe in the course of the war, getting an almost equal number of evaders back to Britain.[18]

Admin officers at stations throughout 5 Group were busy as a new day dawned after the carnage at Wesseling, beginning the process that would result in a telegram to relatives telling them their airman husband or son was missing from operations. It was less likely the Red Cross would be able to follow up with the good news that the airman was a prisoner of war and, in fact, of the 260 missing after Wesseling only thirty-seven went behind the wire and nine evaded.

David Bailey, the brother of F/Sgt Reginald Bailey, wireless operator in F/Lt Walker's crew, remembers the telegram arriving at his own home in Malmesbury, Wiltshire.

> There were eight of us, four boys and four girls. My brother was very good at Morse code and when he came home on leave he used to listen to it on the wireless and tell us what it meant. I was 13 when he was killed and he was 21, the second-oldest boy. It was a terrible day for the family when we heard he was missing. I used to deliver telegrams myself, but I wasn't on that Saturday. The lad next door was also a telegram boy and he delivered it. We were all in the house when the telegram arrived. It just said Reg was missing. We did hear at one stage from the Red Cross it was thought he might be in the hands of the Dutch Underground, because it was known the pilot was. We thought, knowing him, my brother would be able to get home, but the Red Cross told us on 3 November he had been killed. He had met a WAAF while on operations and had got married and his wife was expecting. His death was confirmed by an officer from the Air Ministry who came to see us on 27 December, the day after his son was born.[19]

BOMBER Command's oil campaign continued through June, July and August, nearly 200 aircraft returning to Wesseling on 18 July and causing great damage for the loss of only one Halifax, and 234 going to Sterkrade

---

* This flag now hangs in the thirteenth-century St Michael's Church in Coningsby, handed over by the Resistance in honour of the executed airmen.

on 18 August, again bringing serious destruction for minimal loss, in this case one Halifax and one Lancaster.

The full range of deviations, diversions and aggressive patrols of 100 Group were now being exhibited over Europe. It was so on the night of 20 July when 147 Lancasters, mainly from 3 Group, hit Homberg, further reducing its fluctuating output from between 120 and 970 tons of aviation fuel a day, which was already drastically down from the peak of 6,000 tons a day before the USAAF and RAF had started their attacks. The raid researchers at Bomber Command later reported:

> 42 Mosquitos of 100 Group and seven of Air Defence Great Britain carried out Serrate and intruder patrols, destroying two Me 110, one Ju88, and probably a fourth aircraft. Fourteen Stirlings and four Fortresses operated a Mandrel screen, four Fortresses operated Jostle and two more ABC aircraft, two Halifaxes, three Fortresses and four Stirlings dropped Window. 108 medium and heavy bombers carried out a diversionary sweep over the North Sea.[20]

F/O Harry Reed, the 169 Sqn Mosquito pilot who had claimed his first victory with Serrate equipment at the end of June, was one of the successful fighter pilots. He remembers:

> The score of Hun aircraft shot down by 100 Group Mosquitos stood at ninety-nine for quite a time. My squadron was not on ops for a night or so and we thought one of the other squadrons would get the prize 100th. Not so. On the 20/21 July as the only Mossies on ops we bagged three Huns, one by W/Cdr Bromley, one by F/Lt Fifield and one by myself. We were positioned at or near one of the night-fighter assembly beacons where they were directed into the bomber stream and on this night I was ordered to patrol the Homberg area.
>
> It was no good being in the bomber stream itself because there were too many contacts. My navigator got a Serrate contact, then an AI contact. It was my usual tactic to ask the navigator to place the enemy aircraft against the light part of the sky for the interception and myself in the dark. There's always a lighter piece of sky at 20,000–30,000 feet and I could see a Ju88 outlined against it. The reason the score stuck at ninety-nine for 100 Group was there had been one or two dubious shootings-down where it was a question of whether a Mosquito had been shot down, so we had to go in and visually identify a contact. I

got in quite close and saw it was a Ju88. The crew weren't aware I was there. I then dropped behind, throttled back and set my aim shortly below then pulled back on the stick as I fired, bringing my cannon fire through the mass of the enemy aircraft. In a moment there was an explosion, which lit up the German crosses on the enemy fuselage, and it went into a dive on fire. There was a great party in our mess at Great Massingham to celebrate the score of 100. It was a memorable occasion to which the bigwigs were not invited because we wanted to let our hair down.[21]

Hauptmann Heinz Rokker, a night-fighter pilot on I/NJG2, who would end the war with sixty-four victories and the Knight's Cross with Oak Leaves, remembers what it was like for the hunter to become the hunted that summer.

In the beginning of 1944 my Ju88 c-6 was equipped with the FuG 220 SN-2 radar interception system. Initially the SN-2 could not be jammed and it did lead to more shoot-downs, but the biggest danger to the German night fighters starting from that period were the English long-distance night fighters, the Beaufighter and Mosquito. We could not interfere with their radar systems and those Beaufighters and Mosquitos could track the German aircraft at high altitude. In my *Gruppe* seven crews were shot down by Mosquitos.

Another reason for the high losses among Luftwaffe *Nachtjäger* in that period was that many crews came directly out of training into combat without experience in night fighting itself and especially having to fly long-distance missions.[22]

Despite all the countermeasures and aggressive patrols of 100 Group the German controller was able occasionally to sort wheat from the chaff and assemble enough *Nachtjäger Gruppen* in time at the correct point to severely maul the bomber force. He got it right on the Homberg raid and twenty Lancasters were shot down. It was a particular disaster for 75 (New Zealand) Sqn, the adjutant's office later recording laconically in the operational record book: 'Twenty-six aircraft took off, nineteen were successful in bombing with the aid of markers which seemed well concentrated. Two good explosions were seen and smoke came up from the target area. Heavy AA fire was moderate, but fighters were very active, eight combats taking place. Seven aircraft failed to return.'[23]

*

AS the USAAF continued its daylight attacks on oil installations deep into Germany with Mustang fighter escort, in August the lighter-armed heavies of Bomber Command were employed on short-haul daylight raids to oil targets in France and Belgium when they weren't being used in a tactical role in Normandy or hitting V-weapon sites in the Pas-de-Calais.

Flight engineer Sgt Ken Down, of 550 Sqn, found that the insistence of the squadron commander W/Cdr Alan Sisley on formation flying similar to the Americans made strikes on oil targets by day almost as dangerous as those such as the one on heavily defended Sterkrade by night. He remembers:

> On 5 August we went to Pauillac, an oil refinery near Bordeaux. We took off in the afternoon and flew in formation right down across the West Country almost to Land's End, then made a sharp left turn and descended to 100 feet across the Bay of Biscay. We ascended to about 500 feet to make a left turn into the target. Formation flying was very worrying and a great strain on the pilot and engineer. We were really flogged to death trying to keep in formation because the response from control surfaces isn't very rapid on a heavily laden aircraft. I did fifteen formation ops out of the thirty-two of my tour. At Pauillac there was quite a bit of flak coming up. We were routed back over Brest. Most of the German flak units had been cleared by then, but there was this one isolated battery near Brest. They had a field day as the force flew home. I don't think they shot anybody down, but they put the wind up a lot of people.[24]

Navigator F/Sgt Vic Farmer, of the same squadron, was on a daylight raid to Bordeaux a week later. He says:

> Only thirty-six aircraft were detailed for this eight-hour trip on oil installations. We were the first aircraft over the target, coming in from the sea. It was defended by radar-controlled flak and they concentrated on us. We were only at about 8,000 feet and we went over the target with no change of direction or speed, so we should have been a sitting duck. But our skipper, showing skill and courage, gently lifted the aircraft so that the flak burst below us. We could smell the cordite it was so close. When we arrived back at base we found dozens of small

holes on the underside of the aircraft, but no serious damage. Skip's skilful piloting had saved our lives.[25]

Sgt Frank Etherington, the flight engineer who had found the Nuremberg losses so daunting when he was in training at the end of March, was by now on 166 Sqn in 1 Group in North Lincolnshire. His was one of 108 Lancaster crews briefed to attack an oil depot and storage tanks at Ertvelde/Rieme in Belgium on 18 August, from which all returned safely, the same night as 210 Halifaxes from 4 Group successfully attacked the Sterkrade synthetic oil plant, losing one aircraft. He found for himself how the oil campaign was now reducing the quality of Luftwaffe pilots for lack of training.

While we were circling base to gain height before setting course we lost power on the starboard outer at about 8,000 feet. I wanted to feather it, but the pilot wouldn't let me because it was powering a generator, so we just let it windmill. It was useless as a means of propulsion, but the pilot, who was a French Canadian, F/O Arthur Laflamme, was a very press-on type and went on with just three engines because it was only a short hop to Belgium. The whole trip only took about three hours.

We were just over the coast when we were attacked by a night fighter. The rear gunner spotted it coming in and warned the mid-upper and called a corkscrew to starboard. But of course we had no starboard inner and you don't dive into a dead engine, so the pilot went to port. The rear gunner screamed his head off, 'I said starboard, starboard,' but it was too late. Both gunners started firing and as I wasn't strapped in I grabbed the hook for my collapsible seat and hung on as we went down. I could see our own tracer going across the top of the Perspex as the fighter went over us, but he didn't return fire and disappeared. Our moment of glory was all over in about ten seconds. The German was either very inexperienced or a real dumb-bell. I think at that time a lot of German night-fighter pilots were pretty inexperienced and a bit hesitant.[26]

The main raid that night had been by 288 aircraft to Bremen, which devastated the port area, sinking eight ships, but from which only one Lancaster was missing; another 144 bombers, mainly Halifaxes, had attacked rail yards at Connantre in eastern France without loss; and a third force of 158 Lancasters had attacked the L'Isle-Adam V-weapon storage depot near Paris, which S/Ldr Owen had marked in a Mosquito with great accuracy after the marking had begun badly, later writing in his diary, 'Had to mark the target myself in a hurry and went down to 100 feet. Luckily no defences opened up and we got away with it. Quite a lot of flak from Rouen on return and we followed a Lanc down and saw it belly land in a field. Went down to have a look and saw the pilot* climb out and wave.'*27 So out of a total of 1,220 heavy night bombers on six important targets only six had failed to return. It was clear to Harris that the Luftwaffe had now been so reduced in efficiency as that of Bomber Command soared, he could risk a raid on Germany in daylight.

On 27 August he sent more than 200 Halifaxes of 4 Group back to the oil target of Homberg, which had proved so costly to 75 Sqn only five weeks before. The RAF had built fighter strips in Normandy within weeks of the invasion and this, plus the ability of extending the range of fighters with the ubiquitous drop tank – a British invention – meant the raid was escorted, nine squadrons of Spitfires protecting the bombers on the outward journey and seven on the withdrawal. There was intense flak over the target, but not one bomber was lost.[28] It was Bomber Command's first major daylight raid to Germany since August 1941 and an important psychological blow to the Luftwaffe hierarchy, that they could not now prevent damage to an important target in daylight by an RAF force that had been compelled to spend four years operating by night. A very few fighters approached, but were seen off.

Sgt Frank Jones, the 76 Sqn flight engineer, was on the raid in a Halifax III.

On approaching the target both gunners saw a fighter coming in and the rear gunner told the pilot to corkscrew. He responded immediately, but as the port wing came up a flak shell exploded underneath and tipped us on our back. We found ourselves going down with a full bomb load. Everyone was thrown about in the aircraft and our intercom leads were pulled out. One minute my head was in the astrodome and the next it was my feet. I tried to grab my parachute, but as I pulled the retaining bungee cord over, it disappeared down the tail. I sat down

* This was F/Lt A. J. Saunders (RAAF) of 83 Sqn, who evaded.

and thought, 'This is it and there's nothing I can do about it.' The captain was quite a short-legged chap, but amazingly he managed to right the aircraft and I could feel it coming out of its dive. We had gone down from 18,000 feet to 6,000 feet. How on earth the skipper managed to pull us out we never knew. Over the next few minutes all we could hear was heavy breathing over the intercom. All our loose equipment, logs, maps and pencils were now lying in the back of the aircraft. We gained a bit of height and could see the target being bombed ahead, so we went in, dropped our load and turned for home. I hadn't a log and the navigator hadn't a log and everything had to be done by rule of thumb, but we got back OK.[29]

Oil refineries would feature on the target lists at High Wycombe every month until the closing few weeks of the war, reaching a peak in March and April 1945. The initial impact, however, on German fuel resources was made by the USAAF in May 1944, and by both the USAAF and RAF together in the subsequent June, July and August. In July the Reich Armaments Minister Albert Speer wrote to Hitler that the losses in aviation spirits might be as much as nine-tenths. Without better fighter protection and an increased effort to quickly repair damage, he warned, 'it will be absolutely impossible to cover the most urgent of the necessary supplies for the Wehrmacht by September'.[30] In fact, the Luftwaffe was now in a spiral of defeat whereby lack of fuel meant fewer fighters to defend the synthetic oil plants and less defence meant less oil to fuel those very same fighters.

By September German oil production had fallen to 35 per cent of the level before the campaign had begun and aviation fuel was down to 5.4 per cent.[31] The three-month Bomber Command offensive against oil had taken 16,716 tons of bombs from their constantly resupplied dumps on the airfields of eastern Britain. All the time Harris had felt particularly deprived of his squadrons to achieve what he thought was their true purpose: to blitz Germany's industrial cities and prove his case that such bombing could bring the war to an end by a collapse from within. Harris admitted in his post-war memoirs that when told in the middle of June to join the USAAF oil campaign he had been opposed because it 'would only prolong the respite which the German industrial cities had gained from the use of bombers in a tactical role'. The C-in-C saw it as 'swopping horses in mid stream'.[32]

When not striking at oil targets in June, July and August, Bomber

Command was supporting the armies in Normandy by making night attacks on fortified villages and other strong points holding up the Allied advance, and hitting V-weapon sites. At the heart of the oil campaign in July as Harris obeyed SHAEF's bidding, all the while looking for an opportunity to return to raiding Germany's city industry, he was diverted from his main aim yet again by new, more far-reaching demands in the Transportation Plan. With the Allies still trying to force a breakthrough in Normandy and the need to deny the enemy his supplies as keen as ever Harris was asked by SHAEF in early July to destroy several railway junctions in north-eastern France. There would be no better place for a new bottleneck than the railway at Revigny, in the Meuse department 150 miles east of Paris, where lines east to west and north to south crossed. Harris promised success. In fact, it would take three raids, not one, to wreck the rail yards at Revigny, the first two operations alerting the enemy to eventual intention. The third raid would be third time unlucky for those squadrons making a return visit to the small railway town.

16

One-way Tickets in the Transportation Plan

There were few nights off station for aircrew in July. The constant call for the bomber boys' services in many directions in Normandy, in striking at oil targets, in furthering the reaches of the Transportation Plan, all often at short notice, and in eventually bombing Germany in force again, kept them at a state of readiness more familiar to Fighter Command in 1940. As warm air eddied and climbed, tightening to cloud in a colder altitude then releasing torrents of rain which meant another scrub and a further wait for the possibility of an alternative target, crews idly turned the pages of *Picture Post*, *Blighty* or *Tee Em* in the mess, or gathered in the smoky heat of the station cinema where calls to briefing were inevitably flashed on screen at the key moment of a film to the groans, whistles and shouts of the audience.

F/Sgt Vic Farmer, the 550 Sqn navigator, remembers the atmosphere at North Killingholme.

> Some of the Commonwealth aircrew could be a bit bawdy and they didn't like the station adjutant who had flown in the First World War and had an Observer's badge.* I and some of these chaps were sitting a few rows behind him in the station cinema one day and the Australian and Canadian airmen had a pick at him, shouting comments about his brevet. He took one glance over his shoulder and obviously marked me. A warm summer evening a few nights later he stopped me for

---

* Because of its winged 'O' design the Observer's brevet was known throughout Bomber Command as the 'Flying Arsehole'.

failing to salute him. Of course, you didn't normally salute on operational squadrons apart from reporting to the flight office at the start of the day. He told me I would be charged. I was up for a commission and if the charge had been substantiated my commission would have been put back for six months or scrubbed altogether. I was brought before the CO and I told him I failed to salute the adjutant because I was walking westward and the sun was in my eyes. A flicker of a smile came across his face and he said: 'Admonishment.' An admonishment didn't count for very much, so later the commission came through. I didn't blame the adjutant, in his case I might have done the same.[1]

Crews not on ops or on standby could visit the pub, and at Kirmington, where Sgt Frank Etherington was stationed as a flight engineer in the late summer of 1944, they could do so without even leaving the main gate. Etherington remembers:

The Marrowbone and Cleaver was actually within the RAF station. It was across the road from sick quarters. Aircrew didn't seem to go to the Marrowbone and Cleaver much, Brigg just down the road was the place we went to most times and to Scunthorpe, where there was a great pub called the Oswald. I used to go fairly often with my rear gunner. Our pilot didn't care for his crew to go on the razzle and in fact the vast majority of crews were fairly sober people like us.[2]

It was a time of rapid tours and a quick turnover in personnel. F/Sgt Farmer had three COs in his quick fourteen-week tour at North Killingholme, two of them being shot down and killed. In those days of midsummer bomber aircrew occasionally operated twice, the war diarist of 427 (RCAF) Sqn recording on 27 June that aircrew had taken off at 12.30 a.m. to hit Wizernes returning at dawn, then in the light evening, after a short sleep, swept away for Metz. 'Enemy fighters on the job and three aircraft reported attacks while others reported numerous fighter flares on track,' the diary reads. 'Considered a successful attack, but a little too long for such a bright moonlight night. WHAT A DAY!'[3] What a requirement. W/O A. J. King had successfully completed the first raid, then been shot down on the second, his thirty-first trip. He became a prisoner of war. There were only eight days or nights in July when Bomber Command didn't operate in force, often on three or four targets at once, and crews were now regularly expected to operate in moonlight, unthinkable in 1943 or the early winter months of 1944.

The few opportunities to get off station meant a more intensive effort in wooing the WAAFs who by now made up about 10 per cent of the personnel on any bomber base, filling a variety of roles from telephonist to parachute packer. Some were batwomen for officers. At Metheringham, which 106 Sqn had taken over at the height of the Battle of Berlin – its Lancasters taxiing past rows of concrete mixers as construction continued – there were 150 WAAFs. The decision to make Metheringham one of the fifteen UK bases to be FIDO-equipped, where pipelines were installed alongside runways to allow blazing oil to burn off fog and let returning bombers land in safety, had continued the building-site aspect of the station as spring struggled into summer. In fact, the construction teams who had built an underground pipeline from the railway tanker siding at Metheringham station to supply the 2,500 gallons of petrol needed for each aircraft to land, didn't leave until July.

Metheringham was not an uplifting prospect for the WAAFs who had moved there from the 1930s permanency of Syerston, where 106 Sqn had previously been based. They were lucky, however, in Metheringham's commander, G/Cptn Bill McKechnie, a holder of the George Cross and one of the RAF's more enlightened pre-war officers. He instituted a self-help scheme to improve the station's appearance and encouraged the creation of flower beds on section and headquarters sites, and had roads lined with rhododendrons and silver birch. As on other RAF bases rows of vegetables were planted for airmen to tend, playing their part in the Dig for Victory campaign that was now producing one million vegetables annually from domestic plots. WAAFs, who had found the official drab brown interior of their billets dispiriting, were handed pots of a more pleasing green paint to improve them. Eventually they took part in a competition created by High Wycombe to find the best WAAF site in Bomber Command. Sadly, the inscribed silver cup went to another camp.

A station dance was held on 28 June to mark the fifth anniversary of the formation of the Women's Auxilliary Air Force. A female officer handed round slices of birthday cake and teams of WAAFs, ground crew and aircrew competed in a Bomber Command quiz. The bar opened forty-five minutes before a quickstep started the dancing and airmen jockeyed for position round the bar to buy the girls a drink, despite the usual wartime shortage of glasses (the programme stipulating: 'One person will be served with not more than two glasses at any one time. Experience shows that if you ask for four glasses you will drop at least one and upset the other'). Inevitably relationships developed between WAAFs and the airmen who flew from Metheringham that summer and autumn. Many were predictably short-lived, but marriages were a regular feature, four taking place in July. Station cinemas were a popular place for aircrew and the women in uniform to meet.[4]

Sgt Etherington remembers the official picture house at Kirmington:

It was an all-ranks effort at the camp cinema including WAAFs. It was always full, so people weren't going out a lot. They used to show the same kind of films you could see in town and change the programme about three times a week. Occasionally there would be a live show. The seats weren't very comfortable, but it saved aircrew from going down to Lincoln or places like that.[5]

Very occasionally low cloud would prevent all operations over the Continent and actually allow a run into the nearest town. The crew of flight engineer Dennis Goodliffe were now approaching their last operation on 101 Sqn. He says:

We occasionally went into Louth on a night off. It was full of airmen, including some Americans. I didn't drink at that time and I used to go off in my Singer Bantam and rescue the crew from dances at Louth Corn Exchange. Everybody would get sloshed in there and start a fight with the Americans. All eight of us managed to squeeze in that little Singer. The Service Police didn't bother us, they just used to patrol areas where they thought crews might get VD, which would take them off ops.[6]

It was against this background of long days and intensive effort, relieved occasionally by a high-spirited jaunt, that aircrew taxied out in their Lancasters in the double-summer-time light on the late evening of 12 July, for the first of the three raids on Revigny as stage two of the Transportation Plan continued. It was the fourth attempt to mount the raid in four days, each time bad weather forcing a late scrub. The raid was to be an operation solely for 1 Group, which had suffered so much at Mailly-le-Camp. The pre-op meal was known as the propaganda meal by aircrew and that night it had been been particularly good on 166 Sqn – steak and fried potatoes. It would be the last operational feast for four crews from Kirmington. From Elsham Wolds, 6 miles away – the sound of whose own bombers could also be heard moving along the perimeter track – another three aircraft would be missing and a fourth abandoned over England for lack of fuel after the long 1,550-mile trip, routed to avoid the Normandy battlefield. Canadian F/O Redmond Banville, one of the 166 Sqn skippers who would not be returning, recorded shortly after the war the last moments of his final operational take-off.

> As we swung onto the runway Singleton's* V-Victor was facing us, having taxied up the perimeter track on the other side ... I had my side window open and gave him the old 'finger' sign as we swung on. I let her roll until my tail wheel was straight, and held her on the brakes ... My hands always sweated at this time – this is when you think, 'My God, suppose an engine cuts out at 90 to 100 mph and we do a ground loop with 9,000 lbs of explosives and 1,800 gallons.'
>
> Another green from Control. I waved to the usual collection of spectators (my bat-girl among them – she never missed a take-off) and closed my window ... I opened the inner throttles wide and we started to roll.

At 120 mph he heaved the Lancaster off the ground, bouncing once 'and then we were away'. Three miles into his journey he rocked the aircraft's wings over his favourite pub. 'Sure enough there were the proprietor and his wife way down below, waving.'[7] Four hours later F/O Banville's Lancaster was hit by a night fighter just after bombing, crashing near Montiers-sur-Saulx. He evaded with three others of his crew, the rest being killed.

The raid had been a complete failure, the master bomber being unable to find the target because of cloud, a faulty H2S set and haze at low level when he descended. Then as the 100-plus Lancasters orbited an assembly point waiting to be called in his VHF radio set went down and his deputy had to rapidly order the bombers to go home. Two collided in a red flash as they circled, no one surviving from the 550 Sqn and 103 Sqn aircraft. After so long a trip some persisted to identify the target through gaps in the cloud and bombed, but by that time the Luftwaffe had arrived with fighter flares. The assembly point was only 5 miles from the *Nachtjäger* airfield at St Dizier where I/NJG5 were based and a total of ten Lan-

---

* F/O Bernard Singleton was killed with all his crew on a Stuttgart raid thirteen days later.

casters failed to return. F/O Dennis Goodliffe, flying with 101 Sqn, remembers: 'As you approached the target your eyes were out on stalks as you looked for other Lancs – we didn't weave on our squadron; weaving caused a lot of collisions. It was also my job to push out the Window strips. A lot of engineers stopped as they got to the target, but I kept it up.'[8]

Sgt Ken Down, flight engineer in the 550 Sqn crew of F/O Jim Lord, was on his thirteenth trip and would still be in the air, returning, as the date passed into the 13th of the month, unlucky omens for superstitious aircrew, where survival so often could be an unfathomable mystery. He says:

Fortunately it wasn't a Friday, but we weren't too keen about doing it because of the date. It was a nine hour and thirty minute trip for us. With careful engine handling you normally had enough fuel for ten hours in a Lancaster, at 50 gallons per engine per hour. The force had to circle this green marker over a wooded area while the master bomber tried to find the target. I saw the two Lancasters collide as we circled. There was a fearful explosion and it was obvious what had happened. The fighters arrived and I saw one air-to-air combat in the distance.

The weather was pretty foul. There was nine-tenths cloud cover over the target. Only half the force bombed, but we were one of the few. Our bomb aimer suddenly spotted an opening in the cloud and got them away. We had some flak damage over the target and on the way back I realised we were losing coolant from the port inner and I had to feather it. So we came back on three, which meant we used a lot more fuel because the revs were so high on the remaining engines. The route we had been given also used quite a lot of petrol.[9]

As the crews of the ninety or so bombers that did reach the coast of eastern England prepared to let down after another risky trip they discovered that other great danger on bombing operations, the weather, was about to raise the stakes. FIDO landings now became a distinct possibility as the Lincolnshire airfields disappeared into mist one by one. Instead the weary crews were diverted to air bases in East Anglia, the seventeen aircraft of 550 Sqn landing at no fewer than ten different airfields.

The Lancaster of F/O Lord didn't make it. Sgt Down remembers:

When we got back to North Killingholme it was fogged in. We were diverted back down to Norfolk, but that was covered in fog too. People were milling around trying to find an airfield they could see to land at. We saw a church tower not too far away below us and as we only had about ten minutes' fuel left by this time Jim, the pilot, said: 'It's time to go out.' He pointed the aircraft out to sea, the Australian rear gunner went out through the back of his turret and the rest of the crew through the escape hatch at the front. We were only about 2,000 feet up and it was quite nerve-racking. I put Jim's parachute on for him, then went out and he followed me immediately afterwards. As I pulled the ripcord I saw the bundle of silk shoot up in front of my face and I thought at first it wasn't working. I was amazed by the utter silence after the roar of the engines. I came down in a cornfield near Needham Market and in the fog it looked like rippling water, so, to avoid getting trapped, at about 12 feet up I punched the quick-release buckle and hit the ground with quite a bang.

Apparently the aircraft came down in a barley field only a couple of minutes after we baled out, so we must have been on the last few gallons. I got up and was wandering around when I saw a farmworker. He took me back to his cottage for a cup of tea and on the stairway of his house a door opened and out peeked three little girls, very wide-eyed at seeing an airman. It was about 7 a.m. and I went to the village post office to telephone the authorities and hammered on the door for them to open up. A dear old lady pulled back the blind, saw a peculiar fellow with a bundle of parachute silk under his arm and refused to unlock the door. Eventually a taxi came along the street containing an American airman and his girlfriend and they took me back to the USAAF base at Wattisham. The rest of the crew also ended up there and we were treated high, wide and handsome. We got a very good breakfast, though the marmalade served with the bacon we found a bit daunting. They had stuff in their PX that hadn't been available in Britain for years, such as enormous bars of chocolate. We were able to stock up with those before we took the train to London to travel back up to North Killingholme, where we were back in the air within an hour to make sure we hadn't lost our nerve.

Our aircraft had a cartoon figure on the front and had been named 'We Doodit' after a Canadian strip cartoon our Canadian navigator knew about. We got a brand new aircraft to replace the one we had lost and it was a vast improvement on the old one, which had seen so much service it had bits of wire sticking out. We christened it 'We Doodit II'.[10]

Sgt Tony McKernan, the wireless operator in F/O Les Wareham's 550 Sqn crew, who had taken part in the daylight raid on Le Havre, remembered arriving over North Killingholme 'just as the sea wrack covered the drome' and being diverted further south.

But as fast as we arrived at the diversion drome there was more sea wrack. We eventually arrived at Hethel, still with a full bomb load on board. Unable to see the runway we flew around the perimeter from Drem light to Drem light. We were planning to fly one more circuit then climb to bale out when the Yanks suddenly fired flares from their caravan at the beginning of the runway. Les banked Q-Queenie sharply and made the most superb landing.

R-Robert, in the same circuit, pranged on landing and spewed his bombs all over the place – miraculously none went off. We got back to base at about 3 p.m. the next day and were met by W/Cdr Connolly. He wanted to stand Les down and take us and Q-Queenie back to Revigny the same night. Les refused, Connolly went off with a scratch crew and Q was the only aircraft of 550 Sqn not to return.[11]

Shortly after the weary Revigny raiders had clambered from their bombers in the dawn and told their stories at debriefing it had become obvious the railway town would have to be attacked again. Dennis Goodliffe, who as he began operations in March had been ordered at 19 to make his will because the chances of completing a tour were so low, knew he wouldn't be included. The crew's tour was now over, though the skipper still had one to do. He says:

On this last operation we had to land away at Waddington. It was a great relief when our tour ended. We were dancing a jig at dispersal. The Australian squadrons at Waddington thought we had gone mad. When we told them we had done thirty-three trips, they said, 'Some of our chaps have done forty-five and are still going.'

Despite the odds, Sgt Goodliffe never doubted that he would survive. 'I remember people at briefing sometimes saying, "I don't think we will be coming back tonight," and some of them didn't,' he says. 'Unless you're a positive thinker you are not going to get any-where. I always expected to return.'[12]

THE second Revigny raid, on the night of Friday, 14 July, was no more successful than the first and for the same reasons. Near total cloud forced the master bomber to make three runs over the target after each time ordering the Pathfinders to drop their white flares to illuminate it, and the night fighters from St Dizier such a short distance away were already in contact. Again poor visibility at low level meant the raid had to be called off for fear of killing French civilians. The only gain was to the Luftwaffe, which shot down seven Lancasters of the 125, mainly from 1 Group, that had set out. 103 Sqn, which lost four aircraft on the first raid, now lost another two and 550 Sqn lost its commanding officer. The scratch crew W/Cdr Connolly had gathered included his gunnery leader Ken Fuller, a flight lieutenant at 21 with the DFC, who had only been posted into his new role four days before. All were killed when Q-Queenie was shot down by an FW190 as the bombers circled the target.

Tellingly, the Operational Research Section's report into the night's raids, which included an attack on marshalling yards at Villeneuve, near Paris, concluded that the 'plan of operations looked somewhat similar to that of two nights previously'.[13] There could now be no doubt that Bomber Command would have to return to Revigny and when they did so the Luftwaffe would be waiting.

The third raid was mounted four nights later. This time the target was handed to 5 Group and its low-level markers in 627 Sqn. Now that the Luftwaffe were forewarned it cost Cochrane's group 22 per cent of the aircraft dispatched: twenty-four Lancasters. From Dunholme Lodge, 619 Sqn, which had seen six of its aircraft disappear on the Wesseling raid less than a month before, lost five of the thirteen Lancasters it had sent to Revigny. The chances of completing a tour on 619 Sqn by those who had started shortly before D-Day had now virtually disappeared.

A quicker, more direct route to Revigny had been chosen after so many aircraft had run short of fuel on the previous raid and the force entered enemy air space just north of Dieppe, returning the same way. There were many other operations that night, but the Luftwaffe plotted the Revigny force less than an hour and a half after it took off and there was little doubt it was heading for the railway town. The night fighters at St Dizier were alerted. The first Lancaster, from 619 Sqn, was shot down an hour later and seven more were lost as the yellow night-fighter flares fell, before the final, 90 degree turning point at the River Aube, which took the bombers right past the Luftwaffe airfield.

Another eleven were then lost on the final leg while the Mosquito marker crews of 627 Sqn tried to find the aiming point in the low summer haze – which again bedevilled accuracy – beneath the lazily swinging, white flares of the Pathfinders. The master bomber, in a USAAF-loaned Lightning, put back Main Force's attack by five minutes, but some crews, perhaps confused by fires on the ground that looked like the target but were in fact burning Lancasters, unloaded. At the same time a red spot-fire flare was placed within 50 yards of the aiming point and the first Lancasters, many now orbiting, straightened up and began successfully to plaster the railway yards. Many crews reported seeing a huge explosion at 0144.[14]

In Revigny itself a bomb aimer from 103 Sqn, who had been evading since being shot down while returning from Mannheim the previous September, found himself among the bombed. F/Sgt Denys Teare was being sheltered by and assisting the Maquis in the small town. He had gone to bed after establishing the credentials of another 103 Sqn bomb aimer, F/Sgt Dick Greenwood, shot down on the first Revigny operation six days before, when the sirens sounded for the third raid. The townsfolk had already noted that an ammunition train had pulled into the west sidings that evening and wondered if the RAF would return. The train was only a few hundred yards from where F/Sgt Teare and now F/Sgt Greenwood were hiding.

They heard the sound of aircraft engines, then saw the white flares of the first illuminator Pathfinders beginning to fall. Teare, Dick Greenwood and Louis Chenu, the Resistance chief who was hiding them, dashed outside where they found scores of other people running along beneath the roaring engines and falling flares, heading for the shelter of a dried-up canal bed. Sgt Teare wrote after the war:

> Everyone was running in the same direction, men, women and children. I suddenly became aware of a uniformed figure at my side. I turned and saw it was a German soldier, probably from the nearby barracks. Glancing round as I went down the grassy side into the canal, I saw the most amazing sight. The first bomb, possibly weighing 4,000 lb, had dropped right on the ammunition train and in the enormous sheet of orange flame I could actually see the wagons blown about 50

feet into the air. Down I went into the trench, helped on my way by the blast, and lay, panting for breath and trying to keep as flat as possible, wishing I could burrow into the ground like a rabbit. By my side lay Dick; probably some of his old messmates were circling overhead.[15]

Two aircraft were lost from Waddington, where Sgt Goodliffe had found the Australians so keen to keep operating. One of them, skippered by 467 Sqn's F/O David Beharrie was shot down on its bombing run, F/O Beharrie failing to get out in time. The English flight engineer Sgt Bill Johnson evaded and was later sheltered in the same safe house as Sgt Teare. Back in England in September after the Revigny area's liberation he was able to cryptically relate to MI9 what had happened.

We were attacked by a Ju88 and our starboard engine caught fire. The motor fell out and the petrol tanks exploded. We received orders to bale out at 0215. I landed about 2 km east of Revigny. I had my equipment [the Perspex box of escape materials including compasses and maps all aircrew carried in their battledress] and made contact at once with my bomb aimer Sgt John Brown who was talking to a Frenchman near by in a field. This Frenchman took us to his house and after giving us food supplied us with a map showing the roads leading to Switzerland. As Brown's foot was badly sprained we were unable to go very far, so we stopped at the church in Laheycourt where we remained until the evening of 19 July. Through an old lady who came into the church we made contact with an English-speaking girl who took us to the priest. We remained with the priest until 21 July. The priest got us in touch with the FFI. We were taken to a house in Revigny where we remained about a month. There we met our rear gunner F/Sgt White and F/Sgt Teare, who had been there eleven months. Later three more airmen arrived and we asked to be moved. We were liberated by the Americans on 21 August and were back in England on 7 September.[16]

The three others were Red Banville, his flight engineer John Nicolson and his mid-upper gunner Fred Hoyle, all of whom were suffering from burns, Sgt Hoyle particularly so. F/Sgt Charles Kroschel, the Australian bomb aimer, walked all the way to Switzerland 150 miles away. While Banville, his crew members and Teare were hiding in the house of the two Chenu brothers, delayed-action bombs from the final Revigny operation were still going off, their fuses timed for as long as thirty days to hold up the Germans clearing the wreckage from the devastated yards. The last bomb didn't go off until 8 August.[17] The Germans retreated from Revigny and the immediate area in late August as the Americans advanced, but not before the SS had shot fifty French men and boys held hostage at nearby Robert Espagne the day before the liberators arrived.

The final raid on Revigny had indeed caused much damage, but as the last bomber left the blazing, exploding wreckage in the rail yards the night fighters harried them, and a further eight Lancasters went down before the Channel was reached. At the end of the night a total of 129 crewmen had been lost in twenty-four bombers, another eleven would become prisoners of war and twenty-nine would evade.[18] In Revigny more than 2,000 men were rapidly employed by the Germans in clearing the rail yards' wreckage, Denys Teare later recording that the Chenu brothers were among those conscripted on 20 July. 'They told us that the damage at the junction was unimaginable; the whole area was covered with immense craters which would require hundreds of tons of earth to fill,' he wrote. 'Already squads of German Pioneer Corps were hard at work, together with groups of French prisoners.'[19]

Within five days of the raid the Germans had the east–west line open again, though the north–south line remained cut. The raids on Revigny had added to the total chaos of the Transportation Plan, but so far back from the battle lines there had been no separate quantifiable effect and the raids had cost more than forty bombers – a price undoubtedly too high for what had been achieved. Comparatively, in the first stage of the offensive against northern French and Belgian rail targets before D-Day, a little over 200 bombers had been lost in nearly 9,000 sorties. The three Revigny raids had cost 43 bombers in 337 sorties.

THERE were few such raids in the Transportation Plan that cost a lot for a little. Overall it had been a great success, crucial to victory in Normandy, and as the second stage continued into August considerable forces were attacking railway yards for negligible loss. On 11 August only one Halifax was lost out of 459 heavy bombers that hit, in daylight, railway targets at Étaples, Lens, Somain, Douai and Cambrai. The attack on Cambrai was a mistake, which was rapidly covered up. It was an example of how easy it was for a bomber raid to go wrong, despite the best efforts of those taking part.

F/Sgt Vic Farmer remembers:

We had recently had some formation-flying training on 550 Sqn and
I thought what a daft idea it was. What was the point of night bombers
indulging in formation flying? Our CO had gone missing while we
were on leave in July and W/Cdr Sisley took over shortly after. I liked
him, but many – especially Commonwealth members of the squadron –
thought he was a bit stuffy. On 11 August we found W/Cdr Sisley had
chosen our whole crew including our pilot for the job of flying with
him to bomb the Douai marshalling yards. Earlier we had seen that
six of the squadron aircraft, including X, our own, had had their twin
fins painted with glaring white stripes over the black. At briefing we
were told that the six painted aircraft would fly in Vics of three to the
target in daylight and we would be leading the rest of the stream, so
there was I, a 20-year-old navigator, with the job of showing the way
to the target for about 100 others.

We took off, flying south to Beachy Head, and my navigation was
far from perfect and the Wingco complained. I asked to be left in
peace to sort it out. We did reach Beachy Head on time and set course
for France to make landfall at the Somme estuary, which again we
reached on track and on time. Good navigation. We had to fly to a
map reference 25 miles south of Douai where I gave W/Cdr Sisley a
calculated course for the target, necessitating a turn of about 90
degrees. Halfway through the turn the bomb aimer [F/Sgt Harry
Stack] said he could see the target. I pointed out we were not yet on
the course I had given, but the Wingco, who obviously felt my navigation was suspect because of poor navigation on the first leg, tersely
said: 'Take over, bomb aimer.' He then followed his instructions and
our formation of six aircraft went off to bomb the marshalling yards
in Cambrai.[20]

F/Sgt Stack remembers that at briefing the crew had been told that
not only the wing commander would be coming with them, but also
high-ranking officers from the army and navy to 'show them how it was
done' by Bomber Command.

Just prior to turning onto the target run-up W/Cdr Sisley took the two
officers with him and parked themselves in the bombing compartment,
pointing out things to them ... Getting near to turn onto the target I

asked W/Cdr Sisley to leave the nose and let me get down there with my target map. He didn't appear to take much notice of my request, so I asked him again and again but he didn't take any notice of me and just went on talking to those with him. As Vic gave the skipper the course to run up to the target I almost shouted for them to get out of the nose; they did so grudgingly. By the time I had got plugged into the intercom and spread out my map of the target area we were turning on. I set the latest wind we had found, the mean between Vic and I, and looking around thought we were overshooting the target. There were no markers or TIs. I hadn't expected any as we were the first to bomb. Naturally there were no other planes in front of us or around us, but I was certain in my own mind that this was the target. It looked perfect, marshalling yards, little village, rolling stock at station. Great, the only worry I thought we were overshooting or turning away from it to port, so I said, 'Hold her, Skip, turn back about 15 degrees to starboard, we are overshooting the target,' which meant that instead of running directly up the railway lines we would be cutting across them.

As this was going on W/Cdr Sisley said to the Skip, 'Don't you think you had better circle the target, Thomas?' The skipper said: 'No, my bomb aimer has never been wrong before,' so we went ahead. I called 'Open bomb doors', gave a few quick corrections, had the rolling stock in sight and bombs away. On releasing the bombs W/Cdr Sisley* said: 'I order you, Thomas, to circle the target.' As soon as he started to comply I could see the rest of the kites bombing to the left, Douai, and knew I had bombed the wrong target. I was so sure before that I was right, but what could I do? it was too late then. Nothing was said on the way home, it was all deathly silence. As a matter of fact I thought of baling out. Then I thought, 'Well, they can't shoot me, so what the Hell.'[21]

F/Sgt Farmer recalls:

We got back OK and when we were down the CO grabbed my collar as we were going in to debriefing and told me, 'This is what we say,'

---

* W/Cdr Alan Sisley, 27, was killed in action with his entire crew on 31 August, bombing a V2 rocket store at Agenville in the Pas-de-Calais and is buried in Abbéville cemetery.

so I believe squadron records indicate Pathfinder flares were late going down on the target. Frankly the squadron records aren't correct, but Air Chief Marshal Harris didn't accept cock-ups. Next day we saw all the tail fins of the squadron aircraft had been repainted black.[22]

The operational record book for 550 Sqn for 11 August in fact reads:

Sixteen aircraft and crews were provided and briefed for an attack on Douai. Nearing the target some 6/10–7/10s cloud was encountered and with the markers being a few minutes late the leading aircraft found some difficulty in locating the target with the result that they bombed the marshalling yards at Cambrai. Immediately after this the markers were seen to go down over Douai and were very accurately placed. Both the targets were well and truly bombed as the photographs show.[23]

The operation to Douai was memorable for different reasons for wireless operator Tony McKernan and his crew. 'Our last trip. We bombed Cambrai in error. Got thoroughly Brahms and Liszt that night,' he wrote after the war.[24]

The 11th also marked the end of the Transportation Plan. Now Bomber Command returned to targets in western France to help the armies capture ports and to assist in the planned break-out from Normandy, and also to bombing two targets in Germany: Brunswick and Rüsselsheim. Throughout the summer Harris had itched to return to his main aim of bombing Germany's industrial base. In late July he finally got his chance.

17

Back to Basics

The three heavy raids on Stuttgart launched in late July were a harbinger of what would come to Germany as the second phase of the RAF and Commonwealth bomber offensive closed and the third, final and most terrible phase began. Harris got his wish to return in force to a city target, which had eluded the true destructive power of his command so far, and now show what could be done. Each of the successive raids would be made with the power of more than 400 aircraft.

Stuttgart had been hit by Bomber Command many times, the first on 24 August 1940 when four people were killed in a small operation by Wellingtons and Whitleys, but more recently by nearly 600 aircraft in February, again at the beginning of March and finally, by more than 850 heavy bombers on the night of 15 March. In no case did the results justify the effort expended. The Württemberg capital's location in a series of valleys made it susceptible to cloud and had prevented any attack developing. Harris had had to turn aside for other city targets and the demands of SHAEF had shelved a return until now.

Those who lived in rural southern Germany in the winter of 1944 did not suffer as much as the city dwellers in the north. The heavy bombers largely passed them by. The villagers of Bavaria and Saxony knew no food shortages, nor did those of the Black Forest to which Stuttgart was the gateway. The German diarist Ils Garthaus visited Baden-Baden in the foothills of the Black Forest, and little over 40 miles from Stuttgart, in early July 1944. She described dining at the historic Kurhaus casino restaurant in the spa town. 'Food was still good, wine excellent and the desserts exotic and delicious,' she recorded. 'Extras like American chocolate and cigarettes (12 Reichsmark a packet) were always available from the waiters. They came filtering from the Hotel Stefani where the American officers were held prisoners of war.'[1] While the residents of southern German villages and resorts could feel complacent, however, the citizens of Stuttgart fretted. The raids on their city in February and March, though largely unsuccessful, had demonstrated the might of Bomber Command that was available and the devastating raid on that other south German state capital, Munich, on 24 April, had shown what could be achieved when conditions were right. Few doubted that Stuttgart's night of fire was also coming.

There were many reasons why Bomber Command would want to return to Stuttgart now that the force was temporarily freed from the demands of Eisenhower, and the cities and towns of Prussia and the Ruhr were showing such evidence of the damage the Command could wreak. Stuttgart was the sixth largest city in Germany, the centre of a rail network and among its other attractions as a major target were the Daimler-Benz plant and the Bosch factory in the suburb of Feuerbach, which made dynamos, magnetos and injection pumps – considered to be one of the most important factories in the Reich. Some observers in Germany later considered the three raids a retaliation for the V1 programme, since some parts of this weapon were also produced in the city.

Stuttgart's defences were considerable, ranks of flak battalions staffed in part by expert Luftwaffe gunners, supplemented heavily by Hitler Youth teenagers, Russian prisoners of war who had elected to fight for Germany rather than starve, and now that the demands of fighting land campaigns against the Soviets, in Normandy and on the Italian Front were making such inroads into available German manhood, more and more girls. On 12 July the journalist Ursula von Kardorff had been sent to interview German girls who had recently been called up to work in the anti-aircraft defences of the Reich as manpower declined.

They had fitted up their barrack room very nicely and pinned up photographs of their boyfriends, brothers and fiancés on the doors of their lockers. All the girls I interviewed were cheerful. They are young, most of them are plump, indeed almost fat. The *Maidenführerin* [a rank in the League for German Girls] whom I talked to was at 18 in charge of all the computations for the whole battery and was doing the job of a woman officer. I wrote that they shone with cheerfulness.[2]

Her words echoed the atmosphere in WAAF quarters in Britain as the bombers were prepared in the afternoon of 24 July to try to take Stuttgart out of the war. At Kelstern, in the Lincolnshire-based 1 Group, flight engineer Sgt Norman Jones got ready for his twenty-first raid in a tour with 625 Sqn which had begun less than eight weeks before. In the Halifax-equipped 4 Group F/O Robert Vollum, a wireless operator posted to 158 Sqn at Lissett, found himself down for the first operation of a second tour that would prove vastly different from his first because of the technical developments in the air war. He had begun operational flying on Hampdens way back in April 1942, taking part in the first 1,000-bomber raid to Cologne and the next to Essen, finally finishing his tour on Halifaxes in June 1943. And in 5 Group south of Lincoln Sgt Alf Ridpath, the wireless operator who had been so surprised on the night before D-Day to see the mass of the invasion armada on his fighter-warning Fishpond radar set, made his last-minute checks at Coningsby. He and his crew were now on 83 Sqn, having been spotted one dawn on 49 Sqn by PFF's recruiter-in-chief G/Cptn Hamish Mahaddie, known as the 'horse thief' by squadron commanders. 'After we had done twenty trips we were veterans,' Sgt Ridpath remembers. 'G/Cptn Mahaddie came round and said I want you and you for Pathfinders. He took us and another crew captained by an Australian.'[3]

At their briefings in widely different groups, the flight engineer and the two wireless operators each heard the same story. They were taking a long route to Stuttgart across the Normandy battle area, south of Paris and the expert *Nachtjäger* at St Dizier, then heading towards Mannheim where it was hoped the night fighters would gather as the force of nearly 600 heavy bombers abruptly turned south-east to hit Stuttgart at 0130. They would return in a series of dog-legs by almost the same route. By the end of the week Stuttgart would have claimed one of the three men as a prisoner of war.

As dusk gathered and the huge force thundered southwards to the east of London and out over the Channel the Luftwaffe at first supposed it to be aimed at an inland target in France and only four *Nachtjäger Gruppen* reacted, night fighters in the north being held by the threat of a diversionary sweep over the North Sea by 154 aircraft. But as the main bomber force roared past the German positions in Normandy their course and heading were reported to Luftwaffe control centres and night fighters were swished into the stream due south of Paris making attacks on seven aircraft and shooting down two. The *Nachtjäger* then followed the force all the way to Stuttgart, pecking at the laden bombers over the target itself and back to the point where they had first made contact. A total of seventeen Lancasters and four Halifaxes were lost. Alf Ridpath saw one of the Halifaxos destroyed. He remembers:

> We weren't terribly happy about going back to Germany. We were just running in to the target when the mid-upper gunner screamed 'dive, dive, dive' and the next thing we were going down with a *whoosh* when the Halifax above us exploded. The tail fell down with the rear gunner still in it and the bits were falling all around us as we dived. We went down from 17,000 to 6,000 feet to get away from all the burning pieces.[4]

The bomb aimer from the exploding Halifax, F/Sgt K. W. Campbell, found himself falling through the sky above woods at Plattenhardt, 8 miles south of Stuttgart, with his parachute attached to his harness by one hook. F/Sgt Campbell* landed unhurt and quickly became a prisoner of war, but the rest of the mainly Australian crew, including the unfortunate rear gunner, were killed.

W/O Ron Smith, a PFF rear gunner on 156 Sqn, witnessed the end of one of his fellow Pathfinder crews just after his own had released their flares. He saw two enemy fighters

> streak down way behind a four-engined aircraft entering the now brightly illuminated arena. Their victim dived away to the right, climbed steeply to hang almost stationary, or so it seemed, as flames began to stream back from the wings. Then a terrific explosion, here and there the sparkle of target indicators, identifying the stricken aircraft as one of our group.[5]

There had been total cloud over the target and the Pathfinders had been reduced to a skymarker attack with drifting parachute-held indicators. 'Nothing could be seen of the bombing except a glow of fire beneath the cloud,' the operational record book of 102 Sqn later reported. 'The master bomber was jammed and only heard for a short time.'[6]

---

* In Australia many years after the war Sgt Ridpath's Australian navigator, F/Sgt Robert Brooks, met Campbell, a friend from training days, and discovered it was his aircraft that had exploded above their own.

Flak was intense, one 35 Sqn aircraft plunging into the centre of Stuttgart, but it was the night fighters that proved the greatest menace. Canadian F/Lt Jim Weaver of 102 Sqn had just bombed when he was attacked by a Ju88. 'My gunners claimed to have shot down the Ju88, the port motor was on fire and he was seen to break up in the air,' he reported at debriefing.[7] But that wasn't the full story. Weaver had had to dive from 19,000 to 7,000 feet to put out the flames streaking back from his port engine. He also had damage to the port fin, rudder, elevators and aileron and could not climb. His aircraft was attacked again, this time from ahead and below, leaving a row of bullet holes across where the bomb aimer had been lying a short time before. Weaver finally brought his badly damaged machine into land eight and half hours after leaving Pocklington where he ground-looped as the aircraft revealed it had a shot-up tyre.[8]

The long, fraught journey had taken its toll on each of the crews who returned from Stuttgart. F/O Vollum remembers:

It was a seven hour and forty-five minute trip for us all told. As a wireless operator I was tucked away. There was flak coming up, but it was pretty straightforward for me. I was glad to get that first one in. Having done one tour that was pretty scary I didn't know what to expect, but I knew the aircraft would be pretty good, being a Halifax III, and I found as the tour went on there wasn't the same kind of tension as with my first tour. I didn't feel as keyed up and I think it was because by that stage we knew we were winning the war. I flew with eleven different pilots all told before finishing the tour and many of those I flew with were later killed. I didn't have a crew because I had been posted in just as a spare wireless operator.[9]

Sgt Jones also recalls:

Afterwards I wrote in my log book 'Good Blitz', but it was the length of the trip that was particularly memorable. It was eight hours and twenty-five minutes there and back. There was the usual flak, but you only took special note of it if it looked likely to hit you. The next day there was another trip to Stuttgart, but we were up doing a practice with our H2S equipment over the North Sea.[10]

*

THAT second operation on Stuttgart in two nights had a special significance for F/Sgt Cliff Hill, rear gunner to Canadian F/Lt Harold Hoover. In the warm briefing hut at Graveley in the early evening of 25 July virtually the same route as the night before was unravelled by the red thread stretching across the map at the end of the room. Again its duration would test the fuel capacity of some aircraft and this time an added twist of wrongly forecast winds would mean several bombers crashing in England on return as their tanks ran dry. But the disturbing aspect for F/Sgt Hill was to hear that his crew had a role that would mean them spending extra time over the target, risking the dangers of flak and fighter. 'Hoov, with his infectious grin, gave us the news, "We're deputy master bomber,"' Hill wrote in a diary later. 'Having done this job twice before I secretly hoped the MB would survive.'[11]

The food at Graveley did not have a high reputation and the pre-op meal by no means measured up to that of the steak at Kirmington, a large part often consisting of beans, which caused embarrassing gas expansion in the gut as aircraft climbed. It was something for F/Sgt Hill to reflect on as his and the other fifteen crews of 35 Sqn operating that night ambled across the hot tarmac to the crew room where they emptied their lockers of flying kit and handed the key to the corporal in charge in case of a non-return. F/Sgt Hill wrote:

I checked my letter to my parents was there, just in case. Closing the locker door I turned and joined the noisy banter in the smoke-laden atmosphere. Jimmy Bremner our Glaswegian wireless operator forever singing the latest Sinatra number; Bill Lloyd our flight engineer – I liked his sardonic humour; Jock our mid-upper gunner always with a cigarette in his mouth; Les the Yorkshire navigator, a man of accuracy, ever cheerful; Jack the former wireless operator who had taken over as bomb aimer; Hoov always eager for action shouting, 'For Christ's sake where's the transport?' It arrived in the shape of a good-looking WAAF in a heavy truck, who called out, 'Come on, who's for tennis?'[12]

At other bases, from the Canadian 6 Group in Yorkshire and Durham to 5 Group south of Lincoln, crews were also climbing aboard transport to be taken out to their bombed-up, waiting Lancasters and Halifaxes. They went out to their dispersal points in a rag-taggle line, buses joining utility trucks, open wagons trailing battered lorries. And the airmen themselves showed an equal individuality – some sported lucky scarves, others displayed once-white aircrew roll-neck sweaters hanging below battledress, a few, easily identified as gunners, wore the full protection of both Irvin jacket and trousers in sheepskin. It always seemed there should have been more dignity in it somehow for men embarking on what could prove a final journey.

On 433 (RCAF) Sqn at Skipton-on-Swale thirteen aircraft had taken off successfully in the low evening light past the throng of waving WAAFs, who had recently taken part in slow-bicycle races and rolling-pin-throwing competitions in the squadron's first sports day, when I-Item swung as it gathered speed and crashed off the runway, sending the crowd racing for cover. The crew scrambled clear and joined the sheltering WAAFs before it exploded. F/O Wilbur Pierce, who less than two weeks later would lose two engines in his trip to a flying-bomb storage site, was making his operational debut with 433 Sqn that night, as a second-dickey pilot. That first trip did not go well. 'The crew got lost due to a duff H2S and terribly wrong Met winds,' he remembers. 'We ended up in the Swiss Alps – snow caps both sides of us. We turned north round Lake Constance and Friedrichshafen then drew a straight line to Ford. We lost some aircraft that ran out of fuel.'[13]

THOSE of the 450-strong force who did make it to Stuttgart despite problems with the forecast winds, ten-tenths cloud en route, electrical storms and icing, were met by fierce defence. There were walls of intense flak-box barrages bursting in red-centred puffs of smoke. Searchlights peered deceptively innocently through gaps in the cloud, occasionally flicking onto an unlucky aircraft, more beams of light then eagerly following to form a cone that held the silver shape at its apex until the shape turned into an orange glow and disintegrated. F/Sgt Hill had an unparalleled view from his rear turret. He later wrote:

> As we commenced our bombing run the scene can only be described as horrific, bomb bursts flickering down below between breaks in the cloud. It was patchy and hazy, the target identified on H2S by a good picture, confirmed by target indicators, then visually by the river and railway. On our first run we dropped flares and bombs into the centre of the TIs. A few greens were down and one yellow.

F/Sgt Hill's nagging worry then became reality.

The master bomber was not heard, either he was down or his R/T wasn't working. Hoover decided to take over, quickly assessing the situation he began broadcasting to the Main Force and PFF backers-up and supporters. I can still hear his voice today with its strong Canadian accent, 'Bomb on the red TIs. Come on, fellas, get right in, bomb on the red TIs, I repeat, bomb on the red TIs.' He switched off momentarily, saying to us, 'OK, we're going round again.'

We circled the target and came in on our second run timed at 0154 hours and at 16,500 feet. As always Hoov flew the aircraft dead straight and level through flak bursting on either side. Our bomb aimer's instructions seemed to take forever as he deliberated before dropping our TIs. We pulled out of our run, Hoov continued to talk to the Main Force, 'Come on now, get right in, some of you are undershooting. Bomb the centre of the greens and reds.' The first target indicators were north-west of the aiming point, our own were closer, calculated at 200 yards south. Hoov brought the majority of the aircraft right in and after some wild bombing by the 'fringe merchants' he pulled the raid round giving it a consistency and concentration. On the ground it was a devil's cauldron as the unmerciful pounding continued and the German anti-aircraft gunners laid out a carpet of flak for the incoming bombers. Hoov went round again, making our third run.

Behind his four Browning machine guns in the rear turret F/Sgt Hill expected a night fighter to come in at any time, but they were curiously absent and not one bomber was lost in combat over Stuttgart that night. A large area of fire was burning the heart out of the Württemberg capital.

At 0202 hours a huge explosion followed by a large column of smoke was seen rising to about 8,000 feet obliterating most of the target. Hoov called, 'Can you see any other aircraft back there, rear gunner?' I answered, 'No I guess that's about it.' I think that was the first time I had spoken since arriving at the enemy coast. Back came his retort, 'Right, let's get the hell out of here.' I suddenly realised we were alone over Stuttgart. As we turned for home Hoov gave it all he had, cutting corners off the prescribed navigation route we quickly caught up with the other aircraft homeward bound.[14]

Thousands of feet below the fires had linked into a concentration of crackling, multi-coloured flame, tongues bursting out from burning buildings to catch other structures still untouched, clouds of sparks shooting into the choking, smoke-laden air to fall hundreds of yards away on other, yet spared combustible material. The pulsating glow was visible for 150 miles to the homeward-bound bombers. The scene in the cellar shelters of Stuttgart was now the same as it had been in Germany's northern cities months earlier. The final alert for raiders approaching had wailed across the city at 1 a.m. and Stuttgart's sleepy citizens, still catching up on the lost slumber caused by the raid the night before, had tumbled in bedraggled numbers to the white metal entrance of their bunkers with the gothic script in black '*Eschukraum fur Personen*'. The early lucky ones found a space in one of the two-tier wooden bunks that lined the lime-washed concrete walls. There was nothing to do but read the routine posters: one warning about careless talk showed a Wehrmacht officer talking to a civilian while behind him a spy listened behind his newspaper; the other, entitled '*Brandbomben – Bejamafung*', detailed in nine drawings how to douse the RAF's small but so effective 4-lb incendiary bomb, at this precise time cascading by the thousand into the city. Nothing to do but read and stare at the standard few wooden chairs in the middle of the room clustered round the white metal table supporting a white enamel bowl for wound cleansing. Nothing to do but tremble and listen to the percussive blockbusters shaking the concrete roof despite its supporting, quivering wooden pit props and hope there would be no need for the metal, strap-laden stretcher, leaning against the wall next to the huge metal air pump with its heavy handle to pull in air from the outside.[15]

Reinhold Maier, one of those who took shelter from the rain of RAF bombs on Stuttgart in late July, describes what it was like.

> I just had time to dress and run down to the cellar when the first bomb fell ... Soon the bomb hail was underway. The biggest amount of bombs came not as usual straight from up above, but in a sort of gliding flight ... They crashed in every corner in the area. A couple dropping near by made the house shake. The windows burst. At 2 o'clock the civil air defence sent me up and out. I came back with bad news ... conflagrations everywhere, especially in the west in the direction of Hasenberg and Botnanger Sattel. A strange sight was the burning police broadcasting station in the Moltkestrasse. It looked as if a fire-red Eiffel Tower had been built downtown. The fire brigade from Stuttgart couldn't help because of a water shortage. The Katherinen

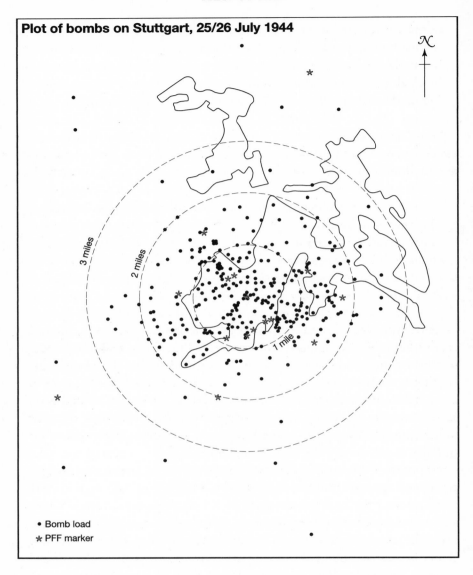

Plot of bombs on Stuttgart, 25/26 July 1944

3 miles

2 miles

1 mile

• Bomb load
∗ PFF marker

hospital was burning, the Hotel Zeppelin was once again blown out, the main railway station was externally still an unbroken stronghold, but its lateral tract was burned out. In many cases the streets were blocked. 'Caution dud', every quarter of an hour new detonations followed ... Stuttgart was newly bleeding out of every wound.[16]

Some managed to save their homes by risking the bombs. A woman resident wrote to an exhibition in Stuttgart many years later about the destruction of the city centre.

I can remember that night in July when everything around us burned. Our row of houses kept standing only because of my father ... His opinion was, 'If I cannot save my house I have nothing to live for anymore.' Therefore he was on stage during the attacks so that he could throw firebombs straight on the street. That is why our house did not burn.[17]

As dawn broke after the appalling weather of the night the relieved crews of Bomber Command let down over the lessening shadows of what was now a peaceful English summer's day and joined the circuits for landing at the bases they had set off from in daylight approximately seven and a half hours before. Their reports at debriefing showed it had been an enormously successful attack, not least because of the lack of night fighters, nearly all combats occurring in a cluster in the same area south of Paris as on the previous night, but this time not repeated until the same point in the return journey. Only twelve aircraft were missing – not counting those that ran out of fuel over England – an impressively small number for such a large force on a well-defended German target and only seven were thought to have fallen to the *Nachtjäger*. Two had been the result of collision. The multi-tasked 100 Group could also claim the destruction of a Me110 – shot down by S/Ldr Harold 'Micky' Martin. The Dams Raid hero now 'resting' by flying a Mosquito with 515 Sqn had been briefed to fly a Ranger patrol to Stuttgart and Böblingen that night. On return to his base, named so beguilingly Little Snoring, he reported:

After crossing the coast at Knocke at 0350 on 350 degrees true an aircraft burning navigation lights was seen at about a mile to port flying very fast on a heading of 163 T. The Mosquito was swung round, and below at 3,000 feet at about 70 yards dead astern the [enemy aircraft] tail light [was] blocking out the spot on the ring sight. With the ring sight in the starboard engine a burst of cannon was delivered which set the engine on fire. The e/a dived and another burst was directed on the port wing. It blew up the wing and the e/a went down in a screaming dive.[18]

The cloud and icing along the route had undoubtedly hampered the enemy night fighters, but there was another important reason why they had done so badly. Less than two weeks before a Ju88 equipped with SN-2 airborne interception radar – deadly in combination with Schräge Musik and unjammable by the currently used Window strips – had landed by mistake in England. It was quickly discovered the wavelength of its SN-2 equipment could be jammed by Window of a new, longer length and this had been hurriedly prepared and rushed to the bomber stations. It was with some satisfaction, therefore, that the academics of Bomber Command's Operational Research Section were able to report in their analysis of the second Stuttgart raid:

Surprisingly little fighter opposition was encountered, especially since the enemy guessed Stuttgart to be the main target over 30 minutes before H-hour and since the attack lasted 43 minutes. No bomber was lost in combat over Stuttgart at all and most of the opposition occurred in the Châteaudun area. The weather hampered fighters – there was much cloud along the route – and a new type of Window was carried which hampered the enemy's long wavelength AI.[19]

The report practically dripped with complacency.

It was this sense of irrevocable supremacy that led the planners at High Wycombe to stick to the same route when Bomber Command returned to Stuttgart in the final of the three raids three nights later, now in the moon period. But this time, as with the third raid on Revigny, the Luftwaffe had read all the signs. They would not be caught napping and it would be one operation too many.

The plan would cost thirty-nine bombers, a loss rate of 7.9 per cent, which the squadrons had not approached on a city target since Schweinfurt in April. Another heavy raid, using Halifaxes as well as Lancasters, was mounted on Hamburg that night and it had been hoped to divide the *Nachtjäger* resources, but the losses here were little better, 7.2 per cent. They were particularly felt by the Halifax-equipped Canadian 6 Group, 431 Sqn losing five of its seventeen aircraft dispatched.

THERE was definite unease among those who had been to Stuttgart at least once that week as they discovered at briefing that Friday evening it was the now familiar path to the same target. Sgt Norman Jones, who had been there on the Tuesday, says:

> When we saw in the briefing room it was Stuttgart again on the same route we definitely thought it was a bit crazy. We wondered what Bomber Command was trying to do, but I think headquarters thought the Germans would never dream we were daft enough to go to the same place on the same track a third time. It was a double bluff that misfired.[20]

F/Sgt Cliff Hill was also surprised when the curtain was drawn back at Graveley and hoped the trip wouldn't be his last. 'It would be my fifty-seventh op and my last visit to Germany. The end of our tour was drawing to a close and I suppose we had been together too long, the strain was beginning to show, slight cracks were appearing in the thin veneer of false gaiety,' he later wrote.[21] The Lancaster crew had been named as Primary Blind Illuminator to open the proceedings over Stuttgart.

Another aircrew had been selected to take off from Graveley in a Mosquito: 692 Sqn of 8 Group's Light Night Striking Force shared Graveley with 35 Sqn and F/Lt Tom Beal had been asked to assess the damage of the two previous raids because cloud had prevented photograph reconnaissance. Among the LNSF's more usual tasks was to continue the RAF's night-time aerial assault on Berlin after it had proved too tough a nut for Bomber Command's lower-altitude heavy bombers in the winter. 'We weren't very keen on going to Berlin because it meant about four and a half hours over the other side, which was a long time in a Mossie,' Tom Beal remembers. 'I did twelve Berlin trips in all.'

Less than three weeks before the CO of 692 Sqn had been lost in a raid involving thirty-five Mosquitos on Berlin and F/Lt Beal had been coned. He remembers:

> I think we were a bit off track and the searchlights came bang, straight

on to us. We were coned for two or three minutes. I was blinded and my neck turned round immediately to see if a night fighter was on my tail. I yelled out to my navigator to chuck out some Window. There was no point trying to evade the cone, the quickest way out was to just keep on the same course and hope for the best. Fortunately as the Window strips went down the searchlights slowly dropped away following them, so it did the trick.

On the night of 28 July he prepared to fly to the Württemberg capital at 30,000 feet as his colleagues on 35 Sqn operated 2 miles below.

It was our forty-fifth operation out of the fifty we had to do for a Mosquito tour. I believe our Mosquito was the only one sent to Stuttgart that night. We were sent out with a special camera to see what damage the heavies had done and to drop a 4,000-lb bomb at the same time. We took off two or three hours after 35 Sqn had taken off for Stuttgart and I was back in bed at Graveley before they got home. You really could feel the 4,000-lb bomb leave a Mosquito. You went up 300–400 feet with the greatest of ease.[22]

Sgt Tom Howie, the 625 Sqn flight engineer whose anoxia-afflicted rear gunner had inadvertently lit up their aircraft over Duisburg, was also over Stuttgart that night – and worrying about aircraft above. He says:

It was described to us as a blitz attack on a rail junction and factories. I remember it was rumoured at that time that the Polish bomber crews always tried to get above briefed heights. If you were told to go in at 20,000 feet they would be at 21,000 feet. They thought they would be safer, but we always thought if you got above the stream you would be exposed to night fighters. The wireless operator would be in the astrodrome looking for the fighters and we always got him to look out for any planes at all, just in case any of our own were above and likely to bomb.[23]

The moonlight and the predictable route proved a deadly combination for the Luftwaffe and as before they fell on the force of nearly 500 Lancasters due south of Paris, near Châteadun. They then shot down bomber after bomber, following the stream towards the target where the carnage would reach a crescendo of burning aircraft screaming earthwards, their crews desperately trying to get out before they were burned alive.

F/Sgt Hill recorded:

It was soon evident that the Luftwaffe had infiltrated the stream early, two explosions on the ground lighting up the sky with a brief red glow ... On the last leg into the target combats became frequent and aircraft with their full bomb loads were being blown to pieces. Behind, fighter activity became intense and as it crept closer the last leg became a nightmare.[24]

No less than twenty-three combats were reported by surviving crews in this final leg between Karlsruhe and Stuttgart as up to 200 night fighters weaved in and out of the stream knocking down bombers as they came across them.

One of those attacked was the 625 Sqn Lancaster of engineer Norman Jones. He remembers:

That night the sky was full of fighters. We had corkscrewed our way out of various situations, but the last attack was quite persistent. We kept corkscrewing and his fire was just missing us, going over the top. The tracer stopped and everything went quiet so we levelled off, but he was waiting for us to do just that and he hit us in the starboard wing. Sparks started coming out of the manifold of the starboard inner engine and in seconds those sparks became flames and the starboard undercarriage dropped down with the tyre blazing away. It was right at the side of my position and I froze with fear. The flames from the engine were by that time passing the tail. We feathered the propeller and used the Graviner extinguisher, but it had no effect. We dropped the bombs to reduce the weight and smoke started to come in the fuselage from the bomb bay because the doors were still open. The pilot, P/O Collett, was wrestling with the controls and he said: 'I think you'd better get out, chaps, I can't hold it much longer.' Nobody wanted to go because we still had something solid under our feet and we knew it meant we wouldn't be going back home. I was always brought up to believe Germans were horrible people and I thought, 'What's going to happen to me?' I thought I would be shot if I reached the ground alive. The pilot said again, 'Come on, chaps.'

I looked at the pilot and he had the control yoke completely over one way and we were falling the other way, so I thought, 'We're going to have to let him have a chance to get out of this,' because once he let go of the control column it was obvious he would have to move fast. I had already found my chute and clipped it in place. I indicated to the bomb aimer, William Lott, at my feet to get out and when he pulled at the parachute exit hatch to bring it in and turned it onto the diagonal to drop it out it jammed in the slipstream as they always did. From my higher position to him I was able to kick it out and he went out head first, I followed him head first also and the navigator, Joe Stephenson, was behind me. I suppose we were at about 10,000 feet.

I saw the aircraft go over my head and the blaze from the wing was spreading right beyond the tail. I pulled the ripcord and I was very frightened as I came down about what was going to happen to me when I got on the ground. I really thought I would be shot. I could see the ground coming up in light and dark patches and I imagined the light was water, so I had one hand on the gas-bottle trigger for my Mae West and the other on the parachute quick-release box to get out if it was water. I thought: 'This is taking a long time, I've got time to say a prayer.' I wasn't much of a man for praying, but I thought it was worth a try. All of a sudden I hit the ground with a bump.[25]

The Lancaster of F/Sgt Cliff Hill had arrived over Stuttgart to find it totally covered in cloud. The green-yellow starred identification of the target his aircraft and others were meant to provide was ineffective and Pathfinders following on had to resort to skymarkers, with the inevitable inaccuracy. 'Thick cloud obscured both ground and skymarkers,' the post-raid analysis noted. 'Crews were eventually directed to aim at the skymarkers, but the bombing was reported to be scattered with much undershooting.'[26] Not surprising considering the intensity of the night-fighter attacks. It didn't all go the Luftwaffe's way, however – more victories were claimed by Bomber Command gunners that night than on any previously, twenty-seven in all. But the damage in Stuttgart would be nothing like that of three nights before.

F/Sgt Hill's bomb aimer dropped his flares at 0145, but could see the marking was becoming scattered and his skipper F/Lt Hoover decided to go round again. The rear gunner later recorded:

The air was full of aircraft as Main Force came in. I sweated as I saw two fighters, an Me110 and an FW190 diving in amongst their own flak. A murderous barrage was coming up, much more than two nights ago. Two Lancasters coming in close behind distracted my attention momentarily, one just above with its bomb doors open. Bremner in the astrodome shouted a warning to Hoov. The other, flying slightly below at port quarter down straight and level, was so close I could see the pilot's and engineer's faces. The sky was lit up in an orange glow and as my eyes took this in I saw tracer ripple across the aircraft to port.

I couldn't believe it, their port engine was on fire, the flames small and then increasing, but they still flew on as if nothing was happening. The two helmeted white faces seemed oblivious. Neither gunner was firing. The flames grew stronger, the other port engine was now on fire. Suddenly they slid right across our tail from port to starboard just below me and went down vertically as bits of the tail fell off. I looked away, searching everywhere for fighters. All this took place faster than it takes to write it down. I can only assume they never knew what hit them.

The fighters continued their attacks as the bombers turned for home, finally breaking away to refuel as the stream passed south of the *Nacht-jäger* base at St Dizier. 'Aircraft were hitting the deck as they were intercepted after releasing their bomb load as Me110s and FW190s lay in wait,' F/Sgt Hill wrote.[27]

F/Sgt Vic Farmer, the 550 Sqn navigator who had got into trouble for not saluting at North Killingholme, was returning from his second Stuttgart raid in a week.

German fighters began dropping flares along our route and other fighters homed into the streams. About thirty minutes after leaving Stuttgart our gunners spotted one coming in for an attack and the pilot was told: 'Corkscrew port, go.' Skip Thomas reacted immediately and down to the left we went, but he didn't complete the corkscrew manoeuvre. He just carried on going down and turning to the left, then he started climbing so he was flying the circumference of a large circle the plane of which was angled to the earth below. It meant that after about two minutes or so we were back where we started and on course. We reached base without further incident. I believe our pilot had pre-determined the move he would make if attacked and it was certainly not what the night-fighter crew would have expected. His skill and cool-headedness saved our lives.[28]

F/Sgt Hill remembers:

The welcoming beacon at Graveley could not come soon enough. We landed to a dawn chorus and what looked like the start of a beautiful day. At debriefing the CO Pat Daniels brought the Duchess of Kent in Wren's uniform to our table and introduced her to Hoover. I can still remember his jerky little bow and boyish grin. All aircraft from 35 Sqn had returned safely ... but it was a different picture when we heard on the news forty [sic] aircraft in total were missing.[29]

IT was a different picture indeed as the losses were calculated on the bases and sent by teleprinter to High Wycombe. The Hamburg force also had been mauled, pursued on the way home, especially north of Heligoland, and four Lancasters and eighteen Halifaxes were shot down. They were all from the Canadian 6 Group, the now dead rear gunner in one 405 Sqn Lancaster, P/O Charles Gray, a former wing commander in the RCAF accounting branch who had remustered as an air gunner at 36 to do his bit towards victory. The operation had been an accurate attack, the first since the Battle of Hamburg the previous summer in which a firestorm had burned out a large section of the city, but the post-raid analysis had to admit: 'So much irreparable damage has been caused in Hamburg by the great 1943 raids that fresh incidents were difficult to distinguish.'[30]

A reconnaissance was also flown to Stuttgart the day after the raid and the photographs its pilot brought back were remarkable, but as with Hamburg there was no way to distinguish what had been achieved with the latest strike and no distinction was made by Bomber Command's Operational Research Section. Its analysis read:

The old city suffered most heavily, especially the central area south-west of the main station. Many parts of this district were completely flattened. The old Bosch works, the VKF Norma ball-bearing factory, the Alred Knecht petrol filter plant and about twelve other factories were damaged. The main railway station, the chief post and telegraph office, the large Reichsbank block, an infantry barracks and many other public buildings were hit, some severely. Eight outlying districts were seriously affected.[31]

As the RAF reconnaissance aircraft banked high over Stuttgart Norman Jones was meeting the enemy for the first time. He had lain where he had landed not far from the city's suburb of Esslingen 'too frightened to even light a cigarette' and waited for the dawn. 'A Heinkel 111 went over and I thought, "There's no doubt where I am now,"' he remembers. 'I buried my chute and Mae West and found I was on the side of a valley.' Sgt Jones was eventually spotted and taken to the home of a policeman in a nearby village, who was 'quite a loudmouth'. The particularly youthful appearance of the 19-year-old then worked in his favour.

A lady with a baby, I think it was his wife, came in the room, looked at me, shook her head and said: '*Kind*' [Child]. I think because of her sympathy I began to be treated better. The policeman wanted to know how I had got there and took me back to where I had buried my chute. I bundled it up with my Mae West and carried it over my shoulders in front of him. When I got back to the village the news about me had been passed round and everybody was up. I walked down the street with curious people on all sides looking at me. I was put on board a beer wagon with this crowd all around me and a blonde girl in the crowd smiled at me. I thought, 'That's quite encouraging.'[32]

Sgt Jones was taken for interrogation at Dulag Luft where – like so many others before him – he was amazed to find out how much the Germans knew about his squadron, then eventually to Stalag Luft VII at Bankau. He discovered that, remarkably, all his crew had survived.

THE assessments of what had happened in the last raid on Stuttgart and to 6 Group on Hamburg were soon filed away and forgotten, but sixty-five aircraft lost in one night shocked the squadrons affected and there is no doubt both raids had cost greatly for questionable benefit. The same route to Stuttgart three times in a week, the last in moonlight, could have only one outcome whether the Luftwaffe was in decline or not. The raids on Stuttgart that week of storms in July had first shown a 4.6 per cent loss, then 2.2 and finally a savage 7.9 per cent. Stuttgart was heavily raided again on 12 September for the loss of only four Lancasters, and on 19 October for the loss of six. Both raids caused new heavy damage, but it was the July raids – particularly that of the 25th – which had so shocked Stuttgart's citizens, though thanks to its good shelter system only 1,171 people were killed. A letter written to a relative by a Stuttgart resident only three days after the 28 July raid reads: 'No Leonhards church anymore! No Stifts church! No Market Place! No Königstrasse! You cannot imagine how it looks in Königstrasse.'[33]

Another written report by Thusnelda, Countess of Luxburg, after the three raids reads:

> The closer I got downtown the worse the sight of the collapsed houses out of which still dense smoke came because under the stones and debris new fire sources generated ... The roads did not exist anymore for they were full of debris and everywhere were bomb craters ... Curiously refreshment stands had been established that sold water and suchlike and possibly bread because there were no shops anymore.[34]

Never again would so many bombers be lost in one night or day as on 28 July though the Luftwaffe would continue to inflict occasional high percentage losses when German cities themselves were attacked, right until the closing weeks of the war. The reaction in the moonlight to the final Stuttgart raid of July was not the last gasp of a dying Luftwaffe by any means, but from then there would be few peaks, and as August flicked by Bomber Command assisted the armies in the break-out from Normandy, devastated one German city for the loss of only one aircraft and carried out two heavy raids on another at extreme range. It was within 70 miles of the Russian lines and demonstrated finally to those in Germany who cared to listen that the forces of East and West would crush the Nazi monster sooner rather than later.

18

The Beginning of the End

If January was the nadir of Bomber Command's fortunes in 1944, then August was the zenith as the second phase of the bomber offensive came to an end. Each group was expanding, target-finding and bombing techniques were improving, and the percentage loss rate per number of sorties was still only two-thirds of the winter figure, despite the fact that sorties had increased by a third as Harris was asked to conduct four different campaigns at the same time. As with July, August was a month of extreme variety for his crews – night ops preceded day raids, city attacks followed tactical support. The contribution the Command had made to the invasion armies and subsequent breakthrough had been considerable, and at the same time as Harris conducted an oil campaign, fulfilled the demands of the Transportation Plan and tackled the V-weapon menace. From June to the middle of August the demands of SHAEF stretched aircrew and ground crew to the limit, rapidly changing orders making sleep a solace swiftly snatched.

The month that saw the bomber-assisted break-out by the Allied armies in Normandy and the flight by the Wehrmacht back towards the German border also saw scores of aircrew on the run now returning home as former occupied territory was seized. It was a period in which the Command was stretched as never before, but it was what was happening on the ground in Normandy that naturally dominated the front pages that summer, much to Harris's irritation.

He had complained in a note to the Chief of the Air Staff in July: 'I think you should be aware of the full depth of feeling that is being aroused by the lack of adequate or even reasonable credit afforded to Bomber Command for their efforts in the invasion of Normandy."[1] Harris's missive was sent 24 hours after an operation that had demonstrated just how crucial heavy bomber support could be to the success of field operations. Montgomery's Twenty-first Army Group was stalled before Caen and the Germans planned an attack on the night of 30 June by tanks of the 2nd and 9th Panzer Divisions. The intention was to burst through the point where the British and American armies met and divide them. Bomber Command was ordered up only hours before to bomb the crossroads at Villers-Bocage, through which the tanks would have to pass.

The master bomber brought the force of 256 Lancasters and Halifaxes down to 4,000 feet to see the 8 Group Mosquito markers in the smoke and more than 1,000 tons of bombs were dropped with great accuracy. The Panzer attack did not take place, to the gratitude of British troops only yards from the German front. One Halifax and one Lancaster were lost, hit by flak. Another Lancaster, flown by S/Ldr N. A. Williamson of 75 Sqn, made a heartstopping landing at a new Allied fighter strip on the beachhead because his flight engineer had been wounded, then Williamson found himself grounded by poor visibility. However, it meant that the next day he was able to go forward to the front line to hear the news of the troops about the attack. He made a broadcast on the BBC's *War Report* four days later, which must have gratified Harris. He told an avid wireless audience:

> Our troops had seen our attack the previous evening – they told us it was a wonderful show. Immediately they heard that we had been one of the attacking force they clustered round to shake hands and slap our backs. Cups of tea appeared as if by magic, from foxholes, slit trenches, and from behind hedges. The spirit of the men was truly amazing, considering the guns were blazing away, and even as we spoke we were sprayed by earth kicked up by shells ... On our way back we stopped at an estaminet, but the French madame coolly told us she hadn't any wine left. An army officer whispered the words '*aviateur anglais*', and to my embarrassment the lady threw her arms around me, kissed me and repeatedly cried, '*Bon, bon,*' and most important of all, produced bottles of wine. When we finally returned to the landing strip the weather had cleared.[2]

The swiftly changing demands of this period created a feverish uncertainty hour by hour for Bomber Command aircrew and for those at the airfields who supported them. Grace Watson, a WAAF intelligence officer at 166 Sqn's base of Kirmington, kept a diary at the time, capturing that atmosphere.

In the morning of 7 July we were Stood Up for two targets, one to be a daylight with 42 aircraft and the other to be a night attack with a further 12 aircraft. At 0945 we were briefed for the daylight op, but just as briefing was over it was indefinitely postponed. At midday it was scrubbed altogether and we were then asked to provide every available aircraft on the station for an early raid. We were able to offer 30 aircraft, a record number for this squadron. There was much speculation as to what the target would be, and when the gen came through it thrilled everybody; it was Caen, where our troops were having such a tough time to dislodge the Germans.[3]

The young officer went out to watch the Lancasters take off on the 'most glorious evening, with brilliant sunshine'. Only a short time before, waiting for the Caen briefing to begin, she had talked to 'Red Mac', the Canadian navigator in S/Ldr Weston's crew. 'He said, "I've got a load of candy in my room – would you like some?" I said, "Yes, please if you can spare it." "Right," he said, "I'll see that you get some tomorrow."'[4]

The raid was controlled by W/Cdr Pat Daniels, the CO of 35 Sqn, who to ensure accuracy on German strong points and avoid hitting troops of the Canadian First and British Second Armies only a mile and a half away allowed only two-thirds of the aircraft to bomb. Air Chief Marshal Sir Arthur Tedder, SHAEF's Deputy Supreme Commander, had been against bombers being used to break the stalemate before Caen because of the danger to Allied troops. As an airman he knew how inaccurate bombing could be under a hail of light flak, but Montgomery asked Churchill for the heavies' support and Churchill agreed and, in fact, forced it through.[5] French soil was being bombed by Frenchmen in the attack, the two Free French squadrons at Elvington, 346 and 347, each sending nine aircraft. The power displayed had been a tremendous morale booster for the troops and impressed the generals mightily, showing the courage of the bomber boys pressing through to the right target despite the effective German gunners. The next day a message from Second Army SHAEF was displayed at all Bomber Command stations that had taken part. It read: 'Heavy attack just taken place. A wonderfully impressive show and enormously appreciated by the Army.

The Army would like their appreciation and thanks sent to all crews.'[6]

Sgt Ken Down, the 550 Sqn flight engineer, who would find himself baling out after a Revigny trip a week later, remembers how strictly crews had been briefed to bomb accurately, despite the risks at low level.

We actually went in at 300 feet. There were a lot of Canadians on the ground near the target and we were told to go in low to definitely hit the right place. We followed the marker aircraft and it looked as if the target was getting quite a pasting. There was quite a lot of light flak coming up and a piece came through the Plexiglass on the port side, just missed the pilot, bounced off the armour plating on the back of his seat and hit my flying helmet by the left temple, gouging a furrow in the leather. I was standing up at the time and it knocked me out for a few seconds, but fortunately most of its force had been spent. I felt a bit groggy and went down and I heard Jim the pilot call out, 'Ken's been hit,' but by the time people arrived to help I was back on my feet again.

After landing I had a search round for the piece of flak before leaving the aircraft. It was wedged under one of the stays of my seat. I poked it out and put it in my pocket. I've still got it. It's a rectangular bit about an inch long by three-quarters wide. I had to go to sick bay to be checked over, the shrapnel had given me a bruise on the side of the head, but they said I was OK. I kept the same flying helmet even though it was damaged. I wouldn't want to change it because I thought it brought me good luck.[7]

The light flak had claimed ten of the 1,000-plus aircraft on the raid and one of them was S/Ldr Weston's Q-Queenie of 166 Sqn, whose navigator F/O Ernest Macintosh had promised Canadian confectionery to Grace Watson. 'Poor "Red",' she wrote in her diary, 'for him there won't be a tomorrow. I don't care about the candy; I just wish that he and the rest of the crew were still here with us. Perhaps, just perhaps, they had time to bale out, but it doesn't seem very likely.'[8] In fact the flak-damaged Q-Queenie came down in the Channel and no one survived.

Eleven days later W/Cdr Daniels took part in another accurate daylight attack by nearly 1,000 bombers on five fortified villages east of Caen, through which the British Second Army was about to launch Operation Goodwood, but this time one of his flight commanders was the master bomber. F/Sgt Cliff Hill, the 35 Sqn rear gunner, found he and his crew were flying with the CO and were somewhat nervous about it. Hill remembers:

> Our pilot was collecting his DFC from the King. We were waiting with W/Cdr Daniels in a huddle outside the aircraft to have a last cigarette before getting in when the flight engineer Bill Lloyd produced his home-made lighter, constructed from a cartridge case. He flicked it a couple of times and nothing happened. The third time it really flared up and singed the Wingco's eyebrows. He just looked and said: 'That's a good lighter, engineer.' It lessened the tension considerably.
>
> After we had bombed, W/Cdr Daniels said, 'We will go and cheer up the troops.' We went down to about 200 feet and flew across the front line. All the troops were waving their mess tins and anything that came to hand. Pat Daniels did three runs and they were absolutely delighted. It was a wonderful morale-boosting gesture on his part.[9]

There were other key raids by sometimes more than 1,000 aircraft, to assist the armies' progress through Normandy on 30 July, 7 August, 12 August and 14 August. Sgt Arthur Madelaine, a flight engineer who had just joined 12 Sqn at Wickenby, was on the raid of 12 August, the smallest in the series, involving 144 Lancasters, Halifaxes and even Stirlings, bombing a German troop concentration caught at a road junction in the chaos of the Falaise Gap through which the Wehrmacht was now in headlong flight. He remembered:

> It was what they called a quickie. They got a few crews that were knocking about, hurriedly briefed them and sent them. You had to be fast when it was your turn to turn off the perimeter track onto the runway to take off and I remember one pilot being a bit slow in front of us and the WAAF in the control tower told him: 'Finger out, S-Sugar.' We didn't see any flak coming up at Falaise. We bombed on red flares the army had fired to mark the positions they wanted bombing.'[10]

The final army support operation two days later, designed to help the Canadians who had opened the way towards Falaise, had tragic consequences. The worst fears of the generals now came true and of the

800-strong bomber force approximately seventy-seven, several from the Canadian 6 Group, unloaded on Canadian troops sheltering in preparation for attack and sixty-five were killed. Harris circulated a personal report into the incident eleven days later in which he concluded the crews at fault had not maintained their time check from the coast to prevent such an error. The report stated the two PFF crews involved had lost their badges and acting ranks and the squadron and flight commanders had relinquished their commands.[11]

AMONG the happier aspects of the Normandy campaign was the thrill of liberation the Allied armies brought to the scores of Bomber Command aircrew on the run in France, desperate to see the first khaki uniforms of forward elements as they hid surrounded by field grey. F/O Bob Farnbank, the 158 Sqn navigator shot down on the Trappes operation four days before D-Day, was one of those who experienced that joy. He had been travelling south until he heard the invasion had taken place then retraced his steps. He says:

> After about five or six days I came to a farm where they were involved in the Resistance. They gave me some food and put me in a hidden room and moved me the next day to a place where an Englishman took over. He was a soldier who had been left behind after Dunkirk and become an agent. Over two or three days my identity was established. If this had not been OK I would have been shot. I was then moved to a safe house at Verneusses, about 30 miles south-east of Lisieux, where I changed into civilian clothes, but kept my uniform. I was there for several weeks because of enemy troop movements in the immediate locality.[12]

In the third week of August two Americans arrived from another safe farm one afternoon because of the presence of Germans near by.

> It now made quite a little band of escapers – two RAF, five American airmen and a French Resistance lady who the Germans were onto so she had had to hide. The Americans were told they could stay the night, but that same evening two German armoured cars and a scout car arrived, seeking cover in the orchard. We had a pre-arranged rendezvous for such emergencies – a hide that had been prepared a couple of fields away from the house. Most of our party were able to

make themselves scarce, but I was trapped in the house and the next morning I sat down to breakfast in the company of nine German soldiers. Fortunately their suspicions were not raised and after breakfast I took some tools, as if to work in the fields, and rejoined the Americans.

Late that same afternoon the farmer's young son came and said it was safe to return to the farm for a meal. However, as we walked back towards the farm, a German staff car pulled up in the yard of our neighbour. The occupants, an SS officer and another, senior officer, soon spotted us and the SS chap followed us into the farm kitchen. He obviously couldn't understand what three young men were doing there instead of being in Germany working as forced labour. Facing us across the table he drew his pistol and commenced shouting at us in rapid, fluent French. We were trapped, but I decided to act as natural as possible, so I just stood up and helped myself to more food from the stove. It worked. The SS man left with the two Americans, but they subsequently were released on the orders of the senior officer. We all met up again, much later. These narrow shaves prompted me to take my leave of the farm, though I remained near by in hiding. During this time I contacted another farm worker and spent the next week lying up in a cornfield and being fed by the Resistance, including the farmer.[13]

By this time the Allies were getting very close and F/O Farnbank decided to risk crossing the front line in uniform.

As I walked up a road in my battledress towards where I knew there were some English troops two men in German uniform jumped out of the hedge. They frightened me to death, but they had their hands up and asked me to take them along. I think they might have been Russians or some other nationality serving in the German Army. They just wanted to get out of it. There was a British Army detached headquarters off the main road and I just walked in with the prisoners. They kept the prisoners, but said, 'We're a bit busy at the moment, can you go back to where you were and wait to be collected in a couple of days?' I was eventually collected by a Royal Artillery unit and taken to a holding unit at Bayeux on 26 August. Within two or three hours of my arrival four other members of my crew who had also evaded walked in. It was amazing. There was actually a tentful of evaders gathered together. I suppose that if you had to be shot down we were shot down in the right place. We were taken to a nearby airfield the next day and flown back to Britain in a Dakota.

I rang my father when I got back to London to say I was safe and I think the telegram arrived at my home the next day, saying I was back in England. I was given survivor's leave and extended sick leave because I hadn't been able to have a bath for three months and had terrible skin trouble. I was sent back to Training Command as a safety navigation officer at an air gunnery school at Inverness. I applied to go back on operations, on Mosquitos, but the CO tore it up. He said, 'You've been down in France, you can't go again.' It could have just been an excuse to keep me.[14]

THE German armies, in bloody and battered retreat from Normandy with thoughts of *Heim ins Reich* (home to Germany) uppermost, were squeezed further by the invasion of southern France on 15 August. It was the salvation for another evader, P/O Harry Fisher, shot down in April in a raid on marshalling yards at Laon, now in a civilian prison in Toulouse after being captured by the Germans with other evaders within sight of freedom in the Pyrenees on 4 June. The guards were German military and conditions in the prison were dire. P/O Fisher remembers:

The Germans wouldn't officially recognise we were RAF, saying we were spies who they were going to take out and shoot. The Allies had just landed in Normandy and they used to taunt us about this secret weapon they had which they said had destroyed the south of England and that London was now simply rubble. We used to think, 'Nonsense,' but of course it was the V1.

We were in one cell and only taken out to wash in a trough. It was pretty basic and toilet facilities were just a bucket in the cell. There were mosquitoes, lice and bed bugs. We got a piece of black bread each morning with a bowl of ersatz coffee, and then for lunch a bowl of boiled cabbage leaves in water and the same again in the evening. The diet never changed. I went down from about 10 stone to under 8. Our salvation was the invasion of southern France. The Germans were being cut off in the Toulouse area and one morning they went in such a hurry they even left food still hot in the kitchens. We woke up that morning to hear the Marseillaise being sung. We thought: 'The Germans will soon put a stop to that,' then we heard running footsteps in the corridors and our cell was opened by a member of the French Forces of the Interior, the Maquis, who had broken into the prison. We were taken by the Maquis to a house outside and given something to eat and got a wash and fresh clothes. They gave me a pass saying I was a British officer liaising with the FFI. They were quite keen we should go out with them to fight, but that didn't appeal to us as airmen one little bit. There were no American forces around at that time and we were with the Maquis for a while. One day French women who had collaborated with the Germans were marched through the streets of Toulouse. Their heads had been shaved and they were stripped to the waist.

The FFI had contact with London and knew a special-duties squadron aircraft from England was coming in to land Resistance supplies one night in a field somewhere outside Toulouse, so on the night of 2 September we were taken out to this field. We hung around and then right enough I heard the sound of an aircraft and these Resistance boys ran out and lined up with torches on either side of the field to make a runway. A Hudson came round and landed. As it got to the end of the field the FFI said to us, 'Right, go.' We tore across the grass to where the guys from the aircraft were rapidly dumping supplies. When we got there, I don't know if they had any knowledge of us because one said, 'Where the hell have you come from?' But we clambered aboard and the engines opened up. My first thought was: 'Here I am in an aircraft without a parachute,' but as we left the ground it was wonderful. I thought, 'We're almost safe, almost safe, hopefully nothing will happen this time.' As dawn broke we crossed the Channel and it was still full of ships, even so long after D-Day. It was chock-a-block. As the wheels touched the runway at the base at Tempsford it was a tremendous feeling. I thought, 'Here we are back and at times I had thought we were never going to make it home and that I was going to be shot.'

From Tempsford we were taken to London, to MI9, where we were given a form saying on no account were we to divulge any information about what happened to us. I went on leave and then to a rehabilitation centre and I was told I wouldn't be going back on operations in the European theatre because I had been in German hands. I was instructing for the rest of the war.[15]

*

THERE were others still falling into the hands of the Resistance as operations continued in northern France in August to follow up Patton's right turn into Brittany and seize the port of Brest, to take pressure off the Allied supply chain. The 617 Sqn pilot F/O Don Cheney, whose mid-upper gunner had baled out after his bomber was badly damaged by flak in the V-weapon attack on Watten on 25 July, was shot down on 5 August in a daylight attack with the squadron's Tallboys on the submarine pens at Brest. He heard the 'whump, clang, whump, clang' of radar-predicted flak striking the Lancaster as it made its bomb run and the aircraft filled with blue smoke. The navigator and wireless operator had been badly wounded and blue-orange flames were licking up from several holes in the starboard wing. The starboard engine failed and as fire spread along the wing Cheney ordered the crew to bale out.

The only way he was able to get out himself after they had left, as 'yellowish brown bubbles and blisters' broke out on the flight engineer's panel with the heat, was through the escape hatch in the canopy above his head as the aircraft went into a dive. He tried, failed, then tried again. 'I flipped the chute pack upwards away from my body and stuffed it out of the hatch just before putting my chest out. It worked!' he wrote in an unpublished account after the war, which graphically describes what it meant to escape from a burning bomber.

> Once more with my feet on the arm rests of the pilots' seat I proceeded to get one knee on the outside edge of the escape hatch. Now I had to get the other foot higher. I felt around for the back of the seat, raised my foot until I could get a grip on the topmost part, then pushed with all my strength. I shot out into the slipstream. The blurred lump of the mid-upper turret flashed past ... the two big tail fins zipped by and I was tumbling in space ... the roar of the aircraft had disappeared and was replaced by the rushing of air in my ears.

His chute now open he saw his crippled aircraft, KC-V, which carried the nose art Dark Victor, spin towards the Channel, motors still revving and trailing flame and black smoke.

> It seemed to take an eternity for the plane to hit the water. Finally there was a thunderous roar as it dived nose first into the sea. For a few seconds red flames mixed with black smoke towered 50 metres

into the air, billowing and swirling. Then came a bubbling, boiling circle of churning, hissing sea water, a column of water vapour, a shower of splashes from pieces of flying debris and silence.

Reflecting on his 'miraculous escape' the pilot, who had just celebrated his 22nd birthday, waited for his own entry into the Channel.

Splash! I went under water for a brief second then bobbed to the surface like a cork, my Mae West life jacket already fully inflated. It felt tight around my body and supported the back of my neck and head. I felt the unpleasant pain of having taken water up my nose. The chute was billowing out behind me in the breeze ... my feet and legs were heavy as my flying boots filled with water.

F/O Cheney released his chute and boots with difficulty and began swimming towards the shoreline about half a mile away, coughing and spluttering and becoming very tired. After what seemed like an hour in which he kept telling himself to 'keep going' he saw 'a small fishing boat ... It headed straight for me.' The French fishermen landed him on the jetty of the small port of Douarnenez, on the outskirts of which the Resistance had been fighting the Germans all morning.

People came up to me to grasp my hand or pat me on the back. One or two motherly types bussed me on both cheeks. I could make out *'aviateur anglais!'* repeated over and over. Someone thrust a pear into my hand and another handed me an opened can of small fish in olive oil similar to sardines but large. As my stomach contained only a little sea water this generous offering smelled terrible to me. I laid the tin aside and promptly threw up, much to my embarrassment.

F/O Cheney was eventually taken by the Resistance to a safe house where a woman handed him civilian clothes and he was given a spare room where he collapsed into bed. He awoke in the dark, worrying about his crew and 'felt the cold hand of fear and loneliness. What I would not give to be going off to the pub with the boys tonight.' The young pilot found the next few days 'very anxious ones. The Germans knew their situation was rapidly becoming untenable from both pressure by the Resistance and the advance of the American forces on Brest. Several houses were burned to the ground on various pretexts.' Before the Germans left and still in hiding from them F/O Cheney was taken by the Resistance to identify the body of his wireless operator, F/Sgt Reg Pool, found floating in the bay, his chute spread out behind him, the severe wounds he had received in the aircraft very obvious. After the Germans left F/O Cheney was able to attend his funeral.

> The emotion of these occasions was indescribable. I kept thinking I would soon wake up and find that the whole episode had never happened. It was not until I left Douarnenez that the bodies of P/O Noel Wait and P/O Roy Welch, the rear gunner and navigator respectively, were found at different points along the shore of the bay.

P/O Welch had left the aircraft severely wounded and P/O Wait is thought to have drowned.*

F/O Cheney left Douarnenez in mid-August with the Resistance and an American evader and after a while met US tanks, whose commander refused to help, 'shouting that they still had a f—ing war to fight'. He eventually made for Bayeux and on the way entered Caen, days after its destruction by the RAF. 'Not a house or building of any kind was left standing for as far as I could see. We wound our way through and amongst great piles of rubble which had once been rows of houses and shops. More than once I noticed tanks buried in rubble with only their turrets and guns protruding.'

On arrival at the depot for evaders in Bayeux he was strictly interrogated and locked up, but eventually after his details had been confirmed was allowed to go into the town. He wrote:

> I overtook a long column of German prisoners, perhaps several hundred. I stopped to observe this latest, and I must say, most satisfying scene, when my attention was diverted by a wild, whining roar just over the treetops ahead. Every split second the terrifying noise became louder. I was rooted to the spot. Three Typhoon fighter bombers in their green and brown camouflage and the

---

* Of F/O Cheney's crew three survived – the flight engineer F/Sgt Jim Rosher and mid-upper gunner W/O Ken Porter also evaded and the bomb aimer F/Sgt Len Curtis was captured by the local garrison, but freed when American troops arrived later.

distinctive white invasion stripes on fuselages and wings, swept past in line abreast. As they passed overhead I lowered my gaze in time to behold the last third of the German column sweeping into the roadside ditch like a line of toppling dominos. They would not soon forget those fearsome low-level strafing attacks which they had endured only days earlier.

F/O Cheney was flown back to England an hour later, twenty-four days and a lifetime of experience since he had last seen its green fields. He was soon repatriated to Canada.[16]

THE evidence of German defeat by Allied airpower witnessed by F/O Cheney was equally clear at Bomber Command in the dawn of 19 August. The previous night they had dispatched 1,037 aircraft, nearly all to five major targets, two of them in Germany, and only four aircraft had been lost, one of those in taxiing. The airmen who had fought the night-bomber war two seasons before would not have believed it possible. The Operational Research Section's report into the night's operations glowed with self-satisfaction over the 'most successful results, devastating the heart of Bremen and causing great damage to the oil refineries at Sterkrade and Ertvelde/Rieme and the marshalling yards at Connantre. Berlin and Cologne were among the other targets bombed. This rate of loss is almost unprecedentedly low for so large an effort.'[17]

The major target had been Bremen, 274 Lancasters and Halifaxes arriving over the city in clear visibility to carry out a textbook attack on the glowing red and green Pathfinder TIs and creating huge fires, which rapidly linked. Day reconnaissance showed that immense damage had been caused, vastly more than the important port, or many cities in Germany, had ever seen before. The ORS analysis ran:

A large area stretching for over 5,000 yards from the north-west outskirts of the old city and comprising two-thirds of the Doventor district and Utbrenner and Herdentor was quite devastated. Forty warehouses in the Weser dockyards were destroyed, two merchant vessels set on fire. The large Geber Nielson rice and starch mills, six other factories, three loco sheds and many smaller railway buildings, the main tramway depot and goods sheds in the city yards were damaged.[18]

All that the defences had to show for it was one Lancaster downed by flak.

Bomber Command's route planners were now experts, having learned much from previous mistakes – particularly in July – and the previous night the enemy had been badly deceived by a diversion along the route towards Bremen. 'Reacting, he made no attacks on our bombers except two at the target,' the analysis continued. 'The Sterkrade force met little stronger opposition and aircraft visiting French and Belgian targets hardly figured at all.'[19]

The diarist Ils Garthaus was a resident of Bremen. She was a dancer at the Staatstheater, although Goebbels was now closing German theatres following the 20 July bomb plot as part of the even tighter grip being imposed by the Nazis to completely control what citizens said and heard. She had been appearing in *Opera Ball*, an operetta of the kind the management had lately concentrated on to cheer people up, when the first alarm came over the radio at about 10 p.m. 'More and more bomber formations were reported over Heligoland. When they reached Cuxhaven and turned we knew we were going to get it,' she wrote. She made for the nearest shelter and

at three minutes before midnight the first wave of carpet-bombing started. People looked at each other in silence and nodded. Some prayed, others held their breath and listened. Children started to cry. A puppy started whining in a bag trying to get out. This was one customer not allowed into the shelter. Its owner, an old man, started to cough loudly. No one had seen anything of course. Outside the flak tried desperately to defend the city, but disturbing devices like strips of foil defeated their action.

Ils Garthaus remained pressed shoulder to shoulder with her fellow citizens, listening to the sounds of war outside the bunker's walls. Most feared was the pushing then sucking sensation of a blockbuster landing near by and the rustle as numerous 4-lb stick incendiaries fell in groups through the sky, each to start an individual small fire in the immediate vicinity. 'Still the bombs kept dropping, rolling along and exploding everywhere,' she wrote. 'Thirty-five minutes later the bombers turned back, leaving Bremen burning. A fantastic firestorm raged through the city spreading disaster among those who left their shelter too early. There was smoke everywhere.'[20]

The raid had indeed devastated the city. More than 8,500 residential units, which could include a whole block of flats, were destroyed that night and up to 1,500 people are thought to have died, many in their shelters asphyxiated behind the 6-foot-thick walls as in the firestorm raid on Hamburg a year before. The Nazi Party controlled all air raid relief in a cynical effort to display humanitarian credentials, and cards for special rations issued to help restore morale included spirits and real coffee, although Martin Bormann, head of the Reich Chancellery, had been trying for months to have rations reduced.

IN terms of demonstrating that Bomber Command could now attack industrial or commercial targets almost with impunity in the face of a declining Luftwaffe, Bremen had been an astounding success, but more was to come. Two operations at the very end of the month showed just how far Bomber Command could now risk reaching into Germany and still count on bringing the great majority of its bombers home. Königsberg in East Prussia had not been bombed by the RAF before. It was a major port, shipbuilding and engineering centre, but at 1,900 miles in a round trip from eastern England, much of it across enemy territory, it was considered too far to make it a viable objective. It had been put forward as a possible target in March, then discarded – a wise decision considering the then strength of the Luftwaffe night-fighter arm. But its importance as a supply route to the Eastern Front had grown and after the Soviet offensive had stalled before Warsaw directly to the south, the encircled Soviet III Tank Corps suffering 90 per cent casualties by 11 August as the Polish Home Army still fought on in Warsaw Old Town, it was considered imperative that Bomber Command show Stalin how much Britain was prepared to do to aid that offensive.

Flight engineer Sgt Edwin Watson began his tour of operations in this period in which Königsberg would figure so crucially and rapidly discovered how much his crew had to learn.

Just after we arrived on 630 Sqn in early August we went up on an air test with a flight lieutenant and did one or two corkscrews for mock fighter attacks. He told us in very strong language that unless we improved on them we would not survive. He then got in the pilot's seat and threw the Lancaster around like a fighter. Of course in training all the aircraft we had flown in were clapped out and the instructors were a bit wary of them falling apart. What the flight lieutenant told us did make us think. From then on we practised as often as we could and on operations we banked and searched, corkscrewing whenever in doubt. We experienced various sightings in our tour of fighters coming after us and one time the rear gunner saw a glowing object coming towards us and we went into a screaming dive and it missed us. We were told back at base it was a rocket projectile with vanes which could follow you into a corkscrew. We were advised to take the most vicious action we could.[21]

The removal of Königsberg as the main supply port to the Eastern Front was handed to 5 Group, which had achieved so much in the past. But it would not be the major target of the night. A total of 372 Lancasters and ten Mosquitos of 1, 3 and 8 Groups were briefed for another Baltic port, Kiel, also part of the supply line to the Russian Front. Only 174 Lancasters would be going to Königsberg and it was known, even at this more efficient stage of the war, what a risk was being taken with fuel consumption.

Sgt Watson remembers:

We were briefed twice in the week before we did the first raid on Königsberg and it was cancelled each time. Then on the day we went, a few hours before take-off we ran up the engines, taxied and parked behind each other at the threshold of the runway. The tanks were topped up to the brim with 2,154 gallons of petrol and we had a bomb load of 8,000 lbs. I remember at briefing we were told it was the first time the RAF had been routed over Sweden. We were told the searchlights would be vertical as a sign of neutrality and if flak was fired it would be 'token flak', which wouldn't harm us.[22]

Both the Kiel and Königsberg forces swept out over the North Sea together and Mosquitos carried out spoofs on Hamburg and Berlin as thirty Lancasters and fifteen Halifaxes laid mines as a diversion off Kiel and Danzig. The two main forces were plotted early by the Luftwaffe controller and seven *Nachtjäger Gruppen* were scrambled, but as Königsberg had not been attacked before it was thought that force was heading for Berlin or Stettin and only four of its Lancasters were lost. The Kiel force was not so fortunate and seventeen were shot down, mainly in the Baltic, and the mining force in Kiel Bay fared even worse proportionately, five of the thirty Lancasters sent out being shot down. However, the results had been dramatic. In Kiel, the Operational Research Section reported, 'The groundmarking was punctual and appeared accurate. Bombing was well directed at the markers and large fires were started.' At Königsberg bombing was 'most concentrated, but centred some way north of the aiming point'.[23]

Sgt Tom Howie, the 625 Sqn flight engineer, who was on the Kiel raid, now saw the fearsome new Luftwaffe weapon Sgt Watson had been warned about. Howie says:

It was the first time I'd seen the Germans use rockets. While we were on the bomb run I saw a pair leave the ground and I was sure as these red balls came up they were going to hit the wing. The bomb aimer was reeling off his instructions, 'Left, left,' and I was so desperate I pressed the intercom switch and said ' Left, left' again and the bomb aimer shouted out, 'No, no, right, right.' Thank God the rockets passed by us and I never saw them on ops again.[24]

Sgt Watson, on the Königsberg operation, found himself carefully checking engine efficiency against fuel consumption knowing there was no margin for error.

We actually went over Denmark and Sweden then across the Baltic to the target, which was 70 miles from the Russian Front. Neutral Sweden was a different world, awe-inspiring in fact – no blackout, searchlights still, Swedish fighters flying around with navigation lights, pretty, multi-coloured non-damaging flak. It even seemed to smell nice. We went on to Königsberg and after bombing we made a gradual descent to conserve fuel. It was an eleven and a quarter-hour flight in all and a shaky experience across the North Sea wondering if we would have enough petrol. We were diverted to an airfield at Longtown in Cumbria. We got a rum ration at debriefing, but they were short of glasses and I remember washing out a mustard pot and taking mine in that.[25]

Reconnaissance the next day showed a considerable part of the attack on Königsberg had fallen across the eastern half of the town where business and residential property suffered heavily. Twenty buildings of a barracks had been destroyed or damaged, considerably reducing the number of troops en route to the Russian Front it could house. 'The Russians should be well pleased with this effort and it should help them quite a lot,' the adjutant's staff at 467 (RAAF) Sqn noted. 'Everyone succeeded in keeping awake long enough and got back in time for breakfast, but not at this station. Today was a stand-down, it had to be, we had no aircraft.'[26] In Kiel, where widespread fires were fanned by a strong wind, the town hall was burned out together with several other public buildings.[27]

However, much of Königsberg's commercial and dock area remained and another attack was mounted three nights later at the same time as a bigger raid was carried out on another Baltic port, Stettin. The Luftwaffe, who had expected Stettin to be attacked on the previous Königsberg raid, was not fooled this time and both forces suffered heavily, the Königsberg element losing 7.9 per cent of those that had set out. This time 5 Group were determined to strike a killer blow and the master bomber, W/Cdr John Woodroffe, aware that the 188 Lancasters he was leading carried only 480 tons of bombs because they needed so much fuel, delayed the opening of the attack as he orbited Königsberg amid its furious light flak, ensuring the four aiming points were accurately marked amid gaps in the clouds. The result was a textbook raid, which created linking fires, destroying more than half the buildings in Königsberg over 400 acres, including forty-four warehouses packed with much needed supplies for the Eastern Front. A total of 65 per cent of the city's fully built-up zone was now devastated. But there had been a price, fifteen Lancasters failed to return to their bases. From Waddington 467 Sqn had sent nineteen crews and the next morning three were missing. 'Most crews had to orbit for 20 minutes and this no doubt accounted for the losses,' the adjutant's staff later reported. 'It is hoped some if not all of these crews were able to get down safely in Sweden as that country was near the route followed.'[28] It was, in fact, part of the route followed, but none of the three 467 Sqn crews crashlanded there – two vanished over the sea and the third crashed near the target. Among the other crews missing that night two had skippers who had already made a name for themselves – S/Ldr Neville Sparks, who had walked home after being shot down in the Mailly-le-Camp raid, this time becoming a prisoner of war after being hit by flak; and G/Cptn Bill McKechnie, who had proved such an enlightened commander to the WAAFs at Metheringham, vanishing without trace. Typically McKechnie, who as a station commander didn't need to fly operationally at all, had gone to Königsberg with a new crew to give them confidence.

Weather conditions that night were dreadful for the time of year, icing conditions over the Baltic following electrical storms en route. Sgt Watson was on the raid, making his second maximum-range trip in a week. He remembers:

Again all the fuel tanks had been topped up. We had problems with the compass this time. The ground crew warned us before take-off that another crew had reported the compass had become de-synchronised from the master compass. Approaching the target there was quite a bit of cloud and we saw a Ju88, so nipped into cloud as smartly as we could. After bombing and coming away from the target we saw another Ju88 and he looked a bit more aggressive so we corkscrewed like hell and again managed to get into cloud.

When we came out we thought we were heading for the Baltic to return home, but saw flashes in the cloud ahead and thought we were heading back to the target. We thought the compass had become toppled in the corkscrew and turned round, sending our wireless operator to check the DR master unit. But he said it was OK, so we realised it must have been lightning we saw in the cloud. We were quite lost by then and headed across the Baltic and Sweden and as I could see the fuel getting low we decided to go low down and try to pick up a landmark. We were only about 50 feet over Denmark and as the coastline came up we flew over an army camp. We could see chinks of light as billet doors were opened. A 20 mm flak battery on the cliffs opened up at us. I can see the flashes to this day. They were hosepiping flak towards us, but luckily we didn't get hit. I rammed the throttles forward and we went right down to the sea. We were very concerned about whether our fuel would last, but we got back after a flight of ten hours and fifty minutes.

Others were not so lucky, many of the fifteen missing believed to have run out of fuel after battle damage and to have gone down in the sea.

Sgt Alf Ridpath, the wireless operator who had seen a Halifax explode above him over Stuttgart, was on both the Königsberg operations and his crew of 83 Sqn Pathfinders helped to mark the target each time. He remembers thinking, 'Oh, my God,' when he saw how far the tape stretched at briefing, and the second trip took even longer than the first.

We took off at 2033 and were back at 0600. We flew over Swedish territory and up came the searchlights, but they were waving away from us and the flak was going where the searchlights were and we figured, 'The Swedes are on our side.' We made two runs on the target on the second op. Both raids were carried out at 15,000 feet. We were illuminators and had clusters of flares and photoflashes. We ran in and dropped flares and orbited, then at 0122 the controller asked for more flares west of a green TI and we had to make another run-in. We weren't able to see a green TI, so we dropped them by H2S. There was considerable flak and when we were asked to make a second run some wag asked, 'Does this count as two trips?' We were specifically asked not to come back across Sweden, but as it had proved so successful going out we thought we would come back the same way. The Swedes were more cunning this time. Up came the searchlights and the flak and this time they were trying to hit us. It was a long haul back and we were totally exhausted by the time we landed.[29]

That Swedish flak was later blamed for downing several bombers on the second Königsberg raid, the Operational Research Section even concluding as many as seven could have gone down to flak over the neutral country, though lack of fuel is a more likely cause.[30]

The Stettin raiders were those who suffered most that night, however, mainly from fighters. Sgt Howie, of 625 Sqn, was lucky. He remembers:

We were told we were going to Stettin because troop ships were coming in from Russia. We flew over Sweden and could see its lights below. The Swedish flak fired in our direction, but it was well below our height and I think it was just to keep the German embassy quiet. We headed down over the island of Borholm and slid into Stettin. We didn't see any night fighters.[31]

But others did, in great numbers. The Königsberg force was slightly in front and its thundering passage over Denmark alerted the Luftwaffe. 'By the time the Stettin force arrived over the Danish coast fighters were already airborne,' the post-raid analysis noted. 'Other fighters were probably moved here from Northern areas. Combats were numerous between here and Stettin.'[32] The 400 Lancasters that arrived over Stettin carrying 1,200 tons of bombs caused great damage to parts of the port, which had so far escaped, and one ship was sunk and seven damaged, but a total of twenty-three bombers were shot down, a loss rate of 5.7 per cent, a figure many squadrons hoped was confined to the bad old days of winter. The crews setting out for Stettin and Königsberg were well aware what might face them from an enraged populace, now that Goebbels was encouraging lynch law and the account of a young airman downed that night over Stettin gives some indication of the terror of bale-out and being on the run.

Sgt Arthur Madelaine, the 19-year-old flight engineer on 12 Sqn who had begun his tour seventeen days before with a trip to Falaise, was on his fourth operation. It would claim the lives of his two gunners and make the rest of the crew prisoners of war. He remembered:

We had been briefed for Stettin twice before and it had been cancelled. When we were given the details the third time another chap in the briefing room said, 'I don't fancy the chances on this one.' But I had no thoughts like that, I thought I was fireproof.

We were attacked by a night fighter about half an hour before the target. I saw level tracers fly past between the fuselage and the starboard inner, near to my position. I tapped the pilot on the shoulder and he immediately went into a corkscrew to port. As he went down he shouted to the rear gunner, 'Which way corkscrew?' I think the rear gunner was asleep, when he saw the tracers coming towards him he shouted so hard in the intercom you couldn't tell what he said, whether it was port or starboard. As the wing came up I could see the rounds thumping into the main spar. At the bottom of the corkscrew as the skipper made his climbing turn to starboard we realised we had lost the fighter, but we had severe damage to the tailplane and starboard wing and could not trim the aircraft.

We were heading into the target when we saw a Lanc to port alongside us display a small orange ball of fire that ended in an enormous white flash. We saw the wings fall off and the engines burst from the wings as it disintegrated. We knew nobody could have got out. On the bombing run we all seemed to be trying to get on the same TI, then suddenly the mid-upper shouted: 'There's a bloody great fire under me, Skipper.' The skipper didn't answer because we were on the bombing run, but I shouted back: 'Well put the bloody thing out then.' I felt the bombs go. Apparently we had been hit by bombs from above, setting our incendiaries alight. You couldn't see down the fuselage for white smoke. The navigator came out of his curtained office and as he went past it knocked my oxygen tube and intercom cord out, so I never did hear any instructions. I bent down behind the pilot to get an emergency oxygen bottle. I put it on and turned round to tackle the fire and met the wireless operator. He pointed towards the front hatch to bale out. I thought we could tackle the fire because we had a brand-new, latest type Lanc with a device that filled the petrol tanks with nitrogen as they emptied so they wouldn't explode. I don't think the skipper knew about this.

I baled out very reluctantly. Everybody got out except the two gunners and I think they were overcome by smoke because when I looked down the fuselage you couldn't see anything except a white blanket working its way up the plane. You couldn't see your hand in front of your face. I was falling through the sky on my back and I saw the wireless operator bale out of the escape hatch. He immediately opened his chute and I saw it spread out underneath the plane. I was sure it was going to catch the tail wheel, but it didn't. I had no sensation of falling. We baled out at about 12,000 feet, but by the light of the fires below I could see the ripcord handle and pulled it. There was a great big column of smoke coming up from an oil tank on fire and I tried to slip the chute away from it, but I didn't have the strength. I landed thump between the river and the canal in a bit of wooded land near the dock area. I thought I was still about 100 feet up and fell over, then I stood up, grabbed my chute and dashed into these bushes and hid the chute there. Civilians had seen me come down and I could hear them shouting as they searched for me. I could see they were carrying pick-axe handles, so I kept quiet. The strip of land ended in a gorge down to the river and I thought, 'If they come close I'll run and jump over the edge into the water,' but eventually they went away. Half an hour later I came out and hid in some reeds by the canal. I lay hidden all day and eventually fell asleep, waking when an FW190 zoomed over. I opened my escape kit and used the rubber bottle to get water from the canal.

As night fell Sgt Madeleine decided to try to make his way out of the target area. But his RAF uniform was soon spotted by civilians. They protected him from attack by a woman who 'wanted to kill me' and he was eventually marched by a Hitler Youth boy to police headquarters, not far from damage caused by the air raid.

A bomb-blasted building was illuminated by carbon arc lights as they searched for bodies. I thought, 'Oh my God, let's hope we don't go near there,' and we didn't. We got to the police station and he took me into a room where there were a lot of typical square-headed Prussians. There was a child's pram in it with broken dolls and I thought, 'I hope the kid who owns it is all right.' They took me to the cells and I had to strip off. The bed was full of lice, so I slept on the floor. To get washed I lined up with the civilian prisoners. There was a bath that looked as if a hundred colliers had been in it. They treated me reasonably well considering that I had been dropping bombs on them. The next day they brought a civilian woman who spoke English and asked if I had anything to do with dropping the bombs. I assured her I had nothing to do with dropping the bombs.

Eventually Sgt Madeleine was taken to Dulag Luft near Frankfurt where he steadfastly refused to answer any questions, though he was shocked to find out just how detailed was the Luftwaffe information about his base and squadron. 'I was shown an aerial photograph of Wickenby by the interrogator and he pointed to my exact billet in a field full of Nissen huts,' he remembers. 'It mystified me because it used to take me all my time to find it. I thought somebody in the group must have been sending them information.'[33]

AS Sgt Madeleine was sent off to Stalag Luft VII in early September to wait out the rest of the war Bomber Command was about to begin its third and most destructive phase. Even at the beginning of 1944 Germany had lacked 11 million homes because of bombing raids. Many were now living in hutted accommodation in the bombed cities. When the Nazi Labour Minister Robert Ley also assumed responsibility for housing he had promised airy, sunny homes for all Germans. Survivors of the air raids joked bitterly in 1944: 'Well, now we have all the sun and air we need.'[34]

Königsberg, Bremen and other recent raids had proved that Bomber Command could now reach further, attack by day or by night, and had so improved in technique it could carry out devastating attacks by individual groups. In eight months there had been a reversal in the fortunes of the men of Bomber Command. From the dogged depression of inevitable doom in the Battle of Berlin they had survived the adversities of Nuremberg and Mailly-le-Camp to savour the triumphs of the invasion, in which the Wehrmacht high command had been fooled and defeated, and then pursued the V-weapon and early oil campaigns to eventually take the air war almost to the Russian lines. The bomber force was far more flexible as summer ended in the harvest of autumn, able to fulfil the obligations of different campaigns at the same time if asked. The loss rate per sortie was falling, though in total numbers the sacrifice was still harrowing. In August, a month of intense effort, 1,266 Bomber Command aircrew were killed and 249 made prisoner, compared to 1,792 and 464 in the first month of the year. At the same time the number of front-line bombers was increasing, availability rising by 50 per cent in 1944.[35]

The Luftwaffe was also in steady decline, both by day and by night. The investment in the V1 and V2 programme had denied essential resources to aircraft manufacture and by September the first of the V-weapons, which had proved so vulnerable in static sites, was a spent force. By the time the Luftwaffe jets made their appearance it would be too late. The entire production of V1s and V2s did not exceed 3,700 tons of high explosives, compared to the 8,000 tons dropped by more than 4,000 British and American bomber fleets in a single 24-hour period.[36] For as August closed the USAAF was an equal partner with Bomber Command over Europe and within months would be greater in size, if not bomb-carrying capacity. That bombing was causing constant interruptions as autumn approached in all areas of arms production. In the aircraft industry alone reliance on a small number of contractors, which deepened after the dispersal forced by bombing, led to constant interruptions in the flow of parts for assembly.[37]

Many thought the war might now be over by Christmas. The failure of the Arnhem campaign put paid to such an illusion as Germany's troops fought on to the end, encouraged by the plan of the US Treasury Secretary Henry Morgenthau to return the Fatherland to an agrarian – seen as slave – nation, and in the knowledge that after what they had done in Russia merciless retribution was arriving from the east. Any doubts a soldier might have about continuing to support Hitler in the post-bomb-plot period were quickly answered by the Gestapo, who were now carrying out death sentences on boys as young as 14.

The scene was set, therefore, for the final stage in the bombing war, which would push Germany towards eventual defeat on the ground, squeezed between East and West. In late September the use of mobile RAF units now operating in liberated France would extend Oboe cover, which had made the Battle of the Ruhr such a success in 1943, to a line east of Kassel and well to the east of Strasbourg and Frankfurt. It would bring the production centres of central and southern Germany, where many factories had been dispersed, within range of its phenomenal accuracy for target marking.

And what of Harris? As August ended and September began he was in disagreement with the Air Ministry as he looked after his experienced, brave flyers, facing pressure as a result of the army's manpower crisis. The Air Ministry wanted to insist that bomber crews automatically carry out a second tour. Harris correctly argued that their 'chances of survival were very small'.[38] In mid-September while the row went on, never to be resolved, he was handed back his command from SHAEF, as control once more reverted to the Air Ministry, but with the proviso that all operations still fit into overall Allied planning. Harris was determined to return to bombing the cities and towns that were the centres of German industrial production and believed the six-month diversion of Bomber Command to invasion needs had been a mistake, considering that so much damage had been caused to the Reich in 1943 it 'showed that if the available bombing forces – ourselves and the Americans – went on and developed the weight of attack that was by then possible, Germany would then without a shadow of doubt be knocked right out within a few months'.[39] This isn't necessarily as erroneously partisan as it sounds. Germany's armaments manufacture reached its apogee between June and August 1944, while Bomber Command was largely engaged elsewhere.[40]

That peak was the final fulfilment of the expansion plans laid in the middle of 1941 when it was realised the comparatively low level of economic mobilisation would be embarrassingly inadequate for sustained warfare. Bombing finally placed a ceiling on German war production in 1944. In that year plans were laid for an annual rate of production of 80,000 aircraft a year in Germany in 1945. The peak, in fact, was 36,000 in 1944.[41]

As we now know, it was the denial of oil supplies that finally brought the German war machine grinding to a halt, but hindsight knows no myopia. Asked to switch the main weight of his effort to bombing synthetic oil installations, more important than ever after the over-running of the Ploesti oil fields in August, Harris was wrong not to realise that this was the key to victory and to devote the overwhelming part of his force's effort in the remaining months of the war to bombing oil plants. He did, after all, by now have GH, the navigational aid that proved so effective in leading vics of three aircraft to small targets – such as oil refineries. But all generals make mistakes and none of them in the Second World War has been so pilloried as Harris has for his. Harris's strength was also his weakness; he was intractable and it was that stubbornness that had saved Bomber Command when it could so easily have been hived off in 1942 to become an adjunct to the navy and the army.

The Command he had saved was about to show conclusively its innovative, terrible strength. More than 45 per cent of the total bomb tonnage dropped by Bomber Command in the whole war would tumble onto Germany in the next eight months. After the failure of Arnhem in September the Allies knew they would have to find another way to quickly finish the conflict before Germany came up with a new and terrible weapon, or even used an atomic bomb. It was after all because Germany first started research into producing such a weapon that America had been persuaded to begin its own Manhattan Project.

As summer made way for autumn and then the first icy warnings of winter, the mayor of Stuttgart, a place that had suffered much as a result of the Nazi need for war, described the conditions in his own ruined Reich city, in which people lived 'in cellars without heat and light, in the corners of the walls, often in the sinister and horrifying neighbourhood of those who had been buried'. Dr Karl Strolin went on: 'In this last stage of the war life in these great cities affected by the bombing attacks was perhaps more dangerous and harder than on the Front.'[42] The road to Dresden lay ahead.

19

Reflection

It is more than sixty years since the events described in these pages took place, yet the evidence of the RAF and Commonwealth bomber offensive, which made such a vital contribution to victory, is still surfacing. Across Europe the remains of Bomber Command aircraft, and often their crews, may be found as a plough strikes wartime aluminium. Occasionally roadworks might disturb what was once Perspex, last peered through in an age as obscure to today's generation as the Victorian period was to the airmen who fought and died.

In September 2005 the remains of five members of Halifax T-Tommy of 640 Sqn were laid to rest in the Commonwealth War Cemetery in Berlin, where 3,584 of their comrades lost over Germany now lie. The men had been missing since setting out from Leconfield in the late afternoon of 24 March 1944 to take part in the last raid of the Battle of Berlin. They were finally unearthed with their aircraft in a field north of Torgau, like so many of their colleagues the victims of a night fighter.[1] Two months after the Torgau airmen were buried, the Netherlands Air Force uncovered near the village of Hank, south of Amsterdam, the remains of crew members of W-Willie of 78 Sqn, missing since being shot down on their way home to Breighton from Aachen on 26 May 1944. The search for them was due to the initial determination of a local man, Mr van der Pluijm, who saw the wreckage the day after the Halifax came down and knew most of the crew were still under the soil.[2]

In fact, it is in the former occupied countries where the memories of bomber airmen who died for freedom are kept alive when many veterans feel their own nation has forgotten them. At Rebréchien, near Orléans, a new marble memorial was unveiled in July 2004 to the crew of Victor 2 of 101 Sqn, lost on the last of the July Stuttgart raids exactly sixty years before.[3] In November 2005 relatives of airmen of 83 Sqn were tracked down and invited to a special service at Morkhoven, Belgium, where villagers have tended the RAF men's graves since their Lancaster crashed returning from Frankfurt.[4]

André Guillet, who saw M-Mother of 207 Sqn crash near Dontilly on the Mailly-le-Camp raid of 3 May, killing P/O Cyril Bell and his crew, says:

> A monument to their memory was erected in 1946 near the spot where their aircraft crashed. The monument was paid for thanks to a fund started by the Network of Resistance Guerin-Buckmaster, of which I was a member. Every 4 May a celebration organised by the town council takes place. Veterans of the war and former members of the Resistance join in.[5]

There is precious little equivocation among those in the former occupied countries about why the bomber offensive was fought; the humming of hundreds of Lancasters and Halifaxes heading east over their heads night after night was the sound of hope in a world of darkness, the audible proof that liberation from a terrible tyranny where human life that was not Aryan was worthless, would one day come. In Britain, which remained free to carry on the air battle, there has been a condemnation of that campaign in recent years by some pundits of succeeding generations, who suggest it was a waste of resources that brought needless suffering to Germany. Yet when the bomber offensive began in 1943 it was the prime hope of winning the war and in much of 1944, the subject of this book, the path to victory.

General Karl Koller, final Chief of the Luftwaffe Air Staff, had no illusions why Germany lost the war. In a transcript of an interrogation by the Americans in September 1945 he details several causes of defeat, none of which, he says, was singularly crucial. 'However the loss of air superiority ... was alone decisive,' he says and adds that if the Nazi hierarchy had concentrated on overwhelming air power, 'The casual mass concentration of heavy air forces in England – as actually happened – would not have been possible. There would have been no invasion, or at most only one which would have been repulsed with considerable bloodshed.'[6] It was that mastery of the air which was realised by Bomber Command in the summer of 1944 after the sacrifices of the winter.

In the soul-searching that followed the attack on Dresden in February 1945 – a target Harris did not want to bomb at that time, but which he was ordered to by Churchill, who then abandoned him – the brave men of Bomber Command were denied a separate campaign medal. It still rankles, among a body of men known for their stoicism. In July 2005 the UK Prime Minister announced the awarding of an Arctic Emblem to those who served on convoys to Russia in the Second World War. Just under 3,000 Royal Navy sailors and merchant seamen were killed during attacks by U-boats and the Luftwaffe in getting vital supplies through to Russia in a brutally harsh campaign. Yet 55,500 died in Bomber Command and all attempts to recognise their sacrifice have been resisted, perhaps for fear of offending former enemies. Among the young men who were denied these past sixty years, the flower of a generation, there was no such prevarication.

The pain of their passing is still felt by those they left behind. David Bailey, brother of Sgt Reginald Bailey, a married wireless operator killed in June 1944, and whose evading skipper was executed by the Gestapo, remembers the effect on his family when confirmation came of Reg's death the day after the airman's only child was born: 'My father, who had been gassed in the First World War, died a little while after,' he says. 'He had hung on thinking Reg was going to come home and then he sort of gave up all hope. He was only 51. My mother was devastated.'[7]

Even members of the British public, who had so enthusiastically cheered the bomber boys as they took the war to Germany, were quick to forget once the conflict was over. Dennis Goodliffe, the 101 Sqn flight engineer, soon found that the rumbustious behaviour of young men about to die had left a film of resentment in some towns near bomber bases, such as Doncaster. 'I was a sales rep after the war and one chap wouldn't have me in his shop when he heard I'd been in bombers,' he remembers. 'He said, "I saw the way you chaps behaved." I told him he hadn't seen the way Bomber Command boys behaved, being shot up over a target. He only saw the way they behaved trying to get over it.'[8]

The mounting of the bomber offensive had taken millions of man-hours – those not flying in or maintaining the bombers often involved in some way in building them – and swallowed millions of pounds. The monetary cost has only just been settled. The last payment on the war loan from the United States after it cancelled the financial lifeline of Lend-Lease was made on the last day of 2006.[9]

The bomber boys who survived the war paid for that debt in austerity during the immediate years that followed. But before post-war cynicism crept in to peer suspiciously round the corner of a hard-wrested peace there was another time, a period when those who were young then neither saved nor planned. It is summed up by F/O L. H. Kennedy, the squadron diarist of 432 (RCAF) Sqn at East Moor, near Thirsk – with whose airmen this story began in January 1944 – writing amid the frenzy of mid-August. He provides a snapshot from a lost age of enthusiasm and innocence when to be brave and loyal to comrades was enough and a day could be a lifetime.

He wrote:

We were on and we were off all day and evening. Finally the pending operation was scrubbed. The ladies of Sutton village run a little canteen behind the village church and it is getting a very popular spot in the evening, particularly around 9 o'clock when the lads congregate to hear the news broadcast. It is also noted that some of them bring their WAAF friends and strangely enough these couples seem to pick the darker corners to sit in. A good many will remember the canteen behind the church in their old age.[10]

I wonder if they do?

Notes

1: AN OP TOO MANY

1. Interview with author
2. Ibid.
3. F/Sgt Hill's recollections
4. Dennis Thorman's private memoirs, 'Per Ardua Ad Sitomagus'.
5. Interview with author
6. Ibid.
7. National Archives: AIR 27–1850
8. Interview with author
9. National Archives: AIR 27–1858
10. Hajo Herrmann, *Eagle's Wings*, p. 209
11. National Archives: AIR 27–1858
12. Interview with author
13. *Eagle's Wings*, p. 209
14. National Archives: AIR 27–2152
15. Interview with author
16. National Archives: AIR 27–2152
17. Marie Vassiltchikov, *Berlin Diaries 1940–45*

2: THE CAULDRON

1. *Yorkshire Evening Press*, 3 Jan. 1944
2. *Lincolnshire Echo*, 3 Jan. 1944
3. Ibid.
4. *Stamford Mercury and Guardian*, 5 Jan. 1944
5. *Boston Guardian*, 5 Jan. 1944
6. *Northern Echo*, 3 Jan. 1944
7. Dudley Saward, *'Bomber' Harris*, p. 218
8. Roger Freeman, *The Mighty Eighth*, p. 113
9. Roger Freeman, *The Mighty Eighth War Manual*, p. 195

10. Dennis Thorman's private memoirs
11. Interview with author
12. Ibid.
13. National Archives: AIR 14–3411
14. Dennis Thorman's private memoirs
15. Interview with author
16. Ibid.
17. Ibid.
18. Lali Horstmann, *Nothing for Tears*
19. Account to author
20. Ibid.
21. Wilhelm Johnen, *Duel Under the Stars*, p. 114
22. National Archives: AIR 27–971
23. Interview with author
24. *It's Suicide But It's Fun*, p. 113
25. Interview with author
26. Ibid.
27. John Hennessey's diary, in John Ward, *Beware of the Dog at War*, p. 301
28. Interview with author
29. Roy Child's personal papers
30. Max Hastings, *Bomber Command*, p. 260
31. National Archives: AIR 14–3411
32. Interview with author
33. Ibid.
34. Roy Child's personal papers
35. Interview with author
36. Dennis Thorman's personal memoirs
37. Ursula von Kardorff, *Diary of a Nightmare*
38. Dennis Thorman's personal

memoirs
39. *Diary of a Nightmare*
40. Ibid.
41. Ingeborg Wells, *Enough No more*, p. 48

3: THE COST OF COURAGE
1. Interview with author
2. National Archives: AIR 14–3411
3. Ibid.
4. Interview with author
5. National Archives: AIR 14–3411
6. Account to author
7. Peter Hinchliffe, *The Other Battle*, p. 243.
8. Interview with author
9. National Archives: AIR 27–1049
10. Marie Vassiltchikov, *Berlin Diaries 1940–45*, p. 141
11. Interview with author
12. Ibid.
13. Ibid.
14. Ibid.
15. Ibid.
16. Ibid.
17. Ibid.
18. National Archives: AIR 20–3082
19. Ibid.
20. Sir Arthur Harris, *Bomber Offensive*, p. 215
21. National Archives: AIR 20–3082
22. Ibid.
23. National Archives: AIR 27–587
24. Interview with author
25. National Archives: AIR 27–587
26. Ibid.
27. Report by W/Cdr J. Lawson, Air Historical Branch, RAF
28. Interview with author
29. Ibid.
30. Report by W/Cdr J. Lawson, Air Historical Branch, RAF
31. National Archives: AIR 18–21
32. Interview with author
33. Ibid.
34. Account to author

4: THE LESSON OF LEIPZIG
1. Max Hastings, *Bomber Command*, p. 266
2. Interview with author
3. Ibid.
4. Ibid.
5. National Archives: AIR 27–482
6. Interview with author
7. Ibid.
8. Ibid.
9. National Archives: AIR 14–3420
10. Interview with author
11. Roy Child's personal papers
12. Interview with author
13. Ibid.
14. Ibid.
15. Ibid.
16. Ibid.
17. Ibid.
18. Ibid.
19. Dennis Thorman's personal memoirs
20. Interview with author
21. Dennis Thorman's personal memoirs
22. Interview with author.
23. Ibid.
24. National Archives: AIR 40–554
25. Ibid.
26. Ilse McKee, *Tomorrow the World*
27. Interview with author
28. Ibid.
29. Ibid.
30. Ibid.
31. Ibid.
32. National Archives: AIR 14–4136
33. *Daily Express*, 14 April 1944
34. Interview with author
35. Ibid.

5: REVENGE AND RECRIMINATION
1. *Daily Mail*, 19 Feb. 1944
2. Lord Alanbrooke's *War Diaries*, p. 523
3. Roy Jenkins, *Churchill*, p. 732
4. *Daily Express*, 25 Feb. 1944
5. Hilary St George Saunders, *Royal Air Force 1939–45*, Vol. III, *The Fight Is Won*, p. 98
6. *Daily Express*, 27 March 1944

7. *Royal Air Force, 1939–45*, Vol. III, p. 387
8. Dudley Saward, *'Bomber' Harris*, p. 218
9. National Archives: AIR 19–170
10. Ibid.
11. *'Bomber' Harris*, p. 223.
12. Ethell and Price, *Target Berlin*, p. 142
13. *Daily Express*, 27 Jan. 1944
14. Max Hastings, *Bomber Command*, p. 171
15. Ibid.
16. *The Times*, 10 Feb. 1944
17. Ibid.
18. Ibid.
19. *Daily Mail*, 10 Feb 1944
20. *Church Times*, 18 Feb 1944
21. National Archives: AIR 14–843
22. Ibid.
23. Ibid.
24. *Cambridge Daily News*, 22 Feb. 1944
25. National Archives, AIR 14–843
26. *Lincolnshire Echo*, 3 April 1944
27. *Blighty*, 15 Jan. 1944
28. *Tit-Bits*, 2 Feb. 1944
29. Ibid., 25 March 1944
30. National Archives: AIR 20–3082

6: BERLIN OR BUST

1. Interview with author
2. National Archives: AIR 14–3420
3. National Archives: AIR 14–3411
4. Martin Middlebrook, *The Berlin Raids*, p. 277
5. *Daily Express*, 24 March 1944
6. Interview with author
7. F/Sgt Hill's recollections
8. Ibid.
9. Ibid.
10. Alan W. Cooper, *Bombers Over Berlin*, p. 185
11. F/Sgt Hill's recollections
12. Interview with author
13. Ibid.
14. Roy Keen, 'An Airman's War', www.airscene.uk.org.uk/nostalgia
15. John Hennessey's diary in John

Ward, *Beware of the Dog at War*, p. 318
16. F/Sgt Hill's recollections
17. Interview with author
18. Account to author
19. *Oberdonau Zeitung*, 31 March 1944
20. National Archives: AIR 27–380
21. Interview with author
22. Ibid.
23. F/Sgt Hill's recollections
24. National Archives: AIR 14–3420
25. Interview with author
26. Jonathan Falconer, *Bomber Command Handbook 1939–45*, p. 205
27. Roy Keen, 'An Airman's War'
28. Interview with author
29. National Archives: AIR 27–482
30. Hajo Herrmann, *Eagles Wings*, p. 216
31. *Oberdonau Zeitung*, 31 March 1944
32. Interview with author
33. F/Sgt Hill's recollections
34. Account to author
35. Picture on p. 256 of author's previous work, *Bomber Boys*
36. Interview with author
37. Ibid.
38. F/Sgt Hill's recollections
39. Interview with *Bournemouth Daily Echo*
40. Account to F/Sgt Cleary's niece Helena Lee
41. Interview with author
42. National Archives: AIR 14–3411
43. National Archives: AIR 27–482
44. National Archives: AIR 27–833
45. National Archives: AIR 27–1921
46. John Hennessey's diary in *Beware of the Dog at War*, p. 318
47. Interview with author
48. Ibid.
49. National Archives: AIR 14–341
50. John Terraine, *The Right of the Line*, p. 554
51. Sir Arthur Harris, *Bomber Offensive*, p. 244
52. Richard Overy, *The Air War 1939–45*, p. 123
53. *The Right of the Line*, p. 553

54. National Archives: AIR 14–3411

7: THE UNDERGROUND AIR WAR
1. Interview with author
2. Anton Gill, *The Great Escape*, p. 85
3. Camp History of Stalag Luft III, compiled for the Air Ministry, RAF Museum Dept of Records
4. Lord Alanbrooke's *War Diaries*, p. 328
5. Imperial War Museum Dept of Documents
6. National Archives: 'The Official History of the North Compound', Stalag Luft III, AIR 40-2645
7. Interview with author
8. Evidence in post-escape court-martialling of camp staff, quoted in B. A. James, *Moonless Night*
9. Interview with author
10. Ibid.
11. Imperial War Museum File 99/82/1
12. Interview with author
13. Ibid.
14. Ibid.
15. Ibid.
16. Ibid.
17. Ibid.
18. IWM File 99/821
19. Ibid.
20. Interview with author
21. Ibid.
22. Ibid.
23. Ibid.
24. Ibid.
25. Ibid.
26. Ibid.
27. IWM File 99/821
28. Interview with author
29. Ibid.
30. Ibid.
31. Ibid.
32. *The Great Escape*, p. 187
33. Interview with author
34. Ibid.
35. Ibid.
36. Ibid.
37. Ibid.

38. Ibid.
39. Ibid.
40. Paul Brickhill, *The Great Escape*, p. 209
41. Gill, *The Great Escape*, p. 196
42. National Archives: WO 235–426
43. Interview with author
44. Gill, *The Great Escape*, p. 212
45. Interview with author
46. Ibid.
47. *Moonless Night*, p. 199
48. Interview with author
49. Ibid.
50. Gill, *The Great Escape*, p. 206
51. National Archives: 'Secret Camp History of Stalag Luft III', AIR 40–2645
52. *Evening Standard*, London, 20 May 1944
53. Gill, *The Great Escape*, p. 251

8: MASSACRE IN THE MOONLIGHT
1. National Archives: AIR 14–780
2. National Archives: AIR 24–269
3. C. Webser and N. Frankland, *The Strategic Air Offensive Against Germany 1939–45*, pp. 54–7
4. Martin Middlebrook, *The Nuremberg Raid*, p. 85
5. Interview with author
6. National Archives: AIR 24–269
7. Ibid.
8. *The Nuremberg Raid*, p. 102
9. *Lincolnshire Echo*, 31 March 1944
10. Interview with author
11. Ibid.
12. Ibid.
13. Ibid.
14. Ibid.
15. Ibid.
16. Ibid.
17. National Archives: AIR 24–269
18. Interview with author
19. *Jägerblatt* magazine, Nov./Dec. 1963
20. Ibid.
21. Interview with author
22. Ibid.

23. Ibid.
24. Ibid.
25. Ibid.
26. Ibid.
27. Account to author
28. National Archives: AIR 24–269
29. Interview with author
30. National Archives: AIR 14–3411
31. *Oberdonau Zeitung*, 31 March 1944
32. National Archives: AIR 27–2050
33. Interview with author
34. Ibid.
35. Ibid.
36. Ibid.
37. Ibid.
38. Ibid.
39. Ibid.
40. John Hennessey's diary in John Ward, *Beware of the Dog at War*, p. 321
41. Interview with author
42. Ibid.
43. Ibid.
44. Ibid.
45. Ibid.
46. Ibid.
47. Account to Wolfgang Scholz
48. Henry Probert, *Bomber Harris: His Life and Times*, p. 266
49. A. C. Grayling, *Among the Dead Cities*, p. 48

9: MAKING A MARK

1. D. C. T. Bennett, *Pathfinder*, p. 154
2. Andrew Boyle, *No Passing Glory*, p. 166
3. Sound Archive; Imperial War Museum 9861/1
4. National Archives: AIR 27–2128
5. National Archives: AIR 27–768
6. National Archives: AIR 14–3411
7. Ken Hulton's wartime diary
8. Interview with author
9. National Archives: AIR 27–768
10 Sir Arthur Harris, *Bomber Offensive*, p. 162
11. *Berlin Then and Now*, p. 148
12. *No Passing Glory*, p. 219
13. Cheshire Papers, Vol. IV, IWM,

Dept of Documents, 71/31/1
14. Ibid.
15. Russell Braddon, *Cheshire VC*, p. 113
16. Ibid., p. 116
17. National Archives: AIR 14–3411
18. Cheshire Papers, Vol. IV
19. National Archives: AIR 27–688
20. Cheshire Papers, Vol. IV
21. Account to author
22. Interview with author
23. IWM Sound Archive ; 9861/3
24. Ute Vallance, *A Girl Survives*, p. 187
25. Interview with author
26. Ibid.
27. Ibid.
28. National Archives: AIR 27–768
29. Ibid.
30. Interview with author
31. Account to author
32. National Archives: AIR 27–2150
33. Account to author
34. Interview with author
35. Dudley Saward, *'Bomber' Harris*, p. 228
36. Ibid.
37. Ibid., p. 229
38. National Archives: AIR 14–3411
39. National Archives: AIR 27–481
40. Max Arthur, *Lost Voices of the Second World War*
41. Information supplied by historian Wolfgang Scholz, of Schweinfurt
42. Interview with author
43. National Archives: AIR 27–2150

10: ESCAPE LINES IN THE RAILWAY DESERT

1. Henry Probert, *Bomber Harris: His Life and Times*, p. 290
2. Sir Arthur Harris, *Bomber Offensive*, p. 196
3. *Sunday Express*, September 1944
4. *Daily Telegraph*, 19 May 1944
5. Charles Carrington, *A Soldier at Bomber Command*, p. 134
6. Probert, *Bomber Harris*, p. 291
7. Hilary St George Saunders, *Royal*

Air Force 1939–45, Vol. III, *The Fight Is Won*, p. 87

8. Ibid., p. 88
9. Martin Middlebrook and Chris Everitt, *Bomber Command War Diaries*, p. 490
10. National Archives: AIR 27–1859
11. Interview with author
12. Ibid.
13. Ibid.
14. Ibid.
15. Ibid.
16. *Bomber Command War Diaries*, pp. 503 and 509
17. F/Sgt Patfield's personal account, 61 Sqn Museum, Skellingthorpe
18. Account to author
19. *Daily Telegraph*, 30 May 1944
20. *Daily Telegraph*, 3 June 1944
21. Interview with author
22. National Archives: AIR 14–3411
23. F/Sgt Hill's recollections
24. Interview with author
25. F/Sgt Hill's recollections
26. National Archives: AIR 27–1049
27. *Sunday Express*, September 1944
28. Ibid.
29. F/Sgt Hill's recollections
30. Interview with author
31. National Archives: AIR 27–1049
32. Ibid.
33. F/Sgt Hill's recollections
34. *Royal Air Force, 1939–45*, Vol. III, p. 88
35. Zuckerman diary, 9 July 1944, p. 215, Decision in Normandy

11: TRAINING AND TERROR

1. *The Times*, 16 Feb. 1944
2. RCAF Ex-Air Gunners' Association magazine *Short Bursts*, May 2001
3. *The Times*, 14 Feb. 1944
4. National Archives: S99180
5. John Terraine, *The Right of the Line*, p. 605
6. National Archives: AIR 28–680
7. Interview with author
8. Ibid.

9. Juliet Gardiner, *Wartime: Britain 1939–1945*, p. 470
10. *A People at War: Life in Britain Today*, British Information Services, Washington
11. Barry Holt, Mailly-le-Camp fiftieth anniversary booklet
12. Imperial War Museum, Dept of Documents, 71/31/1
13. National Archives: AIR 14–3411
14. Jack Currie, *Battle Under the Moon*
15. National Archives: AIR 14–3411
16. *Battle Under the Moon*, p. 65
17. Interview with author
18. Ibid.
19. National Archives: AIR 27–1931
20. Interview with author
21. National Archives: AIR 14–3411
22. National Archives: AIR 27–2128
23. National Archives: AIR 27–688
24. Interview with author
25. Ibid.
26. Ibid.
27. National Archives: AIR 27–482
28. National Archives: AIR 27–688
29. IWM, Dept of Documents, 71/31/1
30. National Archives: AIR 27–688
31. Interview with author
32. Ibid.
33. Ibid.
34. Ibid.
35. National Archives: AIR 27–2145
36. National Archives: AIR 27–688
37. National Archives: AIR 27–2037
38. National Archives: AIR 27–688
39. Claims book for III/NJG 3/4 May, Bundesarchiv
40. Article by Chris Goss in *Flypast*, December 2004
41. National Archives: AIR 27–2037
42. Interview with author
43. Ibid.
44. 21 Panzer Div., abt, 1a 2526/44 geh
45. *Battle Under the Moon*, p. 141
46. John Ward, *Beware of the Dog at War*, p. 337
47. National Archives: AIR 27–482
48. Ibid.

49. *Weekend* magazine, 12 Jan. 1972
50. Account to author, via Sandrine Sosinski
51. National Archives: AIR 27–1931
52. Ibid.
53. Interview with author
54. *Battle Under the Moon*, p. 64
55. IWM Sound Archive, 9861/3
56. Interview with author
57. National Archives: AIR 27–688
58. Interview with author
59. National Archives: AIR 14–1017

12: RETURN TO THE REICH

1. *Daily Mail*, 5 May 1944
2. Interview with author
3. National Archives: AIR 27-482
4. Interview with author
5. Ibid.
6. W. R. Chorley, *Bomber Command Losses*, p. 237
7. Interview with author
8. Martin Middlebrook and Chris Everitt, *The Bomber Command War Diaries*, pp. 488 and 520,
9. Peter Hinchliffe, *The Other Battle*, p. 262

13: THE LONGEST NIGHT

1. Hilary St George Saunders, *Royal Air Force, 1939–45*, Vol. III, *The Fight Is Won*, p. 95
2. Account to author
3. 101 Matters newsletter, summer 2004
4. Interview with author
5. Ibid.
6. L. F. Ellis, *Victory in the West, Vol. I, p. 212*
7. *Interview with author*
8. *Ibid.*
9. *Ibid.*
10 *Ibid.*
11. *Ibid.*
12. *Ibid.*
13. *Imperial War Museum Dept of Documents, 85/16/1–3754*
14. *Robin Neillands and Roderick de Normann, D-Day 1944, p. 475*

15. Bill Middleton's personal account in Frank and Joan Shaw, *We Remember D-Day*, p. 17
16. *Victory in the West*, p. 161
17. *War Report*, 'D-Day to VE Day', p. 59
18. DEFE 3/1545–NA
19. Interview with author
20. Ibid.
21. Ibid.
22. Ibid.
23. Ibid.
24. Account to author
25. Ibid.
26. Interview with author
27. Grete Paquin and Renate Hagan, *Two Women and a War: Diary*
28. Charles Carrington, *A Soldier at Bomber Command*
29. F/O Donald Cheney, 'Adventure in France 1944'
30. Account to author
31. Interview with author
32. Letter to F/O Vic Farmer
33. Interview with author
34. Sir Arthur Harris, *Bomber Offensive*, p. 210

14: SQUASHING THE DOODLEBUG

1. *The Cinema* magazine, 7 June 1944
2. Juliet Gardiner, *Wartime: Britain 1939–45*, p. 126
3. Lord Alanbrooke's *War Diaries*, p. 315, among others
4. *Lincolnshire Echo*, 12 June 1944
5. *Cambridge Daily News*, 12 June 1944
6. *Yorkshire Evening News*, 10 June 1944
7. ARP and NFS *News Review*, June 1945
8. Hilary St George Saunders, *Royal Air Force, 1939–45*, Vol. III, *The Fight Is Won*, p. 147
9. *Wartime:Britain 1939–45*, p. 556
10. Lord Alanbrooke's *War Diaries*, p. 563
11. Roy Jenkins, *Churchill*, p. 747

12. Earl R. Beck, *Under the Bombs*, p. 135
13. *Churchill*, p. 747
14. *Royal Air Force, 1939–45*, Vol. III, p. 159
15. John Terraine, *The Right of the Line*, p. 653
16. Account to author
17. *Royal Air Force, 1939–45*, Vol. III, p. 162
18. Churchill, p. 747
19. National Archives: AIR 27–1931
20. *Royal Air Force, 1939-45*, Vol. III, p. 163
21. Interview with author
22. Ibid.
23. Account to author
24. Sir Arthur Harris, *Bomber Offensive*, p. 217
25. Interview with author
26. *Royal Air Force, 1939–45*, Vol. III, p. 171
27. *Barnes Wallis*, by J. E. Morpurgo, p. 336
28. Interview with author
29. National Archives: AIR 27–2128
30. F/O Donald Cheney, 'Adventure in France 1944'
31. *Royal Air Force, 1939–45*, Vol. III, p. 171
32. National Archives: AIR 27–2128
33. *Royal Air Force, 1939–45*, Vol. III, p. 167
34. Ibid., p. 164
35. *Churchill*, p. 746
36. *Royal Air Force, 1939–45*, Vol. III, p. 164
37. Interview with author
38. Account to author
39. Interview with author

15: THROTTLING THE LUFTWAFFE

1. Sir Arthur Harris, *Bomber Offensive*, p. 225
2. Ibid., p. 228
3. Ibid., p. 220
4. Account to author
5. Ibid.
6. National Archives: AIR 27–1858
7. Interview with author
8. Ibid.
9. National Archives: AIR 14–3412
10. Peter Hinchliffe, *The Other Battle*, p. 290
11. Ibid.
12. Imperial War Museum, Dept of Documents, 85/16/1–3754
13. Interview with author
14. W. R. Chorley, *Bomber Command Losses, 1944*, p. 290
15. Interview with author
16. Letter to F/O Goodliffe
17. *Behind the Wire* video, prepared for the Bomber Command Association by DD Videos, 1997
18. Derek Tilney, *The Story of the Dutch Flag*
19. Interview with author
20. National Archives: AIR 14–3412
21. Interview with author
22. Account to author
23. National Archives: AIR 27–647
24. Interview with author
25. Ibid.
26. Ibid.
27. IWM, Dept of Documents, 85/16/1
28. Martin Middlebrook and Chris Everitt, *Bomber Command War Diaries*, p. 574
29. Interview with author
30. Hilary St George Saunders, *Royal Air Force, 1939–45*, Vol. III, *The Fight Is Won*, p. 269
31. Ibid.
32. *Bomber Offensive*, p. 224

16: ONE-WAY TICKETS IN THE TRANSPORTATION PLAN

1. Interview with author
2. Ibid.
3. National Archives: AIR 27–1849
4. Metheringham Airfield Visitor Centre Archives
5. Interview with author
6. Ibid.
7. F/O Banville's private account in

Oliver Clutton-Brook, *Massacre Over the Marne*, p. 27
8. Interview with author
9. Ibid.
10. Ibid.
11. Letter to F/O Farmer
12. Interview with author
13. National Archives: AIR 14–3412
14. Ibid.
15. T. D. G. Teare, *Evader*, p. 181
16. National Archives: AIR 14–2073
17. *Massacre over the Marne*, p. 79
18. W. R. Chorley, *Bomber Command*, p. 335–8
19. *Evader*, pp. 183–4
20. Interview with author
21. Account to author
22. Interview with author
23. National Archives: AIR 27–2037
24. Letter to F/O Farmer

17: BACK TO BASICS
1. Ils Mar Garthaus, *The Way We Lived in Germany During World War II: A Personal Account*, p. 89
2. Ursula von Kardorff, *Diary of a Nightmare*
3. Interview with author
4. Ibid.
5. Ron Smith, *Rear Gunner Pathfinders*, p. 93
6. National Archives: AIR 27–810
7. Ibid.
8. Chris Goss, *It's Suicide But It's Fun*, p. 125
9. Interview with author
10. Ibid.
11. F/Sgt Hill's recollections
12. Ibid.
13. Account to author
14. F/Sgt Hill's recollections
15. Museum Exhibit, Hamburg
16. Heinz Bardua, *Stuttgart im Luftkrieg, 1939–1945*, p. 94
17. Letter from Miss H. P. to the exhibition project Stuttgart in der 2. Weltkrieg, 30 April 1988
18. National Archives: AIR 27–1981
19. National Archives: NRR 672,

AIR 14–3412
20. Interview with author
21. F/Sgt Hill's recollections
22. Interview with author
23. Ibid.
24. F/Sgt Hill's recollections
25. Interview with author
26. National Archives: NRR 675, AIR 14–3411
27. F/Sgt Hill's recollections
28. Interview with author
29. F/Sgt Hill's recollections
30. National Archives: NRR 675, AIR 14–3412
31. Ibid.
32. Interview with author
33. *Stuttgart im Luftkrieg, 1939–1945*, p. 429
34. Ibid.

18: THE BEGINNING OF THE END
1. Yorkshire Air Museum Archives
2. BBC *War Report*, 4 July, in *War Report*, BBC Books, p. 107
3. Vera Lynn, Robin Cross and Jenny de Gex, *Unsung Heroines: The Women Who Won the War*, p. 85
4. Ibid., p. 87
5. National Archives: AIR 37–1057
6. Yorkshire Air Museum Archives
7. Interview with author
8. *Unsung Heroines: The Women Who Won the War*, p. 87
9. Interview with author
10. Ibid.
11. Henry Probert, *Bomber Harris: His Life and Times*, p. 298
12. Interview with author
13. F/O Farnbank's own account, made after the war
14. Interview with author
15. Ibid.
16. F/O Donald Cheney, 'Adventure in France 1944'
17. National Archives: AIR 14–3412
18. Ibid.
19. Ibid.
20. Ils Mar Garthaus, *The Way We Lived in Germany During World*

War II: A Personal Account, p. 94
21. Interview with author
22. Ibid.
23. National Archives: NRR 698, AIR 14–3412
24. Interview with author
25. Ibid.
26. National Archives: AIR 27–1931
27. National Archives: NRR 698, AIR 14–3412
28. Ibid.
29. Interview with author
30. National Archives: NRR 698, AIR 14–3412
31. Interview with author
32. National Archives: NRR 698, AIR 14–3412
33. Interview with author
34. Charles Whiting (ed.), *The Home Front: Germany*
35. Martin Middlebrook and Chris Everitt, *The Bomber Command War Diaries*, p. 568
36. Joachim Fest, *Speer: The Final Verdict*, p. 221
37. R. J. Overy, *The Air War 1939–1945*
38. National Archives: AIR 20–2859
39. Sir Arthur Harris, *Bomber Offensive*, p. 224
40. *Speer: The Final Verdict*, p. 220
41. *The Air War 1939–1945*, p. 123
42. *Stuttgart im Welzkrieg, 1939–1945* (Bleicher Verlag, 1989)

19: REFLECTION
1. *Daily Telegraph*, 2 Sept. 2005
2. *Saga* magazine, Oct. 2005
3. *Yorkshire Post*, 10 July 2004
4. *Yorkshire Post*, 28 Nov. 2005
5. Account to author
6. National Archives: AIR 40–1470
7. Interview with author
8. Ibid.
9. *Daily Telegraph*, 17 Dec. 2005
10. National Archives: AIR 27–1860

Acknowledgements

I am particularly grateful to the following British, Commonwealth and Allied aircrew and WAAFs who participated in various ways in the preparation of this book. It is their unstinting help that made it all possible, and some of them allowed me to quote from their unpublished manuscripts. Ranks and awards are those when they left the services and only air forces other than RAF are shown after names: 7 Sqn: W/O Roy Child. 9 Sqn: F/Lt Gordon Penfold (deceased); S/Ldr James Hancock DFC (RAAF); P/O Cliff Williams; F/Lt John Simpson; LACW Dorothy Mason. 10 Sqn: S/Ldr John Walker AFC (deceased). 12 Sqn: Sgt Arthur Madelaine (deceased). 15 Sqn: W/O Arthur Edgley. 25 Sqn: F/Sgt Walter Craine. 35 Sqn: S/Ldr Gordon Carter DFC and bar, Legion of Honour (RCAF); W/O Robert Gill DFM; W/O Clifford Hill DFM (deceased). 44 (Rhodesia) Sqn: F/Lt Raymond Worrall; F/Lt Gerry Mitchell; W/O Albert Bracegirdle. 49 Sqn: F/Sgt Alan Morgan. 50 Sqn: W/O Donald Gray; W/O Allan Campbell; W/O George Stewart (deceased). 57 Sqn: W/O Ken Hulton (deceased). 75 Sqn: P/O Ron Brown. 77 Sqn: F/Lt Dennis Thorman; W/O Geoffrey Haworth; W/O Frank Jones. 78 Sqn: W/O Kenneth Dobbs; F/Lt Bernard Downs DFC. 83 Sqn: F/Lt Ken Lane DFC; W/O Dick Raymond; W/O Alfred Ridpath. 88 Sqn: S/Ldr Vincent Hughes AFC. 97 Sqn: W/Cdr Jim Wright DFC; F/Lt John Greening; W/O Patrick Bell (RCAF). 100 Sqn: F/O Douglas Hudson DFC. 101 Sqn: F/O Dennis Goodliffe; F/O Ralph Laurie (RAAF); F/Sgt Gordon Wallace (deceased); W/O Peter Kaye; W/O Graham Boytell (RAAF); W/O Cyril Rowbottom; W/O Jim Davies. 102 Sqn: W/O Montague Clarke; S/Ldr Alan Dearden. 105 Sqn: W/Cdr Robert Bray DFC. 106 Sqn: W/O Harry Stunell; W/O John Harrison; W/O Bob Burns; F/Lt Richard Starkey. 115 Sqn: F/Lt Tom Dugdale DFC; F/Sgt Joe Cleary; F/Lt Kenneth Turnham. 139 Sqn: F/Lt Eric Atkins DFC and bar, Polish Cross of Valour and Bar; F/Lt Frederick Crawley DFC. 142 Sqn: F/Lt Ken Tempest DFC. 156 Sqn: W/O Lawrence Woolliscroft. 158 Sqn: S/Ldr Bob Brackenridge; F/Lt Joe Hitchman DFC (deceased); F/Lt W. T. J. Clark; W/O Harry Ball; S/Ldr Robert Vollum DFC; F/Lt Bob Farnbank. 166 Sqn: W/O Frank Etherington; W/O Barry Wright CGM; F/O Fred Sim DFC (RCAF); W/O Tom Hall DFM; F/Lt Jack Gagg DFC; W/O James Wright; F/Sgt Paul Grant; F/Lt Len Isaacson, Croix de Guerre (RCAF); LACW Marian Smith. 169 Sqn: F/Lt Harry Reed DFC. 218 Sqn: F/Lt Harry Fisher; F/O Rowland Mason; Sgt John Simpson; F/O Reg Johnson. 347 Sqn: Sgt Leonce Vaysse (FFAF). 408 (Goose) Sqn, RCAF: F/O Kenneth Blyth. 433 (Porcupine) Sqn, RCAF: S/Ldr Wilbur Pierce DFC (RCAF). 460 (RAAF) Sqn: F/Lt David Francis DFC; P/O

Edney Eyres; W/O Tom Howie; W/O Donald Gray DFM. 466 Sqn: F/Lt Arnold Derrington DFC. 487 Sqn: S/Ldr Charles Patterson DSO, DFC. 515 Sqn: W/O Alfred Rogers; F/Lt Alan Shufflebottom. 544 Sqn: W/O Francis Bayliss, CdG (Belge), AFM. 550 Sqn: F/O Vic Farmer; W/O Ken Down; W/O Tony McKernan (deceased); F/Lt Jim Lord DFC; W/O Harry Stack (RAAF). 571 Sqn: F/Lt S. D. Perks DFC. 605 Sqn: S/Ldr Robert Muir DFC. 613 Sqn: F/Lt Tony Brandreth. 617 Sqn: S/Ldr Les Munro DSO, DFC (RNZAF); S/Ldr Nicky Ross DSO, DFC; F/O Donald Cheney DFC. 622 Sqn: P/O Bruce Sutherland (RCAF). 625 Sqn: W/O Russell Margerison; W/O Norman Jones; S/Ldr Alex Flett DFC and bar; F/Sgt Frank Tolley; F/Lt William Porter. 626 Sqn: F/O Ron Wood (deceased); W/O Roy Ollerhead DFM. 630 Sqn: W/O William Isaacs; W/O Edwin Watson; F/O Tony Leyva. 692 Sqn: S/Ldr Tom Beal DFC. 1667 HCU: F/Lt Peter Johnson DFC. 306th BG, USAAF, Lt Howard Roth. Stalag Luft III: W/Cdr Ken Rees; S/Ldr B. A. 'Jimmy' James; F/Lt Alan Bryett; F/Lt Sydney Dowse; F/O Albert Wallace (RCAF); F/Lt James Howard; F/Lt Ron Heatherington (deceased).

I am also grateful to the following civilian sources: M. André Guillet; Mdme Sandrine Sosinski; Herr Lars Biester; Herr Wolfgang Scholz; Herr Heinz Bardua; David Bailey. I have received much appreciated assistance from Stephen Walton, Archivist at the Imperial War Museum Department of Documents; John Ward, historian of 49 Sqn; and Keith Lowe, a military historian of considerable reputation, who proved a wise editor yet again.

The following ex-Luftwaffe aircrew have also been generous with their assistance, for which I am grateful: II/JG26: Uffz Ottomar Kruse, Iron Cross Second Class; VIII/NJG3: Major Paul Zorner, Knight's Cross; I/NJG2 Hptmn Heinz Rokker, Knight's Cross with Oak Leaves.

Glossary

ABC	Airborne equipment for spot-jamming of night-fighter transmissions
AP	Aiming point
Appell	Inspection parade of POWs
ASR	Air Sea Rescue
Corona	Ground-based listening and broadcasting system for sending false instructions to German night-fighter crews
Erk	Aircraftsman 2nd Class, the lowest RAF rank
ETA	Estimated time of arrival
DD	Duplex drive, amphibious tanks
DFC	Distinguished Flying Cross
DFM	Distinguished Flying Medal
DSO	Distinguished Service Order
Experten	A recognised Luftwaffe ace with five or more confirmed victories
Feldwebel	Sergeant in the Wehrmacht or Luftwaffe
Feldpolizei	German military police
FFI	French forces of the interior; the Resistance
FIDO	Runway fog dispersal system using burning petrol
F/Lt	Flight Lieutenant
F/O	Flying Officer
F/Sgt	Flight Sergeant
FW190	Focke Wulf single-engined fighter, a favourite of Wilde Sau pilots
Gee	Airborne device receiving signals from one master and two slave radio stations by which a navigator was able to plot his exact course on a grid
Graviner	Fire extinguisher device in an aircraft engine
Gremlin	Fictitious, RAF imp-like figure, expert at putting a spanner in the works
Grossfahndung	German national alert employing civilians as well as armed forces
HCU	Heavy Conversion Unit
Himmelbett	Box fighter-control system introduced by General Kammhuber
H2S	Radar scanner carried underneath bombers supplying features of terrain below to operator inside

Ju88	Twin-engined multi-purpose Junkers aircraft, often used in the Zahme Sau night-fighter role
Jostle	Continuous wave-jamming of German R/T transmissions by equipment in 100 Group aircraft
Kammhuber Line	String of Luftwaffe fighter boxes made defunct by Window
Korfu	Ground-based radar equipment that could lock onto bomber H2S transmissions
LMF	Lack of moral fibre, the harsh judgement made by the RAF on those who felt unable to continue operational flying. Their files were stamped.
Mandrel	Transmission equipment to jam enemy early-warning radar
Me109	Single-engined Messerschmitt day fighter adapted for Wilde Sau role
Me110	Twin-engined Messerschmitt night fighter, lethal with Schrage Musik
Monica	Tail-mounted RAF device to warn of approaching night fighter
NAAFI	Navy, Army and Air Force Institutes – clubs-cum-cafés for other ranks
Nachtjäger	Night-fighter aircraft or aircrew. The command structure was in *Staffels* of nine aircraft, three *Staffels* making a group, three groups making a *Geschwader*. In abbreviated form the Third Group of the First Night Fighter *Geschwader* would be III/NJG1
Naxos	Airborne radar equipment that could track bomber H2S transmissions
Newhaven	Pathfinder marking by visual identification of the target
Oboe	Highly accurate radar tracking and transmission system, signalling to a PFF aircraft the exact point at which to drop its TIs
Occult	A light signal to assist navigation
Offset marking	Technique of dropping TIs outside an aiming point to avoid obscuring by smoke and setting bomb sights for an overshoot, so bombs actually hit the target
OKW	Wehrmacht high command
ORS	Operational Research Section at Bomber Command headquarters
OTU	Operational Training Unit
Parramatta	Pathfinder ground marking by the use of H2S
PFF	Pathfinder Flare Force
P/O	Pilot Officer
Pundit	A flashing light identifying an airfield in Morse
Schrage Musik	Upward-firing guns in the fuselage of German night fighters
Serrate	Night-fighter airborne radar hunting *Nachtjäger* transmissions
S/Ldr	Squadron Leader
SN-2	Luftwaffe airborne radar operating on 90 megacycles that could not be jammed by Window
Sqn	Squadron
T and D	A bombing technique developed by 5 Group where a force

	bombed blind after counting off the time from an identifiable, distant landmark
TI	Target indicator
U/S	Unserviceable
VC	Victoria Cross
WAAF	Womens' Auxiliary Air Force. Members known by the same name
Wad	The air force name for a sandwich, invariably more bread than filling
Wanganui	Skymarking in very poor visibility. The prefix 'musical' meant the use of Oboe
Wilde Sau	Freelance night fighters, usually over targets and single-engined
Window	Metallised paper producing spurious responses on Luftwaffe radar
W/Cdr	Wing Commander
W/O	Warrant Officer
Zahme Sau	'Tame boar' fighters controlled by means of a running commentary

Bibliography

ANDREAS-FRIEDRICH, Ruth, *Berlin Underground* (Latimer House, 1948)
ARTHUR, Max, *Forgotten Voices of the Second World War* (Ebury Press, 2004)
BALL, Harry, *Two Brothers At War* (privately published)
BARDUA, Heinz, *Stuttgart im Luftkrieg 1939–45* (Klett Verlag Stuttgart, 1985)
BECK, Earl R., *Under the Bombs: German Home Front, 1942–1945* (University Press of Kentucky, 1986)
BENNETT, D. C. T., *Pathfinder* (Frederick Muller Ltd, 1958)
BOWMAN, Martin W. and CUSHING, Tom, *Confounding the Reich* (Patrick Stephens, 1996)
BOYLE, Andrew, *No Passing Glory* (Fontana Books, 1959)
BRADDON, Russell, *Cheshire VC* (Evans Brothers Ltd, 1954)
BRICKHILL, Paul, *The Great Escape* (Cassell Military Paperbacks, 2000)
CARRINGTON, Charles, *A Soldier at Bomber Command* (Leo Cooper, 1987)
CHORLEY, W. R., *Bomber Command Losses, 1944* (Midland Counties Publications, 1997)
CLUTTON-BROOK, Oliver, *Massacre over the Marne* (Patrick Stephens, 1994)
COOPER, Alan W., *Bombers Over Berlin* (Harper Collins, 1989)
CURRIE, Jack, *Battle Under the Moon* (Airdata Publications, 1995)
DANCHEV, Alex and TODMAN, Daniel (eds.), *War Diaries 1939–1945, Field Marshal Lord Alanbrooke* (Weidenfeld & Nicolson, 2001)
DAVIES, James Arthur, *A Leap in the Dark* (Leo Cooper, 1994)
ELLIS, L. F., *Victory in the West* (London, 1962)
ETHELL Jeffrey and PRICE, Alfred, *Target Berlin* (Jane's, 1980)
FALCONER, Jonathon, *The Bomber Command Handbook 1939–1945* (Sutton Publishing Ltd, 1998)
FEST, Joachim, *Speer: The Final Verdict* (Alexander Fest Verlag, 1999)
FISCHER, Josef, *Köln 1939–45* (J. P. Bachem, 1970)
FREEMAN, Roger A., *The Mighty Eighth* (Macdonald and Jane's, 1970)
GARDINER, Juliet, *Wartime: Britain 1939–45* (Headline, 2004)
GARTHAUS, Ils Mar, *The Way We Lived in Germany During World War II: A Personal Account* (Arale Books, 1977)
GILL, Anton, *The Great Escape* (Review, 2002)
GOSS, Chris, *It's Suicide But It's Fun* (Crecy Books, 1995)
GRAYLING, A. C., *Among the Dead Cities* (Bloomsbury, 2006)
HARRIS, Sir Arthur, *Bomber Offensive* (Collins, 1947)
HASTINGS, Sir Max, *Bomber Command* (Michael Joseph, 1979)

HERRMANN, Hajo, *Eagle's Wings* (Airlife Publishing, 1991)

HINCHLIFFE, Peter, *The Other Battle* (Airlife Publishing, 1996)

HORSTMANN, Lali, *Nothing for Tears* (Weidenfeld & Nicolson, 1953)

HUDSON, Douglas, *There and Back Again. A Navigator's Story* (Tucann Books, 2001)

JAKOBSSON, John M. and NORTON, Robin D. W., *S/Ldr Robert C. Muir DFC* (Norton Publishing, 2004)

JAMES, B. A., *Moonless Night* (William Kimber, 1983)

JENKINS, Roy, *Churchill* (Macmillan, 2001)

JOHNEN, Wilhelm, *Duel Under the Stars* (William Kimber and Co., 1957)

KARDORFF, Ursula von, *Diary of a Nightmare* (Rupert Hart-Davis, 1965)

LYNN, Vera, CROSS, Robin and DE GEX, Jenny, *Unsung Heroines: The Women Who Won the War* (Sidgwick & Jackson, 1990)

MARGERISON, Russell, *Boys at War* (Ross Anderson Publications, 1986)

MAYNARD, John, *Bennett and the Pathfinders* (Arms and Armour Press, 1996)

MCKEE, Ilse, *Tomorrow the World* (J. M. Dent & Sons, 1960)

MIDDLEBROOK, Martin, *The Berlin Raids* (Viking, 1988)

MIDDLEBROOK, Martin, *The Nuremberg Raid* (Allen Lane, 1973)

MIDDLEBROOK, Martin and EVERITT, Chris, *The Bomber Command War Diaries* (Viking, 1985)

MORPURGO, J. E., *Barnes Wallis* (Longmans, 1972)

NEILLANDS, Robin and DE NORMANN, Roderick, *D-Day 1944* (Weidenfeld & Nicolson, 1994)

OVERY, Richard, *The Air War 1939–1945* (Europa Publications, 1980)

OVERY, Richard, *Bomber Command, 1939–45* (Harper Collins, 1997)

PAQUIN, Grete and HAGEN, Renate, *Two Women and a War: Diary* (Muhlenberg Press, Philadelphia, 1953)

PARTRIDGE, Eric, *Dictionary of RAF Slang* (Michael Joseph, 1945)

PROBERT, Henry, *Bomber Harris: His Life and Times* (Greenhill Books, 2003)

REES, Ken, *Lie in the Dark and Listen* (Grub Street, 2004)

RICHARDS, Denis, *Royal Air Force, 1939–45*, Vol. I, *The Fight At Odds* (Her Majesty's Stationery Office, 1953)

RICHARDS, Denis, *The Hardest Victory* (Hodder & Stoughton, 1994)

RICHARDS, Denis and ST G. SAUNDERS, Hilary, *Royal Air Force 1939–45*, Vol. II, *The Fight Avails* (Her Majesty's Stationery Office, 1954)

RUMPF, Hans, *The Bombing of Germany* (Frederick Muller, 1961)

ST G. SAUNDERS, Hilary, *Royal Air Force, 1939–45*, Vol. III, *The Fight Is Won* (Her Majesty's Stationery Office, 1954)

SAWARD, Dudley, *'Bomber' Harris* (Cassell, 1984)

SHAW, Frank, and SHAW, Joan, *We Remember D-Day* (Isis Publishing Ltd, 1994)

SMITH, Ron, *Rear Gunner Pathfinders* (Crecy Publishing, 1997)

SPEER, Albert, *Inside the Third Reich* (Weidenfeld & Nicolson, 1970)

STARKEY, Richard, *A Lancaster Pilot's Impression on Germany* (Compaid Graphics, 1999)

TEARE, T. D. G., *Evader* (Hodder and Stoughton, 1954)

TERRAINE, John, *The Right of the Line* (Hodder and Stoughton, 1985)

VALLANCE, Ute, *A Girl Survives* (Macgibbon & Kee, 1958)

VASSILTCHIKOV, Marie, *Berlin Diaries* (Alfred A. Knopf, 1987)

WARD, John, *Beware of the Dog at War* (JoTe Publications, 1997)

WARD-JACKSON, C. H., and LUCAS, Leighton, *Airman's Song Book* (William Blackwood and Sons, 1967)

WEBSTER, Charles and FRANKLAND, Noble, *Strategic Air Offensive Against Germany*, Vol. III (HMSO, London, 1961)

WELLS, Ingeborg, *Enough No More* (Herbert Joseph, 1948)

WHITING, Charles (ed.), *The Home Front: Germany* (Time Life Books, 1982)

Index